McDougal Littell Science

Earth's Waters

water cycle

ocean

HABITAT

hydrosphere

Credits
5B Illustration by Stephen Durke; **5C** Illustrations by Richard Bonson/Wildlife Art Ltd.; **71B** © AFP/Corbis/NASA; **71C** Illustration by Raymond Turvey.

Acknowledgments
Excerpts and adaptations from *National Science Education Standards* by the National Academy of Sciences. Copyright © 1996 by the National Academy of Sciences. Reprinted with permission from the National Academies Press, Washington, D.C.

Excerpts and adaptations from *Benchmarks for Science Literacy: Project 2061*. Copyright © 1993 by the American Association for the Advancement of Science. Reprinted with permission.

ISBN: 0-618-33418-1   2 3 4 5 6 7 8 DSC 08 07 06

Internet Web Site: http://www.mcdougallittell.com

McDougal Littell Science

Effective Science Instruction Tailored for Middle School Learners

Earth's Waters
Teacher's Edition Contents

Consultants and Reviewers

Science Consultants

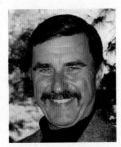

Chief Science Consultant

James Trefil, Ph.D. is the Clarence J. Robinson Professor of Physics at George Mason University. He is the author or co-author of more than 25 books, including *Science Matters* and *The Nature of Science*. Dr. Trefil is a member of the American Association for the Advancement of Science's Committee on the Public Understanding of Science and Technology. He is also a fellow of the World Economic Forum and a frequent contributor to *Smithsonian* magazine.

Rita Ann Calvo, Ph.D. is Senior Lecturer in Molecular Biology and Genetics at Cornell University, where for 12 years she also directed the Cornell Institute for Biology Teachers. Dr. Calvo is the 1999 recipient of the College and University Teaching Award from the National Association of Biology Teachers.

Kenneth Cutler, M.S. is the Education Coordinator for the Julius L. Chambers Biomedical Biotechnology Research Institute at North Carolina Central University. A former middle school and high school science teacher, he received a 1999 Presidential Award for Excellence in Science Teaching.

Instructional Design Consultants

Douglas Carnine, Ph.D. is Professor of Education and Director of the National Center for Improving the Tools of Educators at the University of Oregon. He is the author of seven books and over 100 other scholarly publications, primarily in the areas of instructional design and effective instructional strategies and tools for diverse learners. Dr. Carnine also serves as a member of the National Institute for Literacy Advisory Board.

Linda Carnine, Ph.D. consults with school districts on curriculum development and effective instruction for students struggling academically. A former teacher and school administrator, Dr. Carnine also co-authored a popular remedial reading program.

Donald Steely, Ph.D. serves as principal investigator at the Oregon Center for Applied Science (ORCAS) on federal grants for science and language arts programs. His background also includes teaching and authoring of print and multimedia programs in science, mathematics, history, and spelling.

Sam Miller, Ph.D. is a middle school science teacher and the Teacher Development Liaison for the Eugene, Oregon, Public Schools. He is the author of curricula for teaching science, mathematics, computer skills, and language arts.

Vicky Vachon, Ph.D. consults with school districts throughout the United States and Canada on improving overall academic achievement with a focus on literacy. She is also co-author of a widely used program for remedial readers.

Content Reviewers

John Beaver, Ph.D.
Ecology
Professor, Director of Science Education Center
College of Education and Human Services
Western Illinois University
Macomb, IL

Donald J. DeCoste, Ph.D.
Matter and Energy, Chemical Interactions
Chemistry Instructor
University of Illinois
Urbana-Champaign, IL

Dorothy Ann Fallows, Ph.D., MSc
Diversity of Living Things, Microbiology
Partners in Health
Boston, MA

Michael Foote, Ph.D.
The Changing Earth, Life Over Time
Associate Professor
Department of the Geophysical Sciences
The University of Chicago
Chicago, IL

Lucy Fortson, Ph.D.
Space Science
Director of Astronomy
Adler Planetarium and Astronomy Museum
Chicago, IL

Elizabeth Godrick, Ph.D.
Human Biology
Professor, CAS Biology
Boston University
Boston, MA

Isabelle Sacramento Grilo, M.S.
The Changing Earth
Lecturer, Department of the Geological Sciences
San Diego State University
San Diego, CA

David Harbster, MSc
Diversity of Living Things
Professor of Biology
Paradise Valley Community College
Phoenix, AZ

Richard D. Norris, Ph.D.
Earth's Waters
Professor of Paleobiology
Scripps Institution of Oceanography
University of California, San Diego
La Jolla, CA

Donald B. Peck, M.S.
Motion and Forces; Waves, Sound, and Light;
  Electricity and Magnetism
Director of the Center for Science Education (retired)
Fairleigh Dickinson University
Madison, NJ

Javier Penalosa, Ph.D.
Diversity of Living Things, Plants
Associate Professor, Biology Department
Buffalo State College
Buffalo, NY

Raymond T. Pierrehumbert, Ph.D.
Earth's Atmosphere
Professor in Geophysical Sciences (Atmospheric Science)
The University of Chicago
Chicago, IL

Brian J. Skinner, Ph.D.
Earth's Surface
Eugene Higgins Professor of Geology and Geophysics
Yale University
New Haven, CT

Nancy E. Spaulding, M.S.
Earth's Surface, The Changing Earth, Earth's Waters
Earth Science Teacher (retired)
Elmira Free Academy
Elmira, NY

Steven S. Zumdahl, Ph.D.
Matter and Energy, Chemical Interactions
Professor Emeritus of Chemistry
University of Illinois
Urbana-Champaign, IL

Susan L. Zumdahl, M.S.
Matter and Energy, Chemical Interactions
Chemistry Education Specialist
University of Illinois
Urbana-Champaign, IL

Safety Consultant

Juliana Texley, Ph.D.
Former K–12 Science Teacher and School Superintendent
Boca Raton, FL

English Language Advisor

Judy Lewis, M.A.
Director, State and Federal Programs for reading proficiency
and high risk populations
Rancho Cordova, CA

Research-Based Solutions for Your Classroom

The distinguished program consultant team and a thorough, research-based planning and development process assure that *McDougal Littell Science* supports all students in learning science concepts, acquiring inquiry skills, and thinking scientifically.

Standards-Based Instruction

Concepts and skills were selected based on careful analysis of national and state standards.

- National Science Education Standards
- Project 2061 Benchmarks for Science Literacy
- Comprehensive database of state science standards

CHAPTER 1

The Water Planet

the BIG idea

Water moves through Earth's atmosphere, oceans, and land in a cycle.

In what forms does water exist on Earth?

Key Concepts

SECTION 1.1
Water continually cycles.
Learn about how water on Earth moves in a world-wide system.

SECTION 1.2
Fresh water flows and freezes on Earth.
Learn about fresh water in rivers, lakes, and ice.

SECTION 1.3
Fresh water flows underground.
Learn about water under the land surface and how it is used.

Internet Preview

CLASSZONE.COM
Chapter 1 online resources: Content Review, Simulation, Visualization, four Resource Centers, Math Tutorial, Test Practice

C 6 Unit: Earth's Waters

Standards and Benchmarks

Each chapter in **Earth's Waters** covers some of the learning goals that are described in the *National Science Education Standards* (NSES) and the Project 2061 *Benchmarks for Scientific Literacy*. Selected content and skill standards are shown below in shortened form. The following National Science Education Standards are covered on pages xii-xxvii in Frontiers in Science, and in Timelines in Science, as well as in chapter features and laboratory investigations: Understanding About Scientific Inquiry (A.9), Understanding About Science and Technology (E.6), Science and Technology in Society (F.5), Science as a Human Endeavor (G.1), Nature of Science (G.2), and History of Science.

Content Standards

1 The Water Cycle

National Science Education Standards

D.1.f Water, which covers the majority of Earth's surface, circulates through Earth's atmosphere, surface, and crust in what is known as the "water cycle." Water evaporates from the surface, rises and cools as it moves to higher elevations, condenses as rain or snow, and falls to the surface.

D.3.d The Sun is the major source of energy for phenomena on Earth's surface, such as the water cycle.

Project 2061 Benchmarks

4.B.2 Three-fourths of Earth's surface is covered by a relatively thin layer of water, some of it frozen. The entire planet is surrounded by a relatively thin blanket of air.

4.B.7 Water evaporates from Earth's surface, rises and cools, and condenses into rain or snow. The water falling on land as precipitation collects in rivers and lakes, soil, and porous layers of rock, and much of it flows back into the ocean.

2 Freshwater Resources

National Science Education Standards

F.3.b Human activities can induce hazards through resource acquisition, urban growth, land-use decisions, and waste disposal. Such activities can speed up many natural changes.

F.4.b Risks are associated with natural hazards such as floods—which can destroy habitats, damage property, and harm or kill people. Risks are also associated with chemical hazards such as pollution in air, water, and soil, as well as with biological hazards, such as bacteria and viruses.

Project 2061 Benchmarks

4.B.8 Fresh water, limited in supply, is essential for life and also for most industrial processes. Rivers, lakes, and groundwater can be depleted or polluted, becoming unavailable or unsuitable for life.

4.B.11 The benefits of Earth's resources—such as fresh water, air, soil, and trees—can be reduced by using them wastefully or by deliberately or inadvertently destroying them. Cleaning up polluted air, water, or soil or restoring depleted soil, forests, or fishing grounds can be very difficult or costly.

x Unit: Earth's Waters

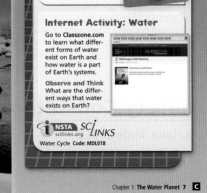

Internet Activity: Water

Go to Classzone.com to learn what different forms of water exist on Earth and how water is a part of Earth's systems.

Observe and Think
What are the different ways that water exists on Earth?

NSTA
scilinks.org SCI LINKS

Water Cycle Code: MDL018

Chapter 1: The Water Planet 7 **C**

T6

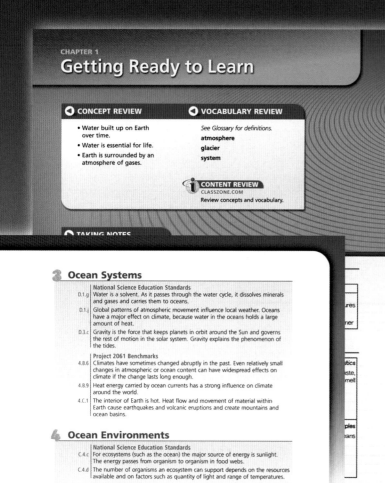

CHAPTER 1

Getting Ready to Learn

◀ CONCEPT REVIEW

- Water built up on Earth over time.
- Water is essential for life.
- Earth is surrounded by an atmosphere of gases.

◀ VOCABULARY REVIEW

See Glossary for definitions.

atmosphere
glacier
system

CONTENT REVIEW
CLASSZONE.COM
Review concepts and vocabulary.

◀ TAKING NOTES

3 Ocean Systems

National Science Education Standards

D.1.g	Water is a solvent. As it passes through the water cycle, it dissolves minerals and gases and carries them to oceans.
D.1.j	Global patterns of atmospheric movement influence local weather. Oceans have a major effect on climate, because water in the oceans holds a large amount of heat.
D.3.c	Gravity is the force that keeps planets in orbit around the Sun and governs the rest of motion in the solar system. Gravity explains the phenomenon of the tides.

Project 2061 Benchmarks

4.B.6	Climates have sometimes changed abruptly in the past. Even relatively small changes in atmospheric or ocean content can have widespread effects on climate if the change lasts long enough.
4.B.9	Heat energy carried by ocean currents has a strong influence on climate around the world.
4.C.1	The interior of Earth is hot. Heat flow and movement of material within Earth cause earthquakes and volcanic eruptions and create mountains and ocean basins.

4 Ocean Environments

National Science Education Standards

C.4.c	For ecosystems (such as the ocean) the major source of energy is sunlight. The energy passes from organism to organism in food webs.
C.4.d	The number of organisms an ecosystem can support depends on the resources available and on factors such as quantity of light and range of temperatures.

Project 2061 Benchmarks

4.B.11	The atmosphere and oceans have a limited capacity to absorb waste and recycle materials naturally.

Process and Skill Standards

National Science Education Standards		Project 2061 Benchmarks	
A.1	Identify questions that can be answered through investigation.	1.A.3	Some knowledge in science is very old and yet is still used today.
A.2	Design and conduct a scientific investigation.	3.B.1	Design requires taking constraints into account.
A.3	Use appropriate tools and techniques to gather and interpret data.	9.B.3	Graphs can show the relationship between two variables.
A.4	Use evidence to predict, explain, and model.	9.C.4	Graphs can show patterns and can be used to make predictions.
A.5	Use critical thinking to find relationships between results and interpretations.	11.C.4	Use equations to summarize observed changes.
A.6	Consider alternative explanations and predictions.	12.B.1	Find what percentage one number is of another.
A.7	Communicate procedures, results, and conclusions.	12.C.1	Compare amounts proportionally.
A.8	Use mathematics in scientific investigations.	12.D.1	Use tables and graphs to organize information and identify relationships.
E.2	Design a solution or product.	12.D.2	Read, interpret, and describe tables and graphs.
E.3	Implement the proposed solution.	12.D.4	Understand information that includes different types of charts and graphs, including circle charts, bar graphs, line graphs, data tables, diagrams, and symbols.

Standards and Benchmarks **xi**

VOCA
fresh w
salt wa
water c
evapora
conden
precipit

MAIN IDEAS AND DETAILS
Make a two-column chart to start organizing information about water.

Water is a unique substance.

Seen from outer space, Earth glistens like a beautiful blue and white marble. Welcome to the "water planet", the only planet in our solar system with a surface covered by a vast amount of liquid water. Because of water, a truly amazing substance, life can exist on Earth.

What is so amazing about water? In the temperature ranges we have on Earth, it is the only substance that exists as a solid, a liquid, and a gas. At a low temperature, water freezes. It becomes a solid, which is ice. At a higher temperature, it flows easily in liquid form. Liquid water can become a gas, especially at higher temperatures. If you have ever noticed how something wet dries out in the hot sunlight, you have observed the effect of liquid water changing into a gas. The gas form is the invisible water vapor in our atmosphere.

Liquid water can fit any container. It can hold its shape in a raindrop, then merge with other drops to flow down a hill or slow down and sit for centuries in a lake.

Chapter 1: **The Water Planet 9** **C**

Content Organized Around Big Ideas

Each chapter develops a big idea of science, helping students to place key concepts in context.

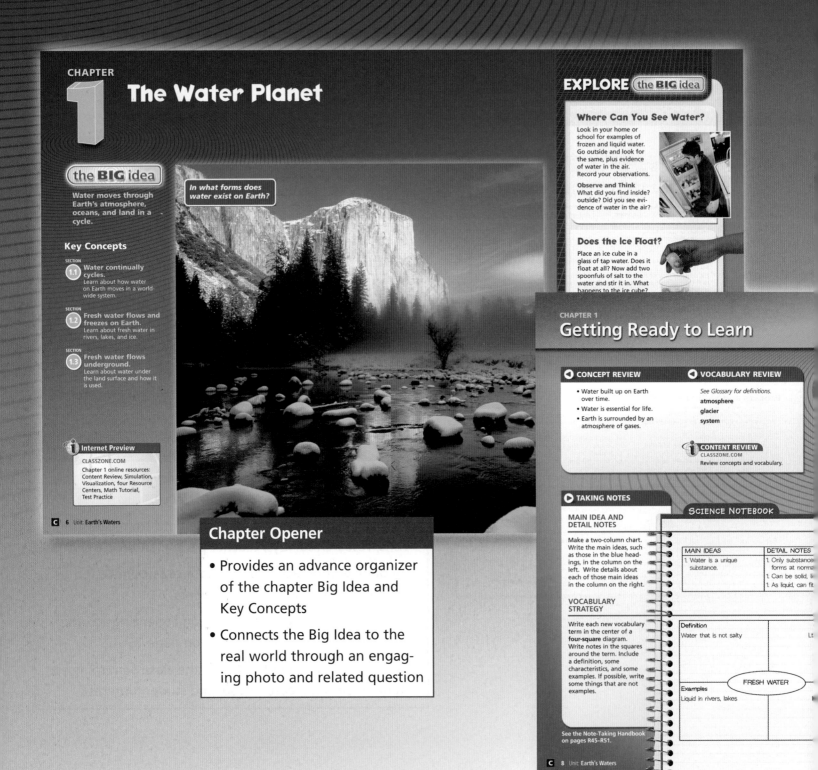

CHAPTER 1

The Water Planet

the BIG idea

Water moves through Earth's atmosphere, oceans, and land in a cycle.

Key Concepts

SECTION 1.1 Water continually cycles.
Learn about how water on Earth moves in a worldwide system.

SECTION 1.2 Fresh water flows and freezes on Earth.
Learn about fresh water in rivers, lakes, and ice.

SECTION 1.3 Fresh water flows underground.
Learn about water under the land surface and how it is used.

Internet Preview

CLASSZONE.COM
Chapter 1 online resources: Content Review, Simulation, Visualization, four Resource Centers, Math Tutorial, Test Practice

C 6 Unit: Earth's Waters

In what forms does water exist on Earth?

EXPLORE the BIG idea

Where Can You See Water?
Look in your home or school for examples of frozen and liquid water. Go outside and look for the same, plus evidence of water in the air. Record your observations.

Observe and Think
What did you find inside? outside? Did you see evidence of water in the air?

Does the Ice Float?
Place an ice cube in a glass of tap water. Does it float at all? Now add two spoonfuls of salt to the water and stir it in. What happens to the ice cube?

CHAPTER 1

Getting Ready to Learn

CONCEPT REVIEW
- Water built up on Earth over time.
- Water is essential for life.
- Earth is surrounded by an atmosphere of gases.

VOCABULARY REVIEW
See Glossary for definitions.
atmosphere
glacier
system

CONTENT REVIEW
CLASSZONE.COM
Review concepts and vocabulary.

TAKING NOTES

MAIN IDEA AND DETAIL NOTES
Make a two-column chart. Write the main ideas, such as those in the blue headings, in the column on the left. Write details about each of those main ideas in the column on the right.

VOCABULARY STRATEGY
Write each new vocabulary term in the center of a **four-square** diagram. Write notes in the squares around the term. Include a definition, some characteristics, and some examples. If possible, write some things that are not examples.

See the Note-Taking Handbook on pages R45–R51.

SCIENCE NOTEBOOK

MAIN IDEAS	DETAIL NOTES
1. Water is a unique substance.	1. Only substance forms at norma
	1. Can be solid, li
	1. As liquid, can fit

Definition
Water that is not salty

FRESH WATER

Examples
Liquid in rivers, lakes

C 8 Unit: Earth's Waters

Chapter Opener

- Provides an advance organizer of the chapter Big Idea and Key Concepts

- Connects the Big Idea to the real world through an engaging photo and related question

Visual Summary

- Summarizes Key Concepts using both text and visuals
- Reinforces the connection of Key Concepts to the Big Idea

Section Opener

- Highlights the Key Concept
- Connects new learning to prior knowledge
- Previews important vocabulary

the BIG idea

Water moves through Earth's atmosphere, oceans, and land in a cycle.

CONTENT REVIEW
CLASSZONE.COM

KEY CONCEPTS SUMMARY

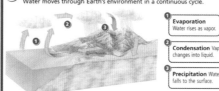

1.1 Water continually cycles.
Water moves through Earth's environment in a continuous cycle.

1 Evaporation Water rises as vapor.

2 Condensation Vapor changes into liquid.

3 Precipitation Water falls to the surface.

VOCABULARY
fresh water p. 11
salt water p. 11
water cycle p. 12
evaporation p. 13
condensation p. 13
precipitation p. 13

1.2 Fresh water flows and freezes on Earth.

Water on land collects and flows in rivers and lakes. Much of Earth's fresh water is frozen.

divide   drainage basins

VOCABULARY
divide p. 17
drainage basin p. 17
turnover p. 19
eutrophication p. 20
iceberg p. 22

1.3 Fresh water flows under
Water collects and moves benea

Gravity pulls water down through **permeable** materials until it reaches an impermeable layer.

The **impermeable** layer prevents water from sinking farther down.

Reviewing Vocabulary

Use the terms in the box below to answer the next nine questions.

evaporation	precipitation	water cycle
turnover	eutrophication	artesian
iceberg	groundwater	permeable

1. Which word describes an increase in nutrients in a lake or pond?

2. Which kind of well does not need a pump?

3. Which term describes a seasonal change in a lake?

4. Which term describes a substance through which water can pass?

5. Which term names the continuous movement of water through Earth's environment?

6. What is the name for an enormous chunk of floating ice?

7. What word means the turning of liquid water into a gas?

8. What is the name of water stored in an aquifer?

9. What word is another name for rain, snow, sleet, and hail?

Reviewing Key Concepts

Multiple Choice Choose the letter of the best answer.

Thinking Critically

Use the photograph to answer the next four questions. There are 4 liters of water in the jug. The hose has been overflowing for about 10 seconds.

21. **OBSERVE** Describe what the water in the hose is doing.

22. **IDENTIFY EFFECTS** Explain what effect the water in the jug has on the water in the hose. Why does the water rise in the hose?

23. **PREDICT** When will the water stop flowing from the hose? Why?

24. **COMPARE AND CONTRAST** How is what is happening in the hose like and unlike what happens in an artesian well?

25. **EXPLAIN** Explain why the water cycle matters to humans and animals.

26. **CONNECT** In a mountainous area, temperatures are lower at higher altitudes. Explain the connection between this fact and the existence of valley glaciers.

27. **COMPARE AND CONTRAST** Explain the difference between clouds and water vapor in the atmosphere.

28. **INFER** Explain why water in a bowl-shaped drainage basin does not eventually flow to the ocean.

29. **APPLY** Name at least two things that you think people could do to lessen eutrophication caused by pollution.

30. **APPLY** Explain why even though evaporation draws water but not salt from the ocean, the ocean does not become saltier.

31. **PREDICT** Fill in the chart with predictions of how water will collect under the stated conditions.

Conditions	Prediction
32. A bed of permeable rock lies atop a bed of impermeable rock; rainfall is plentiful	
33. Heavy snows fall in a region that has year-round freezing temperatures.	
34. A large depression is left in impermeable rock by a glacier.	
35. Water from farm fields and gardens runs off into ponds.	

the BIG idea

36. **SYNTHESIZE** Explain why a raindrop that falls on your head may once have been water in the Pacific Ocean.

37. **MODEL** Draw a diagram of two drainage basins, showing how water flows and collects on the surface of Earth. Label the divide, as well as the bodies of water into which water flows.

UNIT PROJECTS

If you are doing a unit project, make a folder for your project. Include in your folder a list of the resources you will need, the date on which the project is due, and a schedule to keep track of your progress. Begin gathering data.

C 36 Unit: Earth's Waters

KEY CONCEPT

1.1 Water continually cycles.

BEFORE, you learned
- The force of running water causes erosion
- Water can be solid

NOW, you will learn
- What makes water important
- How much of Earth's water is salt water
- How water moves throughout Earth and its atmosphere

VOCABULARY
fresh water p. 11
salt water p. 11
water cycle p. 12
evaporation p. 13
condensation p. 13
precipitation p. 13

EXPLORE Water Vapor

Where does the water come from?

PROCEDURE

1. Put the ice in the glass and fill it with water.
2. Observe what happens to the outside of the glass.

MATERIALS
- clear glass
- ice
- water

WHAT DO YOU THINK?
- Where did the water on the outside of the glass come from?
- What does this activity tell you about the air surrounding you? What conclusion can you draw?

MAIN IDEAS AND DETAILS Make a two-column chart to start organizing information about water.

Water is a unique substance.

Seen from outer space, Earth glistens like a beautiful blue and white marble. Welcome to the "water planet", the only planet in our solar system with a surface covered by a vast amount of liquid water. Because of water, a truly amazing substance, life can exist on Earth.

What is so amazing about water? In the temperature ranges we have on Earth, it is the only substance that exists as a solid, a liquid, and a gas. At a low temperature, water freezes. It becomes a solid, which is ice. At a higher temperature, it flows easily in liquid form. Liquid water can become a gas, especially at higher temperatures. If you have ever noticed how something wet dries out in the hot sunlight, you have observed the effect of liquid water changing into a gas. The gas form is the invisible water vapor in our atmosphere.

Liquid water can fit any container. It can hold its shape in a raindrop, then merge with other drops to flow down a hill or slow down and sit for centuries in a lake.

Chapter 1: The Water Planet 9 C

The Big Idea Questions

- Help students connect their new learning back to the Big Idea
- Prompt students to synthesize and apply the Big Idea and Key Concepts

Many Ways to Learn

Because students learn in so many ways, *McDougal Littell Science* gives them a variety of experiences with important concepts and skills. Text, visuals, activities, and technology all focus on Big Ideas and Key Concepts.

Considerate Text

- Clear structure of meaningful headings
- Information clearly connected to main ideas
- Student-friendly writing style

Hands-on Learning

- Activities that reinforce Key Concepts
- Skill Focus for important inquiry and process skills
- Multiple activities in every chapter, from quick Explores to full-period Chapter Investigations

MAIN IDEA AND DETAILS Record in your notes this main idea and important details about the water cycle.

Water moves in a worldwide cycle.

Water continually moves and changes form. Water from clouds falls over the oceans and on land. Water flows in rivers and collects in lakes and under the ground. Water can be a solid in the form of ice, or it can be an invisible vapor in the atmosphere.

The Water Cycle

Water's movement on Earth is a cycle, or continually repeating process. The **water cycle** is the continuous movement of water through the environment of Earth. In the water cycle, water is constantly changing form, from a liquid on land, to a vapor in the atmosphere, and again to a liquid that falls to the surface. The flow of water on land and underground is also part of the water cycle. As water moves in the water cycle, the total amount of water in Earth's system does not change very much. The water cycle involves three major processes: evaporation, condensation, and precipitation.

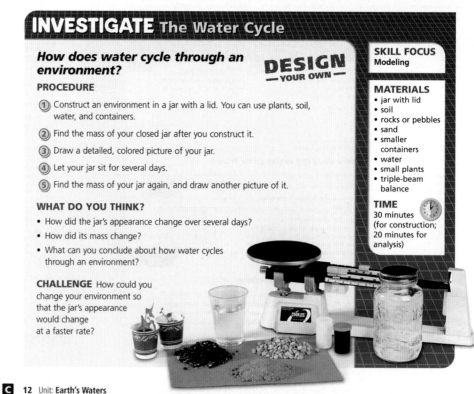

INVESTIGATE The Water Cycle

How does water cycle through an environment? DESIGN —YOUR OWN—

PROCEDURE

1. Construct an environment in a jar with a lid. You can use plants, soil, water, and containers.
2. Find the mass of your closed jar after you construct it.
3. Draw a detailed, colored picture of your jar.
4. Let your jar sit for several days.
5. Find the mass of your jar again, and draw another picture of it.

WHAT DO YOU THINK?

- How did the jar's appearance change over several days?
- How did its mass change?
- What can you conclude about how water cycles through an environment?

CHALLENGE How could you change your environment so that the jar's appearance would change at a faster rate?

SKILL FOCUS Modeling

MATERIALS
- jar with lid
- soil
- rocks or pebbles
- sand
- smaller containers
- water
- small plants
- triple-beam balance

TIME 30 minutes (for construction; 20 minutes for analysis)

The Water Cycle

Water on Earth moves in a continual cycle.

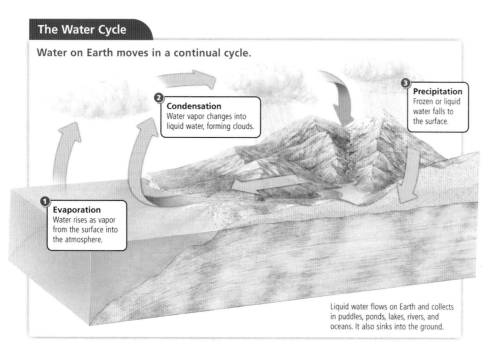

② **Condensation**
Water vapor changes into liquid water, forming clouds.

③ **Precipitation**
Frozen or liquid water falls to the surface.

① **Evaporation**
Water rises as vapor from the surface into the atmosphere.

Liquid water flows on Earth and collects in puddles, ponds, lakes, rivers, and oceans. It also sinks into the ground.

① The process in which water changes from liquid to vapor is called **evaporation.** Heat energy from the Sun warms up the surface of the ocean or another body of water. Some of the liquid water evaporates, becoming invisible water vapor, a gas.

② The process in which water vapor in the atmosphere becomes liquid is called **condensation.** Condensation occurs as air cools. Because cold air can hold less water vapor than warm air, some of the vapor condenses, or turns into droplets of liquid water. These droplets form clouds. At high altitudes clouds contain ice crystals. Unlike water vapor, clouds are visible evidence of water in the atmosphere.

③ Water that falls from clouds is **precipitation.** Inside a cloud, water droplets bump together and merge into larger droplets. They finally become heavy enough to fall as precipitation—rain, sleet, or hail. The water from precipitation sinks into the soil or flows into streams and rivers in the process called runoff. The force of gravity pulls the flowing water downward and, in most cases, eventually to the ocean.

VISUALIZATION
CLASSZONE.COM
See how water moves through Earth's system in the water cycle.

CHECK YOUR READING Why does water vapor in air condense into liquid droplets?

Visuals that Teach

- Information-rich visuals directly connected to the text
- Thoughtful pairing of diagrams and real-world photos
- Reading Visuals questions to support student learning

Integrated Technology

- Interaction with Key Concepts through Simulations and Visualizations
- Easy access to relevant Web resources through Resource Centers and SciLinks
- Opportunities for review through Content Review and Math Tutorials

Differentiated Instruction

A full spectrum of resources for differentiating instruction supports you in reaching the wide range of learners in your classroom.

1.1 INSTRUCT

Real World Example

Identify a 2-mile distance between two local landmarks that are familiar to students, and compare it to the average depth of the oceans.

EXPLORE (the BIG idea)

Revisit "Where Can You See Water?" on p. 7. Have students explain the significance of their results.

Teach from Visuals

To help students interpret the visual showing the water-to-land ratio on Earth, ask:

• How much of Earth's surface is covered by water? *71 percent, or almost three-quarters*

• Why does a globe show the amount of water covering Earth more accurately than a flat map? *A flat map may exaggerate the amount of land in relation to the amount of water.*

Ongoing Assessment

Recognize the importance of water.
Ask: Why is water important? *Water is needed for life to exist on Earth.*

  Answer: in the ocean

Answer: at the bottom, in Antarctica

Water covers most of Earth.

 A Earth looks bluish from space because most of Earth's surface is ocean. If you look at a globe or a world map, you will see the names of four oceans—Atlantic, Pacific, Indian, and Arctic. If you look more closely or trace the four named oceans with your finger, you will see that they are connected to each other. Together they form one huge ocean. Any part of this ocean is called the sea.

The global ocean covers 71 percent, or almost three-quarters, of Earth's surface. Most of the ocean is in the Southern Hemisphere. The ocean is, on average, 3.8 kilometers deep (about 2.4 miles deep). Although most of the water covering Earth is ocean, water also covers some land areas, as rivers, lakes, and ice.

CHECK YOUR READING Where is most of Earth's water?

Water-to-Land Ratio

Almost three-quarters of Earth's surface is covered by water.

29% | 71%

A flat map can make the percentage of land on Earth appear greater than it is.

READING VISUALS Look at the globe and the map. Where is the amount of land most exaggerated on the map?

C 10 Unit: Earth's Waters

Water and Life

Without water, nothing would live on Earth. Living things need water to function. Your own body is two-thirds water. In your body, your blood—which is mostly water—carries nutrients that give you energy and flushes wastes away. Many forms of life live in water. Oceans, lakes, and rivers are home to fish, mammals, plants, and other organisms. Even a single drop of water may contain tiny forms of life.

Fresh Water and Salt Water

When you hear the word *water*, you might imagine a cool drink that quenches your thirst. The water that you drink and depend on for survival is fresh water. **Fresh water** is water that is not salty and has little or no taste, color, or smell. Most rivers and lakes are fresh water.

 The water in the ocean is salt water. **Salt water** is water that contains dissolved salts and other minerals. Human beings and most other land animals cannot survive by drinking salt water, although many other forms of life can live in salt water.

You may be surprised to learn that even though fresh water is important for life, fresh water is actually scarce on Earth. Because most of Earth's water is in the ocean, most of the water on Earth is salt water. The illustration below compares the amount of fresh water and salt water on Earth. Almost all—about 97 percent—of Earth's water is salt water in the ocean. Only about 3 percent of Earth's water, at any given time, is fresh water.

CHECK YOUR READING What is the difference between fresh water and salt water?

VOCABULARY
Remember to write the terms *fresh water* and *salt water* in four-square diagrams in your notebook.

Salt Water vs. Fresh Water

Most water on Earth is salt water.

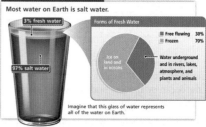

3% fresh water

97% salt water

Forms of Fresh Water

■ Free flowing 30%
■ Frozen 70%

Ice on land and in oceans

Water underground and in rivers, lakes, atmosphere, and plants and animals

 Imagine that this glass of water represents all of the water on Earth.

DIFFERENTIATE INSTRUCTION

? More Reading Support
A What makes Earth look bluish from space? *the ocean*
B How deep is the ocean, on average? *3.8 km (about 2.4 mi)*

English Learners Within this section are a variety of introductory clauses and phrases. Give students these examples and have them identify the subject of each sentence: "Seen from outer space, Earth glistens like a beautiful blue and white marble." "At a low temperature, water freezes." Encourage students to use introductory clauses and phrases in their own writing.

Below Level Display a globe and invite students to compare the amount of blue ocean area with the amount of land area.

DIFFERENTIATE INSTRUCTION

? More Reading Support
C What kind of water is in the oceans? *salt water*
D Which kind of water is scarce? *fresh water*

Advanced Have students consider the question, Why are humans unable to survive by drinking salt water? Have them research the chemistry that answers the question.

 Challenge and Extension, p. 19

Teacher's Edition

• More Reading Support for below-level readers

• Strategies for below-level and advanced learners, English learners, and inclusion students

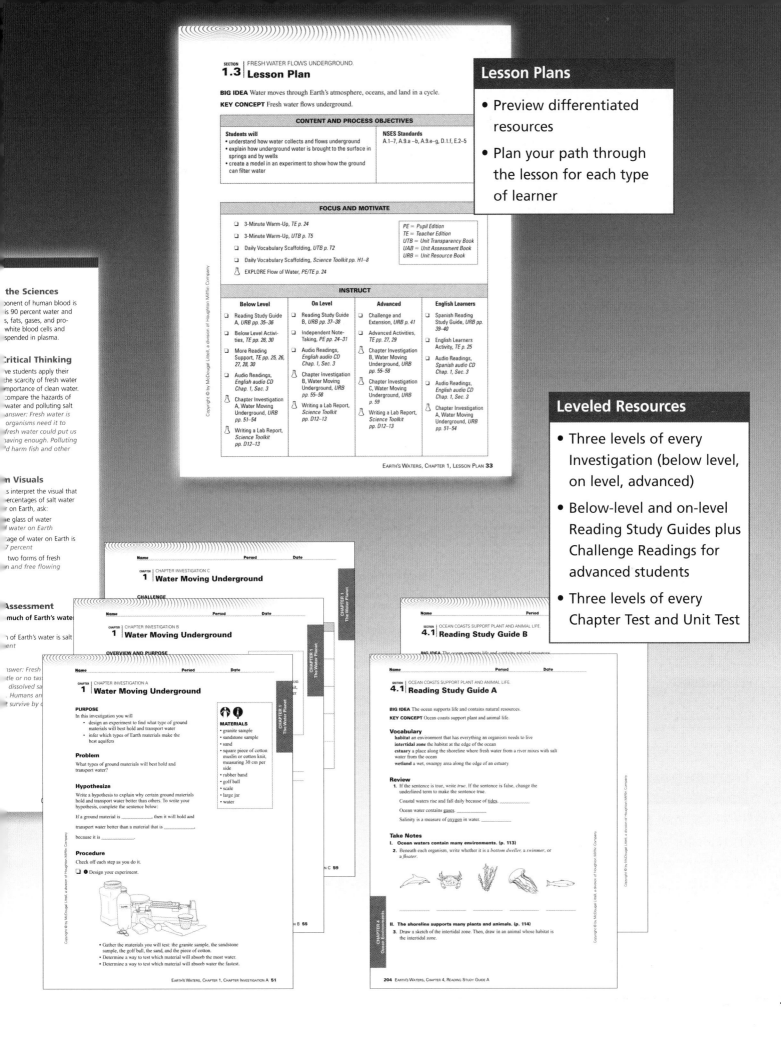

Lesson Plans

- Preview differentiated resources
- Plan your path through the lesson for each type of learner

Leveled Resources

- Three levels of every Investigation (below level, on level, advanced)
- Below-level and on-level Reading Study Guides plus Challenge Readings for advanced students
- Three levels of every Chapter Test and Unit Test

SECTION | FRESH WATER FLOWS UNDERGROUND.
1.3 | Lesson Plan

BIG IDEA Water moves through Earth's atmosphere, oceans, and land in a cycle.

KEY CONCEPT Fresh water flows underground.

CONTENT AND PROCESS OBJECTIVES

Students will
- understand how water collects and flows underground
- explain how underground water is brought to the surface in springs and wells
- create a model in an experiment to show how the ground can filter water

NSES Standards
A.1–7, A.9.a –b, A.9.e–g, D.1.f, E.2–5

FOCUS AND MOTIVATE

- ❏ 3-Minute Warm-Up, *TE p. 24*
- ❏ 3-Minute Warm-Up, *UTB p. T5*
- ❏ Daily Vocabulary Scaffolding, *UTB p. T2*
- ❏ Daily Vocabulary Scaffolding, *Science Toolkit pp. H1–8*
- ⚗ EXPLORE Flow of Water, *PE/TE p. 24*

PE = Pupil Edition
TE = Teacher Edition
UTB = Unit Transparency Book
UAB = Unit Assessment Book
URB = Unit Resource Book

INSTRUCT

Below Level	On Level	Advanced	English Learners
❏ Reading Study Guide A, *URB pp. 35–36*	❏ Reading Study Guide B, *URB pp. 37–38*	❏ Challenge and Extension, *URB p. 41*	❏ Spanish Reading Study Guide, *URB pp. 39–40*
❏ Below Level Activities, *TE pp. 26, 30*	❏ Independent Note-Taking, *PE pp. 24–31*	❏ Advanced Activities, *TE pp. 27, 29*	❏ English Learners Activity, *TE p. 25*
❏ More Reading Support, *TE pp. 25, 26, 27, 28, 30*	❏ Audio Readings, *English audio CD Chap. 1, Sec. 3*	⚗ Chapter Investigation B, Water Moving Underground, *URB pp. 55–58*	❏ Audio Readings, *Spanish audio CD Chap. 1, Sec. 3*
❏ Audio Readings, *English audio CD Chap. 1, Sec. 3*	⚗ Chapter Investigation B, Water Moving Underground, *URB pp. 55–58*	⚗ Chapter Investigation C, Water Moving Underground, *URB p. 59*	❏ Audio Readings, *English audio CD Chap. 1, Sec. 3*
⚗ Chapter Investigation A, Water Moving Underground, *URB pp. 51–54*	⚗ Writing a Lab Report, *Science Toolkit pp. D12–13*	⚗ Writing a Lab Report, *Science Toolkit pp. D12–13*	⚗ Chapter Investigation A, Water Moving Underground, *URB pp. 51–54*
⚗ Writing a Lab Report, *Science Toolkit pp. D12–13*			

EARTH'S WATERS, CHAPTER 1, LESSON PLAN **33**

Copyright © by McDougal Littell, a division of Houghton Mifflin Company

---

Name ___ Period ___ Date ___

CHAPTER | CHAPTER INVESTIGATION C
1 | Water Moving Underground

CHALLENGE

Name ___ Period ___ Date ___

CHAPTER | CHAPTER INVESTIGATION B
1 | Water Moving Underground

OVERVIEW AND PURPOSE

Name ___ Period ___ Date ___

CHAPTER | CHAPTER INVESTIGATION A
1 | Water Moving Underground

PURPOSE
In this investigation you will
- design an experiment to find what type of ground materials will best hold and transport water
- infer which types of Earth materials make the best aquifers

MATERIALS
- granite sample
- sandstone sample
- sand
- square piece of cotton muslin or cotton knit, measuring 30 cm per side
- rubber band
- golf ball
- scale
- large jar
- water

Problem
What types of ground materials will best hold and transport water?

Hypothesize
Write a hypothesis to explain why certain ground materials hold and transport water better than others. To write your hypothesis, complete the sentence below:

If a ground material is ___, then it will hold and transport water better than a material that is ___, because it is ___.

Procedure
Check off each step as you do it.
- ❏ ❶ Design your experiment.

- Gather the materials you will test: the granite sample, the sandstone sample, the golf ball, the sand, and the piece of cotton.
- Determine a way to test which material will absorb the most water.
- Determine a way to test which material will absorb water the fastest.

EARTH'S WATERS, CHAPTER 1, CHAPTER INVESTIGATION A **51**

N B **55**

N C **59**

CHAPTER 1
The Water Planet

CHAPTER 4
Ocean Environments

Name ___ Period ___

SECTION | OCEAN COASTS SUPPORT PLANT AND ANIMAL LIFE.
4.1 | Reading Study Guide B

BIG IDEA The ocean supports life and contains natural resources.

Name ___ Period ___ Date ___

SECTION | OCEAN COASTS SUPPORT PLANT AND ANIMAL LIFE.
4.1 | Reading Study Guide A

BIG IDEA The ocean supports life and contains natural resources.
KEY CONCEPT Ocean coasts support plant and animal life.

Vocabulary
habitat an environment that has everything an organism needs to live
intertidal zone the habitat at the edge of the ocean
estuary a place along the shoreline where fresh water from a river mixes with salt water from the ocean
wetland a wet, swampy area along the edge of an estuary

Review
1. If the sentence is true, write *true*. If the sentence is false, change the underlined term to make the sentence true.

Coastal waters rise and fall daily because of <u>tides</u>. ___

Ocean water contains <u>gases</u>. ___

Salinity is a measure of <u>oxygen</u> in water. ___

Take Notes
I. Ocean waters contain many environments. (p. 113)
2. Beneath each organism, write whether it is a *bottom dweller*, a *swimmer*, or a *floater*.

___ ___ ___ ___

II. The shoreline supports many plants and animals. (p. 114)
3. Draw a sketch of the intertidal zone. Then, draw in an animal whose habitat is the intertidal zone.

204 EARTH'S WATERS, CHAPTER 4, READING STUDY GUIDE A

---

the Sciences

...ponent of human blood is ...is 90 percent water and ...s, fats, gases, and pro- ...white blood cells and ...spended in plasma.

Critical Thinking
...ve students apply their ...the scarcity of fresh water ...mportance of clean water. ...compare the hazards of ...water and polluting salt ...answer: Fresh water is ...organisms need it to ...fresh water could put us ...aving enough. Polluting ...d harm fish and other

Visuals
...s interpret the visual that ...ercentages of salt water ...on Earth, ask:
...e glass of water
...water on Earth
...age of water on Earth is ...7 percent
...two forms of fresh ...and free flowing

Assessment
...much of Earth's wate...
...of Earth's water is salt
...ent
...swer: Fresh
...tle or no tas...
...dissolved sa...
. Humans an...
...survive by...

T13

Effective Assessment

McDougal Littell Science incorporates a comprehensive set of resources for assessing student knowledge and performance before, during, and after instruction.

Diagnostic Tests

- Assessment of students' prior knowledge
- Readiness check for concepts and skills in the upcoming chapter

---

Ongoing Assessment

Explain how water moves throughout Earth and its atmosphere.

Ask: How does water cycle through Earth's environment? *Water evaporates from surface and rises as vapor to atmosphere; it condenses into liquid and forms clouds, then falls to surface as liquid or frozen water; it flows along Earth and collects or sinks into ground.*

EXPLORE (the BIG idea)

Revisit "Internet Activity: Water" on p. 7. Have students compare their findings with the text.

Reinforce (the BIG idea)

Have students relate the section to the Big Idea.

📄 Reinforcing Key Concepts, p. 21

1.1 ASSESS & RETEACH

Assess

📝 Section 1.1 Quiz, p. 3

Reteach

Draw a large circle on the chalkboard. Remind students that a cycle can be represented as a circle. Ask them to come to the board individually to make one contribution that helps you make the circle into a picture of the water cycle. When you have finished, ask students to describe what happens in each section of the circle.

Technology Resources

Have students visit **ClassZone.com** for reteaching of Key Concepts.

ℹ️ CONTENT REVIEW
💿 CONTENT REVIEW CD-ROM

C 14 Unit: Earth's Waters

Most of the water that evaporates on Earth—85 percent of it—evaporates from the ocean. (About 75 percent of this condenses as clouds and falls right back into the ocean.) The remaining 15 percent of evaporating water comes from such sources as damp ground, lakes, wet sidewalks, rivers, and sprinklers. Plants are also part of the water cycle. They pull up water from the ground and then release much of it into the air through their leaves.

Even though the water evaporates into the atmosphere comes from both the salty ocean and from fresh water on land, all the precipitation that falls back to the surface is fresh water. When salt water evaporates, the salt is left behind. Through the water cycle the ocean water that human beings cannot drink becomes a source of fresh water for human beings and other life on Earth.

The Impact of the Water Cycle

The action of the water cycle is easy to spot. When it rains or snows, you can see precipitation in action. When you look at a flowing stream, you see the water cycle returning water to the sea. When a stream dries up, you know that the water cycle in the area has slowed down for a while.

Wet weather can fill reservoirs with drinking water and pour needed water on crops. Wet weather can also bring too much rain. For example, during the wet season in India, winds blow rain clouds inland from the Indian Ocean. Tremendous rains fall over the land for months. The rain is usually welcome after a long and hot dry season. However, these seasonal rains frequently cause devastating floods, covering acres and acres of land with water.

Flooding usually occurs during India's annual rainy season.

1.1 Review

KEY CONCEPTS

1. Name three things about water that make it unique or important.
2. How much of Earth's water is fresh water?
3. Explain the three processes that make up the water cycle.

CRITICAL THINKING

4. **Apply** How can a drop of salt water once have been a drop of fresh water?
5. **Compare and Contrast** What are two differences between salt water and fresh water?

❓ CHALLENGE

6. **Infer** In 1996, the Galileo space probe sent back photographs that showed ice on the surface of one of the moons of Jupiter. Scientists suspected there was water under the ice. Why did this discovery excite some people who thought there was a chance of finding life on that moon?

C 14 Unit: Earth's Waters

ANSWERS

1. Water can exist as liquid, gas, or solid in temperature ranges found on Earth. It can fit any container. It sustains life. It can form into a drop.

2. 3 percent

3. evaporation—liquid water changes into water vapor

(gas); condensation—water vapor (gas) changes into liquid; precipitation—water falls from clouds as rain or snow.

4. The fresh water flowed into the ocean, where dissolved salts and minerals mixed with it.

5. Salt water contains salts and other minerals; it cannot sustain human life. Fresh water has little or no taste.

6. Where there is water, there can be life.

Reviewing Vocabulary

Use the terms in the box below to answer the next nine questions.

evaporation	precipitation	water cycle
turnover	eutrophication	artesian
iceberg	groundwater	permeable

1. Which word describes an increase in nutrients in a lake or pond?

2. Which kind of well does not need a pump?

3. Which term describes a seasonal change in a lake?

4. Which term describes a substance through which water can pass?

5. Which term names the continuous movement of water through Earth's environment?

6. What is the name for an enormous chunk of floating ice?

7. What word means the turning of liquid water into a gas?

8. What is the name of water stored in an aquifer?

9. What word is another name for rain, snow, sleet, and hail?

Reviewing Key Concepts

Multiple Choice *Choose the letter of the best answer.*

10. What are the three forms of water on Earth?
    a. groundwater, lakes, and clouds
    b. liquid water, frozen water, and water vapor
    c. gas, steam, and vapor
    d. groundwater, oceans, and ice

11. How much of Earth's water is fresh water?
    a. almost all
    b. about half
    c. very little
    d. none

12. Which process forms clouds?
    a. evaporation
    b. precipitation
    c. condensation
    d. dehydration

13. What ice formation covers Greenland and Antarctica?
    a. iceberg
    b. landmass
    c. valley glacier
    d. continental glacier

14. Which is a characteristic of a pond?
    a. rooted plants covering the entire bottom
    b. plants only near shore
    c. a layer of impermeable rock
    d. water heated by underground rock

15. How are glaciers like rivers?
    a. They are made of liquid water.
    b. Their water sinks into the ground.
    c. They flow downhill.
    d. They are a mile thick.

16. How is water stored in an aquifer?
    a. in an open underground lake
    b. in cracks and spaces in rocks
    c. in impermeable rock
    d. in wells and springs

Short Answer *Write a short answer to each question.*

17. Explain why most of the water cycle takes place over the ocean.

18. How does an iceberg form?

19. Why are aquifers valuable?

20. What is the difference between a valley glacier and a continental glacier?

Ongoing Assessment

- Check Your Reading questions for student self-check of comprehension
- Consistent Teacher's Edition prompts for assessing understanding of Key Concepts

Section and Chapter Reviews

- Focus on Key Concepts and critical thinking skills
- A full range of question types and levels of thinking

Leveled Chapter and Unit Tests

- Three levels of test for every chapter and unit
- Same Big Ideas, Key Concepts, and essential skills assessed on all levels

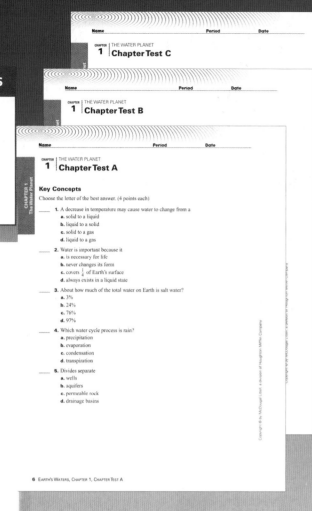

Chapter Test C

CHAPTER 1 THE WATER PLANET

Chapter Test B

CHAPTER 1 THE WATER PLANET

Chapter Test A

CHAPTER 1 THE WATER PLANET

Key Concepts

Choose the letter of the best answer. (4 points each)

1. A decrease in temperature may cause water to change from a
   a. solid to a liquid
   b. liquid to a solid
   c. solid to a gas
   d. liquid to a gas

2. Water is important because it
   a. is necessary for life
   b. never changes its form
   c. covers $\frac{1}{4}$ of Earth's surface
   d. always exists in a liquid state

3. About how much of the total water on Earth is salt water?
   a. 3%
   b. 24%
   c. 76%
   d. 97%

4. Which water cycle process is rain?
   a. precipitation
   b. evaporation
   c. condensation
   d. transpiration

5. Divides separate
   a. wells
   b. aquifers
   c. permeable rock
   d. drainage basins

6 EARTH'S WATERS, CHAPTER 1, CHAPTER TEST A

Thinking Critically

Use the photograph to answer the next four questions. There are 4 liters of water in the jug. The hose has been overflowing for about 10 seconds.

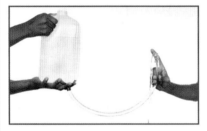

21. **OBSERVE** Describe what the water in the hose is doing.

22. **IDENTIFY EFFECTS** Explain what effect the water in the jug has on the water in the hose. Why does the water rise in the hose?

23. **PREDICT** When will the water stop flowing from the hose? Why?

24. **COMPARE AND CONTRAST** How is what is happening in the hose like and unlike what happens in an artesian well?

25. **EXPLAIN** Explain why the water cycle matters to humans and animals.

26. **CONNECT** In a mountainous area, temperatures are lower at higher altitudes. Explain the connection between this fact and the existence of valley glaciers.

27. **COMPARE AND CONTRAST** Explain the difference between clouds and water vapor in the atmosphere.

28. **INFER** Explain why water in a bowl-shaped drainage basin does not eventually flow to the ocean.

29. **APPLY** Name at least two things that you think people could do to lessen eutrophication caused by pollution.

30. **APPLY** Explain why even though evaporation draws water but not salt from the ocean, the ocean does not become saltier.

31. **PREDICT** Fill in the chart with predictions of how water will collect under the stated conditions.

Conditions	Prediction
32. A bed of permeable rock lies atop a bed of impermeable rock; rainfall is plentiful	
33. Heavy snows fall in a region that has year-round freezing temperatures.	
34. A large depression is left in impermeable rock by a glacier.	
35. Water from farm fields and gardens runs off into ponds.	

the BIG idea

36. **SYNTHESIZE** Explain why a raindrop that falls on your head may once have been water in the Pacific Ocean.

37. **MODEL** Draw a diagram of two drainage basins, showing how water flows and collects on the surface of Earth. Label the divide, as well as the bodies of water into which water flows.

UNIT PROJECTS

If you are doing a unit project, make a folder for

Rubrics

- Rubrics in Teacher's Edition for all extended-response questions
- Rubrics for all Unit Projects
- Alternative Assessment with rubric for each chapter
- A wide range of additional rubrics in the Science Toolkit

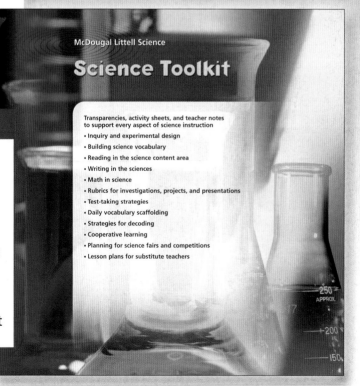

McDougal Littell Science

Science Toolkit

Transparencies, activity sheets, and teacher notes to support every aspect of science instruction

- Inquiry and experimental design
- Building science vocabulary
- Reading in the science content area
- Writing in the sciences
- Math in science
- Rubrics for investigations, projects, and presentations
- Test-taking strategies
- Daily vocabulary scaffolding
- Strategies for decoding
- Cooperative learning
- Planning for science fairs and competitions
- Lesson plans for substitute teachers

McDougal Littell Science Modular Series

McDougal Littell Science lets you choose the titles that match your curriculum. Each module in this flexible 15-book series takes an in-depth look at a specific area of life, earth, or physical science.

- Flexibility to match your curriculum
- Convenience of smaller books
- Complete Student Resource Handbooks in every module

Life Science Titles

A ▶ Cells and Heredity
1. The Cell
2. How Cells Function
3. Cell Division
4. Patterns of Heredity
5. DNA and Modern Genetics

B ▶ Life Over Time
1. The History of Life on Earth
2. Classification of Living Things
3. Population Dynamics

C ▶ Diversity of Living Things
1. Single-Celled Organisms and Viruses
2. Introduction to Multicellular Organisms
3. Plants
4. Invertebrate Animals
5. Vertebrate Animals

D ▶ Ecology
1. Ecosystems and Biomes
2. Interactions Within Ecosystems
3. Human Impact on Ecosystems

E ▶ Human Biology
1. Systems, Support, and Movement
2. Absorption, Digestion, and Exchange
3. Transport and Protection
4. Control and Reproduction
5. Growth, Development, and Health

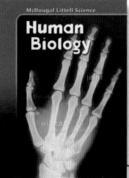

Earth Science Titles

A ▶ **Earth's Surface**
1. Views of Earth Today
2. Minerals
3. Rocks
4. Weathering and Soil Formation
5. Erosion and Deposition

B ▶ **The Changing Earth**
1. Plate Tectonics
2. Earthquakes
3. Mountains and Volcanoes
4. Views of Earth's Past
5. Natural Resources

C ▶ **Earth's Waters**
1. The Water Planet
2. Freshwater Resources
3. Ocean Systems
4. Ocean Environments

D ▶ **Earth's Atmosphere**
1. Earth's Changing Atmosphere
2. Weather Patterns
3. Weather Fronts and Storms
4. Climate and Climate Change

E ▶ **Space Science**
1. Exploring Space
2. Earth, Moon, and Sun
3. Our Solar System
4. Stars, Galaxies, and the Universe

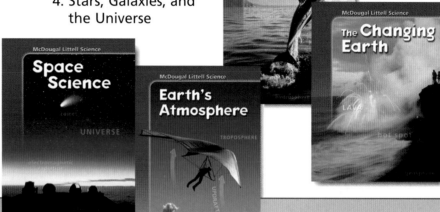

Physical Science Titles

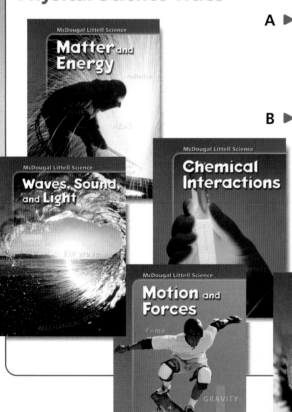

A ▶ **Matter and Energy**
1. Introduction to Matter
2. Properties of Matter
3. Energy
4. Temperature and Heat

B ▶ **Chemical Interactions**
1. Atomic Structure and the Periodic Table
2. Chemical Bonds and Compounds
3. Chemical Reactions
4. Solutions
5. Carbon in Life and Materials

C ▶ **Motion and Forces**
1. Motion
2. Forces
3. Gravity, Friction, and Pressure
4. Work and Energy
5. Machines

D ▶ **Waves, Sound, and Light**
1. Waves
2. Sound
3. Electromagnetic Waves
4. Light and Optics

E ▶ **Electricity and Magnetism**
1. Electricity
2. Circuits and Electronics
3. Magnetism

Teaching Resources

A wealth of print and technology resources help you adapt the program to your teaching style and to the specific needs of your students.

Book-Specific Print Resources

Unit Resource Book provides all of the teaching resources for the unit organized by chapter and section.

- Family Letters
- *Scientific American Frontiers* Video Guide
- Unit Projects
- Lesson Plans
- Reading Study Guides (Levels A and B)
- Spanish Reading Study Guides
- Challenge Readings
- Challenge and Extension Activities
- Reinforcing Key Concepts
- Vocabulary Practice
- Math Support and Practice
- Investigation Datasheets
- Chapter Investigations (Levels A, B, and C)
- Additional Investigations (Levels A, B, and C)
- Summarizing the Chapter

Unit Assessment Book contains complete resources for assessing student knowledge and performance.

- Chapter Diagnostic Tests
- Section Quizzes
- Chapter Tests (Levels A, B, and C)
- Alternative Assessments
- Unit Tests (Levels A, B, and C)

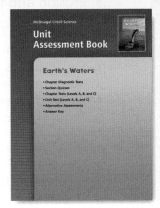

Unit Transparency Book includes instructional visuals for each chapter.

- Three-Minute Warm-Ups
- Note-Taking Models
- Daily Vocabulary Scaffolding
- Chapter Outlines
- Big Idea Flow Charts
- Chapter Teaching Visuals

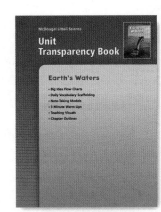

Unit Lab Manual

Unit Note-Taking/Reading Study Guide

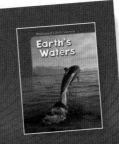

McDougal Littell Science

Unit Resource Book

Earth's Waters

- Family Letters (English and Spanish)
- *Scientific American Frontiers* Video Guides
- Unit Projects (with Rubrics)
- Lesson Plans
- Reading Study Guides (Levels A and B and Spanish)
- Challenge Activities and Readings
- Reinforcing Key Concepts
- Vocabulary Practice and Decoding Support
- Math Support and Practice
- Investigation Datasheets
- Chapter Investigations (Levels A, B, and C)
- Additional Investigations (Levels A, B, and C)
- Summarizing the Chapter

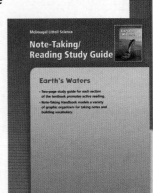

Program-Wide Print Resources

Process and Lab Skills

Problem Solving and Critical Thinking

Standardized Test Practice

Science Toolkit

City Science

Visual Glossary

Multi-Language Glossary

English Learners Package

Scientific American Frontiers Video Guide

How Stuff Works Express
This quarterly magazine offers opportunities to explore current science topics.

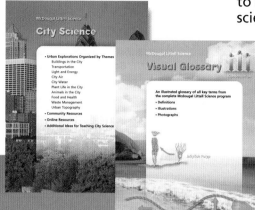

Technology Resources

Scientific American Frontiers **Video Program**
Each specially tailored segment from this award-winning PBS series correlates to a unit; available on VHS and DVD

Audio CDs Complete chapter texts read in both English and Spanish

Lab Generator CD-ROM
A searchable database of all activities from the program plus additional labs for each unit; edit and print your own version of labs

Test Generator CD-ROM

eEdition CD-ROM

EasyPlanner CD-ROM

Content Review CD-ROM

Power Presentations CD-ROM

Online Resources

    ClassZone.com

    Content Review Online

    eEdition Plus Online

    EasyPlanner Plus Online

    eTest Plus Online

Correlation to National Science Education Standards

This chart provides an overview of how the five Earth Science modules of *McDougal Littell Science* address the National Science Education Standards. The complete wording of the standards can be found at the end of this Teacher's Edition.

A   Earth's Surface
B   The Changing Earth
C   Earth's Waters
D   Earth's Atmosphere
E   Space Science

		Book, Chapter, and Section
A.	**Science as Inquiry**	
A.1–A.8	**Abilities necessary to do scientific inquiry** Identify questions for investigation; design and conduct investigations; use evidence; think critically and logically; analyze alternative explanations; communicate; use mathematics.	pp. R2–R44, all Chapter Investigations, all Think Science features
A.9	**Understandings about scientific inquiry** Different kinds of investigations for different questions; investigations guided by current scientific knowledge; importance of mathematics and technology for data gathering and analysis; importance of evidence, logical argument, principles, models, and theories; role of legitimate skepticism; scientific investigations lead to new investigations.	pp. xxii–xxv, A1.4, B1.4, C1.1, D3.3, E3.2
B.	**Physical Science**	
B.1	**Properties and changes of properties in matter** Physical properties; substances, elements, and compounds; chemical reactions.	A2.2, B1.1, C3.1, D1.1 (Connecting Sciences), D1.4, D2.1
B.2	**Motions and forces** Position, speed, direction of motion; balanced and unbalanced forces.	C3.4, C4.1, C4.3, E2.1, E2.2, E2.3
B.3	**Transfer of energy** Energy transfer; forms of energy; heat and light; electrical circuits; sun as source of Earth's energy.	D1.2, D1.3, E1.2, E4.1, E4.2, E4.3, E4.4, B5.3
C.	**Life Science**	
C.3	**Regulation and behavior** Growth, reproduction, and maintenance of stable internal environment; regulation; behavior; evolution of behavior through adaptation to environment.	E1.4 (Connecting Sciences)
C.4	**Populations and ecosystems** Populations; ecosystems; producers, consumers, and decomposers; food webs; energy flow; population size and resource availability; population growth.	B5.1 (Connecting Sciences), C4.1, C4.2, C4.3
C.5	**Diversity and adaptations of organisms** Unity and diversity; similarities in internal structures, chemical processes, and evidence of common ancestry; adaptation and biological evolution; extinction and fossil evidence.	A5.3 (Connecting Sciences), B4.1, B4.2, B4.3
D.	**Earth and Space Science**	
D.1	**Structure of the earth system** Lithosphere, mantle, and core; plate movement and earthquakes, volcanoes, and mountain building; constructive and destructive forces on landforms; soil, weathering, and erosion; water and water cycle; atmosphere, weather, and climate; living organisms in earth system.	A1.1, A2.3, A3, A4, A5, B1.1, B1.2, B1.3, B1.4, B2.1, B2.2, B2.3, B3.1, B3.2, B3.3, C1.1, C1.2, C1.3, C3.1, C3.2, D1.1, D1.2, D1.3, D2.2, D2.3, D2.4, D3.1, D3.2, D3.3, D4.1, D4.2, E3.2
D.2	**Earth's history** Continuity of earth processes; impact of occasional catastrophes; fossil evidence.	A4.3, A5.1, A5.4, B1.2, B2.1, B3.1, B4, D1.1, D4.3, E3.2, E3.4, E (Frontiers in Science)

		Book, Chapter, and Section
D.3	**Earth in the solar system** Sun, planets, asteroids, comets; regular and predictable motion and day, year, phases of the moon, and eclipses; gravity and orbits; sun as source of energy for earth; cause of seasons.	A1.1, B5.1, B5.3, C1.1, C1.2, C3.4, D1.2, D1.3, D2.2, D4.4, E1.1, E2.1, E2.2, E2.3, E3.1, E3.2, E3.3, E3.4

E. Science and Technology

E.1– E.5	**Abilities of technological design** Identify problems; design a solution or product; implement a proposed design; evaluate completed designs or products; communicate the process of technological design.	A5.1, B1.4, B2.3, B5.2, C1.1, C1.3, C4.1, C4.2, D3.4
E.6	**Understandings about science and technology** Similarities and differences between scientific inquiry and technological design; contributions of people in different cultures; reciprocal nature of science and technology; nonexistence of perfectly designed solutions; constraints, benefits, and unintended consequences of technological designs.	All books (pp. xxvi–xxvii) All books (Frontiers in Science, Timelines in Science) A1.1, A1.2, A1.3, A1.4, B5.3, C3.4

F. Science in Personal and Social Perspectives

F.1	**Personal health** Exercise; fitness; hazards and safety; tobacco, alcohol, and other drugs; nutrition; STDs; environmental health.	C2.2, D1.3, D1.4, D4.3
F.2	**Populations, resources, and environments** Overpopulation and resource depletion; environmental degradation.	B5.1, B5.2, B5.3, C1.2, C2.1, C2.2, C2.3, C4.1, C4.2, C4.3, D1.4, D4.3
F.3	**Natural hazards** Earthquakes, landslides, wildfires, volcanic eruptions, floods, storms; hazards from human activity; personal and societal challenges.	A1.1, A5.1, B2.3, B3.1, B3.2, B3.3, B4.3, C2.1, C2.2, C4.1, C4.3, D1.1, D1.4, D3.2, D3.3, D4.3, E3.4
F.4	**Risks and benefits** Risk analysis; natural, chemical, biological, social, and personal hazards; decisions based on risks and benefits.	B2.3, B3.3, B5.1, B5.2, B5.3, C2.1, C2.2, C2.3, C4.1, C4.2, C4.3, D1.1, D3.1, D3.2, D3.3, E (Frontiers in Science)
F.5	**Science and technology in society** Science's influence on knowledge and world view; societal challenges and scientific research; technological influences on society; contributions from people of different cultures and times; work of scientists and engineers; ethical codes; limitations of science and technology.	All books (Timelines in Science) A1.1, A1.2, A1.4, C2.3, C4.2, C4.3, D4.3, E1.2, E1.3, E1.4

G. History and Nature of Science

G.1	**Science as a human endeavor** Diversity of people working in science, technology, and related fields; abilities required by science.	All books (pp. xxii–xxv; Frontiers in Science)
G.2	**Nature of science** Observations, experiments, and models; tentative nature of scientific ideas; differences in interpretation of evidence; evaluation of results of investigations, experiments, observations, theoretical models, and explanations; importance of questioning, response to criticism, and communication.	B4.1, B4.2, E1.2, E1.3, E4.4
G.3	**History of science** Historical examples of inquiry and relationships between science and society; scientists and engineers as valued contributors to culture; challenges of breaking through accepted ideas.	All books (Frontiers in Science; Timelines in Science), B1.2, B4.3, E1.3

Correlations to Benchmarks

This chart provides an overview of how the five Earth Science modules of *McDougal Littell Science* address the Project 2061 *Benchmarks for Science Literacy*. The complete wording of the benchmarks can be found at the end of this Teacher's Edition.

A Earth's Surface
B The Changing Earth
C Earth's Waters
D Earth's Atmosphere
E Space Science

	Book, Chapter, and Section
1. The Nature of Science	
	The Nature of Science (pp. xxii–xxv); A1; Scientific Thinking Handbook (pp. R2–R9); Lab Handbook (pp. R10–R35); Think Science Features: A1.4, B1.4, C1.1, D3.3, E3.2
3. The Nature of Technology	
	The Nature of Technology (pp. xxvi–xxvii); A1, D3.4, E.1.2, E.1.3, E.1.4; Timelines in Science Features

4. The Physical Setting

4.A THE UNIVERSE

4.A.1 The Sun is a medium-sized star on the edge of a disk-shaped galaxy; galaxies contain billions of stars; the universe contains billions of galaxies.	E1.1, E4.1, E4.3, E4.4
4.A.2 Light from the Sun takes a few minutes to reach Earth; some galaxies are so far away that their light takes several billion years to reach Earth.	E1.2, E4.1, E4.3, E4.4
4.A.3 Nine planets of very different size, composition, and surface features move around the Sun in nearly circular orbits.	E2.2, E3.2
4.A.4 Chunks of rock orbiting the Sun sometimes impact Earth's atmosphere and sometimes reach Earth's surface.	E (Frontiers in Science), E3.1, E3.4

4.B THE EARTH

4.B.1 We live on a relatively small planet, the third from the Sun in the only system of planets definitely known to exist.	E3.1, E3.2
4.B.2 Three-fourths of Earth's surface is covered by a relatively thin layer of water; the entire planet is surrounded by a relatively thin blanket of air.	A1.1, A3.1, C1.1, E3.2, E3.3
4.B.3 Everything on or anywhere near the Earth is pulled toward the Earth's center by gravitational force.	E2.1
4.B.4 Because Earth's axis is tilted, sunlight falls more intensely on different regions during the year, producing Earth's seasons and weather patterns.	D2.2, E2.1, E3.2
4.B.5 The moon's orbit around Earth changes what part is lighted by the Sun and how much of that part can be seen from Earth—the phases of the Moon.	E2.3
4.B.6 Climates have sometimes changed abruptly; even small changes in atmospheric or ocean content can have widespread effects on climate.	A3.1, B1.2, B3.3, B4.1, B4.3, C3.2, D1.1, D1.4, D4.3, E3.4
4.B.7 The cycling of water in and out of the atmosphere plays an important role. Water evaporates, rises and cools, condenses, falls again to the surface.	A5.3, C1, D1.1, D2.3, D2.4, D3.1, D3.2, D3.3, D4.1
4.B.8 Fresh water, limited in supply, is essential for life and industry. Rivers, lakes, and groundwater can be depleted or polluted.	B5.1, B5.2, C2.1, C2.2, C2.3

		Book, Chapter, and Section
4.B.9	Heat energy carried by ocean currents has a strong influence on climate around the world.	C3.2, D3.1, D3.2, D4.1
4.B.10	Ability to recover minerals is as important as how abundant or rare they are; as they are used up, obtaining them becomes more difficult.	A2.3, B5.1, B5.2
4.B.11	Benefits of Earth's resources can be reduced by using them wastefully; the atmosphere and oceans have limited capacity to absorb waste and recycle materials naturally; cleaning up pollution can be very difficult and costly.	B5.1, C2.2, C2.3, C4.3, D1.4, D2.4, D4.3
4.C	**PROCESSES THAT SHAPE THE EARTH**	
4.C.1	Earth's interior is hot. Heat flow and movement of material within Earth cause earthquakes, volcanic eruptions, create mountains, and ocean basins.	B1, B3.3, C3.1, D1.1
4.C.2	Some changes in Earth's surface are abrupt (earthquakes, volcanic eruptions) while other changes happen very slowly (motion of wind, water).	A5, B1, B2, B3, B4.3
4.C.3	Sand, smaller particles, and dissolved minerals form solid rock.	A2, A3.3, B3.1
4.C.4	Rock bears evidence of the minerals, temperatures, and forces that created it in the rock cycle.	A3.4
4.C.5	Successive layers of sedimentary rock confirm the history of Earth's changing surface and provide evidence of changing life forms.	B4.1, B4.2, B4.3
4.C.6	Soil composition, texture, fertility, and resistance to erosion are influenced by plant roots, debris, and organisms living in the soil.	A4.2, A5.1, A5.2, A5.3, A5.4, A5.5
4.C.7	Human activities can change Earth's land, oceans, and atmosphere: sometimes rendering the environment unable to support some life forms.	A4.3, B5.1, C2.2, C2.3, C4.1, C4.3, D1.4, D4.3
4.E	**ENERGY TRANSFORMATIONS**	B1.2, B5.1, C3.4, D1.2, E1.2, E2.3, E3.1, E4.1
4.F	**MOTION**	B2.2, E1.2
4.G	**FORCES OF NATURE**	A5.1, C3.4, E1.1, E2, E3.1
5.	**The Living Environment**	
5.D	**INTERDEPENDENCE OF LIFE**	C1.2
5.E	**FLOW OF MATTER AND ENERGY**	A4.2, D1.1
5.F	**EVOLUTION OF LIFE**	B4.1, B4.2, B4.3
8.	**The Designed World**	B5
9.	**The Mathematical World**	All Math in Science Features; A1.2
10.	**Historical Perspectives**	E1, E2.3, E3.1, E4.2
12.	**Habits of Mind**	
12.A	**VALUES AND ATTITUDES**	Think Science Features: A1.4, B1.4, C1.1, D3.3, E3.2
12.B	**COMPUTATION AND ESTIMATION**	All Math in Science Features, Lab Handbook (pp. R10–R35)
12.C	**MANIPULATION AND OBSERVATION**	All Investigates and Chapter Investigations
12.D	**COMMUNICATION SKILLS**	All Chapter Investigations, Lab Handbook (pp. R10–R35)
12.E	**CRITICAL-RESPONSE SKILLS**	Think Science Features: A1.4, B1.4, C1.1, D3.3, E3.2; Scientific Thinking Handbook (pp. R2–R9)

Planning the Unit

The Pacing Guide provides suggested pacing for all chapters in the unit as well as the two unit features shown below.

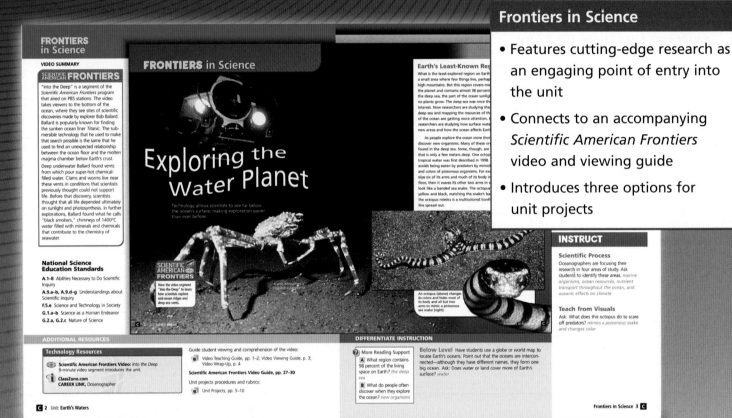

Frontiers in Science

- Features cutting-edge research as an engaging point of entry into the unit
- Connects to an accompanying *Scientific American Frontiers* video and viewing guide
- Introduces three options for unit projects

Timelines in Science

- Traces the history of key scientific discoveries
- Highlights interactions between science and technology

Earth's Waters Pacing Guide

The following pacing guide shows how
the chapters in *Earth's Waters* can be adapted
to fit your specific course needs.

	TRADITIONAL SCHEDULE (DAYS)	BLOCK SCHEDULE (DAYS)
Frontiers in Science: Exploring the Water Planet	1	0.5
Chapter 1 The Water Planet		
1.1 Water continually cycles.	2	1
1.2 Fresh water flows and freezes on Earth.	2	1
1.3 Fresh water flows underground.	3	1.5
Chapter Investigation	1	0.5
Chapter 2 Freshwater Resources		
2.1 Fresh water is an essential resource.	2	1
2.2 Society depends on clean and safe water.	2	1
2.3 Water shortages threaten society.	3	1.5
Chapter Investigation	1	0.5
Chapter 3 Ocean Systems		
3.1 The oceans are a connected system.	2	1
3.2 Ocean water moves in currents.	2	1
3.3 Waves move through oceans.	2	1
3.4 Waters rise and fall in tides.	3	1.5
Chapter Investigation	1	0.5
Timelines in Science: Exploring the Ocean	1	0.5
Chapter 4 Ocean Environments		
4.1 Ocean coasts support plant and animal life.	2	
4.2 Conditions differ away from shore.	2	1
4.3 The ocean contains natural resources.	3	1.5
Chapter Investigation	1	0.5
Total Days for Module	**36**	**18**

Planning the Chapter

Complete planning support precedes each chapter.

Previewing Content

- Section-by-section science background notes
- Common Misconceptions notes

CHAPTER

1 The Water Planet

Earth Science
UNIFYING PRINCIPLES

PRINCIPLE 1
Heat energy inside Earth and radiation from the Sun provide energy for Earth's processes.

PRINCIPLE 2
Physical forces, such as gravity, affect the movement of all matter on Earth and throughout the universe.

PRINCIPLE 3
Matter and move amon rocks and s atmosphere and living t

PRINCIPLE 4

Unit: Earth's Waters
BIG IDEAS

CHAPTER 1
The Water Planet
Water moves through Earth's atmosphere, oceans, and land in a cycle.

CHAPTER 2
Freshwater Resources
Fresh water is a limited resource and is essential for human society.

CHAPTER 3
Ocean Systems
The oceans are system of wate

CHAPTER 1
KEY CONCEPTS

SECTION 1.1	SECTION 1.2
Water continually cycles. 1. Water is a unique substance. 2. Water covers most of Earth. 3. Water moves in a worldwide cycle.	**Fresh water flows and freezes on Earth.** 1. Water flows and collects on Earth's surface. 2. Surface water collects in ponds and lakes. 3. Most fresh water on Earth is frozen

The Big Idea Flow Chart is available on p. T1 in the **UNIT TRANSPARENCY BOO**

Previewing Content

SECTION

1.1 Water continuously cycles. pp. 9–15

1. Water is a unique substance.
- Earth is the only planet with a large amount of liquid water.
- Because of water, Earth can support life.
- Water is the only substance on Earth that exists in all three physical states at normal temperatures.

2. Water covers most of Earth.

SECTION

1.2 Fre Ea

1. Water fl
- The fore tion fall differer side of
- Water i

Previewing Content

SECTION

1.3 Fresh water flows underground.
pp. 24–33

1. Water fills underground spaces.
- Some water sinks into the ground. Plants use some of it, and the rest sinks deeper into Earth and is held underground as **groundwater.**
- Either ground materials are **permeable,** and water can flow through them; or they are **impermeable,** and water cannot flow through them. Some rock, such as sandstone, is permeable. Gravel, sand, and soil are also permeable. Water sinks into Earth until it reaches an impermeable layer. The **water table** is the top of the area that is saturated with water.
- An underground layer of permeable rock or sediment that contains water is an **aquifer.** In an aquifer, groundwater is stored in permeable material located over or beside impermeable rock that prevents the water from draining away. The water is constantly replenished. Aquifers filter and clean water and provide a water source for people on Earth.

2. Underground water can be brought to the surface.
- People collect groundwater from springs and wells. A **spring** is a place where the surface of the land dips below the water table and water bubbles up from the ground. The visual on p. 29 (and in the next column) shows how technology has enabled people to live in more places because they can obtain water more easily.
- A well is a hole drilled into the ground to reach groundwater. The diagram at right shows how a well is drilled.
- An **artesian well** is a well in which water flows to the surface naturally because of pressure exerted below the surface. A hot spring is a place where water heated underground reaches the surface. A geyser is a special kind of hot spring.

How to Make a Well

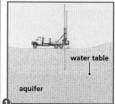

Drill into the ground with special machinery.

water table

aquifer

①

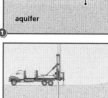

When the drill hole reaches below the water table, lower a pipe into it.

②

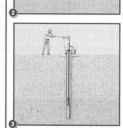

At the top of the well, install a pump powered by a motor or human effort to pull up water.

③

Common Misconceptions

RUNNING WATER Students may think that all water runs downhill. However, pressure may cause underground water to flow upward and form artesian wells, hot springs, or geysers.

This misconception is addressed on p. 30.

MISCONCEPTION DATABASE
CLASSZONE.COM Background on student misconceptions

Previewing Chapter Resources

KEY TO ICONS

🌐 CLASSZONE.COM	💿 CD/CD-ROM	TE Teacher Edition	
ℹ INTERNET	PE Pupil Edition	R UNIT RESOURCE BOC

	INTEGRATED TECHNOLOGY		READING AND REINFORCEMENT	ASSESSMENT

CHAPTER 1
Plate Tectonics

🌐 CLASSZONE.COM
- eEdition Plus
- EasyPlanner Plus
- Misconception Database
- Content Review
- Test Practice
- Visualizations
- Resource Centers
- Internet Activity: Earth's Interior
- Math Tutorial

💿 SCILINKS.ORG

💿 CD-ROM
- eEdition
- EasyPlanner
- Power Presentations
- Content Review
- Lab Generator
- Test Generator

🔊 AUDIO CDS
- Audio Readings
- Audio Readings in Spanish

- Watching a Pot Boil
- Earth's Moving Surface
- Internet Activity: Earth's Interior

R UNIT RESOURCE BOOK
- Family Letter, p. ix
- Spanish Family Letter, p. x
- Unit Projects, pp. 5–10

💿 Lab Generator CD-ROM
Generate customized labs.

- Description Wheel, B20–21
- Supporting Main Ideas, C42
- Daily Vocabulary Scaffolding, H1–8

R UNIT RESOURCE BOOK
- Vocabulary Practice, pp. 57–58
- Decoding Support, p. 59
- Summarizing the Chapter, pp. 80–81

🔊 Audio Readings CD
Listen to Pupil Edition.

🔊 Audio Readings in Spanish CD
Listen to Pupil Edition in Spanish.

PE • Chapter Re
 • Standardiz

A • Diagnostic
 • Chapter Te
 • Alternative

SP A Spanish Cha

💿 Test Genera
Generate cu

💿 Lab Genera
Rubrics for L

SECTION 1.1 Earth has several layers. pp. 9–13
Time: 2 periods (1 block)

T UNIT TRANSPARENCY BOOK
- Big Idea Flow Chart, p. T1
- Daily Vocabulary Scaffolding, p. T2
- Note-Taking Model, p. T3
- 3-Minute Warm-Up, p. T4

PE • EXPLORE Density, p. 9
 • INVESTIGATE Earth's Different Layers, p. 12

R UNIT RESOURCE BOOK
Datasheet, Earth's Different Layers, p. 20

R UNIT RESOURCE BOOK
- Reading Study Guide, A & B, pp. 13–16
- Spanish Reading Study Guide, pp. 17–18
- Challenge and Extension, p. 19
- Reinforcing Key Concepts, p. 21

TE Ongoing Ass

PE Section 1.1

A UNIT ASSES
Section 1.1

of Continents, p. 14
TION, Convection
ovement, pp. 20-21
K
N, Convection
ement, A, B, & C,

R UNIT RESOURCE BOOK
- Reading Study Guide, A & B, pp. 24–27
- Spanish Reading Study Guide, pp. 28–29
- Challenge and Extension, p. 30
- Reinforcing Key Concepts, p. 31

TE Ongoing Ass

PE Section 1.2

A UNIT ASSES
Section 1.2

oundaries, p. 22
ic Reversals, p. 25
9
uctions, p. 41
Reversals, p. 42
ice, pp. 60–61
TION, Magnetic
Floor, A, B, & C,

R UNIT RESOURCE BOOK
- Reading Study Guide, A & B, pp. 34–37
- Spanish Reading Study Guide, pp. 38–39
- Challenge and Extension, p. 40
- Reinforcing Key Concepts, p. 43
- Challenge Reading, pp. 55–56

TE Ongoing Ass

PE Section 1.3

A UNIT ASSES
Section 1.3

es, p. 30
ent Boundaries,
K
Boundaries, p. 53

R UNIT RESOURCE BOOK
- Reading Study Guide, A & B, pp. 46–49
- Spanish Reading Study Guide, pp. 50–51
- Challenge and Extension, p. 52
- Reinforcing Key Concepts, p. 54

TE Ongoing Ass

PE Section 1.4

A UNIT ASSES
Section 1.4

---

flows and freezes
23

cts on Earth's surface.
s water downward. When pre
e that forms a **divide**, it flows
the water flowing downward
to a **drainage basin**.

Previewing Labs

🔖 Lab Generator CD-ROM
Edit these Pupil Edition labs and generate alternative labs.

EXPLORE the BIG idea

Where Can You See Water? p. 7
Students look for different forms of water around them.

TIME 10 minutes
MATERIALS none

Does the Ice Float? p. 7
Students learn about the densities of fresh water and salt water by seeing how ice floats in each.

TIME 10 minutes
MATERIALS glass, water, ice cube, salt, spoon

Internet Activity: Water, p. 7
Students use the Internet to learn about forms of water.

TIME 20 minutes
MATERIALS computer with Internet access

SECTION 1.1

EXPLORE Water Vapor, p. 9
Students put ice in water to observe condensation of water vapor.

TIME 10 minutes
MATERIALS clear glass, ice, water

INVESTIGATE The Water Cycle, p. 12
Students create a closed environment to observe the water cycle.

TIME 30 minutes
MATERIALS jar with lid, soil, rocks or pebbles, sand, smaller containers, water, small plants, triple-beam balance

SECTION 1.2

EXPLORE Water Flow, p. 16
Students pour water into an egg carton when it is flat and then when it is tilted to observe water flowing and collecting.

TIME 10 minutes
MATERIALS plastic-foam egg carton, tray or pan, plastic bottle, water

INVESTIGATE Icebergs, p. 21
Students calculate the densities of water and ice to infer why icebergs float.

TIME 30 minutes
MATERIALS balance, ice cube, graduated cylinder (250 mL), calculator

SECTION 1.3

EXPLORE Flow of Water, p. 24
Students observe water in permeable and impermeable materials to understand that permeability has to do with how porous a material is.

TIME 10 minutes
MATERIALS cup; paper coffee filter; bucket; dishpan, or sink; water

INVESTIGATE Aquifer Filtration, p. 27
Students pour water into a model to observe how ground materials filter water.

TIME 30 minutes
MATERIALS 1 L plastic bottle with bottom cut off, sand, soil, pebbles, water, food coloring, cocoa, pepper, bottle bottom or bucket

CHAPTER INVESTIGATION Water Moving Underground, pp. 32–33
Students design an experiment that compares how different ground materials absorb and transport water in order to infer what Earth materials make the best aquifers.

TIME 40 minutes
MATERIALS granite sample; sandstone sample; sand; square piece of cotton muslin or cotton knit measuring 30 cm per side; rubber band; golf ball; scale; large jar; water

R **Additional INVESTIGATION,** Water Wells, A, B, & C, pp. 60–68; Teacher Instructions, pp. 262–263

Planning the Lesson

Point-of-use support for each lesson provides a wealth of teaching options.

1. Prepare

- Concept and vocabulary review
- Note-taking and vocabulary strategies

2. Focus

- Set Learning Goals
- 3-Minute Warm-up

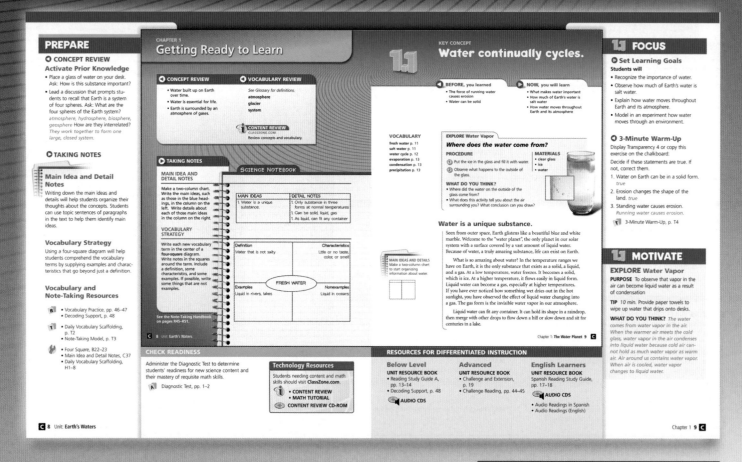

3. Motivate

- Engaging entry into the section
- Explore activity or Think About question

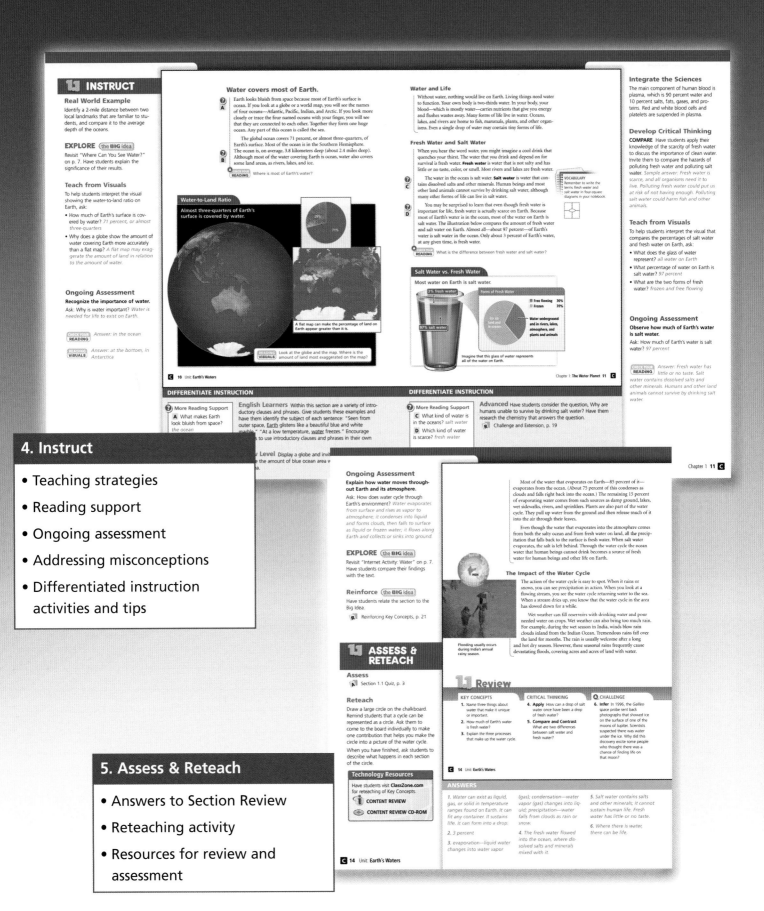

4. Instruct

- Teaching strategies
- Reading support
- Ongoing assessment
- Addressing misconceptions
- Differentiated instruction activities and tips

5. Assess & Reteach

- Answers to Section Review
- Reteaching activity
- Resources for review and assessment

Lab Materials List

The following charts list the consumables, nonconsumables, and equipment needed for all activities. Quantities are per group of four students. Lab aprons, goggles, water, books, paper, pens, pencils, and calculators are assumed to be available for all activities.

Materials kits are available. For more information, please call McDougal Littell at 1-800-323-5435.

Consumables

Description	Quantity per Group	Explore page	Investigate page	Chapter Investigation page
aluminum foil, 6" x 12"	1		87	
baking soda	1 tsp			58
bottle, plastic, 1 liter	1	16		
bottle, plastic, 1 liter with cap	1		27	
clay, modeling	1 stick		125	
cloth, cotton muslin or cotton knit, 30 cm x 30 cm	1			32
cocoa	1 tsp		27	
coffee filter, cone	1	24		
cup, paper, 5–10 oz	1	84		
cup, clear plastic	7	9, 24, 75, 121		
cup, plastic, 20 oz	1		63	
feather	1	130		
food coloring, blue	1 bottle	50, 75, 84	27, 78, 87	
food coloring, red	1 bottle	75	78, 87	
food coloring, green	1 bottle		78, 87	
gravel	1 lb		12, 27	
ice cube	8	9, 84	21	
index card	2–4		78	
indicator strip, litmus paper, acids	8			58
indicator strip, litmus paper, bases	8			58
indicator strip, glucose paper	8			58
paper clip	1		21	
paper fastener, brass	1	98		
pepper	1 tsp		27, 87	
plant, small	2–4		12	
raisin	5	121		
rubber band, large	1			32
salt solution, 10%	2200 mL	75	78, 87	
salt solution, 2.5%	100 mL	75		
salt, table	1–3 tbs			94

Description	Quantity per Group	Explore *page*	Investigate *page*	Chapter Investigation *page*
sand	2 lbs		12, 27	32
soda water	10 oz	121		
soil, potting	1 1/2 lbs		12, 27	
sponge	1		116	
spoon, plastic	1	130		
straw, clear drinking	1	75		
string	3–4 ft	89		
sugar	1 tsp			58
tape, masking	1 roll	84	87	
tape, removable masking	1 roll			138
toothpick	1	84		
vegetable oil	3 tsp	130		
vinegar	1 tsp			58
water, distilled	1 cup			58

Nonconsumables

Description	Quantity per Group	Explore *page*	Investigate *page*	Chapter Investigation *page*
aquarium, small	1	89		94
balance, triple beam	1		12, 21	32
ball, golf	1			32
bottle, plastic dropper	1			94
bowl, small plastic	1	130		
container, plastic, 1/2 pint with lid	2–4		116	
dishpan, plastic	1	16, 24	27, 78	
egg carton, plastic or foam	1	16		
eyedropper	1	50		
film canister	2–4		12	
funnel	1		63	
graduated cylinder, 100 mL	1	50	63	
graduated cylinder, 250 mL	1		21	

Description	Quantity per Group	Explore page	Investigate page	Chapter Investigation page
jar, 26 oz glass	1		12	
jar, baby food	2		78	
jar, plastic, 2 liter	1			32
rock sample, granite	1			32
rock sample, sandstone	1			32
scissors	1	98		
shoebox, clear plastic	1	84	87, 125	
stopper, cork	4	89	21	
stopwatch	1		125	
washer, metal 1"	15–20	89		
water faucet	1		63	

Unit Resource Book Datasheets

Description		Explore page	Investigate page	Chapter Investigation page
Tides Datasheet		98		
Water Use Sheet			43	

Earth's Waters

water cycle

ocean

HABITAT

hydrosphere

EARTH SCIENCE

A ▶ Earth's Surface
B ▶ The Changing Earth
C ▶ Earth's Waters
D ▶ Earth's Atmosphere
E ▶ Space Science

PHYSICAL SCIENCE

A ▶ Matter and Energy
B ▶ Chemical Interactions
C ▶ Motion and Forces
D ▶ Waves, Sound, and Light
E ▶ Electricity and Magnetism

LIFE SCIENCE

A ▶ Cells and Heredity
B ▶ Life Over Time
C ▶ Diversity of Living Things
D ▶ Ecology
E ▶ Human Biology

Acknowledgments: Excerpts and adaptations from *National Science Education Standards* by the National Academy of Sciences. Copyright © 1996 by the National Academy of Sciences. Reprinted with permission from the National Academies Press, Washington, D.C.

Excerpts and adaptations from *Benchmarks for Science Literacy: Project 2061*. Copyright © 1993 by the American Association for the Advancement of Science. Reprinted with permission.

ISBN: 0-618-33417-3   2 3 4 5 6 7 8 DSC 08 07 06

Internet Web Site: http://www.mcdougallittell.com

Science Consultants

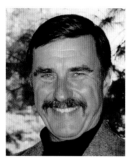

Chief Science Consultant

James Trefil, Ph.D. is the Clarence J. Robinson Professor of Physics at George Mason University. He is the author or co-author of more than 25 books, including *Science Matters* and *The Nature of Science.* Dr. Trefil is a member of the American Association for the Advancement of Science's Committee on the Public Understanding of Science and Technology. He is also a fellow of the World Economic Forum and a frequent contributor to *Smithsonian* magazine.

Rita Ann Calvo, Ph.D. is Senior Lecturer in Molecular Biology and Genetics at Cornell University, where for 12 years she also directed the Cornell Institute for Biology Teachers. Dr. Calvo is the 1999 recipient of the College and University Teaching Award from the National Association of Biology Teachers.

Kenneth Cutler, M.S. is the Education Coordinator for the Julius L. Chambers Biomedical Biotechnology Research Institute at North Carolina Central University. A former middle school and high school science teacher, he received a 1999 Presidential Award for Excellence in Science Teaching.

Instructional Design Consultants

Douglas Carnine, Ph.D. is Professor of Education and Director of the National Center for Improving the Tools of Educators at the University of Oregon. He is the author of seven books and over 100 other scholarly publications, primarily in the areas of instructional design and effective instructional strategies and tools for diverse learners. Dr. Carnine also serves as a member of the National Institute for Literacy Advisory Board.

Linda Carnine, Ph.D. consults with school districts on curriculum development and effective instruction for students struggling academically. A former teacher and school administrator, Dr. Carnine also co-authored a popular remedial reading program.

Donald Steely, Ph.D. serves as principal investigator at the Oregon Center for Applied Science (ORCAS) on federal grants for science and language arts programs. His background also includes teaching and authoring of print and multimedia programs in science, mathematics, history, and spelling.

Sam Miller, Ph.D. is a middle school science teacher and the Teacher Development Liaison for the Eugene, Oregon, Public Schools. He is the author of curricula for teaching science, mathematics, computer skills, and language arts.

Vicky Vachon, Ph.D. consults with school districts throughout the United States and Canada on improving overall academic achievement with a focus on literacy. She is also co-author of a widely used program for remedial readers.

Content Reviewers

John Beaver, Ph.D.
Ecology
Professor, Director of Science Education Center
College of Education and Human Services
Western Illinois University
Macomb, IL

Donald J. DeCoste, Ph.D.
Matter and Energy, Chemical Interactions
Chemistry Instructor
University of Illinois
Urbana-Champaign, IL

Dorothy Ann Fallows, Ph.D., MSc
Diversity of Living Things, Microbiology
Partners in Health
Boston, MA

Michael Foote, Ph.D.
The Changing Earth, Life Over Time
Associate Professor
Department of the Geophysical Sciences
The University of Chicago
Chicago, IL

Lucy Fortson, Ph.D.
Space Science
Director of Astronomy
Adler Planetarium and Astronomy Museum
Chicago, IL

Elizabeth Godrick, Ph.D.
Human Biology
Professor, CAS Biology
Boston University
Boston, MA

Isabelle Sacramento Grilo, M.S.
The Changing Earth
Lecturer, Department of the Geological Sciences
San Diego State University
San Diego, CA

David Harbster, MSc
Diversity of Living Things
Professor of Biology
Paradise Valley Community College
Phoenix, AZ

Richard D. Norris, Ph.D.
Earth's Waters
Professor of Paleobiology
Scripps Institution of Oceanography
University of California, San Diego
La Jolla, CA

Donald B. Peck, M.S.
*Motion and Forces; Waves, Sound, and Light;
Electricity and Magnetism*
Director of the Center for Science Education (retired)
Fairleigh Dickinson University
Madison, NJ

Javier Penalosa, Ph.D.
Diversity of Living Things, Plants
Associate Professor, Biology Department
Buffalo State College
Buffalo, NY

Raymond T. Pierrehumbert, Ph.D.
Earth's Atmosphere
Professor in Geophysical Sciences (Atmospheric Science)
The University of Chicago
Chicago, IL

Brian J. Skinner, Ph.D.
Earth's Surface
Eugene Higgins Professor of Geology and Geophysics
Yale University
New Haven, CT

Nancy E. Spaulding, M.S.
Earth's Surface, The Changing Earth, Earth's Waters
Earth Science Teacher (retired)
Elmira Free Academy
Elmira, NY

Steven S. Zumdahl, Ph.D.
Matter and Energy, Chemical Interactions
Professor Emeritus of Chemistry
University of Illinois
Urbana-Champaign, IL

Susan L. Zumdahl, M.S.
Matter and Energy, Chemical Interactions
Chemistry Education Specialist
University of Illinois
Urbana-Champaign, IL

Safety Consultant

Juliana Texley, Ph.D.
Former K–12 Science Teacher and School Superintendent
Boca Raton, FL

English Language Advisor

Judy Lewis, M.A.
Director, State and Federal Programs for reading proficiency
and high risk populations
Rancho Cordova, CA

iv

Teacher Panel Members

Carol Arbour
Tallmadge Middle School,
Tallmadge, OH

Patty Belcher
Goodrich Middle School,
Akron, OH

Gwen Broestl
Luis Munoz Marin Middle School,
Cleveland, OH

Al Brofman
Tehipite Middle School,
Fresno, CA

John Cockrell
Clinton Middle School,
Columbus, OH

Jenifer Cox
Sylvan Middle School,
Citrus Heights, CA

Linda Culpepper
Martin Middle School,
Charlotte, NC

Kathleen Ann DeMatteo
Margate Middle School,
Margate, FL

Melvin Figueroa
New River Middle School,
Ft. Lauderdale, FL

Doretha Grier
Kannapolis Middle School,
Kannapolis, NC

Robert Hood
Alexander Hamilton Middle School,
Cleveland, OH

Scott Hudson
Covedale Elementary School,
Cincinnati, OH

Loretta Langdon
Princeton Middle School,
Princeton, NC

Carlyn Little
Glades Middle School,
Miami, FL

Ann Marie Lynn
Amelia Earhart Middle School,
Riverside, CA

James Minogue
Lowe's Grove Middle School,
Durham, NC

Joann Myers
Buchanan Middle School,
Tampa, FL

Barbara Newell
Charles Evans Hughes Middle School,
Long Beach, CA

Anita Parker
Kannapolis Middle School,
Kannapolis, NC

Greg Pirolo
Golden Valley Middle School,
San Bernardino, CA

Laura Pottmyer
Apex Middle School,
Apex, NC

Lynn Prichard
Booker T. Washington Middle Magnet
School, Tampa, FL

Jacque Quick
Walter Williams High School,
Burlington, NC

Robert Glenn Reynolds
Hillman Middle School,
Youngstown, OH

Stacy Rinehart
Lufkin Road Middle School,
Apex, NC

Theresa Short
Abbott Middle School,
Fayetteville, NC

Rita Slivka
Alexander Hamilton Middle School,
Cleveland, OH

Marie Sofsak
B F Stanton Middle School,
Alliance, OH

Nancy Stubbs
Sweetwater Union Unified School District,
Chula Vista, CA

Sharon Stull
Quail Hollow Middle School,
Charlotte, NC

Donna Taylor
Okeeheelee Middle School,
West Palm Beach, FL

Sandi Thompson
Harding Middle School,
Lakewood, OH

Lori Walker
Audubon Middle School & Magnet Center,
Los Angeles, CA

Teacher Lab Evaluators

Andrew Boy
W.E.B. DuBois Academy,
Cincinnati, OH

Jill Brimm-Byrne
Albany Park Academy,
Chicago, IL

Gwen Broestl
Luis Munoz Marin Middle School,
Cleveland, OH

Al Brofman
Tehipite Middle School,
Fresno, CA

Michael A. Burstein
The Rashi School,
Newton, MA

Trudi Coutts
Madison Middle School,
Naperville, IL

Jenifer Cox
Sylvan Middle School,
Citrus Heights, CA

Larry Cwik
Madison Middle School,
Naperville, IL

Jennifer Donatelli
Kennedy Junior High School,
Lisle, IL

Melissa Dupree
Lakeside Middle School,
Evans, GA

Carl Fechko
Luis Munoz Marin Middle School,
Cleveland, OH

Paige Fullhart
Highland Middle School,
Libertyville, IL

Sue Hood
Glen Crest Middle School,
Glen Ellyn, IL

William Luzader
Plymouth Community Intermediate School,
Plymouth, MA

Ann Min
Beardsley Middle School,
Crystal Lake, IL

Aileen Mueller
Kennedy Junior High School,
Lisle, IL

Nancy Nega
Churchville Middle School,
Elmhurst, IL

Oscar Newman
Sumner Math and Science Academy,
Chicago, IL

Lynn Prichard
Booker T. Washington Middle Magnet
School, Tampa, FL

Jacque Quick
Walter Williams High School,
Burlington, NC

Stacy Rinehart
Lufkin Road Middle School,
Apex, NC

Seth Robey
Gwendolyn Brooks Middle School,
Oak Park, IL

Kevin Steele
Grissom Middle School,
Tinley Park, IL

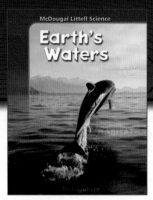

Earth's Waters

eEdition

Unit Features

SCIENTIFIC AMERICAN

1 The Water Planet   6

the **BIG** idea

Water moves through
Earth's atmosphere, oceans,
and land in a cycle.

2 Freshwater Resources   38

the **BIG** idea

Fresh water is a limited
resource and is essential
for human society.

*In what ways do you
depend on water?*
page 38

What causes these waves? page 72

Features

Visual Highlights

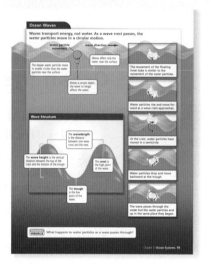

Internet Resources @ ClassZone.com

INVESTIGATIONS AND ACTIVITIES

Standards and Benchmarks

Each chapter in **Earth's Waters** covers some of the learning goals that are described in the *National Science Education Standards* (NSES) and the Project 2061 *Benchmarks for Scientific Literacy.* Selected content and skill standards are shown below in shortened form. The following National Science Education Standards are covered on pages xii-xxvii in Frontiers in Science, and in Timelines in Science, as well as in chapter features and laboratory investigations: Understanding About Scientific Inquiry (A.9), Understanding About Science and Technology (E.6), Science and Technology in Society (F.5), Science as a Human Endeavor (G.1), Nature of Science (G.2), and History of Science.

Content Standards

1 The Water Cycle

National Science Education Standards

D.1.f | Water, which covers the majority of Earth's surface, circulates through Earth's atmosphere, surface, and crust in what is known as the "water cycle." Water evaporates from the surface, rises and cools as it moves to higher elevations, condenses as rain or snow, and falls to the surface.

D.3.d | The Sun is the major source of energy for phenomena on Earth's surface, such as the water cycle.

Project 2061 Benchmarks

4.B.2 | Three-fourths of Earth's surface is covered by a relatively thin layer of water, some of it frozen. The entire planet is surrounded by a relatively thin blanket of air.

4.B.7 | Water evaporates from Earth's surface, rises and cools, and condenses into rain or snow. The water falling on land as precipitation collects in rivers and lakes, soil, and porous layers of rock, and much of it flows back into the ocean.

2 Freshwater Resources

National Science Education Standards

F.3.b | Human activities can induce hazards through resource acquisition, urban growth, land-use decisions, and waste diposal. Such activities can speed up many natural changes.

F.4.b | Risks are associated with natural hazards such as floods—which can destroy habitats, damage property, and harm or kill people. Risks are also associated with chemical hazards such as pollution in air, water, and soil, as well as with biological hazards, such as bacteria and viruses.

Project 2061 Benchmarks

4.B.8 | Fresh water, limited in supply, is essential for life and also for most industrial processes. Rivers, lakes, and groundwater can be depleted or polluted, becoming unavailable or unsuitable for life.

4.B.11 | The benefits of Earth's resources—such as fresh water, air, soil, and trees—can be reduced by using them wastefully or by deliberately or inadvertently destroying them. Cleaning up polluted air, water, or soil or restoring depleted soil, forests, or fishing grounds can be very difficult or costly.

3 Ocean Systems

National Science Education Standards

D.1.g | Water is a solvent. As it passes through the water cycle, it dissolves minerals and gases and carries them to oceans.

D.1.j | Global patterns of atmospheric movement influence local weather. Oceans have a major effect on climate, because water in the oceans holds a large amount of heat.

D.3.c | Gravity is the force that keeps planets in orbit around the Sun and governs the rest of motion in the solar system. Gravity explains the phenomenon of the tides.

Project 2061 Benchmarks

4.B.6 | Climates have sometimes changed abruptly in the past. Even relatively small changes in atmospheric or ocean content can have widespread effects on climate if the change lasts long enough.

4.B.9 | Heat energy carried by ocean currents has a strong influence on climate around the world.

4.C.1 | The interior of Earth is hot. Heat flow and movement of material within Earth cause earthquakes and volcanic eruptions and create mountains and ocean basins.

4 Ocean Environments

National Science Education Standards

C.4.c | For ecosystems (such as the ocean) the major source of energy is sunlight. The energy passes from organism to organism in food webs.

C.4.d | The number of organisms an ecosystem can support depends on the resources available and on factors such as quantity of light and range of temperatures.

Project 2061 Benchmarks

4.B.11 | The atmosphere and oceans have a limited capacity to absorb waste and recycle materials naturally.

Process and Skill Standards

	National Science Education Standards		**Project 2061 Benchmarks**
A.1	Identify questions that can be answered through investigation.	1.A.3	Some knowledge in science is very old and yet is still used today.
A.2	Design and conduct a scientific investigation.	3.B.1	Design requires taking constraints into account.
A.3	Use appropriate tools and techniques to gather and interpret data.	9.B.3	Graphs can show the relationship between two variables.
A.4	Use evidence to predict, explain, and model.	9.C.4	Graphs can show patterns and can be used to make predictions.
A.5	Use critical thinking to find relationships between results and interpretations.	11.C.4	Use equations to summarize observed changes.
A.6	Consider alternative explanations and predictions.	12.B.1	Find what percentage one number is of another.
A.7	Communicate procedures, results, and conclusions.	12.C.1	Compare amounts proportionally.
A.8	Use mathematics in scientific investigations.	12.D.1	Use tables and graphs to organize information and identify relationships.
E.2	Design a solution or product.	12.D.2	Read, interpret, and describe tables and graphs.
E.3	Implement the proposed solution.	12.D.4	Understand information that includes different types of charts and graphs, including circle charts, bar graphs, line graphs, data tables, diagrams, and symbols.

Introducing Earth Science

Scientists are curious. Since ancient times, they have been asking and answering questions about the world around them. Scientists are also very suspicious of the answers they get. They carefully collect evidence and test their answers many times before accepting an idea as correct.

In this book you will see how scientific knowledge keeps growing and changing as scientists ask new questions and rethink what was known before. The following sections will help get you started.

What Is Earth Science?

Earth science is the study of Earth's interior, its rocks and soil, its atmosphere, its oceans, and outer space. For many years, scientists studied each of these topics separately. They learned many important things. More recently, however, scientists have looked more and more at the connections among the different parts of Earth—its oceans, atmosphere, living things, and rocks and soil. Scientists have also been learning more about other planets in our solar system, as well as stars and galaxies far away. Through these studies they have learned much about Earth and its place in the universe.

The text and pictures in this book will help you learn key concepts and important facts about earth science. A variety of activities will help you investigate these concepts. As you learn, it helps to have a big picture of earth science as a frame-work for this new information. The four unifying principles listed below will give you this big picture. Read the next few pages to get an overview of each of these principles and a sense of why they are so important.

- **Heat energy inside Earth and radiation from the Sun provide energy for Earth's processes.**

- **Physical forces, such as gravity, affect the movement of all matter on Earth and throughout the universe.**

- **Matter and energy move among Earth's rocks and soil, atmosphere, waters, and living things.**

- **Earth has changed over time and continues to change.**

Each chapter begins with a big idea. Keep in mind that each big idea relates to one or more of the unifying principles.

Heat energy inside Earth and radiation from the Sun provide energy for Earth's processes.

The lava pouring out of this volcano in Hawaii is liquid rock that was melted by heat energy under Earth's surface. Another, much more powerful energy source constantly bombards Earth's surface with energy, heating the air around you, and keeping the oceans from freezing over. This energy source is the Sun. Everything that moves or changes on Earth gets its energy either from the Sun or from the inside of our planet.

What It Means

You are always surrounded by different forms of energy, such as heat energy or light. **Energy** is the ability to cause change. All of Earth's processes need energy to occur. A process is a set of changes that leads to a particular result. For example, **evaporation** is the process by which liquid changes into gas. A puddle on a sidewalk dries up through the process of evaporation. The energy needed for the puddle to dry up comes from the Sun.

Heat Energy Inside Earth

Underneath the cool surface layer of rock, Earth's interior is so hot that the solid rock there is able to flow very slowly—a few centimeters each year. In a process called **convection,** hot material rises, cools, then sinks until it is heated enough to rise again. Convection of hot rock carries heat energy up to Earth's surface, where it provides the energy to build mountains, cause earthquakes, and make volcanoes erupt.

Radiation from the Sun

Earth receives energy from the Sun as **radiation**—energy that travels across distances in the form of certain types of waves. Visible light is one type of radiation. Radiation from the Sun heats Earth's surface, making bright summer days hot. Different parts of Earth receive different amounts of radiation at different times of the year, causing seasons. Energy from the Sun also causes winds to blow, ocean currents to flow, and water to move from the ground to the atmosphere and back again.

Why It's Important

Understanding Earth's processes makes it possible to

- know what types of crops to plant and when to plant them
- know when to watch for dangerous weather, such as tornadoes and hurricanes
- predict a volcano's eruption in time for people to leave the area

Physical forces, such as gravity, affect the movement of all matter on Earth and throughout the universe.

The universe is everything that exists, and everything in the universe is governed by the same physical laws. The same laws govern the stars shown in this picture and the page on which the picture is printed.

What It Means

What do the stars in a galaxy, the planet Earth, and your body have in common? For one thing, they are all made of matter. **Matter** is anything that has mass and takes up space. Rocks are matter. You are matter. Even the air around you is matter. Matter is made of tiny particles called **atoms** that are too small to see through an ordinary microscope.

Everything in the universe is also affected by the same physical forces. A **force** is a push or a pull. Forces affect how matter moves everywhere in the universe.

- One force you experience every moment is **gravity,** which is the attraction, or pull, between two objects. Gravity is pulling you to Earth and Earth to you. Gravity is the force that causes objects to fall downward toward the center of Earth. Gravity is also the force that keeps objects in orbit around planets and stars.

- **Friction** is the force that resists motion between two surfaces that are pressed together. Friction can keep a rock on a hillside from sliding down to the bottom of the hill. If you lightly rub your finger across a smooth page in a book and then across a piece of sandpaper, you can feel how the different surfaces produce different frictional forces. Which is easier to do?

- There are many other forces at work on Earth and throughout the universe. For example, Earth has a magnetic field. A compass needle responds to the force exerted by Earth's magnetic field. Another example is the contact force between a rock and the ground beneath it. A contact force occurs when one object pushes or pulls on another object by touching it.

Why It's Important

Physical forces influence the movement of all matter, from the tiniest particle to you to the largest galaxy. Understanding forces allows people to

- predict how objects and materials move on Earth
- send spacecraft and equipment into space
- explain and predict the movements of Earth, the Moon, planets, and stars

Matter and energy move among Earth's rocks and soil, atmosphere, waters, and living things.

When a wolf eats a rabbit, matter and energy move from one living thing into another. When a wolf drinks water warmed by the Sun, matter and energy move from Earth's waters into one of its living things. These are just two examples of how energy and matter move among different parts of the Earth system.

What It Means

Think of Earth as a huge system, or an organized group of parts that work together. Within this system, matter and energy move among the different parts. The four major parts of Earth's system are the

- **atmosphere,** which includes all the air surrounding the solid planet
- **geosphere,** which includes all of Earth's rocks and minerals, as well as Earth's interior
- **hydrosphere,** which includes oceans, rivers, lakes, and every drop of water on or under Earth's surface
- **biosphere,** which includes all the living things on Earth

Matter in the Earth System

It's easy to see how matter moves within the Earth system. When water in the atmosphere falls as rain, it becomes part of the hydrosphere. When an animal drinks water from a puddle, the water becomes part of the biosphere. When rainwater soaks into the ground, it moves through the geosphere. As the puddle dries up, the water becomes part of the atmosphere again.

Energy in the Earth System

Most of the energy you depend on comes from the Sun and moves among the four major parts of the Earth system. Think again about the puddle that is drying up. Sunlight shines through the water and heats the soil, or geosphere, beneath the puddle. Some of this heat energy goes into the puddle, moving into the hydrosphere. As the water evaporates and becomes part of the atmosphere, it takes the energy that came from the Sun with it. The Sun provides energy for all weather and ocean currents. Without the Sun, life could not exist on Earth's surface.

Why It's Important

Understanding how matter and energy move through the Earth system makes it possible to

- predict how a temperature change in ocean water might affect the weather
- determine how clearing forests might affect rainfall
- explain where organisms on the ocean floor get energy to carry out life processes

Earth has changed over time and continues to change.

You see Earth changing all of the time. Rain turns dirt to mud, and a dry wind turns the mud to dust. Many changes are small and can take hundreds, thousands, or even millions of years to add up to much. Other changes are sudden and can destroy in minutes a house that had stood for many years.

What It Means

Events are always changing Earth's surface. Some events, such as the building or wearing away of mountains, occur over millions of years. Others, such as earthquakes, occur within seconds. A change can affect a small area or even the entire planet.

Records of Change

What was the distant past like? Think about how scientists learn about ancient people. They study what the people left behind and draw conclusions based on the evidence. In a similar way, scientists learn about Earth's past by examining the evidence they find in rock layers and by observing processes now occurring.

By observing that water breaks down rocks and carries the material away to other places, people learned that rivers can slowly carve deep valleys. Evidence from rocks and fossils along the edges of continents shows that all continents were once joined and then moved apart over time. A **fossil** is the trace of a once-living organism. Fossils also show that new types of plants and animals develop, and others, such as dinosaurs, die out.

Change Continues Today

Every year, earthquakes occur, volcanoes erupt, and rivers flood. Continents continue to move slowly. The Himalayan Mountains of Asia push a few millimeters higher. **Climate**—the long-term weather patterns of an area—may also change. Scientists are studying how changes in climates around the world might affect Earth even within this century.

Why It's Important

Understanding the changing Earth makes it possible to

- predict and prepare for events such as volcanic eruptions, landslides, floods, and climate changes
- design buildings to withstand shaking during earthquakes
- protect important environments for plants and animals

The Nature of Science

You may think of science as a body of knowledge or a collection of facts. More important, however, science is an active process that involves certain ways of looking at the world.

Scientific Habits of Mind

Scientists are curious. They ask questions. A scientist who finds an unusual rock by the side of a river would ask questions such as, "Did this rock form in this area?" or "Did this rock form elsewhere and get moved here?" Questions like these make a scientist want to investigate.

Scientists are observant. They look closely at the world around them. A scientist who studies rocks can learn a lot about a rock just by picking it up, looking at its color, and feeling how heavy it is.

Scientists are creative. They draw on what they know to form possible explanations for a pattern, an event, or an interesting phenomenon that they have observed. Then scientists put together a plan for testing their ideas.

Scientists are skeptical. Scientists don't accept an explanation or answer unless it is based on evidence and logical reasoning. They continually question their own conclusions as well as the conclusions suggested by other scientists. Scientists only trust evidence that can be confirmed by other people or other methods.

Scientists use seismographs to observe and measure vibrations that move through the ground.

This scientist is collecting a sample of melted rock from a hot lava flow in Hawaii.

Science Processes at Work

You can think of science as a continuous cycle of asking and seeking answers to questions about the world. Although there are many processes that scientists use, all scientists typically do the following:

- Observe and ask a question
- Determine what is known
- Investigate
- Interpret results
- Share results

Observe and Ask a Question

It may surprise you that asking questions is an important skill. A scientific investigation may start when a scientist asks a question. Perhaps scientists observe an event or a process that they don't understand, or perhaps answering one question leads to another.

Determine What Is Known

When beginning an inquiry, scientists find out what is already known about a question. They study results from other scientific investigations, read journals, and talk with other scientists. The scientist who is trying to figure out where an unusual rock came from will study maps that show what types of rocks are already known to be in the area where the rock was found.

Investigate

Investigating is the process of collecting evidence. Two important ways of doing this are experimenting and observing.

An **experiment** is an organized procedure to study something under controlled conditions. For example, the scientist who found the rock by the river might notice that it is lighter in color where it is chipped. The scientist might design an experiment to determine why the rock is a different color on the inside. The scientist could break off a small piece of the inside of the rock and heat it up to see if it becomes the same color as the outside. The scientist would need to use a piece of the same rock that is being studied. A different rock might react differently to heat.

A scientist may use photography to study fast events, such as multiple flashes of lightning.

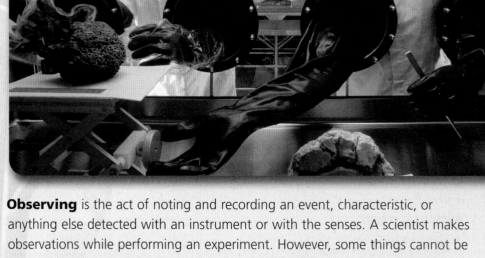

Rocks, such as this one from the Moon, can be subjected to different conditions in a laboratory.

Observing is the act of noting and recording an event, characteristic, or anything else detected with an instrument or with the senses. A scientist makes observations while performing an experiment. However, some things cannot be studied using experiments. For example, streaks of light called meteors occur when small rocks from outer space hit Earth's atmosphere. A scientist might study meteors by taking pictures of the sky at a time when meteors are likely to occur.

Forming hypotheses and making predictions are two other skills involved in scientific investigations. A **hypothesis** is a tentative explanation for an observation or a scientific problem that can be tested by further investigation. For example, the scientist might make the following hypothesis about the rock from the beach:

The rock is a meteorite, which is a rock that fell to the ground from outer space. The outside of the rock changed color because it was heated up from passing through Earth's atmosphere.

A **prediction** is an expectation of what will be observed or what will happen. To test the hypothesis that the rock's outside is black because it is a meteorite, the scientist might predict that a close examination of the rock will show that it has many characteristics in common with rocks that are already known to be meteorites.

Interpret Results

As scientists investigate, they analyze their evidence, or data, and begin to draw conclusions. **Analyzing data** involves looking at the evidence gathered through observations or experiments and trying to identify any patterns that might exist in the data. Scientists often need to make additional observations or perform more experiments before they are sure of their conclusions. Many times scientists make new predictions or revise their hypotheses.

Scientists use computers to gather and interpret data.

Scientists make images such as this computer drawing of a landscape to help share their results with others.

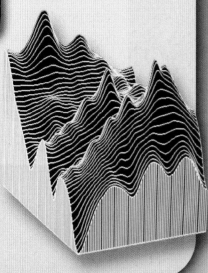

Share Results

An important part of scientific investigation is sharing results of experiments. Scientists read and publish in journals and attend conferences to communicate with other scientists around the world. Sharing data and procedures gives scientists a way to test each others' results. They also share results with the public through newspapers, television, and other media.

The Nature of Technology

When you think of technology, you may think of cars, computers, and cell phones. Imagine having no refrigerator or radio. It's difficult to think of a world without the products of what we call technology. Technology, however, is more than just devices that make our daily activities easier. Technology is the process of using scientific knowledge to design solutions to real-world problems.

Science and Technology

Science and technology go hand in hand. Each depends upon the other. Even a device as simple as a thermometer is designed using knowledge of the ways different materials respond to changes in temperature. In turn, thermometers have allowed scientists to learn more about the world. Greater knowledge of how materials respond to changes in temperature helped engineers to build items such as refrigerators. They have also built thermometers that could be read automatically by computers. New technologies lead to new scientific knowledge and new scientific knowledge leads to even better technologies.

The Process of Technological Design

The process of technological design involves many choices. What, for example, should be done to protect the residents of an area prone to severe storms such as tornadoes and hurricanes? Build stronger homes that can withstand the winds? Try to develop a way to detect the storms long before they occur? Or learn more about hurricanes in order to find new ways to protect people from the dangers? The steps people take to solve the problem depend a great deal on what they already know about the problem as well as what can reasonably be done. As you learn about the steps in the process of technological design, think about the different choices that could be made at each step.

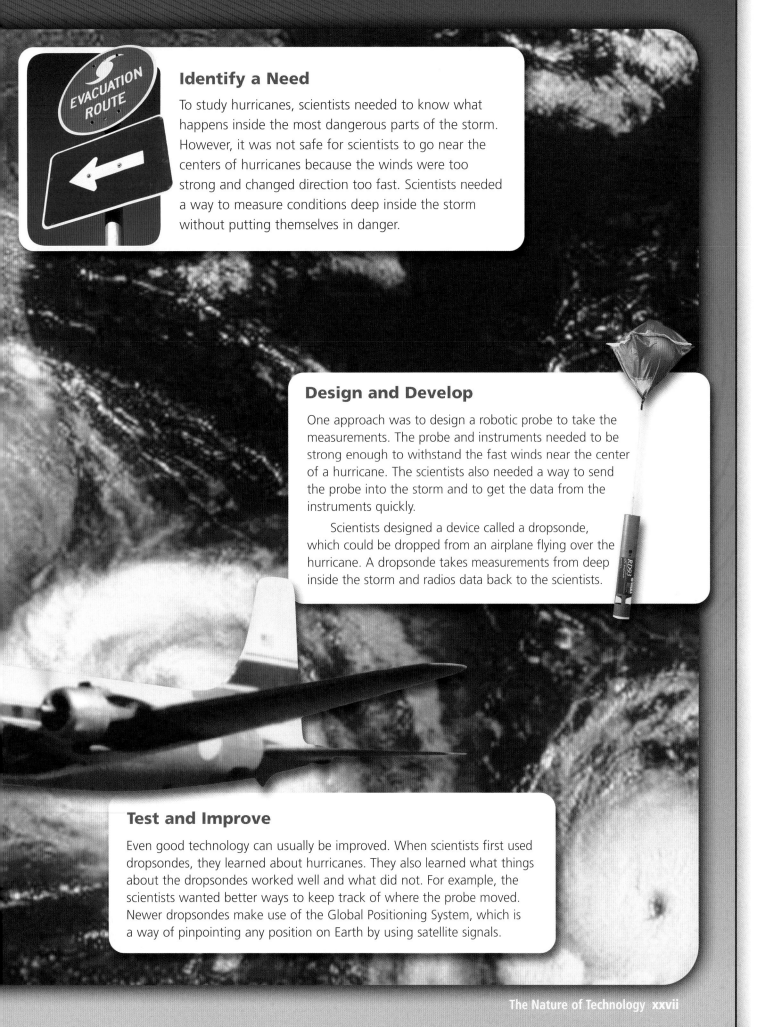

Identify a Need

To study hurricanes, scientists needed to know what happens inside the most dangerous parts of the storm. However, it was not safe for scientists to go near the centers of hurricanes because the winds were too strong and changed direction too fast. Scientists needed a way to measure conditions deep inside the storm without putting themselves in danger.

Design and Develop

One approach was to design a robotic probe to take the measurements. The probe and instruments needed to be strong enough to withstand the fast winds near the center of a hurricane. The scientists also needed a way to send the probe into the storm and to get the data from the instruments quickly.

Scientists designed a device called a dropsonde, which could be dropped from an airplane flying over the hurricane. A dropsonde takes measurements from deep inside the storm and radios data back to the scientists.

Test and Improve

Even good technology can usually be improved. When scientists first used dropsondes, they learned about hurricanes. They also learned what things about the dropsondes worked well and what did not. For example, the scientists wanted better ways to keep track of where the probe moved. Newer dropsondes make use of the Global Positioning System, which is a way of pinpointing any position on Earth by using satellite signals.

Using McDougal Littell Science

Reading Text and Visuals

This book is organized to help you learn. Use these boxed pointers as a path to help you learn and remember the **Big Ideas** and **Key Concepts**.

Take notes.

Use the strategies on the **Getting Ready to Learn** page.

Read the Big Idea.

As you read **Key Concepts** for the chapter, relate them to **the Big Idea**.

CHAPTER 3 — Ocean

the **BIG** idea

The oceans are a connected system of water in motion.

Key Concepts

SECTION 3.1 The oceans are a connected system.
Learn about ocean water and the ocean floor.

SECTION 3.2 Ocean water moves in currents.
Learn about currents and how they interact with climate and weather.

SECTION 3.3 Waves move through oceans.
Learn how waves form and move through the ocean.

SECTION 3.4 Waters rise and fall in tides.
Learn how tides are related to the Sun and the Moon.

Internet Preview

CLASSZONE.COM

Chapter 3 online resources: Content Review, Simulation, Visualization, three Resource Centers, Math Tutorial, Test Practice

C 72 Unit: Earth's Waters

CHAPTER 3
Getting Ready to Learn

◀ CONCEPT REVIEW

- Water covers most of Earth.
- Earth's waters circulate in the water cycle.
- The water in the oceans is salt water.

◀ VOCABULARY REVIEW

salt water p. 11
water cycle p. 12
evaporation p. 13
desalination p. 66

CONTENT REVIEW
CLASSZONE.COM
Review concepts and vocabulary.

▶ TAKING NOTES

OUTLINE

As you read, copy the headings into your notebook in the form of an outline. Then add notes in your own words that summarize what you read.

VOCABULARY STRATEGY

Draw a **word triangle** for each new vocabulary term. At the bottom, write and define the term. Above that, write a sentence in which you use the term correctly. At the top, draw a small picture to represent the term.

See the Note-Taking Handbook on pages R45–R51.

SCIENCE NOTEBOOK

OUTLINE
I. The oceans are a connected system.
  A. Ocean water covers much of Earth.
  B. Ocean water contains salts and gases.
    1.
    2.
  C. Ocean temperatures vary.
    1.
    2.

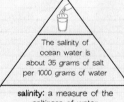

The salinity of ocean water is about 35 grams of salt per 1000 grams of water

salinity: a measure of the saltiness of water

C 74 Unit: Earth's Waters

KEY CONCEPT

3.1 The oceans are a connected system.

BEFORE, you learned

- Most water on Earth is salt water
- The ocean plays an important role in the water cycle

NOW, you will learn

- What ocean water contains
- What the ocean floor looks like
- How people explore the ocean

VOCABULARY

salinity p. 76
density p. 76
continental shelf p. 80
sonar p. 82

EXPLORE Density

Why do liquids form layers?

PROCEDURE

1. Insert the straw into one of the solutions. Cover the top of the straw with your finger and then remove the straw from the solution. The liquid should stay in the straw.

2. Using this technique, try to layer the three liquids in your straw so that you can see three distinct layers.

3. Experiment with the order in which you place the liquids into the straw. Between trials, empty the contents of the straw into the waste cup.

MATERIALS
- 3 solutions— A, B, and C—provided by your teacher
- clear straw
- waste cup

WHAT DO YOU THINK?
Did it matter in what order you layered the liquids? If so, can you explain why?

Ocean water covers much of Earth.

As land animals, we naturally think of our planet as a rocky and solid place. We even named our planet Earth, which means "land" or "soil." But look at a globe and you will see that oceans cover most of Earth. In fact, 71 percent of Earth is covered in seawater.

Looking at a map of the world, you can see the seven continents spread over our planet. These landmasses divide Earth's global ocean into connected sections. Different sections of the ocean have different names, such as Atlantic, Indian, and Pacific. However, all the sections are connected.

OUTLINE
Remember to start an outline for this section.

I. Main idea
  A. Supporting idea
    1. Detail
    2. Detail
  B. Supporting idea

Chapter 3: Ocean Systems 75 **C**

Reading Text and Visuals

Study the visuals.

- Read the title.

- Read all labels and captions.

- Figure out what the picture is showing. Notice colors, arrows, and lines.

The Water Cycle

Water on Earth moves in a continual cycle.

2 Condensation
Water vapor changes into liquid water, forming clouds.

3 Precipitation
Frozen or liquid water falls to the surface.

1 Evaporation
Water rises as vapor from the surface into the atmosphere.

Liquid water flows on Earth and collects in puddles, ponds, lakes, rivers, and oceans. It also sinks into the ground.

1 The process in which water changes from liquid to vapor is called **evaporation.** Heat energy from the Sun warms up the surface of the ocean or another body of water. Some of the liquid water evaporates, becoming invisible water vapor, a gas.

2 The process in which water vapor in the atmosphere becomes liquid is called **condensation.** Condensation occurs as air cools. Because cold air can hold less water vapor than warm air, some of the vapor condenses, or turns into droplets of liquid water. These droplets form clouds. At high altitudes clouds contain ice crystals. Unlike water vapor, clouds are visible evidence of water in the atmosphere.

3 Water that falls from clouds is **precipitation.** Inside a cloud, water droplets bump together and merge into larger droplets. They finally become heavy enough to fall as precipitation—rain, sleet, or hail. The water from precipitation sinks into the soil or flows into streams and rivers in the process called runoff. The force of gravity pulls the flowing water downward and, in most cases, eventually to the ocean.

VISUALIZATION
CLASSZONE.COM

See how water moves through Earth's system in the water cycle.

Read one paragraph at a time.

Look for a topic sentence that explains the main idea of the paragraph. Figure out how the details relate to that idea. One paragraph might have several important ideas; you may have to reread to understand.

CHECK YOUR READING Why does water vapor in air condense into liquid droplets?

Answer the questions.

Check Your Reading questions will help you remember what you read.

Chapter 1: **The Water Planet 13**

Doing Labs

To understand science, you have to see it in action. Doing labs helps you understand how things really work.

① Read the entire lab first.

② Form a hypothesis.

③ Follow the procedure.

④ Record the data.

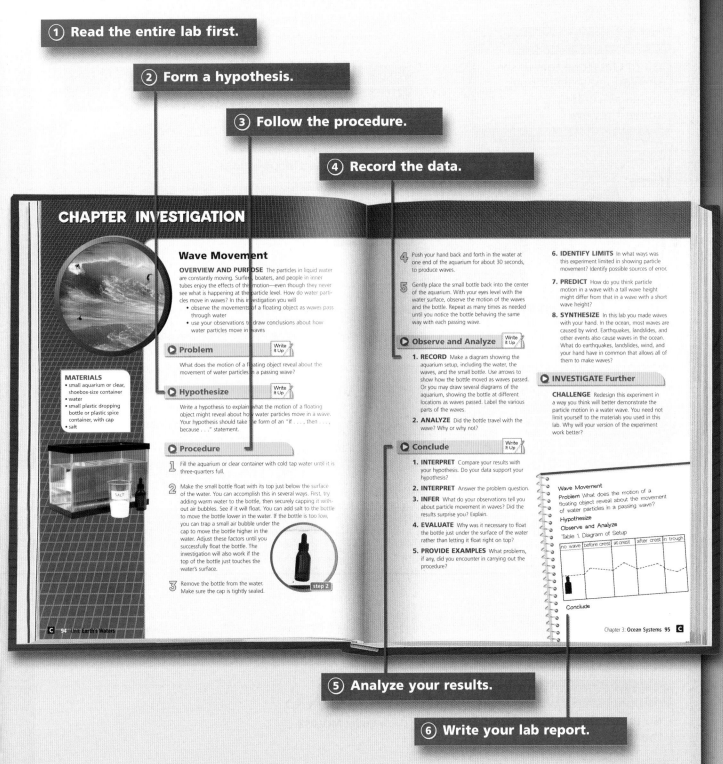

⑤ Analyze your results.

⑥ Write your lab report.

Using Technology

The Internet is a great source of information about up-to-date science. The ClassZone Website and SciLinks have exciting sites for you to explore. Video clips and simulations can make science come alive.

Look for red banners.

Go to **ClassZone.com** to see simulations, visualizations, resources centers, and content review.

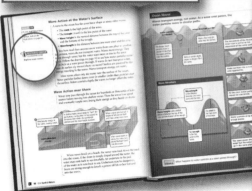

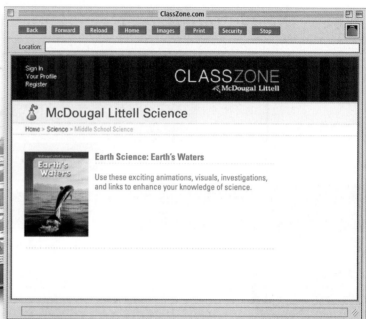

Watch the videos.

See science at work in the **Scientific American Frontiers video.**

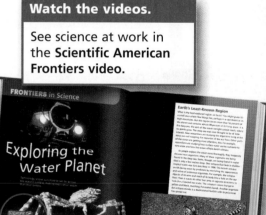

Look up SciLinks.

Go to **scilinks.org** to explore the topic.

Water Cycle **Code: MDL018**

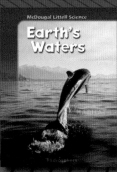

Earth's Waters
Contents Overview

Unit Features

1 The Water Planet   6

the BIG idea

Water moves through Earth's
atmosphere, oceans, and land
in a cycle.

2 Freshwater Resources   38

the BIG idea

Fresh water is a limited resource and
is essential for human society.

3 Ocean Systems   72

the BIG idea

The oceans are a connected system
of water in motion.

4 Ocean Environments   110

the BIG idea

The ocean supports life and contains
natural resources.

VIDEO SUMMARY

SCIENTIFIC AMERICAN FRONTIERS

"Into the Deep" is a segment of the *Scientific American Frontiers* program that aired on PBS stations. The video takes viewers to the bottom of the ocean, where they see sites of scientific discoveries made by explorer Bob Ballard. Ballard is popularly known for finding the sunken ocean liner *Titanic*. The submersible technology that he used to make that search possible is the same that he used to find an unexpected relationship between the ocean floor and the molten magma chamber below Earth's crust.

Deep underwater Ballard found vents from which pour super-hot chemical-filled water. Clams and worms live near these vents in conditions that scientists previously thought could not support life. Before that discovery, scientists thought that all life depended ultimately on sunlight and photosynthesis. In further explorations, Ballard found what he calls "black smokers," chimneys of 1400°C water filled with minerals and chemicals that contribute to the chemistry of seawater.

National Science Education Standards

A.1–8 Abilities Necessary to Do Scientific Inquiry

A.9.a–b, A.9.d–g Understandings about Scientific Inquiry

F.5.e Science and Technology in Society

G.1.a–b Science as a Human Endeavor

G.2.a, G.2.c Nature of Science

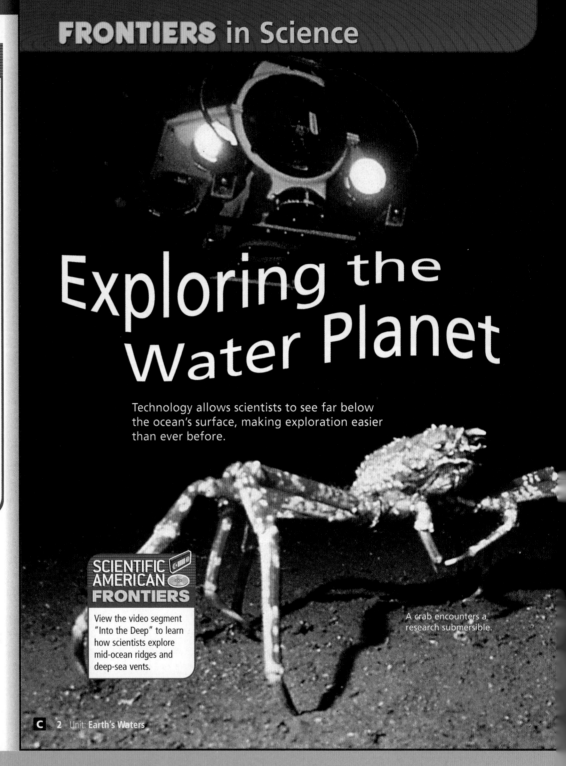

FRONTIERS in Science

Exploring the Water Planet

Technology allows scientists to see far below the ocean's surface, making exploration easier than ever before.

SCIENTIFIC AMERICAN FRONTIERS

View the video segment "Into the Deep" to learn how scientists explore mid-ocean ridges and deep-sea vents.

A crab encounters a research submersible.

C 2 Unit: Earth's Waters

ADDITIONAL RESOURCES

Technology Resources

 Scientific American Frontiers Video: *Into the Deep*
9-minute video segment introduces the unit.

 ClassZone.com
CAREER LINK, Oceanographer

Guide student viewing and comprehension of the video:

 Video Teaching Guide, pp. 1–2; Video Viewing Guide, p. 3; Video Wrap-Up, p. 4

Scientific American Frontiers Video Guide, pp. 27–30

Unit projects procedures and rubrics:

 Unit Projects, pp. 5–10

Earth's Least-Known Region

What is the least-explored region on Earth? You might guess it's a small area where few things live, perhaps in a vast desert or in high mountains. But this region covers more than 50 percent of the planet and contains almost 98 percent of its living space. It is the deep sea, the part of the ocean sunlight cannot reach, where no plants grow. The deep sea was once thought to be of little interest. Now researchers are studying the organisms living in the deep sea and mapping the resources of the sea floor. Other parts of the ocean are getting more attention, too. For example, researchers are studying how surface water carries nutrients to new areas and how the ocean affects Earth's climate.

As people explore the ocean more thoroughly, they frequently discover new organisms. Many of these organisms are being found in the deep sea. Some, though, are being found in water that is only a few meters deep. One octopus that lives in shallow tropical water was first described in 1998. This brown octopus avoids being eaten by predators by mimicking the appearances and colors of poisonous organisms. For example, the octopus slips six of its arms and much of its body into a hole on the sea floor. Then it waves its other two arms in opposite directions, which makes it look like a banded sea snake. The octopus's colors change to yellow and black, matching the snake's bands. Another organism the octopus mimics is a multicolored lionfish with its poisonous fins spread out.

An octopus (above) changes its colors and hides most of its body and all but two arms to mimic a poisonous sea snake (right).

FOCUS

○ Set Learning Goals

Students will

- Explore deep-sea habitats.
- Recognize that ocean currents affect climate.
- Relate eddies to the transport of ocean nutrients.
- Investigate oceans and local bodies of water.

Help students understand why the ocean is the last great frontier on Earth. Tell them that many factors affect ocean exploration, as they'll learn in the "Into the Deep" video. In the deep sea, for example, temperature and sunlight decrease with depth, while pressure increases. Ask: Why must scientists use remotely operated devices or submarines to collect data from the deep sea? *People cannot survive the pressure in the deep ocean, so data must be gathered with the help of technology.*

INSTRUCT

Scientific Process

Oceanographers are focusing their research in four areas of study. Ask students to identify these areas. *marine organisms, ocean resources, nutrient transport throughout the ocean, and oceanic effects on climate*

Teach from Visuals

Ask: What does this octopus do to scare off predators? *mimics a poisonous snake and changes color*

DIFFERENTIATE INSTRUCTION

② More Reading Support

A What region contains 98 percent of the living space on Earth? *the deep sea*

B What do people often discover when they explore the ocean? *new organisms*

Below Level Have students use a globe or world map to locate Earth's oceans. Point out that the oceans are interconnected—although they have different names, they form one big ocean. Ask: Does water or land cover more of Earth's surface? *water*

Scientific Process

After students have read about Robert Ballard, ask:

- What hypothesis did Robert Ballard help prove? *Mountains in the mid-ocean ridge are volcanoes.*

- What evidence helped prove this hypothesis? *underwater photographs taken aboard the submarine* Alvin

Technology Design

Ask students to list the technological challenges in mining ocean resources. Encourage them to brainstorm solutions to these challenges. *Sample answer: Challenges include locating the minerals, extracting them from the ocean floor, and transporting them to the surface. Remotely operated devices may be used to locate the minerals. Drills may be used to extract them. Submarines may be used to bring the minerals to the surface.*

Determining What Is Known

Have students summarize what scientists know about how the ocean and climate interact. *The ocean moves large amounts of heat energy from one area to another. This movement affects climate. The climate affects surface temperatures of the ocean. The warmest layers are generally on top. Ocean water mixes from surface to bottom.*

These scale worms, first described in 1988, live only around deep-sea vents and are thought to feed on the larger tubeworms.

Exploring Deep-Sea Vents

Deep-sea vents support astonishing life forms. These organisms depend on materials dissolved in scalding hot vent water, not on sunlight, for their ultimate source of energy. The superheated vent water contains many dissolved minerals. The minerals become solid as the vent water mixes with cold ocean water. Earth's richest deposits of minerals like copper, silver, and gold may be around some of these vents. To study the minerals that lie beneath thousands of meters of water, researchers use remotely operated devices to collect data and samples.

Exploring the Ocean and Climate

The ocean moves large amounts of heat energy between areas of Earth, affecting the atmosphere and climate. Consider that even though some parts of Alaska and Great Britain are equally close to the North Pole, Great Britain is warmer. Air over the Atlantic Ocean gains heat energy from a warm ocean current, and winds carry this warmth toward Great Britain. In addition to moving across the surface, water also mixes vertically in the ocean. The ocean contains many layers of water, with the warmest generally at the top. But the middle layers of the ocean may now be heating up quickly. Researchers are working to understand how the mixing of water in the ocean affects Earth's atmosphere and climate.

SCIENTIFIC AMERICAN FRONTIERS

View the "Into the Deep" segment of your *Scientific American Frontiers* video to learn how scientists are exploring the deep sea.

IN THIS SCENE FROM THE VIDEO ▶ a deep-sea vent spews out superheated water that is rich in dissolved minerals.

THE DEEPEST DIVES Robert Ballard has made dozens of expeditions in *Alvin,* a three-person submarine. This small vessel can dive deep below the surface to underwater mountain ranges called mid-ocean ridges. Ballard's photographs helped prove that the mountains in a mid-ocean ridge are volcanoes.

While exploring a valley that runs along the top of a mid-ocean ridge, Ballard discovered deep-sea vents. Water that flows out of the vents is very hot and rich in minerals. Ballard was also one of the first scientists to see the giant clams, tubeworms, and other animals that live around the vents. Such life forms are unusual because they depend on energy from within Earth instead of energy from the Sun.

DIFFERENTIATE INSTRUCTION

 More Reading Support

C What is the source of energy for deep-sea vent organisms? *material in vent water*

D What increases Great Britain's warmth? *a warm ocean current*

Advanced Ask students to infer why the warmest layer of ocean water is generally on top. Have them design an experiment to test their hypothesis. *Warm water is less dense than cooler water, and floats on it.*

Exploring Ocean Nutrients

Some water masses move in circular or spiral patterns, as you can see in the photograph below. These spinning water masses are called eddies. Water in eddies mixes slowly with the surrounding water. An eddy that contains nutrient-rich water can drift great distances, mixing with nutrient-poor water over a long time, sometimes years. The added nutrients allow populations of tiny plantlike organisms to grow quickly. These organisms are the base of the ocean food chain, and almost all other ocean organisms depend on them. Researchers are studying how changes in the sizes and numbers of eddies affect ocean organisms. Nutrient-rich eddies may be important to fish, such as salmon, that many people eat.

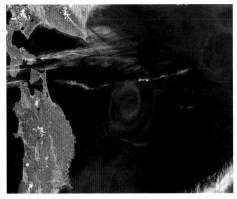

Eddies are mixing seawater from the coast of Japan with water farther from shore.

UNANSWERED Questions

Scientists who study the ocean know that much of it is yet to be explored and that many questions remain.

- How many, and what types of, ocean organisms will be discovered in the next decades?
- How do changes in ocean surface temperatures affect weather?
- What is the best way to maintain populations of fish that people depend on for food?

UNIT PROJECTS

As you study this unit, work alone or with a group on one of the projects listed below.

Track a Drop of Water

Suppose you could follow a drop of surface water as it journeys from your hometown to the ocean.

- Find out which rivers and lakes the drop would travel through, and which ocean it would join.
- Present your findings. You might make a travelogue, a map, or both.

Life in the Water

Investigate the different life forms that live in the water in your area.

- Collect water samples from different sources, such as indoor taps, fountains, puddles, marshes, lakes, and streams.
- Examine a drop from each sample under a microscope. Sketch any living organisms you see.
- Write a lab report to present your findings about the water samples.

Ocean News Report

Imagine that you are part of a news group assigned to report on major discoveries made about the world's oceans over the past 25 years.

- Research the most important or unusual facts uncovered about the oceans. Note what technology was used to gather the data.
- Prepare a special TV or Web-site report about your investigation. Where possible, include photographs or illustrations.

 **CAREER CENTER**
CLASSZONE.COM
Learn more about careers in oceanography.

UNANSWERED Questions

Have students read the questions and think of some of their own. Remind them that scientists always end up with more questions—that inquiry is the driving force of science.

- With the class, generate on the board a list of new questions.
- Students can add to the list after they watch the *Scientific American Frontiers* Video.
- Students can use the list as a springboard for choosing their Unit Projects.

UNIT PROJECTS

Encourage students to pick the project that most appeals to them. Point out that each is long-term and will take several weeks to complete. You might group or pair students to work on projects and in some cases guide student choice. Some of the projects have student choice built into them. Each project has two worksheet pages, including a rubric. Use the pages to guide students through criteria, process, and schedule.

R Unit Projects, pp. 5–10

REVISIT concepts introduced in this article:

Chapter 1
- The water cycle, pp. 9–15

Chapter 2
- Fresh water and life, pp. 41–48

Chapter 3
- Ocean systems, pp. 75–82
- Ocean currents, pp. 84–89

Chapter 4
- Ocean environments, pp. 113–128
- Undersea hot spots, p. 129
- Ocean and natural resources, pp. 130–134

DIFFERENTIATE INSTRUCTION

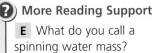 **More Reading Support**

E What do you call a spinning water mass? *an eddy*

F What organisms form the base of the ocean food chain? *tiny plantlike organisms*

Differentiate Unit Projects Projects are appropriate for varying abilities. Allow students to choose the ones that interest them most and let them vary their product. Encourage below level students to give visual or oral presentations or to record audio presentations about their topic.

Below Level Encourage students to try "Track a Drop of Water."

Advanced Challenge students to complete "Ocean News Report."

CHAPTER 1

The Water Planet

Earth Science
UNIFYING PRINCIPLES

PRINCIPLE 1
Heat energy inside Earth and radiation from the Sun provide energy for Earth's processes.

PRINCIPLE 2
Physical forces, such as gravity, affect the movement of all matter on Earth and throughout the universe.

PRINCIPLE 3
Matter and energy move among Earth's rocks and soil, atmosphere, waters, and living things.

PRINCIPLE 4
Earth has changed over time and continues to change.

Unit: Earth's Waters
BIG IDEAS

CHAPTER 1
The Water Planet
Water moves through Earth's atmosphere, oceans, and land in a cycle.

CHAPTER 2
Freshwater Resources
Fresh water is a limited resource and is essential for human society.

CHAPTER 3
Ocean Systems
The oceans are a connected system of water in motion.

CHAPTER 4
Ocean Environments
The ocean supports life and contains natural resources.

CHAPTER 1
KEY CONCEPTS

SECTION 1.1

Water continually cycles.
1. Water is a unique substance.
2. Water covers most of Earth.
3. Water moves in a worldwide cycle.

SECTION 1.2

Fresh water flows and freezes on Earth.
1. Water flows and collects on Earth's surface.
2. Surface water collects in ponds and lakes.
3. Most fresh water on Earth is frozen.

SECTION 1.3

Fresh water flows underground.
1. Water fills underground spaces.
2. Underground water can be brought to the surface.

The Big Idea Flow Chart is available on p. T1 in the **UNIT TRANSPARENCY BOOK.**

Previewing Content

 1.1 **Water continuously cycles.** pp. 9–15

1. Water is a unique substance.
- Earth is the only planet with a large amount of liquid water.
- Because of water, Earth can support life.
- Water is the only substance on Earth that exists in all three physical states at normal temperatures.

2. Water covers most of Earth.
- Earth's four named oceans are all connected to form one huge ocean that covers 71 percent of the planet's surface.
- Life is dependent on water. The human body is two-thirds water.
- Most rivers and lakes contain **fresh water,** which is not salty and has little or no taste.
- The oceans contain **salt water,** which has many dissolved minerals.
- Most water on Earth is salt water. The diagram below shows the percentage of salt water in relation to the percentage of fresh water.

3% fresh water

97% salt water

3. Water moves in a worldwide cycle.
- Water on Earth is continuously moving from one place and form to another. This continuous movement is known as the **water cycle.**
- The water cycle involves three processes. **Evaporation** is the change of water from liquid to vapor. **Condensation** is the change of water vapor in the atmosphere to liquid. **Precipitation** is the water that falls from clouds after condensation has taken place.
- The water cycle impacts our lives through precipitation, which brings needed fresh water for drinking and crops but may also cause flooding or other problems.

 1.2 **Fresh water flows and freezes on Earth.** pp. 16–23

1. Water flows and collects on Earth's surface.
- The force of gravity pulls water downward. When precipitation falls on a high ridge that forms a **divide,** it flows away in different directions. All the water flowing downward on one side of a divide flows into a **drainage basin.**
- Water in a drainage basin forms streams and rivers or sinks into the ground. Most water eventually flows to the sea.

2. Surface water collects in ponds and lakes.
- Water collects in low areas to form ponds and lakes. In some places, the land surface dips below the level of underground water. Water enters lakes and ponds as precipitation and may run in from streams. A lake is larger than a pond and may have water so deep that no sunlight reaches the bottom. A pond is generally filled with plants.
- In places with cold winters, the cool water layers of lakes switch places with the warm water layers. This is known as **turnover.**
- **Eutrophication** is an increase in the nutrient level of a lake or pond, caused by a buildup of dead organisms or by pollution, such as nitrogen from fertilizers and phosphates from detergents. It causes an increase in the amount of algae and other organisms in the water. This leads to oxygen depletion of the water and the death of fish and other animals.

3. Most fresh water on Earth is frozen.
- Two-thirds of the fresh water on Earth is in the form of ice, mostly in huge ice sheets that cover land near the poles. These are continental glaciers. Valley glaciers build up in mountainous areas and flow slowly down between mountains.
- Sometimes a chunk of a glacier breaks off to form an **iceberg** that floats in the ocean. Only about 1/8 of the total volume and weight of an iceberg floats above the water.

Common Misconceptions

CONTENT OF CLOUDS Students may think that clouds are made up of water vapor because they are in the atmosphere and students know that the atmosphere contains water vapor. In actuality,

 MISCONCEPTION DATABASE
CLASSZONE.COM Background on student misconceptions

clouds are made up of many tiny droplets of liquid water that are too small and light to be pulled down to Earth by gravity.

 This misconception is addressed on p. 13.

Previewing Content

1.3 Fresh water flows underground.
pp. 24–33

1. Water fills underground spaces.
- Some water sinks into the ground. Plants use some of it, and the rest sinks deeper into Earth and is held underground as **groundwater.**
- Either ground materials are **permeable,** and water can flow through them; or they are **impermeable,** and water cannot flow through them. Some rock, such as sandstone, is permeable. Gravel, sand, and soil are also permeable. Water sinks into Earth until it reaches an impermeable layer. The **water table** is the top of the area that is saturated with water.
- An underground layer of permeable rock or sediment that contains water is an **aquifer.** In an aquifer, groundwater is stored in permeable material located over or beside impermeable rock that prevents the water from draining away. The water is constantly replenished. Aquifers filter and clean water and provide a water source for people on Earth.

2. Underground water can be brought to the surface.
- People collect groundwater from springs and wells. A **spring** is a place where the surface of the land dips below the water table and water bubbles up from the ground. The visual on p. 29 (and in the next column) shows how technology has enabled people to live in more places because they can obtain water more easily.
- A well is a hole drilled into the ground to reach groundwater. The diagram at right shows how a well is drilled.
- An **artesian well** is a well in which water flows to the surface naturally because of pressure exerted below the surface. A hot spring is a place where water heated underground reaches the surface. A geyser is a special kind of hot spring.

How to Make a Well

Drill into the ground with special machinery.

water table

aquifer

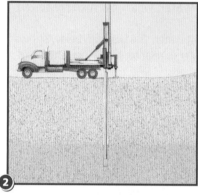

When the drill hole reaches below the water table, lower a pipe into it.

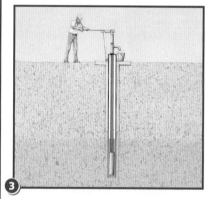

At the top of the well, install a pump powered by a motor or human effort to pull up water.

Common Misconceptions

RUNNING WATER Students may think that all water runs downhill. However, pressure may cause underground water to flow upward and form artesian wells, hot springs, or geysers.

[T E] This misconception is addressed on p. 30.

MISCONCEPTION DATABASE
CLASSZONE.COM Background on student misconceptions

Previewing Labs

Lab Generator CD-ROM
Edit these Pupil Edition labs and generate alternative labs.

EXPLORE the BIG idea

Where Can You See Water? p. 7
Students look for different forms of water around them.

TIME 10 minutes
MATERIALS none

Does the Ice Float? p. 7
Students learn about the densities of fresh water and salt water by seeing how ice floats in each.

TIME 10 minutes
MATERIALS glass, water, ice cube, salt, spoon

Internet Activity: Water, p. 7
Students use the Internet to learn about forms of water.

TIME 20 minutes
MATERIALS computer with Internet access

SECTION 1.1

EXPLORE Water Vapor, p. 9
Students put ice in water to observe condensation of water vapor.

TIME 10 minutes
MATERIALS clear glass, ice, water

INVESTIGATE The Water Cycle, p. 12
Students create a closed environment to observe the water cycle.

TIME 30 minutes
MATERIALS jar with lid, soil, rocks or pebbles, sand, smaller containers, water, small plants, triple-beam balance

---

SECTION 1.2

EXPLORE Water Collection, p. 16
Students pour water into an egg carton when it is flat and then when it is tilted to observe water flowing and collecting.

TIME 10 minutes
MATERIALS plastic-foam egg carton, tray or pan, plastic bottle, water

---

INVESTIGATE Icebergs, p. 21
Students calculate the densities of water and ice to infer why icebergs float.

TIME 30 minutes
MATERIALS balance, ice cube, water, graduated cylinder (250 mL), paper clip, calculator, cork

---

SECTION 1.3

EXPLORE Flow of Water, p. 24
Students observe water in permeable and impermeable materials to understand that permeability has to do with how porous a material is.

TIME 10 minutes
MATERIALS cup; paper coffee filter; bucket; dishpan, or sink; water

---

INVESTIGATE Aquifer Filtration, p. 27
Students pour water into a model to observe how ground materials filter water.

TIME 30 minutes
MATERIALS 1 L plastic bottle with bottom cut off, gravel, sand, soil, water, food coloring, cocoa, pepper, bottle bottom or bucket

---

CHAPTER INVESTIGATION Water Moving Underground, pp. 32–33
Students design an experiment that compares how different ground materials absorb and transport water in order to infer what Earth materials make the best aquifers.

TIME 40 minutes
MATERIALS granite sample; sandstone sample; sand; square piece of cotton muslin or cotton knit measuring 30 cm per side; rubber band; golf ball; scale; large jar; water

---

R **Additional INVESTIGATION,** Water Wells, A, B, & C, pp. 60–68; Teacher Instructions, pp. 262–263

Previewing Chapter Resources

	INTEGRATED TECHNOLOGY	LABS AND ACTIVITIES

CHAPTER 1
The Water Planet

 CLASSZONE.COM
- eEdition Plus
- EasyPlanner Plus
- Misconception Database
- Content Review
- Test Practice
- Visualization
- Simulation
- Resource Centers
- Internet Activity: Water
- Math Tutorial

 SCILINKS.ORG
SCI **LINKS**

 CD-ROMS
- eEdition
- EasyPlanner
- Power Presentations
- Content Review
- Lab Generator
- Test Generator

 AUDIO CDS
- Audio Readings
- Audio Readings in Spanish

PE EXPLORE the Big Idea, p. 7
- Where Can You See Water?
- Does the Ice Float?
- Internet Activity: Water

R UNIT RESOURCE BOOK
- Family Letter, p. vii
- Spanish Family Letter, p. viii
- Unit Projects, pp. 5–10

Lab Generator CD-ROM
Generate customized labs.

SECTION
1.1 Water continually cycles.
pp. 9–15

Time: 2 periods (1 block)
 Lesson Plan, pp. 11–12

 • **VISUALIZATION,** The Water Cycle
• **RESOURCE CENTER,** Evidence of a Water Cycle on Mars

 UNIT TRANSPARENCY BOOK
- Big Idea Flow Chart, p. T1
- Daily Vocabulary Scaffolding, p. T2
- Note-Taking Model, p. T3
- 3-Minute Warm-Up, p. T4

 • EXPLORE Water Vapor, p. 9
• INVESTIGATE The Water Cycle, p. 12
• Think Science, p. 15

 UNIT RESOURCE BOOK
Datasheet, The Water Cycle, p. 20

SECTION
1.2 Fresh water flows and freezes on Earth.
pp. 16–23

Time: 2 periods (1 block)
 Lesson Plan, pp. 22–23

 • **MATH TUTORIAL**
• **RESOURCE CENTER,** Frozen Fresh Water

 UNIT TRANSPARENCY BOOK
- Daily Vocabulary Scaffolding, p. T2
- 3-Minute Warm-Up, p. T4

 • EXPLORE Water Collection, p. 16
• INVESTIGATE Icebergs, p. 21
• Math in Science, p. 23

 UNIT RESOURCE BOOK
- Datasheet, Icebergs, p. 31
- Math Support, p. 49
- Math Practice, p. 50

SECTION
1.3 Fresh water flows underground.
pp. 24–33

Time: 4 periods (2 blocks)
 Lesson Plan, pp. 33–34

 • **SIMULATION,** Aquifers
• **RESOURCE CENTER,** Geysers and Hot Springs

 UNIT TRANSPARENCY BOOK
- Big Idea Flow Chart, p. T1
- Daily Vocabulary Scaffolding, p. T2
- 3-Minute Warm-Up, p. T5
- "Springs and Wells" Visual, p. T6
- Chapter Outline, pp. T7–T8

 • EXPLORE Flow of Water, p. 24
• INVESTIGATE Aquifer Filtration, p. 27
• CHAPTER INVESTIGATION, Water Moving Underground, pp. 32–33

 UNIT RESOURCE BOOK
- Datasheet, Aquifer Filtration, p. 42
- CHAPTER INVESTIGATION, Water Moving Underground, A, B, & C, pp. 51–59
- Additional INVESTIGATION, Water Wells, A, B, & C, pp. 60–68

KEY TO ICONS

 INTERNET   CD/CD-ROM   **PE** Pupil Edition   **TE** Teacher Edition   **R** UNIT RESOURCE BOOK   **T** UNIT TRANSPARENCY BOOK   **A** UNIT ASSESSMENT BOOK   **SP A** SPANISH ASSESSMENT BOOK   SCIENCE TOOLKIT

READING AND REINFORCEMENT

- Four Square, B22–23
- Main Idea and Detail Notes, C37
- Daily Vocabulary Scaffolding, H1–8

 UNIT RESOURCE BOOK
- Vocabulary Practice, pp. 46–47
- Decoding Support, p. 48
- Summarizing the Chapter, pp. 69–70

Audio Readings CD
Listen to Pupil Edition.

Audio Readings in Spanish CD
Listen to Pupil Edition in Spanish.

 UNIT RESOURCE BOOK
- Reading Study Guide, A & B, pp. 13–16
- Spanish Reading Study Guide, pp. 17–18
- Challenge and Extension, p. 19
- Reinforcing Key Concepts, p. 21
- Challenge Reading, pp. 44–45

 UNIT RESOURCE BOOK
- Reading Study Guide, A & B, pp. 24–27
- Spanish Reading Study Guide, pp. 28–29
- Challenge and Extension, p. 30
- Reinforcing Key Concepts, p. 32

 UNIT RESOURCE BOOK
- Reading Study Guide, A & B, pp. 35–38
- Spanish Reading Study Guide, pp. 39–40
- Challenge and Extension, p. 41
- Reinforcing Key Concepts, p. 43

ASSESSMENT

- Chapter Review, pp. 35–36
- Standardized Test Practice, p. 37

 UNIT ASSESSMENT BOOK
- Diagnostic Test, pp. 1–2
- Chapter Test, Levels A, B, & C, pp. 6–17
- Alternative Assessment, pp. 18–19

 Spanish Chapter Test, pp. 153–156

Test Generator CD-ROM
Generate customized tests.

Lab Generator CD-ROM
Rubrics for Labs

 Ongoing Assessment, pp. 10–14

 Section 1.1 Review, p. 14

 UNIT ASSESSMENT BOOK
Section 1.1 Quiz, p. 3

 Ongoing Assessment, pp. 17–22

 Section 1.2 Review, p. 22

UNIT ASSESSMENT BOOK
Section 1.2 Quiz, p. 4

 Ongoing Assessment, pp. 25, 28–29, 31

 Section 1.3 Review, p. 31

 UNIT ASSESSMENT BOOK
Section 1.3 Quiz, p. 5

STANDARDS

National Standards
A.1–8, A.9.a–c, A.9.e–f, D.1.f, D.3.d, E.2–5

See p. 6 for the standards.

National Standards
A.2–7, A.9.a–b, A.9.e–f, D.1.f, D.3.d, E.2–5

National Standards
A.2–8, A.9.a–c, A.9.e–f, D.1.f, D.3.d

National Standards
A.1–7, A.9.a–b, A.9.e–g, D.1.f, E.2–5

Previewing Resources for Differentiated Instruction

CHAPTER INVESTIGATION

Leveled resources present the same concepts for different abilities.

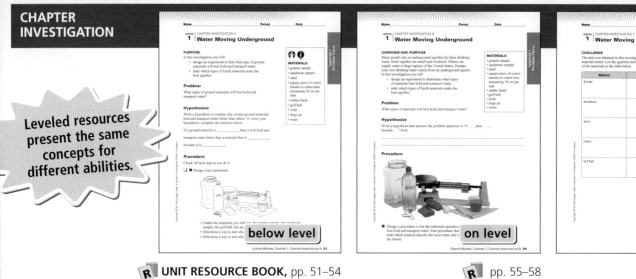

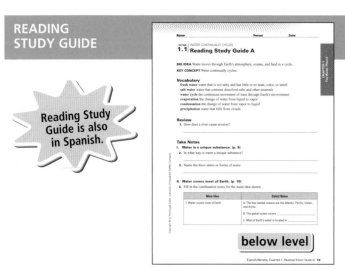

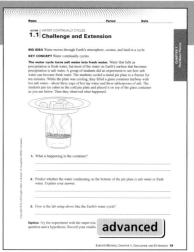

below level

on level

advanced

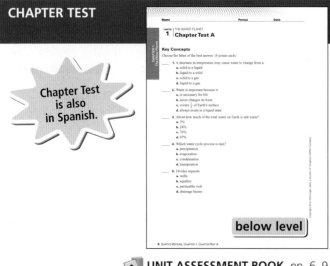 **UNIT RESOURCE BOOK,** pp. 51–54

R pp. 55–58

R pp. 55–59

READING STUDY GUIDE

Reading Study Guide is also in Spanish.

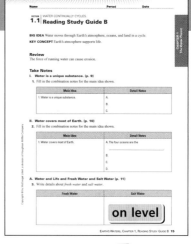

below level

on level

advanced

R UNIT RESOURCE BOOK, pp. 13–14

R pp. 15–16

R p. 19

CHAPTER TEST

Chapter Test is also in Spanish.

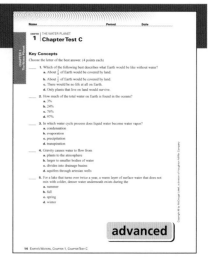

below level

on level

advanced

A UNIT ASSESSMENT BOOK, pp. 6–9

A pp. 10–13

A pp. 14–17

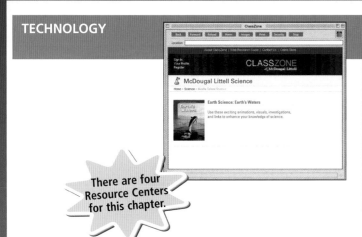

There are four Resource Centers for this chapter.

CLASSZONE.COM

CD/CD-ROMS

CLASSZONE.COM

VISUAL CONTENT

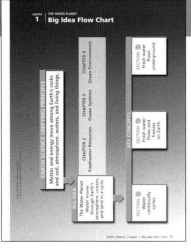

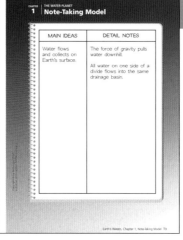

 **UNIT TRANSPARENCY BOOK,** p. T1

 p. T3

p. T6

MORE SUPPORT

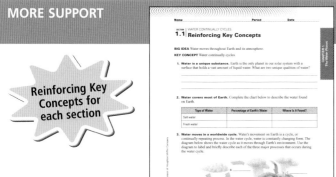

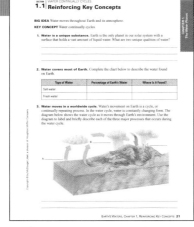

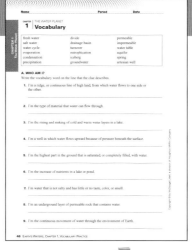

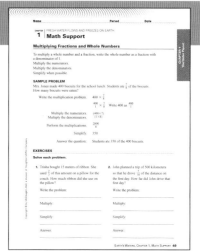

Reinforcing Key Concepts for each section

UNIT RESOURCE BOOK, p. 21

pp. 46–47

p. 49

INTRODUCE

the **BIG** idea

Have students look at the photograph of mountains and different forms of water. Discuss how the question in the box links to the Big Idea:

- What forms of water can you see around you now?
- What other forms of water have you experienced?
- What have you noticed about the characteristics of each form of water that you have experienced?

National Science Education Standards

Content

D.1.f Water, which covers the majority of Earth's surface, circulates through the crust, oceans, and atmosphere in the "water cycle."

D.3.d The Sun is the major source of energy for phenomena on Earth's surface, such as winds, ocean currents, and the water cycle.

Process

A.1–8 Identify questions that can be answered through investigations; design and conduct an investigation; use tools to gather and interpret data; use evidence to describe, predict, explain, model; think critically to make relationships between evidence and explanation; recognize different explanations and predictions; communicate scientific procedures and explanations; use mathematics.

A.9.a–c, A.9.e–g Understand scientific inquiry by using different investigations, methods, mathematics, and explanations based on logic, evidence, and skepticism. Data often result in new investigations.

E.2–5 Identify a problem; design, implement, and evaluate a solution or product; communicate technological design.

CHAPTER

The Water Planet

the **BIG** idea

Water moves through Earth's atmosphere, oceans, and land in a cycle.

In what forms does water exist on Earth?

Key Concepts

SECTION
1.1 Water continually cycles. Learn about how water on Earth moves in a world-wide system.

SECTION
1.2 Fresh water flows and freezes on Earth. Learn about fresh water in rivers, lakes, and ice.

SECTION
1.3 Fresh water flows underground. Learn about water under the land surface and how it is used.

 Internet Preview

CLASSZONE.COM

Chapter 1 online resources: Content Review, Simulation, Visualization, four Resource Centers, Math Tutorial, Test Practice

C 6 Unit: Earth's Waters

 INTERNET PREVIEW

CLASSZONE.COM For student use with the following pages:

Review and Practice
- Content Review, pp. 8, 34
- Math Tutorial: Multiplying Fractions and Whole Numbers, p. 23
- Test Practice, p. 37

Activities and Resources
- Internet Activity: Water, p. 7
- Resource Center: Water Cycle on Mars, p. 15; Frozen Fresh Water, p. 21; Geysers and Hot Springs, p. 31
- Visualization: The Water Cycle, p. 13
- Simulation: Aquifers, p. 26

NSTA *SCiLINKS*
scilinks.org
Water Cycle **Code: MDL018**

Where Can You See Water?

Look in your home or school for examples of frozen and liquid water. Go outside and look for the same, plus evidence of water in the air. Record your observations.

Observe and Think What did you find inside? outside? Did you see evidence of water in the air?

Does the Ice Float?

Place an ice cube in a glass of tap water. Does it float at all? Now add two spoonfuls of salt to the water and stir it in. What happens to the ice cube?

Observe and Think What might the salt do to the water that affects the way the ice cube floats?

Internet Activity: Water

Go to **ClassZone.com** to learn what different forms of water exist on Earth and how water is a part of Earth's systems.

Observe and Think What are the different ways that water exists on Earth?

NSTA scilinks.org **SCiLINKS**

Water Cycle **Code: MDL018**

Chapter 1: **The Water Planet 7** **C**

These inquiry-based activities are appropriate for use at home or as a supplement to classroom instruction.

Where Can You See Water?

PURPOSE To help students recognize that water is present in many places and in different forms in their environment.

TIP *10 min.* Encourage students to check in the refrigerator and freezer.

Ideally students will find water in nonobvious places—plant soil, gutters, etc., and will identify water in different forms, such as ice and in clouds.

REVISIT after p. 10.

Does the Ice Float?

PURPOSE To prepare students for the concepts of freshwater icebergs floating in oceans and the higher density of salt water.

TIP *10 min.* Use cold water to keep the ice cube from melting too quickly.

Students will see how ice floats in fresh water and, depending on how they conduct the experiment, how it floats differently in salt water.

REVISIT after p. 22.

Internet Activity: Water

PURPOSE To see how water exists in different forms and how it cycles.

TIP *20 min.* Students might suggest places on Earth where water is found in each of its different forms.

Water moves throughout the Earth system in different forms and in different ways.

REVISIT after p. 14.

TEACHING WITH TECHNOLOGY

Graphics and Presentation Software After reading p. 18, students can download photographs and diagrams from the Internet and then use presentation software to create a display that compares and contrasts ponds and lakes. After teaching p. 29, have students make diagrams that show the difference between a well and a spring.

CBL and Probeware If students have probeware, they can use a flow-rate sensor to see how steeper inclines generate faster currents in the Explore on p. 16.

◐ CONCEPT REVIEW

Activate Prior Knowledge

- Place a glass of water on your desk. Ask: How is this substance important?
- Lead a discussion that prompts students to recall that Earth is a system of four spheres. Ask: What are the four spheres of the Earth system? *atmosphere, hydrosphere, biosphere, geosphere* How are they interrelated? *They work together to form one large, closed system.*

◑ TAKING NOTES

Main Idea and Detail Notes

Writing down the main ideas and details will help students organize their thoughts about the concepts. Students can use topic sentences of paragraphs in the text to help them identify main ideas.

Vocabulary Strategy

Using a four-square diagram will help students comprehend the vocabulary terms by supplying examples and characteristics that go beyond just a definition.

Vocabulary and Note-Taking Resources

- Vocabulary Practice, pp. 46–47
- Decoding Support, p. 48

- Daily Vocabulary Scaffolding, p. T2
- Note-Taking Model, p. T3

- Four Square, B22–23
- Main Idea and Detail Notes, C37
- Daily Vocabulary Scaffolding, H1–8

Getting Ready to Learn

◐ CONCEPT REVIEW

- Water built up on Earth's surface over time.
- Water is essential for life.
- Earth has an atmosphere of gases.

◐ VOCABULARY REVIEW

See Glossary for definitions.

atmosphere

glacier

system

CONTENT REVIEW
CLASSZONE.COM
Review concepts and vocabulary.

▶ TAKING NOTES

MAIN IDEA AND DETAIL NOTES

Make a two-column chart. Write the main ideas, such as those in the blue headings, in the column on the left. Write details about each of those main ideas in the column on the right.

VOCABULARY STRATEGY

Write each new vocabulary term in the center of a **four-square** diagram. Write notes in the squares around the term. Include a definition, some characteristics, and some examples. If possible, write some things that are not examples.

See the Note-Taking Handbook on pages R45–R51.

SCIENCE NOTEBOOK

MAIN IDEAS	DETAIL NOTES
1. Water is a unique substance.	1. Only substance in three forms at normal temperatures
	1. Can be solid, liquid, gas
	1. As liquid, can fit any container

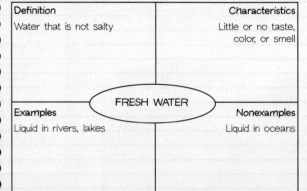

Definition	Characteristics
Water that is not salty	Little or no taste, color, or smell

FRESH WATER

Examples	Nonexamples
Liquid in rivers, lakes	Liquid in oceans

CHECK READINESS

Administer the Diagnostic Test to determine students' readiness for new science content and their mastery of requisite math skills.

 Diagnostic Test, pp. 1–2

Technology Resources

Students needing content and math skills should visit **ClassZone.com**.

- **CONTENT REVIEW**
- **MATH TUTORIAL**

 CONTENT REVIEW CD-ROM

BEFORE, you learned
- The force of running water causes erosion
- Water can be solid

NOW, you will learn
- What makes water important
- How much of Earth's water is salt water
- How water moves throughout Earth and its atmosphere

VOCABULARY

fresh water p. 11
salt water p. 11
water cycle p. 12
evaporation p. 13
condensation p. 13
precipitation p. 13

EXPLORE Water Vapor

Where does the water come from?

PROCEDURE

1. Put the ice in the glass and fill it with water.
2. Observe what happens to the outside of the glass.

MATERIALS
- clear glass
- ice
- water

WHAT DO YOU THINK?
- Where did the water on the outside of the glass come from?
- What does this activity tell you about the air surrounding you? What conclusion can you draw?

Water is a unique substance.

Seen from outer space, Earth glistens like a beautiful blue and white marble. Welcome to the "water planet," the only planet in our solar system with a surface covered by a vast amount of liquid water. Because of water, a truly amazing substance, life can exist on Earth.

What is so amazing about water? In the temperature ranges we have on Earth, it exists commonly as a solid, a liquid, and a gas. At a low temperature, water freezes. It becomes a solid, which is ice. At a higher temperature, it flows easily in liquid form. Liquid water can become a gas, especially at higher temperatures. If you have ever noticed how something wet dries out in the hot sunlight, you have observed the effect of liquid water changing into a gas. The gas form is the invisible water vapor in our atmosphere.

Liquid water can fit any container. It can hold its shape in a raindrop, then merge with other drops to flow down a hill or slow down and sit for centuries in a lake.

MAIN IDEA AND DETAILS
Make a two-column chart to start organizing information about water.

Chapter 1: **The Water Planet 9** C

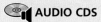
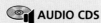

1.1 FOCUS

Set Learning Goals
Students will
- Recognize the importance of water.
- Observe how much of Earth's water is salt water.
- Explain how water moves throughout Earth and its atmosphere.
- Model in an experiment how water moves through an environment.

3-Minute Warm-Up

Display Transparency 4 or copy this exercise on the chalkboard:

Decide if these statements are true. If not, correct them.

1. Water on Earth can be in a solid form. *true*

2. Erosion changes the shape of the land. *true*

3. Standing water causes erosion. *Running water causes erosion.*

 3-Minute Warm-Up, p. T4

1.1 MOTIVATE

EXPLORE Water Vapor

PURPOSE To observe that vapor in the air can become liquid water as a result of condensation

TIP *10 min.* Provide paper towels to wipe up water that drips onto desks.

WHAT DO YOU THINK? *The water comes from water vapor in the air. When the warmer air meets the cold glass, water vapor in the air condenses into liquid water because cold air cannot hold as much water vapor as warm air. Air around us contains water vapor. When air is cooled, water vapor changes to liquid water.*

1.1 INSTRUCT

Real World Example

Identify a 2-mile distance between two local landmarks that are familiar to students, and compare it to the average depth of the oceans.

EXPLORE (the BIG idea)

Revisit "Where Can You See Water?" on p. 7. Have students explain the significance of their results.

Teach from Visuals

To help students interpret the visual showing the water-to-land ratio on Earth, ask:

- How much of Earth's surface is covered by water? *71 percent, or almost three-quarters*

- Why does a globe show the amount of water covering Earth more accurately than a flat map? *A flat map may exaggerate the amount of land in relation to the amount of water.*

Ongoing Assessment

Recognize the importance of water.

Ask: Why is water important? *Water is needed for life to exist on Earth.*

 CHECK YOUR READING *Answer: in the ocean*

 READING VISUALS *Answer: at the bottom, in Antarctica*

Water covers most of Earth.

A Earth looks bluish from space because most of Earth's surface is ocean. If you look at a globe or a world map, you will see the names of four oceans—Atlantic, Pacific, Indian, and Arctic. If you look more closely or trace the four named oceans with your finger, you will see that they are connected to one another. Together they form one huge ocean. Any part of this ocean is called the sea.

The global ocean covers 71 percent, or almost three-quarters, of Earth's surface. Most of the ocean is in the Southern Hemisphere. The ocean is, on average, 3.8 kilometers (2.4 mi) deep. Although most of the water covering Earth is ocean, water also covers some land areas, as rivers, lakes, and ice.

B

CHECK YOUR READING Where is most of Earth's water?

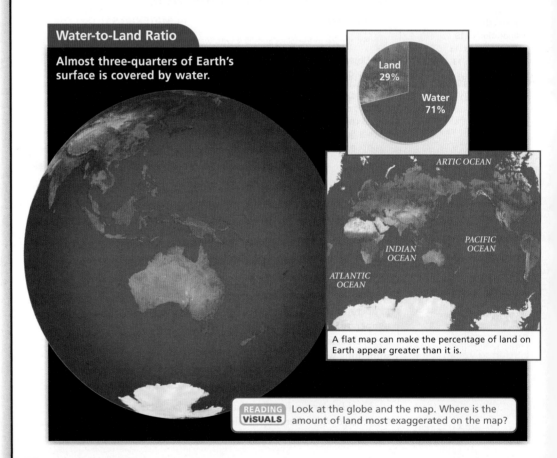

Water-to-Land Ratio

Almost three-quarters of Earth's surface is covered by water.

Land 29%

Water 71%

ARTIC OCEAN

PACIFIC OCEAN

INDIAN OCEAN

ATLANTIC OCEAN

A flat map can make the percentage of land on Earth appear greater than it is.

READING VISUALS Look at the globe and the map. Where is the amount of land most exaggerated on the map?

C 10 Unit: Earth's Waters

DIFFERENTIATE INSTRUCTION

? More Reading Support

A What makes Earth look bluish from space? *the ocean*

B How deep is the ocean, on average? *3.8 km (about 2.4 mi)*

English Learners Within this section are a variety of introductory clauses and phrases. Give students these examples and have them identify the subject of each sentence: "Seen from outer space, Earth glistens like a beautiful blue and white marble." "At a low temperature, water freezes." Encourage students to use introductory clauses and phrases in their own writing.

Below Level Display a globe and invite students to compare the amount of blue ocean area with the amount of land area.

Water and Life

Without water, nothing would live on Earth. Living things need water to function. Your own body is two-thirds water. In your body, your blood—which is mostly water—carries nutrients that give you energy and flushes wastes away. Many forms of life live in water. Oceans, lakes, and rivers are home to fish, mammals, plants, and other organisms. Even a single drop of water may contain tiny forms of life.

Fresh Water and Salt Water

When you hear the word *water,* you might imagine a cool drink that quenches your thirst. The water that you drink and depend on for survival is fresh water. **Fresh water** is water that is not salty and has little or no taste, color, or smell. Most rivers and lakes are fresh water.

 The water in the ocean is salt water. **Salt water** is water that contains dissolved salts and other minerals. Human beings and most other land animals cannot survive by drinking salt water, although many other forms of life can live in salt water.

You may be surprised to learn that even though fresh water is important for life, fresh water is actually scarce on Earth. Because most of Earth's water is in the ocean, most of the water on Earth is salt water. The illustration below compares the amounts of fresh water and salt water on Earth. Almost all—about 97 percent—of Earth's water is salt water in the ocean. Only about 3 percent of Earth's water, at any given time, is fresh water.

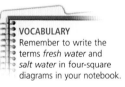

VOCABULARY
Remember to write the terms *fresh water* and *salt water* in four-square diagrams in your notebook.

CHECK YOUR READING What is the difference between fresh water and salt water?

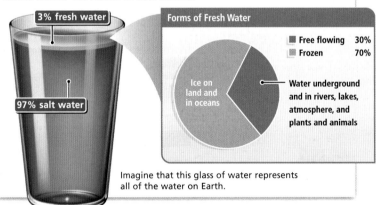

Salt Water vs. Fresh Water

Most water on Earth is salt water.

3% fresh water

97% salt water

Forms of Fresh Water

- Free flowing 30%
- Frozen 70%

Ice on land and in oceans

Water underground and in rivers, lakes, atmosphere, and plants and animals

Imagine that this glass of water represents all of the water on Earth.

DIFFERENTIATE INSTRUCTION

More Reading Support

C What kind of water is in the oceans? *salt water*

D Which kind of water is scarce? *fresh water*

Advanced Have students consider the question, Why are humans unable to survive by drinking salt water? Have them research the chemistry that answers the question.

R Challenge and Extension, p. 19

Integrate the Sciences

The main component of human blood is plasma, which is 90 percent water and 10 percent salts, fats, gases, and proteins. Red and white blood cells and platelets are suspended in plasma.

Develop Critical Thinking

COMPARE Have students apply their knowledge of the scarcity of fresh water to discuss the importance of clean water. Invite them to compare the hazards of polluting fresh water and polluting salt water. *Sample answer: Fresh water is scarce, and all organisms need it to live. Polluting fresh water could put us at risk of not having enough. Polluting salt water could harm fish and other animals.*

Teach from Visuals

To help students interpret the visual that compares the percentages of salt water and fresh water on Earth, ask:

- What does the glass of water represent? *all water on Earth*
- What percentage of water on Earth is salt water? *97 percent*
- What are the two forms of fresh water? *frozen and free flowing*

Ongoing Assessment

Observe how much of Earth's water is salt water.

Ask: How much of Earth's water is salt water? *97 percent*

CHECK YOUR READING *Answer: Fresh water has little or no taste. Salt water contains dissolved salts and other minerals. Humans and other land animals cannot survive by drinking salt water.*

INVESTIGATE The Water Cycle

PURPOSE To investigate how water cycles through the environment

TIPS *50 min.*

- Keep the environments small.
- Make sure students know what kind of plants they have.
- Have students use care with glass jars.

WHAT DO YOU THINK? *Water drops appeared on the inside of the jar. The mass stayed the same. Water in the soil goes into the air as a gas and returns as liquid water that drips down the sides of the jar.*

CHALLENGE *Put it in sunlight.*

 Datasheet, The Water Cycle, p. 20

Technology Resources

Customize this student lab as needed or look for an alternative. Print rubrics to assess student lab reports.

 Lab Generator CD-ROM

Real World Example

Rain, hail, sleet, snow, freezing rain, and fog are all part of the water cycle.

 MAIN IDEA AND DETAILS Record in your notes this main idea and important details about the water cycle.

Water moves in a worldwide cycle.

Water continually moves and changes form. Water from clouds falls over the oceans and on land. Water flows in rivers and collects in lakes and under the ground. Water can be a solid in the form of ice, or it can be an invisible vapor in the atmosphere.

The Water Cycle

Water's movement on Earth is a cycle, or continually repeating process. The **water cycle** is the continuous movement of water through the environment of Earth. In the water cycle, water is constantly changing form, from a liquid on land, to a vapor in the atmosphere, and again to a liquid that falls to the surface. The flow of water on land and underground is also part of the water cycle. As water moves in the water cycle, the total amount of water in Earth's system does not change very much. The water cycle involves three major processes: evaporation, condensation, and precipitation.

INVESTIGATE The Water Cycle

How does water cycle through an environment?

DESIGN —YOUR OWN—

PROCEDURE

1. Construct an environment in a jar with a lid. You can use plants, soil, water, and containers.
2. Find the mass of your closed jar after you construct it.
3. Draw a detailed, colored picture of your jar.
4. Let your jar sit for several days.
5. Find the mass of your jar again, and draw another picture of it.

WHAT DO YOU THINK?

- How did the jar's appearance change over several days?
- How did its mass change?
- What can you conclude about how water cycles through an environment?

CHALLENGE How could you change your environment so that the jar's appearance would change at a faster rate?

SKILL FOCUS
Modeling

MATERIALS
- jar with lid
- soil
- rocks or pebbles
- sand
- smaller containers
- water
- small plants
- triple-beam balance

TIME
30 minutes (for construction; 20 minutes for analysis)

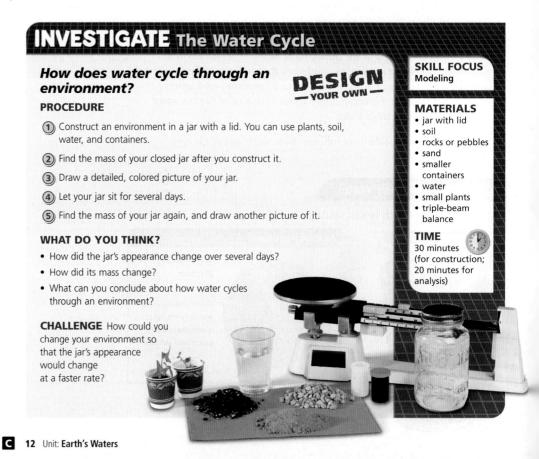

DIFFERENTIATE INSTRUCTION

 More Reading Support

E What is the water cycle? *the continuous movement of water through Earth's environment*

Below Level Read this page and the definitions of *evaporation, condensation,* and *precipitation* out loud to students. Ask them to draw a picture of the water cycle, and have them include arrows to show how water moves. Ask them to try and accurately label the arrows: "evaporation," "condensation," "precipitation." Then have them look at the diagram on p. 13 and revise their drawings.

The Water Cycle

Water on Earth moves in a continual cycle.

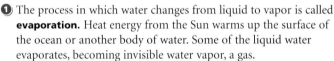

② **Condensation**
Water vapor changes into liquid water, forming clouds.

③ **Precipitation**
Frozen or liquid water falls to the surface.

① **Evaporation**
Water turns into vapor in the atmosphere and rises from the surface.

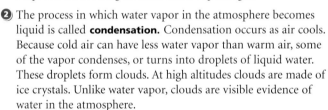

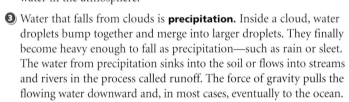

Liquid water flows on Earth and collects in puddles, ponds, lakes, rivers, and oceans. It also sinks into the ground.

① The process in which water changes from liquid to vapor is called **evaporation.** Heat energy from the Sun warms up the surface of the ocean or another body of water. Some of the liquid water evaporates, becoming invisible water vapor, a gas.

② The process in which water vapor in the atmosphere becomes liquid is called **condensation.** Condensation occurs as air cools. Because cold air can have less water vapor than warm air, some of the vapor condenses, or turns into droplets of liquid water. These droplets form clouds. At high altitudes clouds are made of ice crystals. Unlike water vapor, clouds are visible evidence of water in the atmosphere.

③ Water that falls from clouds is **precipitation.** Inside a cloud, water droplets bump together and merge into larger droplets. They finally become heavy enough to fall as precipitation—such as rain or sleet. The water from precipitation sinks into the soil or flows into streams and rivers in the process called runoff. The force of gravity pulls the flowing water downward and, in most cases, eventually to the ocean.

VISUALIZATION
CLASSZONE.COM

See how water moves through Earth's system in the water cycle.

CHECK YOUR READING Why does water vapor in air condense into liquid droplets?

❓ More Reading Support

F What is condensation the opposite of?
evaporation

Advanced Biosphere 2 is a totally enclosed environment that mimics the Earth's environment. Invite students to research the way the water cycle in Biosphere 2 works. Have them create sketches or charts to compare the water cycle in Biosphere 2 with Earth's water cycle.

Have students who are interested in the origin of water read the following article.

 Challenge Reading, pp. 44–45

Teach from Visuals

To help students interpret the visual showing the water cycle, ask:

• What three processes are shown to occur during the water cycle? *evaporation, condensation, precipitation*

• What happens to water that falls from clouds? *It flows along the ground; collects in puddles, ponds, lakes, rivers, and oceans; and sinks into the ground.*

Address Misconceptions

IDENTIFY Ask: What are clouds composed of? If students say "water vapor," they may hold the misconception that clouds are made up of gases.

CORRECT Have students breathe onto the palms of their hands. Explain that their breath contains water vapor. Breathe onto a mirror. Tell students that the droplets on the mirror are caused by the condensation of the water vapor in your breath. Explain that water droplets in clouds are like the droplets on the mirror. Explain that when a cloud's temperature is below freezing, the water droplets become ice crystals.

REASSESS Ask: Is it true that clouds are made up of gases? Explain your answer. *No, clouds consist of water droplets or when below freezing, ice crystals.*

Technology Resources

Visit **ClassZone.com** for background on common student misconceptions.

MISCONCEPTION DATABASE

Ongoing Assessment

CHECK YOUR READING *Answer: because cold air can hold less water vapor than warm air*

Explain how water moves throughout Earth and its atmosphere.

Ask: How does water cycle through Earth's environment? *Water evaporates from surface and rises as vapor to atmosphere; it condenses into liquid and forms clouds, then falls to surface as liquid or frozen water; it flows along Earth and collects or sinks into ground.*

EXPLORE (the BIG idea)

Revisit "Internet Activity: Water" on p. 7. Have students compare their findings with the text.

Reinforce (the BIG idea)

Have students relate the section to the Big Idea.

 Reinforcing Key Concepts, p. 21

1.1 ASSESS & RETEACH

Assess

 Section 1.1 Quiz, p. 3

Reteach

Draw a large circle on the chalkboard. Remind students that a cycle can be represented as a circle. Ask them to come to the board individually to make one contribution that helps you make the circle into a picture of the water cycle.

When you have finished, ask students to describe what happens in each section of the circle.

Technology Resources

Have students visit **ClassZone.com** for reteaching of Key Concepts.

 CONTENT REVIEW

 CONTENT REVIEW CD-ROM

Most of the water that evaporates on Earth—85 percent of it—evaporates from the ocean. (About 75 percent of this condenses into cloud droplets and falls right back into the ocean.) The remaining 15 percent of evaporating water comes from such sources as damp ground, lakes, wet sidewalks, rivers, and sprinklers. Plants are also part of the water cycle. They pull up water from the ground and then release much of it into the air through their leaves.

Even though the water that evaporates into the atmosphere comes from both the salty ocean and from fresh water on land, all the precipitation that falls back to the surface is fresh water. When salt water evaporates, the salt is left behind. Through the water cycle the ocean water that human beings cannot drink becomes a source of fresh water for human beings and other life on Earth.

The Impact of the Water Cycle

Flooding usually occurs during India's annual rainy season.

The action of the water cycle is easy to spot. When it rains or snows, you can see precipitation in action. When you look at a flowing stream, you see the water cycle returning water to the sea. When a stream dries up, you know that the water cycle in the area has slowed down for a while.

Wet weather can fill reservoirs with drinking water and pour needed water on crops. Wet weather can also bring too much rain. For example, during the wet season in India, winds blow moist air inland from the Indian Ocean. Tremendous rains fall over the land for months. The rain is usually welcome after a long and hot dry season. However, these seasonal rains frequently cause devastating floods, covering acres and acres of land with water.

1.1 Review

KEY CONCEPTS

1. Name three things about water that make it unique or important.
2. How much of Earth's water is fresh water?
3. Explain the three processes that make up the water cycle.

CRITICAL THINKING

4. **Apply** How can a drop of salt water once have been a drop of fresh water?
5. **Compare and Contrast** What are two differences between salt water and fresh water?

🔍 CHALLENGE

6. **Infer** In 1996, the *Galileo* space probe sent back photographs that showed ice on the surface of one of the moons of Jupiter. Scientists suspected there was water under the ice. Why did this discovery excite some people who thought there was a chance of finding life on that moon?

ANSWERS

1. Water can exist as liquid, gas, or solid in temperature ranges found on Earth. It can fit any container. It sustains life. It can form into a drop.

2. 3 percent

3. evaporation—liquid water changes into water vapor

(gas); condensation—water vapor (gas) changes into liquid; precipitation—water falls from clouds as rain or snow.

4. The fresh water flowed into the ocean, where dissolved salts and minerals mixed with it.

5. Salt water contains salts and other minerals; it cannot sustain human life. Fresh water has little or no taste.

6. Where there is water, there can be life.

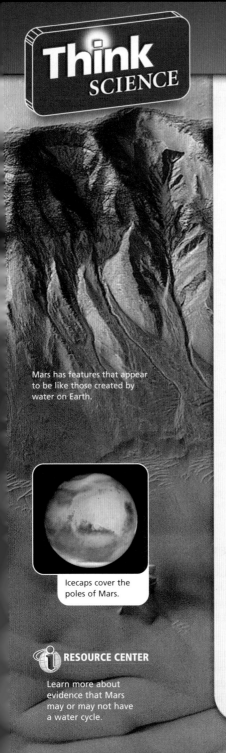

Mars has features that appear to be like those created by water on Earth.

Icecaps cover the poles of Mars.

RESOURCE CENTER

Learn more about evidence that Mars may or may not have a water cycle.

Does Mars Have a Water Cycle?

Mars once had water flowing on its surface. Today, it is a frozen desert. Most astronomers think that there has been no liquid water on Mars for the past 3.9 billion years. Others, though, think that Mars has had flowing water recently—in the last 10 million years. They suggest that Mars may have a multimillion-year water cycle. According to their hypothesis, occasional volcanic activity melts ice, releasing floods of water. After the water evaporates, condenses, and falls as rain, it becomes ice again. And if Mars does have a water cycle, it could have something else that goes with water on Earth: life.

▶ Issues

For Mars to have a water cycle, it would need several features.

- • a source of energy for melting ice into water
- • conditions for water to evaporate
- • conditions for water vapor to condense

▶ Observations

Astronomers have observed several facts about Mars.

- • Mars has water ice at its north and south poles.
- • Mars has had very large volcanoes in the past, although it seems to have no active volcanoes today.
- • Mars takes about 687 Earth days to orbit the Sun.
- • Mars is the fourth planet from the Sun.
- • Mars has an atmosphere that is 100 times thinner than the atmosphere of Earth.
- • Mars has an average surface air temperature of $-55°C$ ($-67°F$).
- • Mars has features that look like ones shaped by water on Earth: ocean shorelines, river valleys, and gullies.
- • Mars has many visible craters—unlike Earth, where most craters get washed away, filled with water, or covered up.

▶ Determine the Relevance of Each Observation

On Your Own Decide whether each observation is relevant in determining whether Mars has a water cycle.

As a Group Discuss the relevance of each observation to the idea of a water cycle on Mars. List other information that might be helpful.

CHALLENGE Research information about Mars. Identify facts that support or oppose the idea of a Martian water cycle.

Chapter 1: **The Water Planet 15** **C**

ANSWERS

On Your Own Mars has ice at poles (ice means water). Mars has had volcanoes (volcanoes could melt ice). Mars has a 687 Earth-day orbit (probably not relevant); Mars has an average temperature of −55°C (too cold for liquid water). Mars has water-shaped features (may mean that water once flowed on planet and could again). Mars is fourth from Sun (not necessarily relevant, except that it may be colder than Earth). Mars has visible craters (probably not relevant).
CHALLENGE Answers will vary, depending on information students gather.

THINK SCIENCE
Scientific Methods of Thinking

Set Learning Goal

To weigh the relevance of observations in order to determine whether Mars has a water cycle

Present the Science

Observations of Mars from Earth and from spacecraft have raised the possibility that there is a regular annual cycle of water vapor in the atmosphere of the planet. The total amount of water that might be in the Martian atmosphere is only enough to make a puddle less than 0.01 cm deep if it all fell as rain at the same time. The top few centimeters of soil contains a significant amount of water. Water is also found in the polar icecaps.

Guide the Activity

- Invite volunteers to review the vocabulary terms in Section 1.1.
- Encourage students to make a chart to help them make a decision. After evaluating whether each observation is relevant to the issue, they should list those observations that support the existence of a water cycle on Mars and those that do not. Students should include what they learn while doing the Challenge activity.

COOPERATIVE LEARNING STRATEGY

Divide the class into groups of three. One member of each group should read an observation aloud and decide whether it is relevant. If it is relevant, another member should decide if it does or does not support the notion of a water cycle on Mars and explain why. The third member should record the conclusions. For each fact, members should switch roles so that all members participate in each role. Finally, the conclusions should be evaluated by the group to reach a single decision.

Close

Ask students to interpret the available information to determine whether Mars has a water cycle. *Students will probably conclude that Mars has a water cycle.*

◉ Set Learning Goals

Students will

- Explain how fresh water flows and collects on land.
- Understand how surface water forms lakes.
- Understand how frozen water exists on Earth.
- Calculate and compare the densities of water and ice in an experiment.

◒ 3-Minute Warm-Up

Display Transparency 4 or copy this exercise on the board:

Draw a diagram of the water cycle that includes water standing and running on land, in clouds, and in precipitation. Add labels and arrows to the diagram. *Diagram should include arrows from standing water to atmosphere, labeled "evaporation"; from atmosphere to clouds, labeled "condensation"; from clouds to running water, labeled "precipitation"; and from running water to standing water.*

 3-Minute Warm-Up, p. T4

1.2 MOTIVATE

EXPLORE Water Collection

PURPOSE To observe the way water flows downhill and collects in depressions

TIP *10 min.* Have students work in pairs.

WHAT DO YOU THINK? *Water flowed downward, collected in bottom cups, and did not collect above them. On land, water flows downhill.*

Teaching with Technology

Have students use a flow-rate sensor when the carton is tipped.

KEY CONCEPT

1.2 Fresh water flows and freezes on Earth.

◁ **BEFORE, you learned**

- Water covers most of Earth's surface
- Water continually cycles
- Water falls to Earth's surface as precipitation

▷ **NOW, you will learn**

- How fresh water flows and collects on land
- How surface water forms lakes
- How frozen water exists on Earth

VOCABULARY

divide p. 17
drainage basin p. 17
turnover p. 19
eutrophication p. 20
iceberg p. 22

EXPLORE Water Collection

How does water flow and collect?

PROCEDURE

1. With the open egg carton on a level tray, pour water slowly into the center of the carton until the cups are three-quarters full.

2. Empty the carton. Tip it slightly, as shown in the photograph, and pour water into the higher end. Stop pouring when the carton is about to overflow.

MATERIALS

- plastic-foam egg carton
- tray or pan
- plastic bottle
- water

WHAT DO YOU THINK?

- How did the water flow when you poured it into the level carton? into the tilted carton? Where did it collect in the carton? Where did it not collect?
- What might your observations tell you about how water flows when it falls on land?

MAIN IDEA AND DETAILS
Record in your notebook this main idea and details about it.

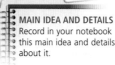

Water flows and collects on Earth's surface.

Imagine you are in a raft on a river, speeding through whitewater rapids. Your raft splashes around boulders, crashing its way downriver. Then the raft reaches a lake. You glide across the surface, slowing down. At the end of the lake, your raft enters a river again and floats down it.

In your raft you are following the path a water drop might take on its way to the ocean. All over the planet, the force of gravity pulls water downhill. Fresh water flows downhill in a series of streams and rivers, collects in lakes and ponds, and eventually flows into the ocean. All of this water flows between high points called divides, in areas called drainage basins.

RESOURCES FOR DIFFERENTIATED INSTRUCTION

Below Level
UNIT RESOURCE BOOK
- Reading Study Guide A, pp. 24–25
- Decoding Support, p. 48

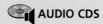 **AUDIO CDS**

Advanced
UNIT RESOURCE BOOK
Challenge and Extension, p. 30

English Learners
UNIT RESOURCE BOOK
Spanish Reading Study Guide, pp. 28–29

 **AUDIO CDS**

- Audio Readings in Spanish
- Audio Readings (English)

Divides and drainage basins affect the way water flows on land. A **divide** is a ridge, or continuous line of high land, from which water flows in different directions. If you were on a skateboard and began at the top of a hill, you would ride in one general direction down the hillside. On the other side of the hill, you would ride downhill in a completely different direction. The top of the hill is like a divide. A divide can be a continuous ridge of high mountains. On flatter ground, a divide can simply be the line of highest ground.

A **drainage basin,** or watershed, is an area into which all of the water on one side of a divide flows. If you pour water into the basin of your bathroom sink, it will flow down the side from high points to low, and eventually down the drain, which is at the lowest point. In mountainous areas, hills and mountains form the sides of basins, and valleys form the low points. Flatter regions also have basins. The basins may not be obvious in these regions, but they still drain water.

When it rains in a drainage basin, the water forms streams and rivers or sinks into the ground. Every stream, river, and lake is in a basin. In most places, the water eventually flows to the sea. In a bowl-shaped basin, the water may collect at the bottom of the basin or evaporate.

Divides and Drainage Basins

Divides separate drainage basins.

Divides exist in mountain ranges as well as in flatter regions.

Water falling on a divide flows into the **drainage basins** on either side of the divide.

Water in a drainage basin flows downhill in streams and rivers, usually to the ocean.

READING VISUALS With your finger, trace each divide in this drawing. Point out four drainage basins.

Chapter 1: **The Water Planet** 17 **C**

DIFFERENTIATE INSTRUCTION

More Reading Support

A What does the water falling on a divide flow into? *drainage basins*

B What happens to rainfall in a drainage basin? *It forms streams and rivers or sinks into the ground.*

English Learners Help students recognize sentences that indicate a cause-and-effect relationship. Have students make a two-column chart in their notebook with the headings "Cause" and "Effect." Give them several cause-and-effect sentences and have them put the parts of each sentence under the correct headings. Begin with the example below.

"When it rains in a drainage basin, the water forms streams and rivers or sinks into the ground."

1.2 INSTRUCT

Teach Difficult Concepts

Some students may have a hard time understanding that a divide is not necessarily a mountain ridge. Point out that within a drainage basin there can be land that rises and falls. Basins can be huge; the Mississippi basin extends from the Rocky Mountains to Appalachia. To help students understand, you might try the following demonstration.

Teacher Demo

Crumple a sheet of paper and spread it a bit in a pan. Add dots of blue water-soluble marker. Have students predict which way the blue will flow when water falls on it. Use an eyedropper to make "rain." Have students observe the flow of the water and identify the "divides" and "drainage basins."

Teach from Visuals

To help students interpret the visual "Divides and Drainage Basins," ask:

• Where are divides found? *along mountain ranges as well as in some flatter regions*

• Where does water falling onto a divide flow? *into the drainage basins on each side*

Ongoing Assessment

Explain how fresh water flows and collects on land.

Ask: Where does water flow when it rains? *from divides into drainage basins; in drainage basins into streams and rivers or into the ground.*

READING VISUALS *Answer: Students should trace the divides that clearly separate at least four basins in the diagram.*

Chapter 1 **17** **C**

Develop Critical Thinking

COMPARE Visually adapt the information about the differences between ponds and lakes by drawing a cross-section diagram of each on the board. Have students help you to determine and add the appropriate features of each. When you have finished, ask: What do these two diagrams have in common?

Teaching with Technology

Have students search the Internet for graphics of ponds and lakes. Have them download photographs and diagrams and then use presentation software to create a display comparing ponds and lakes.

Real World Example

Have students apply their knowledge of ponds and lakes to a specific example. Have students think about a pond or lake with which they are familiar. If they cannot think of one in their area, show them a picture. Ask them to describe the features of the body of water. Then ask how their descriptions can help them determine whether the body of water is a lake or a pond. *If students describe a shallow, small body of water with lots of plants, it is probably a pond. If they describe a larger body of water with no obvious vegetation, it is most likely a lake.*

Ongoing Assessment

Understand how surface water forms lakes.

Ask: What are three ways that water may fill a lake? *Underground water may fill a low area; water may flow in from streams and rivers; some water comes from precipitation.*

CHECK YOUR READING *Answer: A lake is bigger than a pond. Sunlight reaches the bottom of a pond, so that plants grow throughout the pond.*

Surface water collects in ponds and lakes.

 C Lakes and ponds form where water naturally collects in low parts of land. Some lakes were formed during the last ice age. For example, the Great Lakes were formed when huge sheets of ice scraped out a series of giant depressions. Other lakes, such as Crater Lake in Oregon, were formed when water collected inside the craters of inactive volcanoes.

Water can fill a lake in several ways. Where the land surface dips below the level of underground water, the low land area fills with water. Rainfall and other precipitation contribute water to all lakes. Water may flow through a lake from a stream or river. Water may also flow away from a lake through a stream running downhill from the lake. Many lakes maintain fairly steady levels because of the balance of flow in and flow out.

 D The main difference between a pond and a lake is in their overall size. A pond is smaller and shallower than a lake, and there are many plants, such as water lilies and cattails, rooted in its muddy bottom. A lake may have water so deep that sunlight can't reach the bottom. In the deeper part of the lake, plants can't take root, so they grow only around the lake's edges. Ponds and lakes provide homes for many kinds of fish, insects, and other wildlife. They also provide resting places for migrating birds.

CHECK YOUR READING Name two differences between a pond and a lake.

Chicago, Illinois, at the southwest corner of Lake Michigan, is the largest city on a Great Lake. Note that the lake is so wide that from Chicago you cannot see Michigan on the other side.

Lake Michigan

Chicago

Lake Michigan is the third largest of the five Great Lakes, which border eight states and Canada's Ontario province.

DIFFERENTIATE INSTRUCTION

More Reading Support

C Where do lakes and ponds form? *where water collects in low areas*

D What is the main difference between a lake and a pond? *overall size*

Inclusion Help visual learners understand how underground water contributes to the filling of a lake. Half fill a clear baking pan or plastic shoebox with sand. Then slowly pour water over the sand so that it seeps through the sand and collects at the bottom. From the side point out the top of the underground water, which is the water table. Have a student use a spoon to scoop out sand from one area along the side of the pan until the hole reaches below the water level. A "pond" or "lake" will result. Draw a cross section of this model and review the water-filling process.

Lake Turnover

The water in a lake is not as still as it might appear. The changing temperatures of the seasons affect the water and cause it to move within the lake in a yearly cycle.

In a place with cold winters, ice may form on a lake, so that the wind cannot ruffle the surface. The water temperature in the lake remains steady, and the water stops moving. The water just below the surface ice is near freezing, so the fish move to the bottom, where the water is a bit warmer.

In many lakes the water temperatures at different levels vary as the seasons change. In the spring and summer, sunlight can warm a layer of water at the top of a lake. Because the colder water beneath the top layer is denser than the warmer water above it, the water levels do not mix easily. The warm water contains more oxygen, so fish may be more plentiful in the upper part of the lake.

READING TiP

Cold water is denser than (has more mass than the same amount of) warm water.

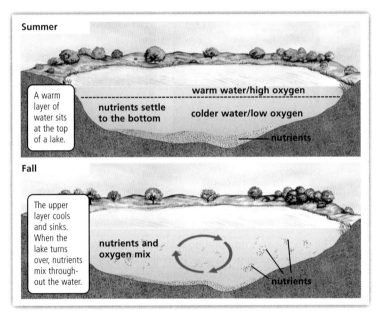

Summer

A warm layer of water sits at the top of a lake.

warm water/high oxygen

nutrients settle to the bottom

colder water/low oxygen

nutrients

Fall

The upper layer cools and sinks. When the lake turns over, nutrients mix throughout the water.

nutrients and oxygen mix

nutrients

In the fall, days cool and the surface water cools too. The upper layer becomes heavy and sinks, so that the lake water "turns over." Nutrients from minerals and from dead plants and organisms are stirred up from the bottom. These nutrients are used by many life forms in the lake. The rising and sinking of cold and warm water layers in a lake is called **turnover.** Turnover occurs twice each year as the seasons change.

CHECK YOUR READING What happens to surface water when the weather cools in the fall?

Integrate the Sciences

The cells of many aquatic animals contain large amounts of glycerol and glucose that keep them from freezing completely in the winter. Animals that cannot survive freezing temperatures may spend the winter at the bottom of a lake, where ice does not form.

Teach from Visuals

To help students interpret the visual that illustrates lake turnover, ask:

• What is the temperature of the lake water in the summer? *The surface is warm, and the bottom is cold.*

• Where are the nutrients and oxygen highest in summer? *The nutrients are highest at the lake's bottom. The oxygen is highest at the lake's surface.*

• What mixes along with the water in the fall? *oxygen and nutrients*

Teacher Demo

To illustrate density differences between warm and cold water, half fill a beaker with hot water. Very slowly, add cold water that is colored with food coloring. Ask: What did you observe? How can you explain this? *The cold water sank because it is denser than the hot water. As it sank, the hot and cold water mixed.* In what climate does lake turnover occur? *four-season regions where waters are warmed and cooled* What is affected by the turnover of the water? *the lake and its living things*

Ongoing Assessment

CHECK YOUR READING *Answer: The surface water cools and sinks.*

DIFFERENTIATE INSTRUCTION

More Reading Support

E What happens to the water temperature at different levels of a lake as the seasons change? *They vary.*

Advanced Tell students that water has a certain property that makes it different from other substances. Because of this property, ice forms on the top of a frozen pond or lake. Challenge students to find out what this property is. *The property is that water becomes less dense as it freezes, unlike other substances, which become more dense as they freeze. Because ice is less dense than liquid water, ice floats on the water in ponds and lakes.*

R Challenge and Extension, p. 30

Teach Difficult Concepts

Some students may have a difficult time understanding that too many nutrients can cause organisms to die. Ask: What organisms grow rapidly when many nutrients are present in a lake? *algae* Explain that when the numbers of algae get very large, oxygen in the water is depleted. Organisms such as fish die in large numbers. The dead organisms, including masses of rotting algae, fill in lakes that would otherwise remain unfilled for a long time. To help students understand, you might try the following demonstration.

Teach from Visuals

To help students interpret the visual of eutrophication, ask:

- How does a lake begin to fill in? *Algae buildup.*
- What happens as organisms die? *The lake gets shallower; water evaporates.*
- What is the end result? *The lake becomes a meadow.*

Teacher Demo

Prepare two algae cultures, add fertilizer to one, and place them in a warm area with plenty of light. Let them sit for several days. Have students observe the cultures. Discuss the differences and their significance.

Ongoing Assessment

CHECK YOUR READING *Answer: Runoff of fertilizers and detergents in wastewater add nutrients such as nitrogen and phosphates to lakes.*

Eutrophication

A lake does not remain a lake forever. Through natural processes that take thousands of years, most lakes eventually are filled in and become meadows—fields covered with grass and other plants. A lake can become filled in as sediments, including the remains of dead fish, plants, and other organisms, pile up on the bottom.

READING TiP
Eutrophication comes from the Greek word *eutrophos*, meaning "well-nourished."

The activity of life in a lake is affected by nutrients. Nutrients are the foods and chemicals that support living things. When the amounts of such nutrients as phosphorus and nitrogen in a lake increase, algae and other organisms in the water grow more rapidly. An increase of nutrients in a lake or pond is called **eutrophication** (yoo-TRAHF-ih-KAY-shuhn). As eutrophication occurs, algae form a thick scum on the water. The amount of oxygen in the water decreases, until fish and other organisms that require oxygen cannot survive. The illustration below shows what happens to a lake when nutrient levels increase.

① When the amounts of such nutrients as nitrogen and phosphorus increase, algae grow faster and form a scum layer at the surface.

② Dead algae, plants, and fish pile up. Plants grow more quickly, leaving more debris as they die. Water evaporates, and the lake becomes shallower.

③ The lake becomes a soggy marsh, then finally a completely filled-in meadow.

The process of eutrophication is usually slow. In some cases, however, eutrophication happens more quickly than it normally would because of pollution from human activities. Nitrogen in fertilizers used on farms and gardens may be washed into lakes. Phosphates from laundry detergents may be present in wastewater that reaches lakes. The extra nutrients cause algae and plants in lakes to grow faster and more thickly than they normally would grow. Eutrophication from pollution causes clear lakes to become clogged with algae and plants.

CHECK YOUR READING How does human activity contribute to eutrophication?

DIFFERENTIATE INSTRUCTION

? More Reading Support

F What is an increase of nutrients in a lake or pond called? *eutrophication*

G What is the result of the process of eutrophication? *The lake fills in.*

Below Level List the following words and phrase in a vertical arrangement on the board in this order: *lake, nutrients, eutrophication, algae, oxygen, dead plants and animals, evaporation,* and *meadow.* Begin with the first word and ask students to tell its relationship to the next word. Write their responses next to the words and phrase.

Most fresh water on Earth is frozen.

If you want fresh water, take a trip to Greenland or the South Pole. Two-thirds of the world's fresh water is locked up in the ice covering land near the poles.

The ice sheet that covers Antarctica is almost one and a half times as big as the United States and is in places more than a kilometer thick. Ice on Earth's surface contains more than 24 million cubic kilometers of fresh water. Just how much water is that? Imagine that you have three glasses of lemonade. If you take one sip from one of the glasses of lemonade, you have drunk the water in all the lakes and rivers on Earth. The rest of the glass represents liquid ground water. The other two glasses of lemonade represent all the frozen water on the planet.

Ice on Land

In Earth's coldest regions—near both poles and in high mountains—more snow falls each year than melts. This snow builds up to form glaciers. A glacier is a large mass of ice and snow that moves over land. There are two types of glaciers. The ice sheets of Antarctica and Greenland are called continental glaciers because they cover huge landmasses. The other type of glacier is a valley glacier, which builds up in high areas and moves slowly down between mountains.

 RESOURCE CENTER
CLASSZONE.COM
Find out more about
frozen fresh water.

INVESTIGATE Icebergs

Why do icebergs float?

PROCEDURE

(1) Find the masses of the empty graduated cylinder and the ice cube.

(2) Add 200 mL of water to the cylinder. Find the volume of the ice cube by measuring how much water it displaces. Make sure the water is extremely cold to prevent the ice cube from melting. Use the point of a paper clip to completely submerge the ice.

(3) Remove the water and let the ice melt in the cylinder.

(4) Calculate the density (Density = mass/Volume) of the ice cube. Now find the mass and volume of the liquid water from the melted ice and calculate its density.

WHAT DO YOU THINK?

• What was the density of the ice cube? the water?

• Why do icebergs float?

CHALLENGE Float a cork in water. How does its behavior compare with that of floating ice?

SKILL FOCUS
Calculating

MATERIALS
• balance
• ice cube
• water
• 250 mL graduated cylinder
• paper clip
• calculator
for Challenge:
• cork

TIME
30 minutes

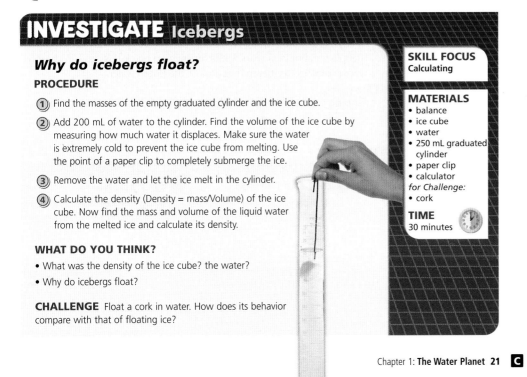

Chapter 1: **The Water Planet 21** C

INVESTIGATE Icebergs

PURPOSE To compare the density of water with the density of ice to show why ice floats

TIP *30 min.* Have students read the water level at the bottom of the meniscus.

OBSERVE AND ANALYZE *Ice cube: 0.75 g/mL; water: 0.96 g/mL. Ice is less dense than water and rises to the surface.*

CHALLENGE *Less of the cork is below the surface of the water, because the cork is less dense than the ice cube.*

Datasheet, Icebergs, p. 31

Technology Resources

Customize this student lab as needed or look for an alternative. Print rubrics to assess student lab reports.

Lab Generator CD-ROM

Metacognitive Strategy

Ask students to discuss how the content of this investigation relates to their experiences with water and ice.

Develop Measuring Skills

Review the procedure using the displacement of water to find volume. See p. R16, Graduated Cylinder.

Ongoing Assessment

Understand how frozen water exists on Earth.

Ask: Where is most of Earth's fresh water? *frozen near the poles*

DIFFERENTIATE INSTRUCTION

 More Reading Support

H How much of the world's fresh water is frozen? *two-thirds*

I What forms where more snow falls each year than melts? *glaciers*

Alternative Assessment Have pairs of students do a peer review of each other's density calculations to check for math errors. If they encounter discrepancies, have them compare the data they obtained. If different data cannot account for the different calculations, have students use each other's data to recalculate and compare.

EXPLORE the BIG idea

Revisit "Does the Ice Float?" on p. 7. Have students explain the significance of their results.

Reinforce the BIG idea

Have students relate the section to the Big Idea.

 Reinforcing Key Concepts, p. 32

1.2 ASSESS & RETEACH

Assess

 Section 1.2 Quiz, p. 4

Reteach

Help students review the concepts in this section by giving them modeling clay and having them create a landscape with a variety of high places and low places.

- Have students identify and label different temperature and climate zones on the landscape.
- Have students create labels that describe how water will behave in each portion of the landscape.
- Remind students to explain how the temperature will affect the way water behaves.

Technology Resources

Have students visit **ClassZone.com** for reteaching of Key Concepts.

 CONTENT REVIEW

CONTENT REVIEW CD-ROM

Icebergs

An **iceberg** is a mass of ice floating in the ocean. An iceberg starts out as part of a glacier. In places such as Antarctica and Greenland, glaciers form ice shelves that extend out over the ocean. When a large chunk of a shelf breaks off and floats away, it becomes an iceberg.

Thousands of icebergs break off from ice sheets each year. In the Northern Hemisphere, ocean currents push icebergs south into the warmer Atlantic Ocean. It may take an iceberg two to three years to float down to the area off the coast of Canada. In that region, it breaks apart and melts in the sea. A North Atlantic iceberg sank the *Titanic*.

Icebergs are masses of frozen fresh water floating in the salt water of the world's oceans.

How big is an iceberg? One iceberg that recently broke off an Antarctic ice shelf was the size of Connecticut. Off the coast of eastern Canada, some icebergs tower 46 meters (150 ft) above the surface of the ocean. This is impressive, because most of a floating iceberg is below the surface. Only about one-eighth of the total weight and volume of the iceberg can be seen above the surface of the sea. When people say "It's only the tip of the iceberg," they mean that a lot of something is unrevealed.

The water in an iceberg may have been frozen for 15,000 years. However, the ice in the center, if melted, can be clean, clear drinking water. And an iceberg can hold a lot of water. An iceberg as big as a city block holds enough drinking water to supply a city of 50,000 people for about ten years. Unfortunately, no one knows how to cheaply move icebergs to cities in order to use the frozen water.

 How much of an iceberg is below the surface?

1.2 Review

KEY CONCEPTS

1. Why is it important that fresh water flows over Earth's surface?
2. Explain the relationship between a drainage basin and a divide.
3. Where and in what form is most of the fresh water on Earth?

CRITICAL THINKING

4. **Apply** If you were going on a fishing trip in a northern state, why would you want to know about lake turnover?
5. **Connect** Explain the connection between living things in a lake and eutrophication.

CHALLENGE

6. **Synthesize** How is the water in icebergs involved in the water cycle on Earth?

ANSWERS

1. Water on the surface supports life. The water cycle continues as water flows on land and into the ocean.

2. A drainage basin is the area on one side of a divide, a ridge of land from which water flows. Water flows from a basin toward the ocean.

3. Most of it is in the polar regions and is frozen.

4. would tell me where oxygen and nutrients were and, because of this, where fish might be

5. Eutrophication is an increase in the amount of nutrients in a lake. Living organisms, such as algae, grow faster and form solid matter in the lake. Eventually the lake fills in.

6. Icebergs are made of frozen fresh water from snow. After they melt, water evaporates and returns to surface as precipitation.

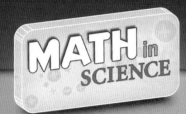

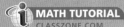

MATH TUTORIAL
CLASSZONE.COM

Click on Math Tutorial for help multiplying fractions and whole numbers.

SKILL: MULTIPLYING FRACTIONS AND WHOLE NUMBERS

How Big Is an Iceberg?

In salt water, the part of an iceberg that is visible above water is only 1/8 of the whole iceberg. The remaining 7/8 of the iceberg is hidden under the water's surface. You can use fractions to estimate how much ice is underwater.

Example

An iceberg is made of 1000 cubic meters of ice. How much of the ice is underwater?

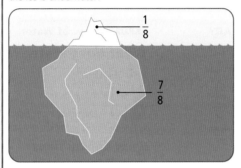

Solution

(1) Write a word equation.

$$\text{Volume of ice underwater} = \text{volume of iceberg} \cdot \text{fraction underwater}$$

(2) Substitute.

$$\text{Volume of ice underwater} = 1000 \text{ m}^3 \cdot \frac{7}{8}$$

(3) Multiply the numerator by the total volume.

$$= \frac{1000 \text{ m}^3 \cdot 7}{8}$$

(4) Calculate and simplify.

$$= \frac{7000 \text{ m}^3}{8} = 875 \text{ m}^3$$

ANSWER About 875 cubic meters of ice are underwater.

Calculate how much ice is underwater.

1. The iceberg is made of 1600 cubic meters of ice.

2. The iceberg is made of 1800 cubic meters of ice.

3. The iceberg is made of 12,000 cubic meters of ice.

CHALLENGE About 500 cubic meters of an iceberg is visible above the water. Estimate the total volume of the iceberg.

Chapter 1: **The Water Planet 23** **C**

Set Learning Goal

To calculate the amount of an iceberg that is underwater by multiplying fractions and whole numbers

Present the Science

Warm weather causes huge chunks of ice to break off glaciers. Some icebergs rise more than 120 meters (390 feet) above the water. After the *Titanic* hit an iceberg and sank, 16 nations involved in shipping in the North Atlantic Ocean established the International Iceberg Patrol to warn ships of icebergs.

Develop Calculation Skills

Remind students that a whole number can be written as a fraction.

To help them understand why a whole number can be shown as a fraction, draw an evenly divided circle on the chalkboard and shade all the parts. Have students count the number of shaded parts in the whole. Then write the whole as a fraction.

DIFFERENTIATION TIP If calculators are not used, provide students who have trouble seeing or making calculations with grid paper. This will help them align place values when multiplying and dividing.

Close

Ask students to use what they have learned about icebergs to explain why they are a danger to ships. *Because icebergs are made of hard ice, much of it underwater, they can damage ships.*

R • Math Support, p. 49
• Math Practice, p. 50

Technology Resources

Students can visit **ClassZone.com** for practice in writing and solving equations.

 MATH TUTORIAL

ANSWERS

1. $1600 \cdot \dfrac{7}{8} = \dfrac{1600 \cdot 7}{8} = \dfrac{11{,}200}{8} = 1400$ *cubic meters of ice.*

2. $1800 \cdot \dfrac{7}{8} = \dfrac{1800 \cdot 7}{8} = \dfrac{12{,}600}{8} = 1575$ *cubic meters of ice.*

3. $12{,}000 \cdot \dfrac{7}{8} = \dfrac{12{,}000 \cdot 7}{8} = \dfrac{84{,}000}{8} = 10{,}500$ *cubic meters of ice.*

CHALLENGE $500 \text{ m}^3 = \dfrac{1}{8}$ *of the volume of the iceberg.*

500 is $\dfrac{1}{8}$ *of what?* $8 \cdot 500 = 4000$ *cubic meters of ice.*

Set Learning Goals

Students will

- Understand how water collects and flows underground.
- Explain how underground water reaches the surface in springs and by wells.
- Create a model in an experiment to show how the ground can filter water.

3-Minute Warm-Up

Display Transparency 5 or copy this exercise on the chalkboard:

Match each definition to the correct term.

Definitions

1. area into which water from a divide flows *b*
2. large body of water *a*
3. series of streams and rivers *e*

Terms

a. lake
b. drainage basin
c. pond
d. divide
e. river system

 3-Minute Warm-Up, p. T5

1.3 MOTIVATE

EXPLORE Flow of Water

PURPOSE To observe permeable and impermeable materials and understand that permeability has to do with spaces in a material

TIPS *10 min.* A measuring cup with a pouring spout helps prevent spillage. Use tepid water.

WHAT DO YOU THINK? *The cup is made of material that water cannot pass through. It went toward the bottom of the filter and through spaces in the material of the filter.*

CHALLENGE *Possible answers: cloth, sponge, paper towel, newspaper*

KEY CONCEPT

1.3 Fresh water flows underground.

◁ BEFORE, you learned

- Water flows in river systems on Earth's surface
- Water collects in ponds and lakes on Earth's surface

▷ NOW, you will learn

- How water collects and flows underground
- How underground water reaches the surface in springs and by wells

VOCABULARY

groundwater p. 24
permeable p. 24
impermeable p. 25
water table p. 25
aquifer p. 26
spring p. 28
artesian well p. 28

EXPLORE Flow of Water

What does water flow through?

PROCEDURE

1. Fill the cup with water.
2. Have a partner hold the filter open over a sink, bucket, or pan while you pour water into it.

WHAT DO YOU THINK?

- Why did the water remain in the cup before you poured it?
- What route did the water take to pass through the filter?

CHALLENGE What other materials might hold water? allow water to flow through?

MATERIALS

- water
- cup
- paper coffee filter
- bucket, dishpan, or sink

 VOCABULARY
In your notebook make four-square diagrams for the terms *groundwater* and *permeable*.

Water fills underground spaces.

After a rainstorm, water does not stay on the ground for long. What happens to this water? It flows along Earth's surface into a river or reservoir, evaporates, or sinks into the soil. Plants use some of the water that sinks into the ground, and the rest of it sinks deeper into Earth. Water held underground is called **groundwater.** The ground under your school may seem too solid to hold water, but it is likely that groundwater sits or moves under the surface.

To understand how groundwater collects, you need to know the difference between permeable and impermeable materials. The ground beneath your feet is made of both permeable and impermeable materials.

A **permeable** substance is a substance that liquids can flow through. Liquids flow through a coffee filter because the filter is permeable. Soil,

---

RESOURCES FOR DIFFERENTIATED INSTRUCTION

Below Level

UNIT RESOURCE BOOK
- Reading Study Guide A, pp. 35–36
- Decoding Support, p. 48

 AUDIO CDS

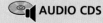 **Additional INVESTIGATION,**
Water Wells, A, B, & C, pp. 60–68;
Teacher Instructions, pp. 261–262

Advanced

UNIT RESOURCE BOOK
Challenge and Extension, p. 41

English Learners

UNIT RESOURCE BOOK
Spanish Reading Study Guide, pp. 39–40

AUDIO CDS

- Audio Readings in Spanish
- Audio Readings (English)

sand, and gravel are permeable because there are spaces between the particles. Water flows into and through these spaces. The bigger the particles, the more easily water can flow. Gravel and larger rocks have large spaces between them, so water flows quickly through. Sandy soil also has many pores, or spaces. Some rocks, such as sandstone, are permeable although the spaces in these rocks are extremely small.

A

An **impermeable** substance is a substance that liquids cannot flow through. A drinking glass holds orange juice because the material of the glass is impermeable. Rocks such as granite are impermeable. Unless granite has cracks, it has no spaces for water to go through. Many impermeable materials are hard, but not all of them. Clay is soft, but it is nearly impermeable. Water can get between its particles, but the overlapping of the particles stops the water from flowing through.

READING TiP

The prefix *im* in *impermeable* means "not."

How does groundwater collect? Gravity causes rainwater to sink into the soil. If it rains heavily, all the spaces in the soil fill with water. Eventually the water reaches impermeable rock. There it is held in place or forced to flow in a different direction.

B

Even when the soil on Earth's surface is dry, huge amounts of groundwater may be stored below. The top of the region that is saturated, or completely filled with water, is called the **water table**. The saturated region below the water table is called the saturation zone.

CHECK YOUR READING What prevents groundwater from sinking farther down?

Groundwater

Pulled down by gravity, water sinks through permeable ground until it reaches an impermeable layer.

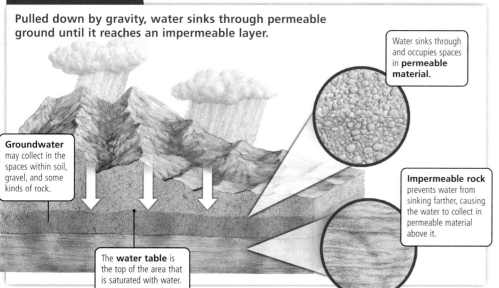

Water sinks through and occupies spaces in **permeable material.**

Groundwater may collect in the spaces within soil, gravel, and some kinds of rock.

Impermeable rock prevents water from sinking farther, causing the water to collect in permeable material above it.

The **water table** is the top of the area that is saturated with water.

Chapter 1: **The Water Planet 25** **C**

DIFFERENTIATE INSTRUCTION

? More Reading Support

A What is an impermeable material? *material that does not let liquid flow through*

B Where is the water table located? *top of the area filled with water*

English Learners Have students write the definitions of *water table, aquifer, spring,* and *artesian well* in their Science Word Dictionaries. Note that the Explore and Investigate activities in this section use the imperative mood; "you" is understood in each direction. For example, "Fill the cup with water" is to be understood as "You fill the cup with water." Be sure that English learners can understand and follow these directions.

Teach Difficult Concepts

Some students may not fully understand that groundwater does not generally sit in large pools or flow like an underground river. Explain that water is instead found within small spaces in rock, gravel, sand, and other underground materials. To help students understand, you might try the following demonstration.

Teacher Demo

Fill a glass beaker with rocks, gravel, and sand. Explain that the material in the beaker represents what is underground. Pour water into the beaker. Ask: Where is the underground water? *between the particles of rock, gravel, and sand*

Teach from Visuals

To help students interpret the visual on groundwater, ask:

• What is the water table? *the top of the area saturated with water*

• Through what kind of materials can water sink? *permeable*

• When does water stop sinking? *when it reaches impermeable rock*

Ongoing Assessment

Understand how water collects and flows underground.

Ask: Where does water flow and collect underground? *In the spaces of permeable materials.*

CHECK YOUR READING *Answer: impermeable rock*

Real World Connection

The Ogallala Aquifer is the part of the Ogallala geological formation that is saturated with water. This formation was deposited about 10 million years ago. For a long time, people thought the area over the Ogallala Aquifer had an unlimited supply of water for irrigation. In 1949, about 4 million acre-feet of water was pumped out of the aquifer for irrigation. In 1980, the amount was 18 million acre-feet. Between the 1950s and the 1970s, water was taken out of the aquifer much faster than it was replenished, and the water table declined as much as five feet per year. The usage of the water was inefficient. Since up to 50 percent was lost to evaporation, more than was needed was pumped out. Today, irrigation methods are better; some equipment is almost 100 percent efficient, and less water is used for irrigation. The rate of depletion of the aquifer has declined.

Teach from Visuals

To help students interpret the visual on aquifers, ask:

• What forms the upper boundary of the water in an aquifer? *the water table*

• What forms the bottom of an aquifer? *a layer of impermeable rock*

• What holds the water in place? *a layer of permeable material*

• Is there an aquifer in your state? *Answers will vary.*

Develop Number Sense

To help students visualize the size of the Ogallala Aquifer, remind them that a kilometer is 1000 meters.

Aquifers

An **aquifer** is an underground layer of permeable rock or sediment that contains water. Some aquifers lie deep under layers of impermeable rock. Other aquifers lie just beneath the topsoil.

SIMULATION
CLASSZONE.COM
Explore how groundwater fills in aquifers.

Aquifers can be found all over the world. They lie under deserts as well as wet regions. As the map below shows, they are found in many areas of the United States. An aquifer might be a bed of sand or gravel only a few meters thick. Or it might be an enormous layer of sandstone, several hundred meters thick, holding water in countless pore spaces. The Ogallala Aquifer is the largest aquifer in North America. It covers 450,000 square kilometers (176,000 mi^2), from South Dakota to Texas.

For an aquifer to form, three things are needed:

• A layer of permeable material holds the water. Groundwater is stored in the pore spaces of gravel, sand, or rock.

• A neighboring area of impermeable rock keeps the water from draining away. Sometimes impermeable rock lies both above and below an aquifer.

• A source of water replenishes or refills the aquifer. Like any body of water, an aquifer can be emptied.

You know that fresh water on land flows toward the ocean. Water that is underground acts like slow-motion streams, rivers, and lakes. Underground water moves slowly. The water is under pressure

Aquifers

Water collects underground in layers of permeable material.

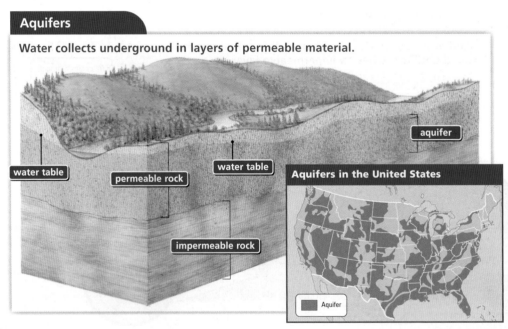

Aquifers in the United States

DIFFERENTIATE INSTRUCTION

? More Reading Support

C Where in the world are aquifers found? *all over the world*

Below Level Make a set of cards for each group of two to four students. On separate index cards, write these phrases: *water table*, *permeable material*, and *impermeable rock*. Write the word *aquifer* in color on another card. Have a student pick one of the first set of cards and place it next to the aquifer card. Have the student explain to the others in the group how the two concepts are related. Have students take turns picking cards.

from all sides, and it must go around endless tiny corners and passageways in rock. Unlike the water in an aboveground river, groundwater moves sideways, down, and even up. In some areas, groundwater is pushed upward so that it flows from a hillside. Because it moves so slowly, much of the water in an aquifer may have been there for thousands of years.

The Importance of Aquifers

When water sinks into land, the ground acts like a giant filter. Stones and sand in the ground can filter out bacteria and other living organisms. This ground filter also removes some harmful chemicals and minerals. The filtering process can make groundwater clear and clean and ready to drink. If it is not polluted, groundwater may not need expensive treatment. It is one of our most valuable natural resources.

Many big cities collect water from rivers and store it in reservoirs above the ground. However, about one-fifth of the people in the United States get their fresh water from underground. Most people who live in rural areas pump groundwater from wells. In many desert regions people depend on sources of underground water.

INVESTIGATE Aquifer Filtration

How can the ground filter water?

PROCEDURE

① Cap the top of the bottle. Invert it and add to it a layer of gravel, then a layer of sand, then a layer of soil.

② Slowly pour water onto the soil until a water table becomes visible in the sand beneath it.

③ Add the pollutants pepper, cocoa, and food coloring to the bottle top. Slowly unscrew the cap so that water trickles into the bucket.

④ Observe the water that filtered through.

⑤ Pour more water onto the soil and let water trickle out.

WHAT DO YOU THINK?

• Which pollutants were filtered out before reaching the "aquifer"? Which ones reached the aquifer?

• What effect does pollution have on drinking water that comes from aquifers?

CHALLENGE What could you do to clean up an aquifer?

SKILL FOCUS
Making models

MATERIALS
• water
• 1L plastic bottle with bottom cut off
• gravel
• sand
• soil
• pepper
• cocoa
• food coloring
• bottle bottom or bucket

TIME
30 minutes

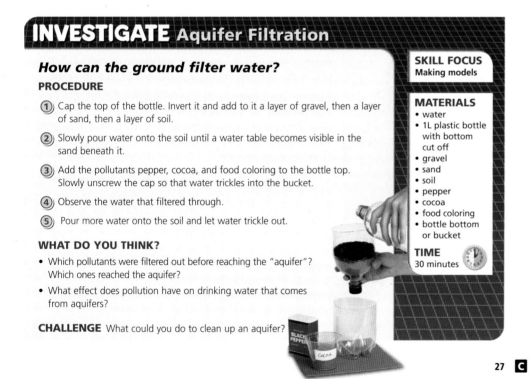

27 **C**

INVESTIGATE Aquifer Filtration

PURPOSE To model an aquifer to observe how ground materials filter water and see how different substances can get into groundwater

TIP *30 min.* Students should take care to unscrew the cap slowly so that only water escapes.

WHAT DO YOU THINK? *Pepper and cocoa; red food coloring. Pollution can seep into the aquifer and pollute the water there.*

CHALLENGE *Take steps to ensure that pollutants do not enter the ground. Over time, water becomes cleaner.*

 Datasheet, Aquifer Filtration, p. 42

Technology Resources

Customize this student lab as needed or look for an alternative. Print rubrics to assess student lab reports.

 Lab Generator CD-ROM

DIFFERENTIATE INSTRUCTION

 More Reading Support

D What happens to water when it sinks into the land? *It is filtered and cleaned by the ground.*

Alternative Assessment Have students use drawings to show the results of the investigation. Then ask them to explain their drawings orally.

Advanced Have students discuss how they can do the investigation differently to find out more about the filtering capacity of various types of ground materials. Have them devise an experimental procedure and carry it out. Have them share their findings with the rest of the class.

Develop Critical Thinking

APPLY Have students apply their knowledge of springs and wells to discuss the advantages and disadvantages of drinking bottled spring water and of drinking water from a well. Explain that much of the water consumed by city dwellers is stored in large reservoirs and does not come from either wells or springs.
Sample answer: Spring water may taste different from well water, but both come from an aquifer and so are essentially the same kind of water. If the water from a well is free, using it may be preferable to buying bottled water.

Ongoing Assessment

CHECK YOUR READING *Answer: pressure caused by the weight of surrounding water in the aquifer*

MAIN IDEA AND DETAILS
In your notebook, fill out a chart for this main idea.

Underground water can be brought to the surface.

If you had lived in colonial America or in ancient Greece, your daily chore might have been to haul water home from a well. You would have lowered a bucket into a pit until it reached the water table, then pulled the filled bucket up with a rope. Or you might have worked at digging a well, hacking away at the ground with a shovel until water flowed into the hole you dug.

Today's technology makes it easier to bring groundwater to the surface. Powerful drills bore through rock, and motors pump groundwater to the surface and to kitchen sinks. Scientists study the sizes and areas of aquifers. They know where to get water and how much to expect.

Springs and Wells

Underground pressure causes this artesian well to shoot water 18 meters (60 ft) into the air.

Groundwater can be collected from springs and wells. A **spring** is a flow of water from the ground at a place where the surface of the land dips below the water table. In some springs, the water bubbles up, then sinks back into the soil. In others, the water flows into a stream or lake. Spring water has a fresh clean taste, and many water companies bottle this water to sell.

A well is a hole in the ground that reaches down to the saturation zone—the wet region below the water table. Usually, a pump is used to draw the water out of the ground, and a screen is used to filter out particles of sand and gravel. If the water table is near the surface, a well can be dug by hand. The part of the well beneath the water table will fill with water.

Most modern wells are dug with motorized drills. A drill digs through soil and rock into the saturation zone; then a pipe is lowered into the drill hole. A pump is used to raise the water from the ground. Some wells are more than 300 meters (1000 ft) deep.

One kind of well does not need a pump. An **artesian well** is a well in which water flows to the surface naturally because it is under pressure. In places where impermeable rock dips into an aquifer, the water directly below the rock is pushed to a lower level than the water on either side. When a well is drilled into the water beneath the rock, the weight of the surrounding water pushes the water upward.

? E

CHECK YOUR READING What makes water flow upward out of an artesian well?

DIFFERENTIATE INSTRUCTION

 More Reading Support

E How does an artesian well differ from other wells? *Water flows to the surface in it naturally.*

Additional Investigation To reinforce Section 1.3 learning goals, use the following full-period investigation:

R 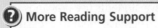 **Additional INVESTIGATION,** Water Wells, A, B, & C, pp. 60–68, 261–262
(Advanced students should complete Levels B and C.)

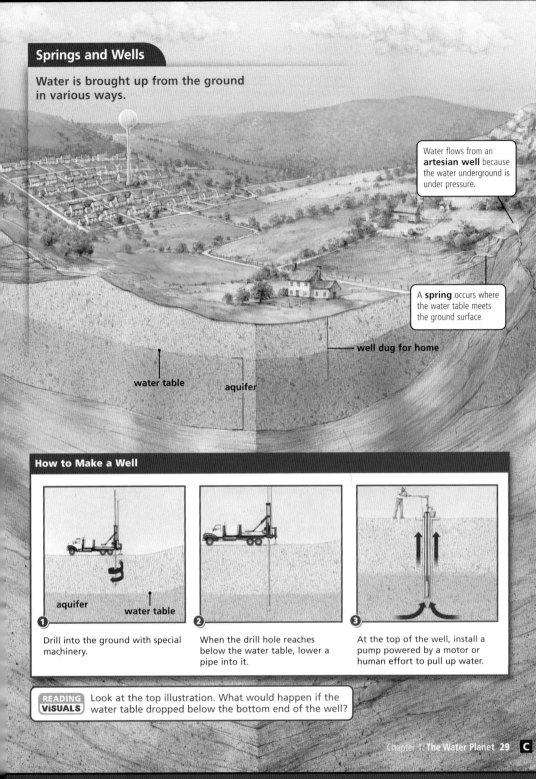

Springs and Wells

Water is brought up from the ground in various ways.

Water flows from an **artesian well** because the water underground is under pressure.

A **spring** occurs where the water table meets the ground surface.

well dug for home

water table

aquifer

How to Make a Well

aquifer

water table

① Drill into the ground with special machinery.

② When the drill hole reaches below the water table, lower a pipe into it.

③ At the top of the well, install a pump powered by a motor or human effort to pull up water.

READING VISUALS Look at the top illustration. What would happen if the water table dropped below the bottom end of the well?

DIFFERENTIATE INSTRUCTION

Advanced Challenge students to make a model of an artesian well. Tell them that one model uses the following materials: plastic shoebox or other container, sand, water, clay, pencil, and drinking straw. Students could half fill the shoebox with sand, saturate it with water, and cover the sand with clay. They could tilt the shoebox slightly, then use the pencil to "drill a well" and insert the straw. Pressure will force the water up through the straw. Ask: What part of the model represents impermeable rock? *the clay and the shoebox*

 Challenge and Extension, p. 41

Teach from Visuals

To help students interpret the visual of springs and wells, ask:

- What are the three steps in making a well? *1. Drill into the ground to below the water table. 2. Lower a pipe into the hole. 3. Install a pump to pull water up through the pipe.*

- Why is drilling not needed to reach the water in a spring? *In a spring, water bubbles up at the surface because the land dips below the water table.*

- What part of a well is not needed to get the water from an artesian well? *the pump*

T This visual is also available as T6 in the Unit Transparency Book.

Teaching with Technology

Have students use graphics creation and production software to make a diagram that compares a well and a spring. Most graphics creation software makes use of tools. Students can use shape tools to create different types of shapes. They can use the text tool to add labels and a title.

Ongoing Assessment

Explain how underground water reaches the surface in springs and wells.

Ask: What are two differences between a well and a spring? *Sample answer: spring—occurs where the water table reaches the surface of the ground, does not need a hole dug; well—brings water from an underground aquifer, needs a hole dug*

READING VISUALS *Answer: The well would go dry.*

F

The depth of the water table in a particular place can vary from season to season, depending on how much rain falls and how much water is used. When water is taken from an aquifer, the water table might drop. When it rains or snows, some of the water filters back into the aquifer, replacing what has been taken. If water is used faster than it is replaced, wells may run dry. Low groundwater levels can also cause the ground to settle and damage the environment.

As more and more people live on Earth, the amounts of groundwater used to irrigate crops increase. In some states where crops are grown in dry areas, as much as 70 percent of all the groundwater brought to the surface is used for irrigation. Water used for irrigation is recycled back into the water cycle. In some places it sinks back into the ground and filters into aquifers. In other regions much of the water evaporates or flows away, and the groundwater levels are lowered.

Hot Springs

Yellowstone National Park sits atop the remains of an ancient volcano. The rain and melted snow that sink into the ground there eventually reach depths of more than 3000 meters (10,000 feet), where the rocks are extremely hot. The water heats up and reaches the boiling point. Then it becomes even hotter while remaining liquid because it is under such great pressure from the rocks pushing on it from all sides.

The hot water deep underground is like water in an enormous boiling pot—with a lid 3000 meters thick. The water expands the only way that it can, by pushing upward through weak places in the rocks. A place where the water surfaces is a hot spring. A hot spring has a continual flow of hot water.

Vapor rises from these hot springs in Yellowstone National Park in Wyoming.

WYOMING

C 30 Unit: Earth's Waters

 In a geyser, water heats underground. The diagram shows the underground "plumbing" of a geyser in Iceland.

 Hot water and steam are pushed up to the surface where they erupt.

A geyser is a kind of hot spring. The illustrations above show how a geyser works. Beneath the surface, there are underground channels in the rock. The rising hot water is forced to travel through these narrow passages. Like water in a garden hose, the water moves with force because it is under pressure. When it finally reaches Earth's surface, the pressure makes it burst out. It shoots into the air as a dramatic fountain of water and steam. In Yellowstone National Park there are more than 300 geysers. One of the largest, Old Faithful, shoots a jet of hot water and steam about 20 times a day. The eruptions last from 1.5 to 5 minutes, and reach heights of 30 to 55 meters (106 to 184 ft).

RESOURCE CENTER
CLASSZONE.COM

Learn more about geysers and hot springs.

CHECK YOUR READING Why does water shoot out of Old Faithful with such great force?

1.3 Review

KEY CONCEPTS

1. Draw a diagram that shows how water collects underground.
2. What is the difference between a spring and a well?
3. What causes water to rise out of the ground in hot springs and geysers?

CRITICAL THINKING

4. **Connect** Is a T-shirt permeable or impermeable? How about a raincoat? Explain why.
5. **Infer** Would you expect to find a spring on the very top of a hill? Why or why not?

CHALLENGE

6. **Sequence** On a blank sheet of paper, draw a cartoon strip that shows how aquifers collect and store water and how people bring the water to the surface. Show at least five steps in the process. Write captions for your drawing to explain the steps.

Chapter 1: The Water Planet **31** **C**

ANSWERS

1. Diagram should show water sinking through permeable sediment and rock until it reaches impermeable rock, where it collects.

2. Spring is place where surface of land meets water table, so that water flows out. Well is hole drilled into

saturation zone. (In artesian well water is forced upward without pump.)

3. Heat underground creates pressure, which forces hot water upward.

4. T-shirt is permeable because spaces in cloth let water through. Raincoat is

impermeable because its material has no such spaces.

5. No, because spring is at level of water table and water table is not likely to be as high as top of hill.

6. Cartoon should resemble graphic on p. 29, showing drilling of well.

Ongoing Assessment

CHECK YOUR READING Answer: The water is pushed with force through narrow passages because it is under pressure.

Teaching with Technology

Have students download graphics from the Internet and use presentation software to create a display of wells, springs, artesian wells, hot springs, and geysers.

Reinforce (the **BIG** idea)

Have students relate the section to the Big Idea.

R Reinforcing Key Concepts, p. 43

1.3 ASSESS & RETEACH

Assess

A Section 1.3 Quiz, p. 5

Reteach

To help students review this section, write "Bringing Underground Water to the Surface" on the board. Ask them to identify and describe the ways underground water comes to the surface. *spring—ground dips below the water table and water bubbles up; well—water is pumped up through a hole drilled into an aquifer; artesian well—water is pushed up and out by pressure beneath the surface; hot spring or geyser—water is forced to the surface by underground heating that builds up pressure.*

Technology Resources

Have students visit **ClassZone.com** for reteaching of Key Concepts.

CONTENT REVIEW

CONTENT REVIEW CD-ROM

Chapter 1 **31** **C**

Focus

PURPOSE To determine the permeabilities of a variety of materials and draw conclusions about why and how water collects and flows underground

OVERVIEW Students will design an experiment, using ground samples, a rubber band, a scale, a jar, and water to determine what types of ground materials best hold and transport water. Students will determine the following:

- Which materials are permeable and how permeability and impermeability affect the way materials hold and transport water.

- How the materials in the experiment relate to materials in the ground that account for the formation of aquifers.

Lab Preparation

- Aquarium gravel and other available materials can be substituted for the ground-material samples.

- Prior to the investigation, have students read through the investigation and prepare their data tables. Or you may wish to copy and distribute datasheets and rubrics.

 UNIT RESOURCE BOOK, pp. 51–59

 SCIENCE TOOLKIT, F12

Lab Management

- Divide students into groups of three or four.

- Warn students not to throw the golf ball or shoot the rubber band.

DIFFERENTIATION TIP Some students may benefit from drawing diagrams to illustrate the procedures they decide upon. Others might benefit from reading their procedures aloud before continuing with the experiment.

CHAPTER INVESTIGATION

Water Moving Underground

OVERVIEW AND PURPOSE

Many people rely on underground aquifers for their drinking water. Some aquifers are small and localized. Others can supply water to huge regions of the United States. Perhaps your own drinking water comes from an underground aquifer. In this investigation you will

DESIGN —YOUR OWN— **EXPERIMENT**

- design an experiment to determine what types of materials best hold and transport water
- infer which types of Earth materials make the best aquifers

MATERIALS
- granite sample
- sandstone sample
- sand
- square piece of cotton muslin or cotton knit, measuring 30 cm per side
- rubber band
- golf ball
- scale
- large jar
- water

 Problem [Write It Up]

What types of materials will best hold and transport water?

 Hypothesize [Write It Up]

Write a hypothesis that answers the problem question in "If . . . , then . . . , because . . ." form.

 Procedure

1. Design a procedure to test the materials samples to determine which will best hold and transport water. Your procedure should be designed to identify both which material absorbed the most water and which material absorbs water the fastest.

2. Record your procedure in your **Science Notebook.**

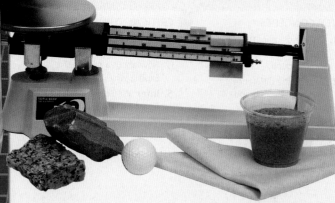

INVESTIGATION RESOURCES

 CHAPTER INVESTIGATION, Water Moving Underground
- Level A, pp. 51–54
- Level B, pp. 55–58
- Level C, p. 59

Advanced students should complete Levels B & C.

 Writing a Lab Report, D12–13

Technology Resources

Customize this student lab as needed or look for an alternative. Print rubrics to assess student lab reports.

 Lab Generator CD-ROM

3. Create a data table to organize the data you will collect.

4. Be sure that you make both qualitative and quantitative observations.

5. Be sure to include a calculations section in your **Science Notebook.**

▶ Observe and Analyze

1. **RECORD OBSERVATIONS** Draw a diagram of your experimental setup.

2. **CALCULATE** Which item absorbed the most water?

3. **SCIENTIFIC METHOD** How did you use the golf ball? What did it represent?

▶ Conclude

1. **INTERPRET** Answer the problem question.

2. **COMPARE** Compare your results with your hypothesis. Do your data support your hypothesis?

3. **IDENTIFY LIMITS** In what ways was this activity limited in demonstrating how water moves underground? How might your experimental setup lead to incorrect conclusions?

4. **APPLY** Look over your data table. Your results should indicate both which material absorbed the most water and which material absorbed water the fastest. How do these two characteristics compare in terms of their importance for an aquifer?

5. **INFER** Which types of Earth materials make the best aquifers?

▶ INVESTIGATE Further

CHALLENGE The data you gathered in this investigation reflect the permeability of each Earth material tested. What qualities and characteristics determine their permeabilities?

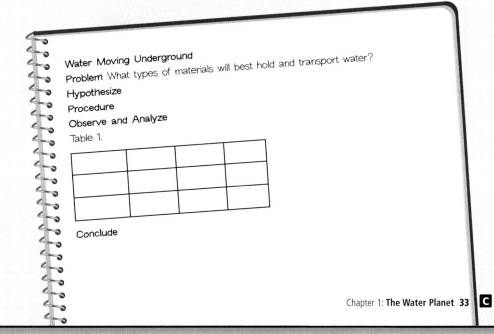

Water Moving Underground
Problem What types of materials will best hold and transport water?
Hypothesize
Procedure
Observe and Analyze
Table 1.

Conclude

Chapter 1: **The Water Planet** 33

▶ Observe and Analyze

Sample data: Data table should record observations about each material, including whether the material could hold water or was impermeable. The best data tables will have measurements for the amount of water that a material could hold.

1. *Check students' diagrams.*

2. *It is likely that either the sandstone or the sand held the most water, but results will depend on the size of each material sample. Student should demonstrate their findings with recorded measurements.*

3. *Sample answer: placed the golf ball in the sand or at the bottom of it, representing impermeable rock (Students should focus on the impermeability of the golf ball.)*

▶ Conclude

1. *Of the materials tested, sandstone, sand, and cotton hold or transport water best.*

2. *Answers will vary. Sample hypothesis: "If material in the ground is rock, it will not hold water because rock is hard." Data do not support hypothesis because sandstone held water.*

3. *The materials that were tested are not necessarily the same as what is found underground. Also, with these materials, it was not possible to make a precise model of what happens underground; these were just samples of materials, not large formations.*

4. *Materials that contain the most water might be found in an aquifer that holds a large amount of water. Where an aquifer's material doesn't hold as much water, the aquifer might be depleted quickly, or water from above will travel away because the aquifer is full. How fast the material absorbs water would affect how quickly water would sink through that material in the ground.*

5. *Materials with more spaces in them, because they hold the most water.*

CHALLENGE Materials with more spaces between particles, like the gravel, are more permeable and hold more water.

Post-Lab Discussion

- Use differences among the students' results to point out the connection between the hypothesis, the procedure, and the conclusion. If the procedure does not match the hypothesis, then the results will be inconclusive.

- Discuss how students would evaluate the procedures they designed.

- Discuss the ways students might communicate a procedure to someone else, who would then test the experimental design. *Students should be able to review the data and give a logical explanation of the cause-and-effect relationships in their results.*

BACK TO

Ask students to describe how their daily lives are affected by how water moves on Earth. Encourage them to use what they have learned in the chapter as they answer the question. *Sample answer: When water condenses and falls as precipitation as part of the water cycle, it affects whether I need an umbrella and what I can do outside. Water from springs and wells is used to irrigate crops that I eat. When the water enters drainage basins, it flows into rivers and lakes where I swim.*

◐ KEY CONCEPTS SUMMARY

SECTION 1.1

Ask: What are the three processes that are part of the water cycle? *evaporation, condensation, precipitation*

SECTION 1.2

Ask: In what form is the water in glaciers? *frozen as ice*

Ask: What happens to water that falls as precipitation? *It flows and collects in rivers and lakes.*

SECTION 1.3

Ask: How does gravity affect water on the land? *It pulls it down into the ground.*

Ask: Where does water collect underground? *in open spaces in soil, gravel, and rock*

Ask: What happens to underground water when it reaches an impermeable rock layer? *It cannot sink any farther.*

Review Concepts

- Big Idea Flow Chart, p. T1
- Chapter Outline, pp. T7–T8

Chapter Review

the BIG idea

Water moves through Earth's atmosphere, oceans, and land in a cycle.

CONTENT REVIEW
CLASSZONE.COM

◐ KEY CONCEPTS SUMMARY

1.1 Water continually cycles.
Water moves through Earth's environment in a continuous cycle.

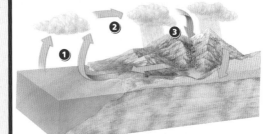

1 **Evaporation** Water becomes vapor.

2 **Condensation** Vapor changes into liquid.

3 **Precipitation** Water falls to the surface.

VOCABULARY
fresh water p. 11
salt water p. 11
water cycle p. 12
evaporation p. 13
condensation p. 13
precipitation p. 13

1.2 Fresh water flows and freezes on Earth.

Water on land collects and flows in rivers and lakes. Much of Earth's fresh water is frozen.

divide

drainage basins

VOCABULARY
divide p. 17
drainage basin p. 17
turnover p. 19
eutrophication p. 20
iceberg p. 22

1.3 Fresh water flows underground.
Water collects and moves beneath the land surface.

Gravity pulls water down through **permeable** materials until it reaches an impermeable layer.

Water collects in open spaces in soil, gravel, or rock.

The **impermeable** layer prevents water from sinking farther down.

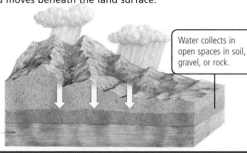

VOCABULARY
groundwater p. 24
permeable p. 24
impermeable p. 25
water table p. 25
aquifer p. 26
spring p. 28
artesian well p. 28

Technology Resources

Have students visit **ClassZone.com** or use the CD-ROM for a cumulative review of concepts.

 CONTENT REVIEW

 CONTENT REVIEW CD-ROM

Engage students in a whole-class interactive review of Key Concepts. Edit content as you wish.

 POWER PRESENTATIONS

Reviewing Vocabulary

Use the terms in the box below to answer the next nine questions.

evaporation	precipitation	water cycle
turnover	eutrophication	artesian
iceberg	groundwater	permeable

1. Which word describes an increase in nutrients in a lake or pond?

2. Which kind of well does not need a pump?

3. Which term describes a seasonal change in a lake?

4. Which term describes a substance through which water can pass?

5. Which term names the continuous movement of water through Earth's environment?

6. What is the name for an enormous chunk of floating ice?

7. What word means the turning of liquid water into a gas?

8. What is the name of water stored in an aquifer?

9. What word is another name for rain, snow, sleet, and hail?

Reviewing Key Concepts

Multiple Choice *Choose the letter of the best answer.*

10. What are the three forms of water on Earth?
    a. groundwater, lakes, and clouds
    b. liquid water, frozen water, and water vapor
    c. gas, steam, and vapor
    d. groundwater, oceans, and ice

11. How much of Earth's water is fresh water?
    a. almost all
    b. about half
    c. very little
    d. none

12. Which process forms clouds?
    a. evaporation
    b. precipitation
    c. condensation
    d. dehydration

13. What ice formation covers Greenland and Antarctica?
    a. iceberg
    b. landmass
    c. valley glacier
    d. continental glacier

14. Which is a characteristic of a pond?
    a. rooted plants covering the entire bottom
    b. plants only near shore
    c. a layer of impermeable rock
    d. water heated by underground rock

15. How are glaciers like rivers?
    a. They are made of liquid water.
    b. Their water sinks into the ground.
    c. They flow downhill.
    d. They are a mile thick.

16. How is water stored in an aquifer?
    a. in an open underground lake
    b. in cracks and spaces in rocks
    c. in impermeable rock
    d. in wells and springs

Short Answer *Write a short answer to each question.*

17. Explain why most of the water cycle takes place over the ocean.

18. How does an iceberg form?

19. Why are aquifers valuable?

20. What is the difference between a valley glacier and a continental glacier?

Reviewing Vocabulary

1. eutrophication

2. artesian

3. turnover

4. permeable

5. water cycle

6. iceberg

7. evaporation

8. groundwater

9. precipitation

Reviewing Key Concepts

10. b

11. c

12. c

13. d

14. a

15. c

16. b

17. Most of Earth's water is in the ocean. Therefore, huge quantities of water evaporate from the ocean and condense and fall as precipitation over it.

18. A piece of a glacier or ice shelf breaks off along a coastline.

19. because they hold enormous quantities of fresh, drinkable water, even in desert areas

20. A valley glacier is found in a mountain region and flows downward between mountains. A continental glacier is more like a great sheet of ice. It covers a land mass in a cold region.

ASSESSMENT RESOURCES

 UNIT ASSESSMENT BOOK
- Chapter Test A, pp. 6–9
- Chapter Test B, pp. 10–13
- Chapter Test C, pp. 14–17
- Alternative Assessment, pp. 18–19

 SPANISH ASSESSMENT BOOK
Spanish Chapter Test, pp. 153–156

Technology Resources

Edit test items and answer choices.

 Test Generator CD-ROM

Visit **ClassZone.com** to extend test practice.

 Test Practice

Thinking Critically

21. *Water is spouting out.*

22. *The weight of the water in the jug creates pressure, pushing water in the hose upward.*

23. *when level in the jug is lower than level of the hose's open end; water is no longer pressing down*

24. *The downward pressure of the mass of the water forcing water upward in the hose is like an artesian well. Unlike an artesian well, the water in the jug is an open pool, not water saturating rock or sediment.*

25. *The water cycle renews the supply of fresh water on Earth, so that there is always fresh water available for life.*

26. *In higher areas, where it is colder, more snow falls each year than melts, and glaciers form as snow builds up.*

27. *Clouds are made up of tiny drops of liquid water or ice crystals. Water vapor is an invisible gas.*

28. *The water flows down into the middle of the "bowl." Because a divide completely surrounds the basin, the water cannot flow out of the basin.*

29. *Use less detergent or detergent that does not contain phosphorus. Use less fertilizer that contains nitrogen.*

30. *Rainwater and water flowing from land is fresh.*

Sample predictions

31. *Water will collect in the permeable rock as groundwater.*

32. *Glaciers will form and build up.*

33. *A lake could form.*

34. *Eutrophication could happen faster than it would naturally.*

the BIG idea

35. *Water could have evaporated from the Pacific, condensed into a cloud that floated over my location, and rained on me.*

36. *Diagram should show a divide and streams flowing into lakes or the ocean.*

UNIT PROJECTS

Give students the appropriate Unit Project worksheets from the URB for their projects. Both directions and rubrics can be used as a guide.

 Unit Projects, pp. 5–10

Thinking Critically

Use the photograph to answer the next four questions. There are four liters of water in the jug. The hose has been overflowing for about ten seconds.

21. **OBSERVE** Describe what the water in the hose is doing.

22. **IDENTIFY EFFECTS** Explain what effect the water in the jug has on the water in the hose. Why does the water rise in the hose?

23. **PREDICT** When will the water stop flowing from the hose? Why?

24. **COMPARE AND CONTRAST** How is what is happening in the hose like and unlike what happens in an artesian well?

25. **EXPLAIN** Explain why the water cycle matters to humans and animals.

26. **CONNECT** In a mountainous area, temperatures are lower at higher altitudes. Explain the connection between this fact and the existence of valley glaciers.

27. **COMPARE AND CONTRAST** Explain the difference between clouds and water vapor in the atmosphere.

28. **INFER** Explain why water in a bowl-shaped drainage basin does not eventually flow to the ocean.

29. **APPLY** Name at least two things that you think people could do to lessen eutrophication caused by pollution.

30. **APPLY** Explain why even though evaporation draws water but not salt from the ocean, the ocean does not become saltier.

PREDICT Fill in the chart with predictions of how water will collect under the stated conditions.

Conditions	Prediction
31. A bed of permeable rock lies atop a bed of impermeable rock; rainfall is plentiful.	
32. Heavy snows fall in a region that has year-round freezing temperatures.	
33. A large depression is left in impermeable rock by a glacier.	
34. Water from farm fields and gardens runs off into ponds.	

the BIG idea

35. **SYNTHESIZE** Explain why a raindrop that falls on your head may once have been water in the Pacific Ocean.

36. **MODEL** Draw a diagram of two drainage basins, showing how water flows and collects on the surface of Earth. Label the divide, as well as the bodies of water into which water flows.

UNIT PROJECTS

If you are doing a unit project, make a folder for your project. Include in your folder a list of the resources you will need, the date on which the project is due, and a schedule to keep track of your progress. Begin gathering data.

MONITOR AND RETEACH

If students have trouble applying the concepts in item 36, suggest that they review the visual on p. 17. Then place a mound of clay in a container. Pour water over the clay. Ask students to identify the divide and the drainage basins in the model.

Students may benefit from summarizing one or more sections of the chapter.

R Summarizing the Chapter, pp. 69–70

Standardized Test Practice

For practice on your
state test, go to . . .
TEST PRACTICE
CLASSZONE.COM

Analyzing Data

In an experiment to study the effect of heating on evaporation, identical pans of water were placed for two hours under different types of lights. The temperature of the air just above each pan was measured with a thermometer every 30 minutes. The amount of evaporation was determined by subtracting the amount of water in the pan at the end of two hours from the amount that was in the pan at the beginning. The data table shows the results. Study the data and answer the questions below.

Pan	Description	Average Air Temperature Above the Water	Evaporation
1	under regular light	22°C (72°F)	30 mL (1.0 oz)
2	under heat lamp on low	25°C (78°F)	40 mL (1.4 oz)
3	under heat lamp on high	28°C (83°F)	50 mL (1.7 oz)

1. What is the relationship between the air temperature and the evaporation rate?
- **a.** There is no relationship between the temperature and the rate.
- **b.** As the temperature increases, the rate decreases.
- **c.** As the temperature increases, the rate stays the same.
- **d.** As the temperature increases, the rate increases.

2. If the air temperature averaged 27°C (80°F), about how much water would evaporate in two hours?
- **a.** 28 mL
- **b.** 38 mL
- **c.** 48 mL
- **d.** 58 mL

3. The constants in this experiment are the factors that stay the same for all three pans. Which of the following is a constant?
- **a.** the type of light
- **b.** the size of the pans
- **c.** the air temperature above the water
- **d.** the amount of evaporation

4. The dependent variable in an experiment is the factor that is measured to gather results. Which is the dependent variable in this experiment?
- **a.** the amount of evaporation
- **b.** the amount of water in each pan in the beginning
- **c.** the type of light
- **d.** the air temperature

5. Which change would make the results of this experiment more reliable?
- **a.** conducting the experiment for four hours
- **b.** decreasing the amount of water in the pans
- **c.** increasing the air temperature for one pan
- **d.** using a fan to blow air on one of the pans

Extended Response

Answer the two questions below in detail. Include some of the terms shown in the word box. In your answers, underline each term you use.

low	eutrophication	meadow
water table	saturation zone	

6. Kori notices that a pond at his summer camp is filled with more soil and plants each year. Explain how this change fits into the pattern of how ponds change over time.

7. Juanita's family gets water from a well on their ranch. Each time a well has gone dry, they have had to dig a new one that was deeper than the old one. Explain why they have needed to go deeper.

Analyzing Data

1. d

2. c

3. b

4. a

5. a

Extended Response

6. RUBRIC

4 points for a response that correctly answers the question and uses the following terms accurately:
- low
- eutrophication
- meadow

Sample: Over time, nutrients continue to enter a pond. This causes growth of plants and other organisms and causes the remains of plants and other organisms to collect in the <u>low</u> parts. The increase of nutrients in a pond or lake is called <u>eutrophication</u>. Over time, the pond can completely fill in and become a <u>meadow</u>.

3 points correctly answers the question and uses two terms accurately
2 points correctly answers the question and uses one term accurately
1 point correctly answers the question but does not use the terms

7. RUBRIC

4 points for a response that correctly answers the question and uses the following terms accurately:
- water table
- saturation zone

Sample: The well runs dry because the <u>water table</u> is dropping and is too low for the well to draw water. For the well to work, the well must extend below the water table, into the <u>saturation zone</u>, which is the area filled with water.

3 points correctly answers the question and uses one term accurately
2 points correctly answers the question but does not use the terms

---

METACOGNITIVE ACTIVITY

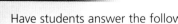

Have students answer the following questions in their **Science Notebook:**

1. What were you surprised to learn about water on Earth?

2. What more do you want to find out about water on Earth?

3. Describe what concepts in this chapter relate to your Unit Project.

CHAPTER

2 Freshwater Resources

Earth Science
UNIFYING PRINCIPLES

PRINCIPLE 1
Heat energy inside Earth and radiation from the Sun provide energy for Earth's processes.

PRINCIPLE 2
Physical forces, such as gravity, affect the movement of all matter on Earth and throughout the universe.

PRINCIPLE 3
Matter and energy move among Earth's rocks and soil, atmosphere, waters, and living things.

PRINCIPLE 4
Earth has changed over time and continues to change.

Unit: Earth's Waters
BIG IDEAS

CHAPTER 1
The Water Planet

Water moves through Earth's atmosphere, oceans, and land in a cycle.

CHAPTER 2
Freshwater Resources

Fresh water is a limited resource and is essential for human society.

CHAPTER 3
Ocean Systems

The oceans are a connected system of water in motion.

CHAPTER 4
Ocean Environments

The ocean supports life and contains resources.

CHAPTER 2
KEY CONCEPTS

SECTION 2.1

Fresh water is an essential resource.

1. Fresh water supports life.

2. Most human activities require water.

3. Dams and other structures alter rivers.

SECTION 2.2

Society depends on clean and safe water.

1. Treatment makes water safe for drinking.

2. Wastewater is treated and released.

3. Water pollution comes from many sources.

4. Water pollution can be prevented.

SECTION 2.3

Water shortages threaten society.

1. Water shortages are a global problem.

2. Overuse can cause water shortages.

3. Fresh water can be conserved.

4. People can balance water needs and uses.

T The Big Idea Flow Chart is available on p. T9 in the **UNIT TRANSPARENCY BOOK.**

Previewing Content

2.1 Fresh water is an essential resource.
pp. 41–49

1. Fresh water supports life.
Humans cannot live without clean, fresh water. As the world's population grows, fresh water becomes more precious.

2. Most human activities require water.
Almost every activity we do requires water, either directly or indirectly. Taking a shower and washing clothes are obvious examples. Indirect examples include eating food, reading a book, and using electricity because these products require much water to produce. Following are major ways people use water:

- **Farming** About 40 percent of the water used in the United States goes toward crops and livestock. Various methods of **irrigation** are often used to draw water from aquifers, rivers, and lakes in places where rain is not sufficient.
- **Industry** Industries that make cars, TVs, and other products are major water users. For example, a paper mill uses 100 to 300 metric tons of water to manufacture one ton of paper.
- **Transportation** The Great Lakes and major rivers of the U.S. provide a convenient and efficient way to transport goods.
- **Recreation** Rafting and swimming are among ways people use rivers and lakes for recreation.
- **Fisheries** Fresh water provides food for people as well as frogs, insects, birds, and larger animals. Fish farming, or **aquaculture,** provides a cheap source of fish.
- **Energy** Electricity is generated by **dams** as falling water spins the blades of a turbine.

3. Dams and other structures alter rivers.
Dams control the flow of water in rivers so that boats can travel on them. Dams separate the rivers into sections of different elevation. Boats traverse these steps through **locks,** which raise and lower the water level. Dams may also cause problems, such as blocking the passage of fish or of rich soil to areas downstream.

2.2 Society depends on clean and safe water. pp. 50–59

1. Treatment makes water safe for drinking.
People get water from a variety of sources, including wells, reservoirs, lakes, and rivers. Fresh water may contain harmful substances. The Environmental Protection Agency sets standards for safe drinking water and determines the **concentration** of various substances that can be in drinking water. Water treatment plants make water safe for drinking by removing harmful substances and killing harmful organisms.

2. Wastewater is treated and released.
Sewage systems collect and treat huge amounts of wastewater from cities and towns. A **septic system** treats wastewater from an individual home or business. Solids are broken down by bacteria or settle to the bottom of the septic tank.

3. Water pollution comes from many sources.
When human activities add so many chemicals, minerals, or organisms to a water supply that it cannot be made safe to drink, it is considered to be polluted.

- **Point-source pollution** enters water from a known source, such as a factory that spills chemicals into a river.
- **Nonpoint-source pollution** is pollution whose source is hard to find or is scattered, such as runoff from streets or farms.

4. Water pollution can be prevented.
Businesses and individuals can do a number of things to prevent or reduce water pollution.

- **Industry and Transportation** Factories and shippers can reduce the use of toxic materials and recycle or reuse wastes. Companies invent nontoxic products and help consumers recycle materials.
- **Agriculture** Farmers can grow crops without pesticides and keep animals away from water sources.
- **At Home** People can properly dispose of hazardous wastes, use nontoxic materials, and eat organic foods so that lower amounts of pesticides and herbicides enter the water supply.

Common Misconceptions

ROLE OF BACTERIA Students might think that all bacteria are harmful pathogens. In fact, some microorganisms play a beneficial role as decomposers and recyclers of basic elements and water. Some bacteria, for example, break down sludge and oils in water treatment facilities.

 This misconception is addressed on p. 53.

MISCONCEPTION DATABASE
CLASSZONE.COM Background on student misconceptions

POLLUTION Many students have the misconception that biodegradable materials and natural materials, such as human waste, are not pollution.

 This misconception is addressed on p. 54.

Previewing Content

2.3 Water shortages threaten society.
pp. 60–67

1. Water shortages are a global problem.

Some dry parts of the world, such as northern Africa and the Middle East, have a constant water problem. Other areas may experience water shortages during **droughts.**

People in regions that are affected by drought or that do not have enough water must import food they cannot grow themselves. Jordan imports 91 percent; Israel, 87 percent; and Egypt, 40 percent of grain needed.

2. Overuse can cause water shortages.

As the world's population grows, water is becoming scarcer. Most fresh water worldwide is used for agriculture. Overuse of ground water for irrigation is depleting aquifers faster than they can be refilled. River water also is being overused to the point that some rivers dry up for parts of the year.

3. Fresh water can be conserved.

Each American uses an average of 168 liters of water each day, broken down as follows:

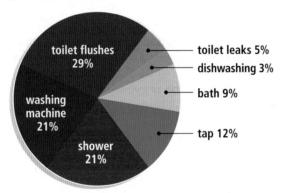

toilet flushes 29%
toilet leaks 5%
dishwashing 3%
bath 9%
washing machine 21%
tap 12%
shower 21%

Knowing how you use water is the first step toward conserving it. Water can be conserved in homes, businesses, and schools, and on farms. Conservation is an urgent issue due to the drying up of aquifers, and people need to find a way to share the water supply. Conserving water can be done by using less, by reusing water, and by recycling water for the same purpose.

4. People can balance water needs and uses.

Different people often have different opinions on how to use water. Public officials and experts can help to manage water use and enforce fair laws. When a river flows between states or countries, people must find a way to share the water rights. The Rio Grande River is an example of this, as its water is shared by three states and Mexico. The Rio Grande sometimes partially runs dry because so many people use its water.

When there is not enough water for a country to grow food, international organizations help to provide food for people. People are investigating different ways in which water can be shared from state to state and country to country.

Pollution also crosses state and international boundaries, causing problems far away from its source. Cooperation among governments is sometimes needed to limit such pollution.

Desalination, making fresh water from salt water, is a source of water in some places, but the process is very expensive. Costs may come down as technology improves. Cheap desalination would solve many water shortage problems.

Previewing Labs

Lab Generator CD-ROM
Edit these Pupil Edition labs and generate alternative labs.

EXPLORE (the BIG idea)

How Much Water Do You Drink? p. 39
Students keep track of how much they drink.

TIME 10 minutes
MATERIALS pencil and paper

What Happens When Salt Water Evaporates? p. 39
Students allow water to evaporate from salt water.

TIME 10 minutes
MATERIALS glass, spoon, water, 1 tsp. salt

Internet Activity: Aquifers, p. 39
Students explore changes in aquifers.

TIME 20 minutes
MATERIALS computer with Internet access

SECTION 2.1

INVESTIGATE Water Usage, p. 43
Students determine how much water they use in a week.

R Water Use Sheet, p. 80

TIME 30 minutes
MATERIALS Water Use Sheet, calculator

SECTION 2.2

EXPLORE Concentration, p. 50
Students dilute food coloring to 1 part per million.

TIME 10 minutes
MATERIALS water, graduated cylinder, eyedropper, food coloring

CHAPTER INVESTIGATION
Monitoring Water Quality, pp. 58–59
Students use systematic testing procedures similar to those used in real life and test known samples for common "pollutants" and then identify unknown water samples based on those tests.

TIME 40 minutes
MATERIALS 8 glucose strips, 16 litmus strips, watch with second hand, about 50 mL weak base made with baking soda and water, about 50 mL mild acid made with vinegar in water, about 50 mL sugar in water mixture, about 50 mL pure distilled water, clear plastic cups

---

SECTION 2.3

EXPLORE The Value of Fresh Water, p. 60
Students compare the prices of bottled water and gasoline.

TIME 10 minutes
MATERIALS calculator

INVESTIGATE Water Conservation, p. 63
Students calculate how much water is wasted by a dripping faucet.

TIME 20 minutes
MATERIALS water faucet, container for collecting dripping water, funnel, 100 mL graduated cylinder

---

R **Additional INVESTIGATION,** Desalination, A, B, & C, pp. 120–128; Teacher Instructions, pp. 261–262

Previewing Chapter Resources

	INTEGRATED TECHNOLOGY	LABS AND ACTIVITIES

CHAPTER 2
Freshwater Resources

 CLASSZONE.COM
- eEdition Plus
- EasyPlanner Plus
- Misconception Database
- Content Review
- Test Practice
- Visualization
- Simulation
- Resource Centers
- Internet Activity: Aquifers
- Math Tutorial

 SCILINKS.ORG
SCI*LINKS*

 CD-ROMS
- eEdition
- EasyPlanner
- Power Presentations
- Content Review
- Lab Generator
- Test Generator

 AUDIO CDS
- Audio Readings
- Audio Readings in Spanish

 EXPLORE the Big Idea, p. 39
- How Much Water Do You Drink?
- What Happens When Salt Water Evaporates?
- Internet Activity: Aquifers

 UNIT RESOURCE BOOK
Unit Projects, pp. 5–10

Lab Generator CD-ROM
Generate customized labs.

SECTION

2.1 Fresh water is an essential resource.
pp. 41–49

Time: 2 periods (1 block)
 Lesson Plan, pp. 71–72

- **RESOURCE CENTER,** Dams
- **MATH TUTORIAL**

 UNIT TRANSPARENCY BOOK
- Big Idea Flow Chart, p. T9
- Daily Vocabulary Scaffolding, p. T10
- Note-Taking Model, p. T11
- 3-Minute Warm-Up, p. T12

- THINK ABOUT How valuable is water? p. 41
- INVESTIGATE Water Usage, p. 43
- Math in Science, p. 49

 UNIT RESOURCE BOOK
- Water Use sheet, p. 80
- Datasheet, Water Usage, p. 81
- Math Support, p. 109
- Math Practice, p. 110

SECTION

2.2 Society depends on clean and safe water.
pp. 50–59

Time: 3 periods (1.5 block)
 Lesson Plan, pp. 83–84

 VISUALIZATION, Water Treatment Plant

 UNIT TRANSPARENCY BOOK
- Daily Vocabulary Scaffolding, p. T10
- 3-Minute Warm-Up, p. T12
- "Sources of Water Pollution" Visual, p. T14

 EXPLORE Concentration, p. 50
- CHAPTER INVESTIGATION, Monitoring Water Quality, pp. 58–59

 UNIT RESOURCE BOOK
CHAPTER INVESTIGATION Monitoring Water Quality, Levels A, B, & C, pp. 111–119

SECTION

2.3 Water shortages threaten society.
pp. 60–67

Time: 3 periods (1.5 block)
 Lesson Plan, pp. 93–94

 RESOURCE CENTER, Water Conservation

UNIT TRANSPARENCY BOOK
- Big Idea Flow Chart, p. T9
- Daily Vocabulary Scaffolding, p. T10
- 3-Minute Warm-Up, p. T13
- Chapter Outline, pp. T15–T16

 EXPLORE The Value of Fresh Water, p. 60
- INVESTIGATE Water Conservation, p. 63

 UNIT RESOURCE BOOK
- Datasheet, Water Conservation, p. 102
- Additional INVESTIGATION, Desalination, A, B, & C, pp. 120–128

KEY TO ICONS

 CD/CD-ROM

 INTERNET

 Pupil Edition

 Teacher Edition

UNIT RESOURCE BOOK

UNIT TRANSPARENCY BOOK

UNIT ASSESSMENT BOOK

SPANISH ASSESSMENT BOOK

SCIENCE TOOLKIT

READING AND REINFORCEMENT

ASSESSMENT

STANDARDS

 • Description Wheel, B20–21
• Supporting Main Ideas, C42
• Daily Vocabulary Scaffolding, H1–8

 UNIT RESOURCE BOOK
• Vocabulary Practice, pp. 106–107
• Decoding Support, p. 108
• Summarizing the Chapter, pp. 129–130

 Audio Readings CD
Listen to Pupil Edition.

 Audio Readings in Spanish CD
Listen to Pupil Edition in Spanish.

 • Chapter Review, pp. 69–70
• Standardized Test Practice, p. 71

 UNIT ASSESSMENT BOOK
• Diagnostic Test, pp. 20–21
• Chapter Test, Levels A, B, & C, pp. 25–36
• Alternative Assessment, pp. 37–38

 Spanish Chapter Test, pp. 157–160

 **Test Generator CD-ROM**
Generate customized tests.

Lab Generator CD-ROM
Rubrics for Labs

National Standards
A.2–8, A.9.a–f, F.3.b, F.4.b, F.5.b–c, G.1.b

See p. 38 for the standards.

 UNIT RESOURCE BOOK
• Reading Study Guide, A & B, pp. 73–76
• Spanish Reading Study Guide, pp. 77–78
• Challenge and Extension, p. 79
• Reinforcing Key Concepts, p. 82

 Ongoing Assessment, pp. 42, 44, 46–47

 Section 2.1 Review, p. 48

 UNIT ASSESSMENT BOOK
Section 2.1 Quiz, p. 22

National Standards
A.2–8, A.9.a–c, A.9.e–f, F.3.b, G.1.b

 **UNIT RESOURCE BOOK**
• Reading Study Guide, A & B, pp. 85–88
• Spanish Reading Study Guide, pp. 89–90
• Challenge and Extension, p. 91
• Reinforcing Key Concepts, p. 92

 Ongoing Assessment, pp. 51–56

 Section 2.2 Review, p. 57

UNIT ASSESSMENT BOOK
Section 2.2 Quiz, p. 23

National Standards
A.2–7, A.9.a–b, A.9.d–f, F.4.b, G.1.b

 **UNIT RESOURCE BOOK**
• Reading Study Guide, A & B, pp. 95–98
• Spanish Reading Study Guide, pp. 99–100
• Challenge and Extension, p. 101
• Reinforcing Key Concepts, p. 103
• Challenge Reading, pp. 104–105

 Ongoing Assessment, pp. 61, 63, 65

 Section 2.3 Review, p. 66

UNIT ASSESSMENT BOOK
Section 2.3 Quiz, p. 24

National Standards
A.2–8, A.9.a–f, F.4.b, F.5.b–c, G.1.b

Previewing Resources for Differentiated Instruction

CHAPTER INVESTIGATION

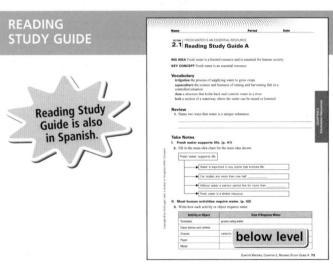

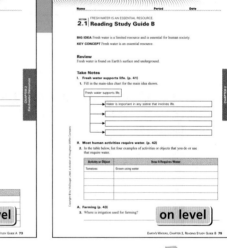

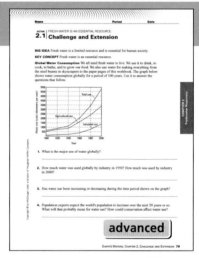

Leveled resources present the same concepts for different abilities.

below level

on level

advanced

R **UNIT RESOURCE BOOK,** pp. 111–114   R pp. 115–118   R pp. 115–119

READING STUDY GUIDE

Reading Study Guide is also in Spanish.

below level

on level

advanced

R **UNIT RESOURCE BOOK,** pp. 73–74   R pp. 75–76   R p. 79

CHAPTER TEST

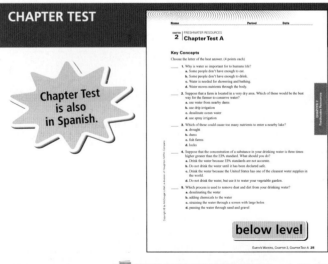

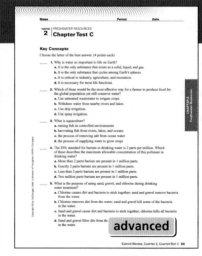

Chapter Test is also in Spanish.

below level

on level

advanced

A **UNIT ASSESSMENT BOOK,** pp. 25–28   A pp. 29–32   A pp. 33–36

TECHNOLOGY

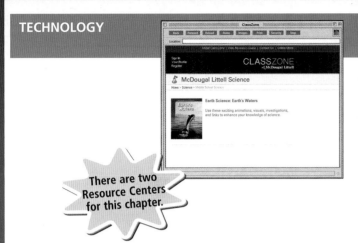

There are two Resource Centers for this chapter.

 **CLASSZONE.COM**

 **CD/CD-ROMS**

 **CLASSZONE.COM**

VISUAL CONTENT

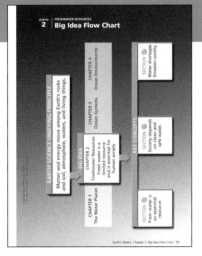

T **UNIT TRANSPARENCY BOOK,** p. T9

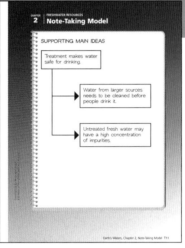

T p. T11

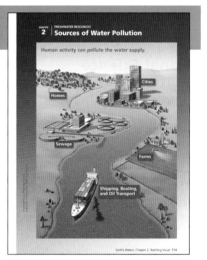

T p. T14

MORE SUPPORT

Reinforcing Key Concepts for each section

R **UNIT RESOURCE BOOK,** p. 82

R pp. 106–107

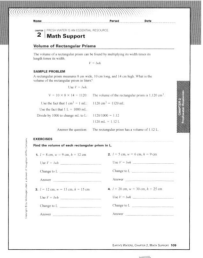

R p. 109

INTRODUCE

the BIG idea

Have students look at the photograph of a running faucet and discuss how the question in the box links to the Big Idea. Ask:

- What are some ways that people use water to produce the things that you need to live?

- Is all fresh water on Earth clean and safe? Why or why not?

- How easy is it for you and for other people in the world to get clean, safe drinking water?

National Science Education Standards

Content

F.3.b Human activities can induce hazards through activities that can accelerate many natural changes.

F.4.b Students should understand the risks associated with chemical hazards (pollutants in air, water, soil, and food).

Process

A.2–8 Design and conduct an investigation; use tools to gather and interpret data; use evidence to describe, predict, explain, model; think critically to make relationships between evidence and explanation; recognize different explanations and predictions; communicate scientific procedures and explanations; use mathematics.

A.9.a–f Understand scientific inquiry by using different investigations, methods, mathematics, technology, and explanations based on logic, evidence, and skepticism.

F.5.b–c Societal challenges inspire scientific research; technology influences society.

G.1.b Science requires different abilities.

CHAPTER

2 Freshwater Resources

the BIG idea

Fresh water is a limited resource and is essential for human society

In what ways do you depend on water?

Key Concepts

SECTION 2.1 Fresh water is an essential resource.
Learn how water is needed for life and how water is used for human activities.

SECTION 2.2 Society depends on clean and safe water.
Learn how water is made safe for drinking and how wastewater is treated.

SECTION 2.3 Water shortages threaten society.
Learn about the causes of water shortages and about ways to conserve water.

Internet Preview

CLASSZONE.COM

Chapter 2 online resources: Content Review, Simulation, Visualization, two Resource Centers, Math Tutorial, Test Practice

INTERNET PREVIEW

CLASSZONE.COM For student use with the following pages:

Review and Practice
- Content Review, pp. 40, 68
- Math Tutorial: Volume of a Rectangular Prism, p. 49
- Test Practice, p. 71

Activities and Resources
- Internet Activity: Aquifers, p. 39
- Resource Centers: Dams, p. 47; Water Conservation, p. 63
- Visualization: Water Treatment Plant, p. 52

Water Pollution
Code: MDL019

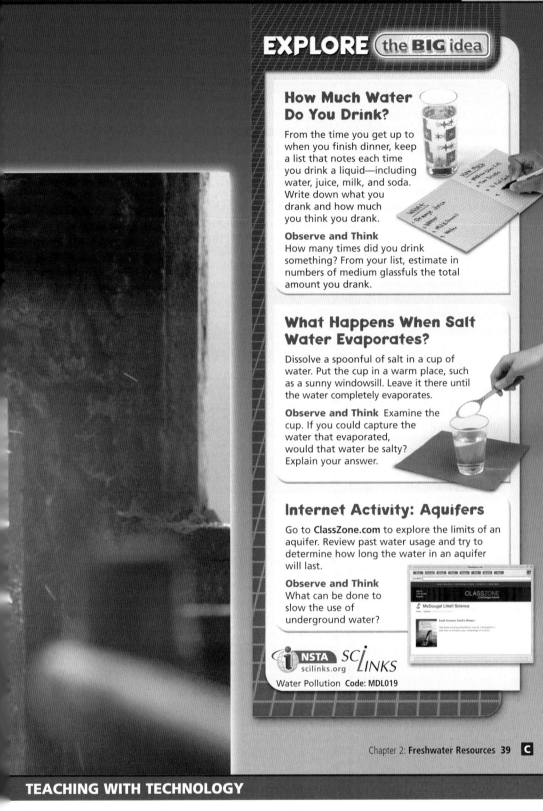

EXPLORE (the BIG idea)

How Much Water Do You Drink?

From the time you get up to when you finish dinner, keep a list that notes each time you drink a liquid—including water, juice, milk, and soda. Write down what you drank and how much you think you drank.

Observe and Think
How many times did you drink something? From your list, estimate in numbers of medium glassfuls the total amount you drank.

What Happens When Salt Water Evaporates?

Dissolve a spoonful of salt in a cup of water. Put the cup in a warm place, such as a sunny windowsill. Leave it there until the water completely evaporates.

Observe and Think Examine the cup. If you could capture the water that evaporated, would that water be salty? Explain your answer.

Internet Activity: Aquifers

Go to **ClassZone.com** to explore the limits of an aquifer. Review past water usage and try to determine how long the water in an aquifer will last.

Observe and Think
What can be done to slow the use of underground water?

NSTA *SCiLINKS*
scilinks.org
Water Pollution **Code: MDL019**

Chapter 2: **Freshwater Resources 39** **C**

These inquiry-based activities are appropriate for use at home or as a supplement to classroom instruction.

How Much Water Do You Drink?

PURPOSE To make students aware of how much water they consume each day, including water in various beverages.

TIP *10 min.* Show students an example of a "medium glassful" (about 8 ounces) to help them determine the volume they drink.

Answer: Students will get a better idea of how much water they consume, especially in drinks other than plain water.

REVISIT after p. 42.

What Happens When Salt Water Evaporates?

PURPOSE To reinforce the concept that when salt water evaporates, only fresh water turns into vapor. Salt is left behind.

TIP *10 min.* This activity will generally require time on two days.

Answer: Students will see that only the water evaporates; the salt is left behind. Therefore, water vapor is fresh water.

REVISIT after p. 66.

Internet Activity: Aquifers

PURPOSE To show students how aquifers can be depleted or replenished.

TIP *20 min.* Review the concept of an aquifer with students.

Answer: Students see how aquifer depletion occurs and how quickly, depending on the amounts of input and output.

REVISIT after p. 61.

TEACHING WITH TECHNOLOGY

Spreadsheet Software Have students use spreadsheet software to record data for the Chapter Investigation on pp. 58–59.

CBL and Probeware If probeware is available, use a pH sensor to determine the pH of water samples in the Chapter Investigation on pp. 58–59. Have students use calculators to make their calculations in "Investigate Water Conservation" on p. 63.

PREPARE

CONCEPT REVIEW

Activate Prior Knowledge

- Remind students that Earth's surface is 29 percent land and 71 percent water. Ask them to create a pie chart that displays this ratio.

- Remind students that only 3 percent of water on Earth is fresh water.

- Draw a diagram of the water cycle on the board. Use the diagram "The Water Cycle" on p. 13 of "The Water Planet" as a model. Ask students to come to the board to label the diagram with arrows and labels for evaporation, condensation, and precipitation.

TAKING NOTES

Supporting Main Ideas

If students have trouble identifying supporting information, refer them to red headings, topic sentences of paragraphs, and vocabulary terms.

Vocabulary Strategy

Students can use as many lines to add as much detail as they want on their description wheels. These wheels are easy study devices when students look back through their notes.

Vocabulary and Note-Taking Resources

R
- Vocabulary Practice, pp. 106–107
- Decoding Support, p. 108

T
- Daily Vocabulary Scaffolding, p. T10
- Note-Taking Model, p. T11

- Supporting Main Ideas, C42
- Description Wheel, B20–21
- Daily Vocabulary Scaffolding, H1–8

Getting Ready to Learn

CONCEPT REVIEW

- Water can be a solid, a liquid, or a gas.
- Water continually cycles on Earth.
- Water flows underground.

VOCABULARY REVIEW

fresh water p. 11
water cycle p. 12
groundwater p. 24
aquifer p. 26

CONTENT REVIEW
CLASSZONE.COM
Review concepts and vocabulary.

TAKING NOTES

SUPPORTING MAIN IDEAS

Make a chart to show main ideas and the information that supports them. Write each blue heading from the chapter in each box. In boxes below it, add supporting information, such as reasons, explanations, and examples.

VOCABULARY STRATEGY

Place each vocabulary term at the center of a **description wheel**. Write some words describing it on the spokes.

See the Note-Taking Handbook on pages R45–R51.

C 40 Unit: Earth's Waters

SCIENCE NOTEBOOK

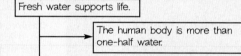

Fresh water supports life.

- The human body is more than one-half water.
- Living cells need water.
- Water is a limited resource.

water drawn is from aquifers, lakes, and rivers

can be spray
can be in canals
process of supplying water
used for crops
used in dry areas

IRRIGATION

CHECK READINESS

Administer the Diagnostic Test to determine students' readiness for new science content and their mastery of requisite math skills.

 Diagnostic Test, pp. 20–21

Technology Resources

Students needing content and math skills should visit **ClassZone.com**.

- CONTENT REVIEW
- MATH TUTORIAL
- CONTENT REVIEW CD-ROM

Fresh water is an essential resource.

◄ **BEFORE,** you learned

- Fresh water is found on Earth's surface and underground
- People use wells to bring ground water to the surface

▶ **NOW,** you will learn

- How water is required for life
- How water is used for many human activities

VOCABULARY

irrigation p. 43
aquaculture p. 45
dam p. 46
lock p. 46

THINK ABOUT

How valuable is water?

In the United States, fresh water seems plentiful. When you want water for a drink or to wash, you can go to a drinking fountain or turn on the tap to get all the water you want. In some parts of the world, water is scarce and difficult to get. In Port-au-Prince, Haiti, this girl is getting her bucket filled with fresh water so that she can take water home. If you had to get your water this way, how might that change the way you think of water? Would you use water differently than you do now?

Fresh water supports life.

Close your eyes and imagine a beautiful place in nature that is full of life. Maybe you think of trees, flowers, and a waterfall and pools where animals come to drink. Water is important in any scene that involves life.

People have always lived near clean, fresh water. Why is water so important to humans? One reason is that our bodies are more than one-half water. Without the water in your blood, your cells would not receive the nutrients they need. Your skin and tissues hold water in your body, but some water is lost every day. As a result, you get thirsty and drink water or something that contains mostly water, such as milk or juice. Without water, a person cannot live for more than a few days. And without water, people wouldn't be able to grow food.

Chapter 2: **Freshwater Resources 41** **C**

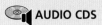

2.1 FOCUS

❶ Set Learning Goals
Students will
- Explain how water is required for life.
- List the ways in which water is used for human activities.
- Analyze data in an experiment to see how much water they use in a day.

◄ 3-Minute Warm-Up
Display Transparency 12 or copy this exercise on the board:

Choose the letter of the best answer.

1. What percent of water on Earth is salt water? *d*
   a. 3 percent   c. 70 percent
   b. 30 percent   d. 97 percent

2. The process in which water vapor changes into liquid water is *c*
   a. evaporation   c. condensation
   b. precipitation d. dehydration

3. The top of an underground area that is saturated is called *b*
   a. impermeable rock. c. an aquifer.
   b. the water table.   d. artesian well.

    3-Minute Warm-Up, p. T12

2.1 MOTIVATE

THINK ABOUT

PURPOSE To make students aware of how scarce water is in some parts of the world

DISCUSS Have students discuss the effort involved in getting clean, fresh water in the way that is shown in the photograph: walking a distance to a community well, maybe waiting in line, walking back home with the heavy load, and trying not to spill any.

Answers: Students would probably think of water as a valuable resource rather than something that's often taken for granted. They would probably conserve water more and use it sparingly.

Teach from Visuals

To help students interpret the visual "U.S. Population Near Water Sources," ask:

• Where is each of the cities shown located? *along a river or lake*

• What does a river provide to a city? *a source of fresh water and transportation*

• Where do the rivers on the map flow? *Willamette to the Pacific Ocean; other rivers to the Gulf of Mexico (Atlantic Ocean)*

Integrate the Sciences

The percentage of the human body that is water varies with age, sex, and physical condition. Infants may contain about 73 percent water, young males about 60 percent, and young females about 50 percent, but the body of an elderly person may be only 45 percent water.

EXPLORE (the BIG idea)

Revisit "How Much Water Do You Drink?" on p. 39. Have students explain the significance of their results.

Ongoing Assessment

Explain how water is required for life.

Identify two ways that water is needed for life. *Sample answer: to drink and to grow food*

CHECK YOUR READING *Answer: As the population grows, water can be used up or can become polluted so that it cannot be used.*

U.S. Population Near Water Sources

Many U.S. cities are located by rivers or lakes.

Portland — Willamette River
Omaha — Missouri River
Pittsburgh — Ohio River
St. Louis — Mississippi River
Cleveland — Lake Erie

Pittsburgh, Pennsylvania, is one of many cities by rivers. Here the Allegheny and the Monongahela rivers come together to form the Ohio River.

You have read that fresh water on Earth is a limited resource. A fixed amount cycles through the atmosphere, flows in rivers, is held in lakes and glaciers, and is stored in aquifers deep under the ground. As more and more people live on the planet every year, our water sources become more precious. If too much water is taken from aquifers, the supply will eventually run out. If the water in rivers and lakes becomes polluted, we can no longer use it.

CHECK YOUR READING What can happen to water as the world population grows?

Most human activities require water.

SUPPORTING MAIN IDEAS Record details about how water is important to human activities.

Almost everything you do requires water. When you take a shower or brush your teeth, you use water. Your dishes and clothes are washed with water. You might exercise in water at a pool.

Some of the ways you use water might surprise you. Let's say you do your homework after school. You grab a slice of pizza from the refrigerator, switch on the light, and sit down to read a book in your favorite chair. Have you used any water so far? The answer is yes, many gallons of water.

On farms water was needed to grow the tomatoes and wheat for your pizza. The cheese topping came from a cow that drank water and ate grain grown with water. The paper in your book was produced at a paper plant that used vast amounts of water to wash and mix wood pulp. When you switch on a light, you are probably using energy that was generated by some form of moving water. And the metal in the lamp was mined from underground, using—you guessed it—water.

DIFFERENTIATE INSTRUCTION

? More Reading Support

A Which activities that you do require water? *Almost everything, from taking a shower to making or eating pizza.*

English Learners English learners rely on patterns in the English language and may not recognize cause-and-effect relationships in sentences beginning with *If* that do not contain *then.* Students might recognize cause-and-effect relationships more easily if they break such sentences into parts, as is done in the following chart:

Cause	Effect
If the water in rivers and lakes becomes polluted,	we can no longer use it.

INVESTIGATE Water Usage

How much water do you use in a week?

PROCEDURE

1. Write down all the ways you use water in a day. Start with the time you get up in the morning. Include things such as brushing your teeth, flushing the toilet, using ice, and taking a shower.

2. Look at the Water Use sheet, and from it, identify other ways that you and others in your household use water.

3. Add up how many liters of water you use in a day, and multiply that by 7. This is how much water you use in a week.

WHAT DO YOU THINK?

- Which of your activities used the most water?
- What are some ways that you could reduce the amount of water you use weekly?

CHALLENGE Based on your weekly water usage, how much water is used by the United States annually? **Hint:** Find the population of the United States in a reference source.

SKILL FOCUS
Analyzing data

MATERIALS
- Water Use sheet
- calculator

TIME
30 minutes

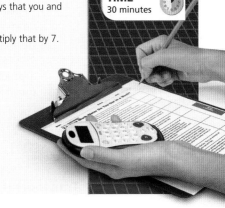

Farming

In the United States, about 40 percent of the water that is used goes to growing crops and raising livestock. Any kind of farm depends on water to grow plants for food and to raise animals. To grow oranges, a farm needs about 0.25 centimeters (0.1 in.) of rainfall a day. To produce one hamburger can require 5000 liters (1300 gal.) of water or more because animals not only drink water but also eat grass and grain that use water.

In many areas, rainfall does not provide enough water to support crops and animals. In these drier areas, farmers draw water from aquifers, rivers, or lakes to grow crops. The process of supplying water to land to grow crops is **irrigation.**

A common method of irrigation pours water through canals and waterways so that it flows through the fields. A little more than half of U.S. farms that are irrigated use this method, which is called flood irrigation. Most of the other farms that irrigate use spray irrigation, which sprays water onto the fields. You can think of lawn sprinklers as an example of spray irrigation for grass. On farms, the water often is delivered by metal structures that roll around entire fields.

These green irrigated fields are circular because the metal sprinklers move like clock hands from a center point

INVESTIGATE Water Usage

PURPOSE To have students collect and analyze data about their own use of fresh water, to exercise skills in collecting and totaling data, to realize just how much water they use

TIPS *30 min.* Have students bring calculators to use when analyzing their data. Allow students to work in pairs to help each other with the calculations.

INCLUSION

- Remind students to align the decimal points when adding decimals.

- Have students keep track of the number of zeros as placeholders when multiplying by the U.S. population figure.

WHAT DO YOU THINK *Answers for water use will vary but will likely include taking showers, taking baths, flushing toilets, or other household use. Ways of reducing water use might include taking shorter showers, putting less water in the bathtub, installing low-flush toilets, not letting the water run while brushing teeth, and watering lawns less and at times when less water is lost to evaporation.*

CHALLENGE *Answers will vary but should be found by multiplying students' weekly consumption by 52 weeks, then multiplying that product by the current U.S. population.*

- Water Use Sheet, p. 80
- Datasheet, Water Usage, 81

Technology Resources

Customize this student lab as needed or look for an alternative. Print rubrics to assess student lab reports.

Lab Generator CD-ROM

DIFFERENTIATE INSTRUCTION

More Reading Support

B Which term describes the process of supplying water to grow crops?
irrigation

Advanced Invite students to use the Internet to find visuals of the various kinds of irrigation. Challenge them to identify those that waste more or those that waste less water. For example, both flooding and spray irrigation waste water through evaporation. With both flood and spray irrigation, much excess water does not reach the plant roots. In a method called drip irrigation, water drips from narrow pipes directly around the base of individual plants and is most efficiently used.

Challenge and Extension, p. 79

Real World Examples

On the Great Lakes, about 65 large, self-propelled vessels carry dry goods and about 20 smaller vessels carry liquid materials. In a typical year, these ships transport more than 111 million tons of cargo, about 1000 pounds for each American. The Great Lakes-St. Lawrence Seaway system includes 15 major international ports and about 50 smaller regional ports in the United States and Canada.

Social Studies Connection

The location of waterways has influenced human activity and settlement throughout history. An example of this influence is the fall line in the eastern United States. The fall line is the boundary between the Atlantic coastal plain and the Piedmont—the rocky foothills of the Appalachian Mountains. The fall line is so called because it is where waterfalls blocked navigation along rivers flowing to the coast. As a result, in the 1700s many pioneers settled in places along the fall line, including Trenton, New Jersey; Richmond, Virginia; Raleigh, North Carolina; and Macon, Georgia. Many of the first American factories sprang up in these places, as the power of falling and fast-moving water was needed to turn water wheels that turned machinery.

Ongoing Assessment

CHECK YOUR READING *Answer: Water is used in various kinds of manufacturing and in mining, to cool machines, to wash things, to make paper, etc.*

A paper mill uses large quantities of water to process wood pulp.

Great Lakes

This freighter carries cargo on the Great Lakes.

Industry

The industries that make our cars, notebooks, jeans, sneakers, skateboards, and TVs are major water users. The manufacture of just about any item you can name probably uses water. Consider these examples.

- The process of making one car can require about 50 times the car's weight in water. This process begins with the mining of minerals and ends with the final washing as the car rolls out of the factory.
- In many industries, huge amounts of water are used to cool down machines.
- In a coal mine, water is used to separate chunks of coal from other clumps of dirt and rock.
- A paper mill uses 100 to 300 metric tons of water to manufacture one ton of paper.

Water used in industry can be used again. Factories can clean the water they use and return most of it to lakes and rivers.

CHECK YOUR READING How is water used in industry?

Transportation and Recreation

?
C

Since the earliest times, rivers and lakes have helped people visit their neighbors and trade food and goods. In the United States, major rivers and the Great Lakes provide an efficient way to transport goods, especially cargo that is bulky and heavy, such as coal. For example, on the Great Lakes, large ships carry iron ore from Minnesota to cities where it is used to make steel. On the Mississippi River, barges haul grain to ports, where the grain may be processed or placed on ships to go overseas.

DIFFERENTIATE INSTRUCTION

? **More Reading Support**

C What are two major water transportation routes in the United States? *Mississippi River and Great Lakes*

Advanced Challenge students to find out about the process used to make paper. Have them illustrate or make a 3-D model of the process while using captions or tags to explain each step. Invite students to use their visuals to explain the process to the class and point out where water is used along the way.

People also use rivers and lakes for recreation. Whitewater rafting, canoeing, and kayaking are popular activities. Many people also like to camp, picnic, swim, and fish along the shores of freshwater rivers and lakes.

Not every section of a river can be navigated by boat. A river may flow too fast or be too shallow for safe travel. To make water transportation easier, people dig channels called canals that bypass rough spots and connect waterways. For example, a 376-kilometer (234-mi) canal lets boats travel between the Tennessee and Tombigbee rivers in Mississippi and Alabama. In Canada, west of Buffalo, New York, the Welland Canal connects two Great Lakes, Ontario and Erie. It is part of the waterway known as the St. Lawrence Seaway, which connects the Great Lakes to the Atlantic Ocean.

Fisheries and Aquaculture

Fresh water is full of life—from tiny one-celled organisms to small shrimp and worms, to trout and salmon. Rivers and lakes provide fish for our food, a living resource that people depend upon. They also provide food for frogs, insects, birds, and larger animals.

When people talk about livestock, do you think of fish? Probably not, but fish farming is a thriving business all over the world. **Aquaculture** is the science and business of raising and harvesting fish in a controlled situation. Freshwater fish farms provide a cheap, ready source of catfish, trout, and salmon. However, aquaculture also causes some problems. The farms can cause excess nutrients and pollution to flow into rivers and lakes.

To help maintain the population of fish in rivers and lakes, fish hatcheries are used to raise fish to release into lakes and rivers. Hatcheries give people who fish something to catch and also help threatened species survive.

READING TiP
You can use word parts to help remember vocabulary terms. *Aqua-* comes from the Latin word for water.

An aquaculture worker tends to a fish farm in Nepal.

NEPAL

45 C

Real World Example

The St. Lawrence Seaway opened to large seagoing vessels in 1959. The seaway extends from the Atlantic Ocean to Duluth, Minnesota, on Lake Superior, a distance of 2038 nautical miles (2345 statute miles or 3775 kilometers). It takes about eight days for a ship to sail all the way from the ocean to Duluth. Since it opened, more than two billion tons of cargo have been shipped along the seaway. Almost half of the ships on the seaway travel to and from overseas ports in Europe, the Middle East, and Africa.

Integrate the Sciences

Aquaculture can seem like a no-lose proposition because fish populations are raised and harvested in abundance, seemingly without depleting fish stocks. However, many kinds of aquaculture have serious pollution issues associated with them. Salmon and catfish farming both can cause harmful pollution. Salmon farming may harm the wild fish population because of pollution. Catfish farming has unleashed a killer, non-native carp species threatening the Great Lakes' ecosystems. Catfish farmers imported the carp to eat weeds in their farms.

DIFFERENTIATE INSTRUCTION

More Reading Support

D Why are canals built? *to bypass rough spots and connect waterways*

E What is the raising and harvesting of fish in a controlled situation? *aquaculture*

Below Level Help students understand the concept of aquaculture by comparing it with agriculture. Ask: What words do you think of when you hear the word *agriculture*? *Possible answers include farming, crops, and fields.* What is agriculture? *the science and business of raising crops and livestock* Which part of the word *aquaculture* is different from *agriculture*? *aqua- instead of agri-* What does *aqua-* mean? *water* How are aquaculture and agriculture similar? *They both involve growing and harvesting food.*

Chapter 2 **45** C

Integrate the Sciences

Some rivers, such as the Columbia River in the Pacific Northwest, have special locks that allow salmon to go around dams. Salmon breed in rivers and then travel to the ocean. Once they have grown to maturity, they swim back upstream to the place where they hatched to lay eggs. Without fish locks, the salmon could not get around the dams and would not be able to reproduce.

Teach Difficult Concepts

Some students may have a difficult time understanding why locks are needed and how they work. Dams break up a river into a series of flowing "pools" in a staircase fashion. Locks allow ships to navigate this staircase. After a ship enters a lock, the open wall closes, the water in the lock is raised or lowered, and then the other wall is opened to allow the ship to float into the higher or lower level side of the dam. Ask: Why are locks needed for ships to go around dams? *because the water level on the two sides of the dam is different*

Ongoing Assessment

CHECK YOUR READING *Answer: Ships need to use locks on rivers that have dams sectioning the river into different levels. Locks allow ships to be raised or lowered to the next level.*

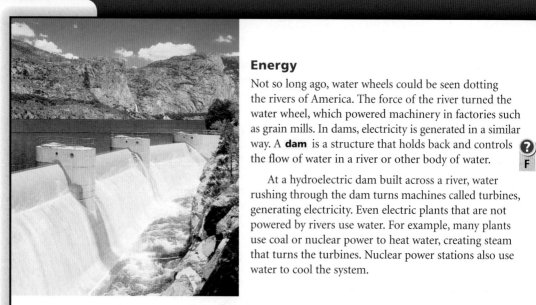

At a hydroelectric plant, water flowing through a dam spins turbines to produce electricity.

VOCABULARY
Add a description wheel for *lock* in your notebook.

Energy

Not so long ago, water wheels could be seen dotting the rivers of America. The force of the river turned the water wheel, which powered machinery in factories such as grain mills. In dams, electricity is generated in a similar way. A **dam** is a structure that holds back and controls the flow of water in a river or other body of water. **F**

At a hydroelectric dam built across a river, water rushing through the dam turns machines called turbines, generating electricity. Even electric plants that are not powered by rivers use water. For example, many plants use coal or nuclear power to heat water, creating steam that turns the turbines. Nuclear power stations also use water to cool the system.

Dams and other structures alter rivers.

When a dam is built on a river, the landscape and the shape of a river are greatly changed. Below the dam, the speed and volume of water flow may change, making a new ecosystem. Behind the dam, water may collect and form a lake covering what once had been a river valley.

In some locations, a lake behind a dam is used as a source of fresh water. A lake that is used to store water is called a reservoir (REHZ-uhr-VWAHR). Some dams are built solely for the purpose of creating a reservoir, and many communities rely on reservoirs for their water needs. Some reservoirs provide opportunities for boating and other recreational activities.

Dams have purposes in addition to providing hydroelectric power and forming reservoirs. Dams may also be built to control rivers that flow too fast or too unpredictably for boats to use them. These dams might separate a river into sections of different elevations, like steps in a staircase. To allow boats to climb or descend these steps and move to the next river section, locks are built at the dams. A **lock** is a section of waterway, closed off by gates, in which the water level is raised or lowered to move ships through. **G**

In addition to rivers with dams, locks are used in canals and rivers that connect lakes of different elevations. Locks are also used in canals that slope upward and then downward, such as the Panama Canal. The Panama Canal is dug into a strip of land between the Atlantic and Pacific oceans, allowing ships a handy shortcut.

CHECK YOUR READING Why do ships need to use locks?

DIFFERENTIATE INSTRUCTION

? More Reading Support

F What controls the flow of water on a river?
dams

G What allows boats to pass through a dam?
a lock

Alternative Assessment The Grand Coulee Dam in Washington is the largest U.S. hydroelectricity plant. Invite students to find out facts about the dam and to illustrate their findings in a poster or chart. Suggest that they diagram a cross-section showing the two water levels, the dam, and where flowing water spins a turbine.

In some cases dams cause problems as well as solve them. For example, in Egypt's Nile valley the giant Aswan Dam stopped floods that happened every year. However, the dam also blocked the flow of rich soil to the valley below the dam. The soil in the Nile valley was fertile for more than 4000 years. Yet today farmers need to add chemical fertilizers to grow their crops.

Dams can also cause problems for fish. When a dam blocks a river, salmon and steelhead cannot reach their breeding grounds. People have tried to solve this problem by installing fish ladder structures along dams that allow fish to climb up the river.

RESOURCE CENTER
CLASSZONE.COM
Learn more about dams.

Locks and Dams

Locks and dams control the flow of rivers and allow boats to pass through.

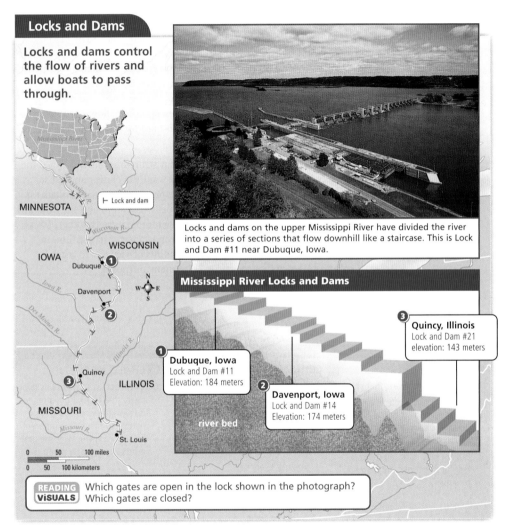

Locks and dams on the upper Mississippi River have divided the river into a series of sections that flow downhill like a staircase. This is Lock and Dam #11 near Dubuque, Iowa.

Mississippi River Locks and Dams

❸ **Quincy, Illinois**
Lock and Dam #21
elevation: 143 meters

❶ **Dubuque, Iowa**
Lock and Dam #11
Elevation: 184 meters

❷ **Davenport, Iowa**
Lock and Dam #14
Elevation: 174 meters

river bed

READING VISUALS Which gates are open in the lock shown in the photograph? Which gates are closed?

Chapter 2: **Freshwater Resources** 47 **C**

Before European settlers arrived, the Mississippi River was a major transportation route for Native Americans. They had built many cities along the river, the largest of which was Cahokia near what is now St. Louis, which was home to about 15,000 people. The first Europeans to explore the upper part of the river were the Jesuit missionary Jacques Marquette and the explorer Louis Joliet in 1673. They passed by the long-abandoned Cahokia ruins without ever seeing them.

Teach from Visuals

To help students interpret the visual showing locks and dams, ask:

• What river is shown here? *Mississippi River*

• What change occurs between locks and dams 11, 14, and 21? *the elevation of the water*

• How many locks and dams are there on the Mississippi between Dubuque and St. Louis? *15*

• What do the dams along the river do? *They change the river into a series of lakes flowing downhill like a staircase.*

• What do the locks do? *They partition the waterway into individual parts that are closed off and raised or lowered to allow ships to go from one elevation to the next.*

• What is in the lock? *a barge*

Ongoing Assessment

List the ways that water is used for human activities.

Ask: What are the ways that humans make use of water? *drinking, bathing, farming, aquaculture, manufacturing, recreation, transportation, energy*

READING VISUALS *Answer: The closed gates are on the left (top) side of the lock; the gates on the right side (bottom) are open.*

DIFFERENTIATE INSTRUCTION

More Reading Support

H What problems can dams cause? *block flow of rich soil, block fish from reaching their breeding grounds*

Inclusion Have students use stacks of books to create a model of the steplike structure of a series of locks and put a small model boat at one step. Then have them explain how they can move the boat up and down the set of locks without picking it up. (Students should slide the boat along each book, while pausing to raise each book to the next level.).

Alternative Assessment Have students create a collage of the ways that water is used from pictures in magazines.

Teach from Visuals

To help students interpret the photograph of the dammed-up waterway, ask:

- In which direction is water flowing? *from the top of the photograph toward the bottom*

- How do you think the landscape looked before the dam was built? *The lake didn't exist and instead was a continuation of the river. Tributaries probably entered the river within the area shown, such as from the upper left. The new river to the left of the dam didn't exist.*

- Why is the newly formed river full of rapids? *The water is flowing over rugged ground.*

Reinforce (the **BIG** idea)

Have students relate the section to the Big Idea.

 Reinforcing Key Concepts, p. 82

2.1 ASSESS & RETEACH

Assess

 Section 2.1 Quiz, p. 22

Reteach

Draw a circle on the board and divide it into sevenths. Then draw two lines radiating out from each section. Label the circle "Human Uses of Water." Have students do the following:

- Identify seven ways that people use water. Write their answers in the seven sections of the circle. *drinking, farming, industry, transportation, recreation, fish, and energy*

- Write two details about each type of usage on the lines radiating outward from each section.

Technology Resources

Have students visit **ClassZone.com** for reteaching of Key Concepts.

 CONTENT REVIEW

CONTENT REVIEW CD-ROM

This dammed-up waterway in Texas spilled around its dam during a flood. It formed a new channel that flows to the left of the dam.

Other changes to rivers can have unwanted effects. The placement of locks and the digging of a channel into a river bottom force a river to follow a constant path. In nature, however, a river changes its path depending on how much water it is carrying. It regulates itself by flooding during the wet season. As people alter rivers and build their homes closer to them, flooding becomes a problem. Some people argue that changing the natural flow makes it hard for a river to regulate itself, causing even more flooding.

People have different opinions about structures on rivers. In some places with hydroelectric dams, people want the dams removed so that salmon can swim upstream. Some people think that habitats for wildlife would be improved on the upper Mississippi and the Missouri rivers if the waters were allowed to flow more naturally. Others stress the value of hydroelectricity and the importance of navigation. In many cases the people with differing points of view try to reach compromises so that rivers can serve many purposes.

2.1 Review

KEY CONCEPTS

1. What are three ways that you directly use fresh water daily?

2. Identify a benefit and a possible disadvantage of aquaculture.

3. Explain why dams are both helpful to people and harmful to a river.

CRITICAL THINKING

4. **Predict** Do you think people will need more or less fresh water in the future? Why?

5. **Provide Examples** Explain how water is used in the manufacture of three products that you use every day.

**CHALLENGE

6. **Connect** In some towns near rivers, the federal government is buying houses and paying people to move to a different location. Explain why the government might be doing this.

ANSWERS

1. Sample answer: bathing/showering, brushing teeth, drinking

2. can supplement natural fish stocks; can cause pollution

3. They can make rivers easier to navigate, can control flooding, and can provide power. Dams can keep fish from swimming upstream and can change ecosystems.

4. As population grows, need grows.

5. Sample answer: A car requires water from time metal is mined until finished car is washed. Paper requires water to wash and mix pulp. The generation of electricity to manufacture things requires moving water.

6. By moving people out, it can allow rivers to flood with fewer harmful effects.

SKILL: VOLUME OF RECTANGULAR PRISMS

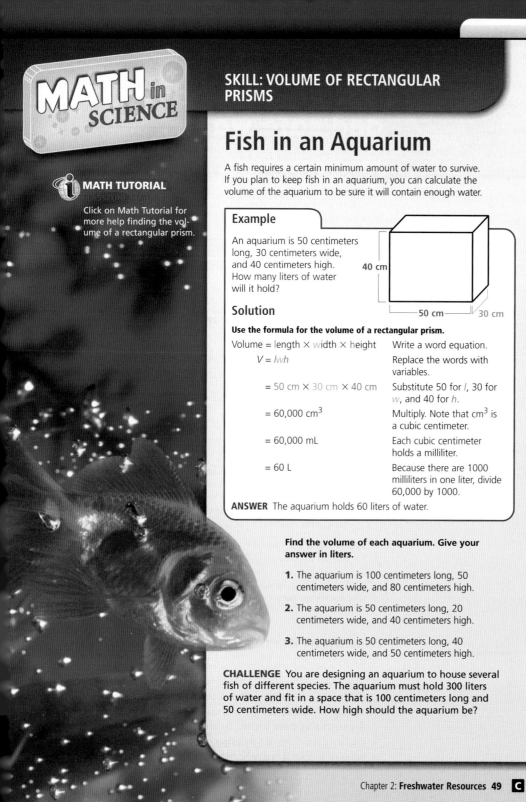

MATH TUTORIAL

Click on Math Tutorial for more help finding the volume of a rectangular prism.

Fish in an Aquarium

A fish requires a certain minimum amount of water to survive. If you plan to keep fish in an aquarium, you can calculate the volume of the aquarium to be sure it will contain enough water.

Example

An aquarium is 50 centimeters long, 30 centimeters wide, and 40 centimeters high. How many liters of water will it hold?

40 cm
50 cm
30 cm

Solution

Use the formula for the volume of a rectangular prism.

Volume = length × width × height	Write a word equation.
$V = lwh$	Replace the words with variables.
$= 50 \text{ cm} \times 30 \text{ cm} \times 40 \text{ cm}$	Substitute 50 for l, 30 for w, and 40 for h.
$= 60{,}000 \text{ cm}^3$	Multiply. Note that cm³ is a cubic centimeter.
$= 60{,}000 \text{ mL}$	Each cubic centimeter holds a milliliter.
$= 60 \text{ L}$	Because there are 1000 milliliters in one liter, divide 60,000 by 1000.

ANSWER The aquarium holds 60 liters of water.

Find the volume of each aquarium. Give your answer in liters.

1. The aquarium is 100 centimeters long, 50 centimeters wide, and 80 centimeters high.

2. The aquarium is 50 centimeters long, 20 centimeters wide, and 40 centimeters high.

3. The aquarium is 50 centimeters long, 40 centimeters wide, and 50 centimeters high.

CHALLENGE You are designing an aquarium to house several fish of different species. The aquarium must hold 300 liters of water and fit in a space that is 100 centimeters long and 50 centimeters wide. How high should the aquarium be?

Set Learning Goal

To calculate the volume of an aquarium by multiplying length by width by height

Present the Science

The number of fish that can survive in an aquarium depends on many factors, including the type of fish, the ratio of the surface area to the volume of water, the type of filtration system for getting rid of wastes, and the amount of food that is put into the tank.

Develop Algebra Skills

Remind students that the multiplication should be done one step at a time: first, the length by the width and then that answer by the height.

DIFFERENTIATION TIPS For visual learners, provide grid paper for them to align their math calculations. For the Challenge question, have students put the information they already know into the formula for volume.

Close

Ask students to make a generalization about the relationship between length, width, and height and volume. *Answer: The greater the length, width, and height, the larger the volume. Containers with different dimensions could have the same volume.*

 • Math Support, p. 109
• Math Practice, p. 110

Technology Resources

Students can visit **ClassZone.com** for practice doing volume problems.

 MATH TUTORIAL

ANSWERS

1. $100 \times 50 \times 80 = 400{,}000 \text{ cm}^3 = 400{,}000 \text{ mL} = 400 \text{ L}$

2. $50 \times 20 \times 40 = 40{,}000 \text{ cm}^3 = 40{,}000 \text{ mL} = 40 \text{ L}$

3. $50 \times 40 \times 50 = 100{,}000 \text{ cm}^3 = 100{,}000 \text{ mL} = 100 \text{ L}$

CHALLENGE $300{,}000 = 100 \times 50 \times h; \; h = \dfrac{300{,}000}{5000}; \; h = 60 \text{ cm}$

Set Learning Goals

Students will

• Explain how drinking water and wastewater are treated.

• Identify ways that fresh water can become polluted.

• Explain how water pollution can be prevented.

3-Minute Warm-Up

Display Transparency 12 or copy this exercise on the board:

Imagine that the water supply is cut off for one day. How would this affect your life and the lives of other people and organisms? *Sample answer: Water would not be available for drinking, cooking, or washing. Farmers would not be able to water their crops or give their animals water. Industries might lack water for production processes.*

3-Minute Warm-Up, p. T12

2.2 MOTIVATE

EXPLORE Concentration

PURPOSE To introduce students to the concept of a concentration and to give them an idea of the relative size of one part per million

TIP *10 min.* Tell students to notice the relationship between the concentration of food coloring and the amount of color they see in the water.

WHAT DO YOU THINK? *Add five drops of food coloring to 1000 mL of water. Then add a drop of that water to a new 1000 mL of water. You have five parts per thousand per thousand, or five ppm.*

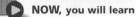

KEY CONCEPT

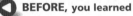

Society depends on clean and safe water.

◀ BEFORE, you learned	▶ NOW, you will learn
• Water supports life • Water is used in many ways	• How drinking water and wastewater are treated • How fresh water can become polluted • How water pollution can be prevented

VOCABULARY

concentration p. 51
sewage system p. 53
septic system p. 54
point-source pollution p. 54
nonpoint-source pollution p. 54

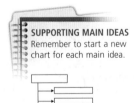
SUPPORTING MAIN IDEAS
Remember to start a new chart for each main idea.

EXPLORE Concentration

What is one part per million?

PROCEDURE

1. Pour 50 mL of water into the graduated cylinder. This is equal to 1000 drops of water.

2. Add one drop of food coloring to the water in the cylinder. This represents one drop of food coloring to 1000 drops of water, or one part per thousand.

3. Fill the eyedropper from the cylinder.

4. Empty the cylinder and pour 50 mL of new water into the cylinder. Add one drop from the eyedropper to the cylinder. The mixture now contains one part food coloring per thousand thousand parts water, or one part per million (ppm).

MATERIALS
• water
• graduated cylinder
• eyedropper
• food coloring

WHAT DO YOU THINK?
The amount of sodium found in clean spring water is five parts per million. How would you conduct this experiment to make a mixture of food coloring in water of five parts per million?

Treatment makes water safe for drinking.

When you wash your face or brush your teeth, do you ever wonder where the water comes from? It depends on where you live. In many places, water is pumped from a nearby well dug into an underground aquifer. If you live in a big city such as New York City or San Francisco, the water may travel a great distance to arrive at your sink. It is piped to the city from reservoirs that may be many miles away. Then it is stored in tanks or in a local reservoir before flowing through pipes to your home.

RESOURCES FOR DIFFERENTIATED INSTRUCTION

Below Level

UNIT RESOURCE BOOK
• Reading Study Guide A, pp. 85–86
• Decoding Support, p. 108

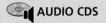 **AUDIO CDS**

Advanced

UNIT RESOURCE BOOK
Challenge and Extension, p. 91

English Learners

UNIT RESOURCE BOOK
Spanish Reading Study Guide, pp. 89–90

AUDIO CDS

• Audio Readings in Spanish
• Audio Readings (English)

Water comes from many different sources, so it may contain impurities or organisms that cause disease. For this reason, drinking water in larger systems is cleaned, or treated, before people can drink it.

Quality Standards

Fresh water can contain a variety of harmful substances and organisms. Certain substances and organisms may be present naturally, but others get into water because of pollution from human activity. Some of the impurities in water are safe for humans to drink in small quantities. However, when impurities reach high concentrations, they can harm people. A **concentration** is the amount of a substance that is in another substance. For example, soft drinks have a high concentration of sugar in water. Concentrations are often expressed in parts per million.

A government agency called the Environmental Protection Agency (EPA) sets standards for safe, clean drinking water. The EPA standards are guidelines for the protection of our natural water sources and the quality of the water that reaches our homes. Government agencies in states and local communities enforce laws based on the EPA standards.

The EPA lists standards for harmful organisms that can cause disease. It also lists safe levels for copper and certain other metals that can be found in water. In addition, the EPA checks for a variety of chemicals and harmful radioactive materials.

Your local water provider regularly tests the water to make sure it meets the EPA requirements. If any concentrations are higher than the EPA standards, the water must be treated. As a result, the United States has one of the safest, cleanest water supplies in the world.

CHECK YOUR READING How does a water provider know that it must treat water?

EPA Standards for Substances in Water

Substance	Common Source	Maximum Allowed, in Parts per Million
Copper	Natural deposits; household pipes	1.3
Cyanide	Various factories	0.2
Lead	Natural deposits; household pipes	0.015
Mercury	Natural deposits; refineries and factories; landfills; crop fields	0.002
Nitrite	Water running off fertilized fields; sewage leaks; natural deposits	1

Students test river water in West Virginia for pollutants.

51 C

DIFFERENTIATE INSTRUCTION

More Reading Support

A What is the amount of a substance that is in another substance called? *the concentration*

English Learners For this section, have students write the definitions for *concentration, point-source pollution,* and *non-point-source pollution* on the Science Word Wall. Students should also draw diagrams of septic systems and sewage systems.

Below Level Have students read aloud the concentrations from the visual, each time using the phrase, "Water is safe to drink as long as it contains no more than [X] parts per million of [substance Y]."

Teach Difficult Concepts

Some students may have a difficult time understanding the standards for drinking water. Explain that although one part per million seems tiny, some poisonous substances are dangerous in very small amounts. Also, the quantities listed are the maximums allowed, not necessarily the amounts that are present in all drinking water. Further explain that the list shown in the chart includes only a small number of the substances that can contaminate water.

Real World Example

Bacteria called giardia cause a disease known as "hiker's disease" because it is often contracted by drinking untreated water in the wilderness. To avoid this disease, hikers should purify water by boiling it, filtering it, or adding iodine tablets to it.

Teach from Visuals

To help students interpret the chart showing the EPA standards for substances in water, ask:

- How many parts per million of cyanide are allowed in drinking water? *0.2*
- Which substance has the lowest allowed concentration in drinking water? *mercury*
- Which substance has the highest allowed concentration? *copper*

Develop Critical Thinking

RANK Have students rank the substances in the EPA standards chart from most harmful to least harmful. If necessary, tell them that more dangerous substances have lesser values (lower numbers) of parts per million allowed. *mercury, lead, cyanide, nitrite, copper*

Ongoing Assessment

CHECK YOUR READING *Answer: The water provider tests the water and compares results with EPA standards.*

Teach from Visuals

To help students interpret the visual of water treatment and distribution, ask:

- What is the source of the fresh water? *a lake or river*

- Where does water go first when in the treatment plant? *through mixers*

- What is added in the mixers? *clumping agents and disinfecting chemicals*

- What do the clumping agents do? *make dirt and bacteria clump together*

- Where does the water go next? *to a clarifying pool*

- What is done to the water here? *Nothing; it just sits.*

- What happens in the clarifying pool? *Lumps of dirt sink to the bottom and are scraped away.*

- Where does the water go next? *through filters*

- What do the filters take out? *bits of dust and dirt*

- What is added to the water at the end? *chlorine*

- What does this substance do? *kills bacteria*

- Where does the water go next? *to huge storage tanks*

- Where does the water go next? *to people when they need it*

Teacher Demo

Make some water dirty by mixing in a variety of substances such as soil, pepper, ketchup, and vegetable oil. Pour some of the dirty water through a strainer containing sand and gravel, and collect the strained water in a clean container. Compare the strained water to the pre-strained dirty water and clean water. Have students describe what happened to the strained water.

Ongoing Assessment

Explain how drinking water is treated.

Ask: What are four major steps in treating water? *adding disinfecting chemicals and clumping agents, letting huge dirt clumps sink out, filtering out dust and dirt, killing bacteria with chlorine*

VISUALIZATION
CLASSZONE.COM

See a water treatment plant in action.

Treatment of Drinking Water

In a water treatment plant, thousands of gallons of water flow through a series of tanks, where the water is filtered and treated with chemicals to remove harmful substances and kill organisms. The major steps are chemical disinfection and the removal of dirt.

Water Treatment and Distribution

Water Source

① Water in a river or lake is piped to the treatment plant.

Storage and Distribution

⑥ The treated water leaves the plant. It is stored in huge water tanks so that there is plenty of water available when people need it.

Water Treatment Plant

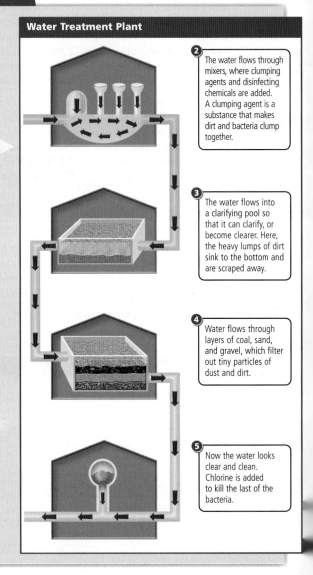

② The water flows through mixers, where clumping agents and disinfecting chemicals are added. A clumping agent is a substance that makes dirt and bacteria clump together.

③ The water flows into a clarifying pool so that it can clarify, or become clearer. Here, the heavy lumps of dirt sink to the bottom and are scraped away.

④ Water flows through layers of coal, sand, and gravel, which filter out tiny particles of dust and dirt.

⑤ Now the water looks clear and clean. Chlorine is added to kill the last of the bacteria.

DIFFERENTIATE INSTRUCTION

Below Level Have students give an oral summary of the process of water treatment. They can first summarize the process generally, then break it into its various steps.

Advanced The water treatment described on this page commonly is provided for water that comes from lakes and rivers. The treatment for groundwater is usually less extensive. Have students research how groundwater is treated at large community wells. Ask them to illustrate their findings in a diagram with captions and labels.

Wastewater is treated and released.

Wastewater is the water that runs down the drain. Before wastewater can be released back into the environment, it needs to be treated. Sewage and septic systems are two ways of treating wastewater.

Sewage System

A **sewage system** is a system that collects and treats wastewater from a city or a town. Sewage pipes carry wastewater from homes and businesses to a water treatment plant.

In the first part of treatment, wastewater is strained to remove large objects. Then the water is pumped into a tank, where it sits until the heaviest sludge sinks to the bottom. The sludge is taken away to decompose in another tank. Then chlorine is added to the water to kill the harmful bacteria. This process removes about half of the pollutants.

During the second part of the process, extra oxygen is pumped into the wastewater. The oxygen causes certain kinds of bacteria to grow in great numbers. These bacteria consume much of the sludge and oil that is still in the water. In other words, these tiny organisms help clean the water. More sludge also settles out, and grease is skimmed off the top. Chemicals clean the water one more time and remove any extra chlorine.

Wastewater Treatment

A sewage system collects and treats wastewater.

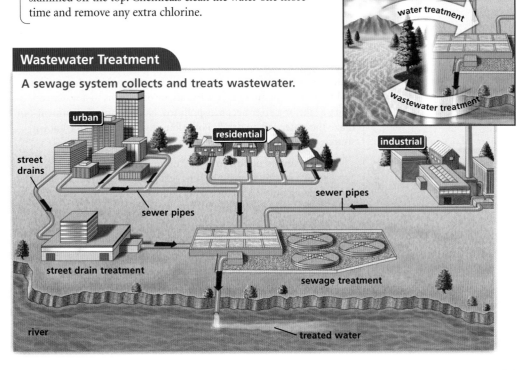

Water Use Cycle

water treatment

wastewater treatment

urban

residential

industrial

street drains

sewer pipes

sewer pipes

street drain treatment

sewage treatment

river

treated water

Chapter 2: **Freshwater Resources 53** **C**

? **More Reading Support**

B What does oxygen do in wastewater treatment? *causes the growth of bacteria that eat sludge and oil*

Advanced Have students research the treatment of wastewater in their community, and compare this information with that in the text and visual. If possible, obtain maps of local areas with streets marked, and ask students to identify the location of any treatment plants.

R Challenge and Extension, p. 91

Address Misconceptions

IDENTIFY Ask: How do bacteria affect people? If students answer only that bacteria make people sick, they may hold the misconception that all bacteria are harmful pathogens.

CORRECT Direct students to the diagram of wastewater treatment. Then have them read the last paragraph on the page, while paying attention to the role of bacteria in the treatment process.

REASSESS What is one way bacteria help people? *Certain kinds of bacteria consume some of the sludge and oil in sewage, helping to clean it before it goes back into the environment.*

Technology Resources

Visit **ClassZone.com** for background on common student misconceptions.

i **MISCONCEPTION DATABASE**

Teach from Visuals

To help students interpret the visual showing a sewer system, ask:

- From where does the water entering a sewage treatment facility come? *street drains, city sewers, residential area sewers, factories*

- Which parts of wastewater treatment are similar to treatment of drinking water? *letting materials settle out, adding chlorine to kill bacteria*

Integrate the Sciences

Helpful bacteria include those that live in the digestive systems of animals, including humans, and help to digest food. Other helpful bacteria live on the roots of plants and take nitrogen out of the air to make it available to the plants. Some soil bacteria are sources of antibiotics.

Ongoing Assessment

Learn how wastewater is treated.

Ask: What are the main steps of cleaning wastewater in a treatment plant? *straining and letting sludge settle out, adding chlorine, pumping in oxygen to help bacteria that eat sludge and oil grow, skimming grease and letting more sludge settle out, and adding chemicals*

To help students interpret the visual of a septic tank, ask:

- Where is a septic tank located? *underground*

- What parts make up a septic system? *septic tank and pipes that carry sewage into the tank and cleaner water out of the tank*

- What would happen if the sludge is not cleaned out periodically? *It would build up so much that wastewater couldn't be cleaned.*

Address Misconceptions

IDENTIFY Tell students to imagine that they are taking a walk. On the ground, they see a soda can, a banana peel, a candy wrapper, and a patch of oil. Ask: Which of these items are sources of pollution? If students do not answer "all of them," they may hold the misconception that biodegradable and natural materials are not pollution.

CORRECT Ask students if they would mind someone throwing any of these items into their yard. Explain that even biodegradable items, such as the banana peel, take a long time to break down.

REASSESS Ask: What is the best way to dispose of a bucket of dirty, soapy water after washing a car? *pouring it down the drain so that it goes to a treatment plant* What method of disposal would be polluting? *dumping it on the lawn or driveway*

Technology Resources

Visit **ClassZone.com** for background on common student misconceptions.

 MISCONCEPTION DATABASE

Develop Critical Thinking

INFER Have students infer how density plays a role in a septic tank. The densest solids sink to the bottom and form the layer of sludge. Oil and other materials less dense than water float to the top to form the layer of scum. Water settles between the two layers and is piped out of the septic tank.

Septic System

A **septic system** is a small wastewater system used by a home or a business. Septic systems are more common in lightly populated areas that do not have central sewage treatment centers. In a house with a septic system, wastewater is carried out through a pipe to an underground tank away from the house. The sludge, or thicker material, in the wastewater settles to the bottom. Much of this sludge is consumed naturally by bacteria, just as in the large sewage treatment plants. Sludge that remains has to be removed from the tank every few years.

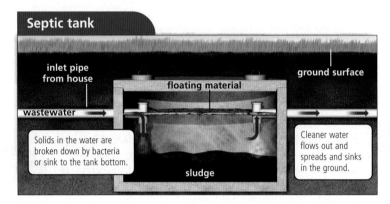

Septic tank

inlet pipe from house

floating material

ground surface

wastewater

Solids in the water are broken down by bacteria or sink to the tank bottom.

Cleaner water flows out and spreads and sinks in the ground.

sludge

Water pollution comes from many sources.

You have learned how fresh water is treated before we drink it. Unfortunately, treatment only works for water that has fairly low concentrations of harmful substances. Sometimes human activities add far too many minerals, chemicals, or organisms to a water supply. Then a lake or a river becomes polluted. No amount of treatment can make the water safe to drink. Pollution can come from one known source, or point, or it can come from many points.

- **Point-source pollution** is pollution that enters water from a known source. It might be sewage flowing from a pipe or chemicals spewing out of a factory. This pollution is easy to spot, and laws can be enforced to stop it.

- **Nonpoint-source pollution** is pollution whose source is hard to find or is scattered. Rain and gravity cause water to wash off streets, lawns, construction sites, and farms. This water, called runoff, can carry oil, gas, pesticides, chemicals, paints, and detergents into storm drains or over land and then to rivers and lakes. If you don't know exactly where pollution comes from, it is hard to enforce laws against it. For this reason, nonpoint-source pollution causes most water pollution.

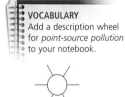

VOCABULARY
Add a description wheel for *point-source pollution* to your notebook.

C

DIFFERENTIATE INSTRUCTION

 **More Reading Support**

C What term describes pollution that enters water from a known source? *point-source pollution*

Below Level Make a chart on the board with the headings *Sewage System* and *Septic System*. Ask students to identify characteristics of both of these systems. Compare and contrast the characteristics and discuss how the systems are similar and how they are different.

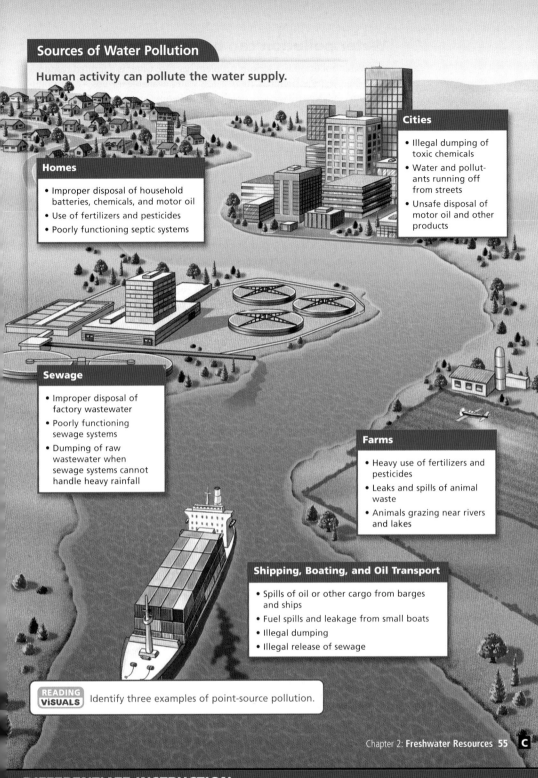

Sources of Water Pollution

Human activity can pollute the water supply.

Homes
- Improper disposal of household batteries, chemicals, and motor oil
- Use of fertilizers and pesticides
- Poorly functioning septic systems

Cities
- Illegal dumping of toxic chemicals
- Water and pollutants running off from streets
- Unsafe disposal of motor oil and other products

Sewage
- Improper disposal of factory wastewater
- Poorly functioning sewage systems
- Dumping of raw wastewater when sewage systems cannot handle heavy rainfall

Farms
- Heavy use of fertilizers and pesticides
- Leaks and spills of animal waste
- Animals grazing near rivers and lakes

Shipping, Boating, and Oil Transport
- Spills of oil or other cargo from barges and ships
- Fuel spills and leakage from small boats
- Illegal dumping
- Illegal release of sewage

READING VISUALS Identify three examples of point-source pollution.

DIFFERENTIATE INSTRUCTION

Below Level Have students create their own illustration to show the five major sources of water pollution. Have them write labels in their own words.

Teach from Visuals

To help students interpret the visual showing sources of water pollution, ask:

- What are five major categories of water pollution sources? *residential, urban, sewage, agriculture, and shipping*
- What causes urban pollution? *illegal dumping of toxic chemicals, runoff from streets, unsafe disposal of motor oil and other products*
- What is the plane doing? *spreading pesticides*
- How is the ship causing water pollution? *Oil or fuel is leaking into the water.*
- Why might a part of the river downstream be more polluted than a part of the river upstream? *Pollution accumulates in the river downstream from various sources upstream.*
- Which sources of pollution have you seen occurring? *Answers will vary. Students may have seen runoff, gasoline leaking from a boat motor, or wastewater coming from a pipe.*

T This visual is also available as T14 in the Unit Transparency Book.

Social Studies Connection

Display a map of your geographic region. Try to find a large-scale map that shows a relatively small area. U.S. Geological Service (USGS) topographic maps work well. Have students locate possible sources of water pollution in your area. Students might first find rivers and lakes on the map, then locate towns, farmland, and ports along the waterways. Compare those sources with those shown in the visual on this page.

Ongoing Assessment

READING VISUALS *Answers should include any three of the bulleted sources in the visual, such as improper factory wastewater disposal, poorly functioning sewage system, and dumping of raw wastewater.*

Teacher Demo

Draw dots with water-soluble marker on a sheet of paper. Spread out a sheet of chart paper. Have a student hold the sheet of paper with the dots on it over the chart paper. Use a spray bottle to spray water onto the paper with the dots until the water begins to run off onto the chart paper. Then take a squeeze bottle of food coloring and drip it onto the chart paper. Ask students whether these two sources of colored water on the chart paper model point-source or nonpoint-source pollution. *The marker dots model nonpoint-source pollution. The food coloring models point-source pollution.*

History of Science

Rachel Carson, a marine zoologist and former editor in chief for the U.S. Fish and Wildlife Service publications, wrote the book *Silent Spring* in 1962, which alerted the world to the dangers of pesticides. Her book inspired the environmental movement and caused state governments to begin to regulate the use of pesticides.

Ongoing Assessment

Identify ways that fresh water can become polluted.

Ask: Describe the two types of sources of pollution. *Point-source pollution is pollution that comes from a known source. Nonpoint-source pollution is pollution whose source is hard to find or is scattered.*

Explain how water pollution can be prevented.

Ask: What can industries do to reduce water pollution? *reuse and recycle chemicals and materials, dispose of toxins and byproducts responsibly*

CHECK YOUR READING *Pavement causes water to run off instead of sinking into the ground. Runoff can carry pollutants to streams and lakes.*

Water pollution can be prevented.

Water pollution is a serious problem because water is a limited resource. When water is polluted, there is less water available for use. Water pollution can also endanger people's health. People and businesses can do a number of things to prevent or reduce pollution of water.

Industry and Transportation Operators of factories and of vehicles that haul cargo can take a number of steps to prevent or reduce water pollution. For example, factories can maintain their pipelines and equipment to ensure that harmful chemicals are not leaking into the ground and contaminating groundwater. Transportation companies can inspect and repair their trucks, planes, and ships to prevent oil and fuels from leaking onto pavement or into water.

READING TiP
A toxic substance is one that is capable of causing harm to health.

Industry can prevent or reduce pollution by reducing the amount of toxic waste it generates. Factories can reuse and recycle chemicals and materials used in manufacturing. Companies can also provide ways for their customers to recycle or return certain products—such as used motor oil or batteries—that can pollute water if they are disposed of improperly.

In the construction industry, builders can design their projects to reduce the pollution that new construction can cause. Builders can use less pavement when they build parking areas for malls and office buildings. Less pavement reduces the amount of water that may run off and carry pollutants from cars and other sources to rivers and lakes. And measures to preserve open land, especially wetland areas, can protect a natural water cleansing system and reduce runoff.

CHECK YOUR READING How does pavement contribute to water pollution?

Pollution can make a lake or river dangerous or unusable. In many places, people are cleaning up and restoring freshwater resources.

DIFFERENTIATE INSTRUCTION

More Reading Support

D Can water pollution be prevented? *yes*

E What kind of chemicals should industry use less of to prevent pollution? *toxic chemicals*

Alternative Assessment Have students find examples of nontoxic cleaners and other products in stores, in catalogs, or on the Internet. If they need help getting started, direct students to search the Internet for environmental groups with sites that list nontoxic products. Make a class list on the board, and have students compare it with a list of products from home.

Agriculture Farming generates chemical and natural waste that can contaminate water. Farmers can follow practices that prevent or reduce pollution from agriculture. On farms with livestock, pastures used by cows and other grazing animals can be fenced off to keep animals away from streams and lakes. Keeping livestock away from water reduces pollution from animal waste. Farms that keep animals in structures can keep waste out of the water supply by storing and disposing of manure properly.

New techniques in farming can reduce pollution. Many farmers grow food without pesticides, which can be toxic and pollute water. The farmers fight insects and other pests by bringing in their natural enemies, such as ladybugs. To fertilize soil, the use of natural substances and the planting of certain crops can take the place of manufactured chemicals. Farming that does not use such chemicals is known as organic.

At home There are a number of things most people can do in their daily lives to prevent or reduce water pollution. People can take their old household chemicals to hazardous waste collection sites. Toxic chemicals should not be poured down the drain or onto the ground. Proper disposal and recycling of electronic devices such as computers can prevent toxic metals contained in them from reaching the water supply.

In shopping for food, consumers can choose organic products to support farming methods that don't use toxic pesticides. People can try to use nontoxic products in their homes. They can also stop using toxic pesticides and weed killers, as well as chemical fertilizers, on lawns and gardens.

These farmers in Vermont use organic methods to produce milk and ice cream.

2.2 Review

KEY CONCEPTS

1. How are EPA standards used to ensure a clean, safe supply of water?

2. What are two ways that wastewater is treated before it can be released?

3. What is the difference between point-source pollution and nonpoint-source pollution?

CRITICAL THINKING

4. **Compare and Contrast** How are sewage systems and septic systems alike? How are they different?

5. **Categorize** Categorize the following as point- or non-point-source pollution: small boat leaking oil; fish farm releasing wastes into a river; person dumping motor oil onto the ground.

⚠ CHALLENGE

6. **Compare** What parts of sewage and septic systems are similar to the way water is naturally cleaned by Earth's water cycle?

Chapter 2: **Freshwater Resources 57** **C**

Develop Critical Thinking

PROVIDE EXAMPLES Challenge students to give examples of ways that they can help to lower pollution levels. *Sample answer: use nontoxic cleaning substances, urge parents to refrain from using pesticides, recycle products*

Reinforce (the **BIG** idea)

Have students relate the section to the Big Idea.

 Reinforcing Key Concepts, p. 92

2.2 ASSESS & RETEACH

Assess

 Section 2.2 Quiz, p. 23

Reteach

Have students identify a river, stream, or lake in their area. Make a two-column chart on the board. Ask volunteers to identify possible sources of pollution that affect this water supply in one column and to suggest ways the water could be made cleaner in the other. *Sources of pollution should include residential or urban areas near the water, any nearby industry or agriculture, and any shipping or boating on the water. Ways of making water cleaner should include recycling and reducing the use of toxic materials by all of the possible sources of pollution.*

Technology Resources

Have students visit **ClassZone.com** for reteaching of Key Concepts.

 CONTENT REVIEW

 CONTENT REVIEW CD-ROM

ANSWERS

1. Water providers test water to see if it meets standards.

2. Sample answers: straining, adding chlorine, pumping in extra oxygen, skimming grease, removing extra chlorine

3. Point-source comes from a known, single place. Nonpoint-source comes from many scattered places.

4. They both settle sludge, use bacteria filtering. Sewage systems use several chemical, mechanical steps.

Septic systems are much smaller and are used for homes.

5. point or nonpoint; point; nonpoint

6. bacteria cleansing, filtering through ground, settling

Focus

PURPOSE To perform systematic testing procedures to identify pollutants in unknown water samples

OVERVIEW Students will use three kinds of indicator strips and perform systematic procedures to test water samples for pollution. They will test a pure distilled water sample, known samples containing common "pollutants," and four unknown mystery samples. Students will find

- certain substances change the color of indicator strips
- indicator strips can be used to determine the presence of certain unknown substances in water

Lab Preparation

- Use red and blue litmus strips for two samples and glucose strips for the third sample.
- Prepare as samples and unknowns a mild base using baking soda in water; a mild acid using vinegar in water; and sugar in water.
- Assign each of the three samples to represent chemical-, bacteria-, and pesticide-contaminated water.
- Prior to the investigation, have students read through the investigation and prepare their data tables, or you may wish to copy and distribute datasheets and rubrics.

 UNIT RESOURCE BOOK, pp. 111–119

SCIENCE TOOLKIT, F15

Lab Management

Divide students into pairs.

SAFETY Remind students to wear safety goggles and use care when handling the water samples, which contain chemicals.

Teaching with Technology

If probeware is available, use a pH sensor to determine the pH of the water samples.

CHAPTER INVESTIGATION

Monitoring Water Quality

OVERVIEW AND PURPOSE Water pollution in some amount seems to happen wherever people live. That's why water for home drinking is almost always treated. Proper water treatment depends on knowing what forms of pollution water contains. This two-part activity models the process of monitoring for water quality. In this investigation you will

- perform systematic testing procedures similar to those used to test the water supply
- test known samples for common "pollutants," and then identify unknown water samples based on those tests

▶ Procedure

PART ONE

1. Make a data table for Part One like the one shown on the sample **Science Notebook** page on page 59.

2. Test the three different known contaminated water samples with the three types of indicator strips. Dip one of each strip into the solution and instantly remove it. A positive result causes a color change. Make your observations of color changes exactly 30 seconds after dipping the strip. Observe and note the results in your table so you know what a positive result looks like for each contaminant. Do not reuse test strips. You need fresh strips for each water sample.

3. Test the pure distilled water with the three types of indicator strips and note your results.

PART TWO

1. A water-testing company has mixed up four water samples taken from the following locations: a runoff stream from an agricultural field, a river near a factory, a pond on a dairy farm, and a mountain stream. You will test the four unknown samples using the same procedures as above to determine which sample has which contaminant. You will then determine which location the sample most likely came from.

MATERIALS

- 8 each of three types of indicator strips
- watch with second hand
- "pesticide-contaminated" water sample
- "bacteria-contaminated" water sample
- "chemical-contaminated" water sample
- pure distilled water sample
- 4 unknown water samples

INVESTIGATION RESOURCES

 CHAPTER INVESTIGATION, Monitoring Water Quality
- Level A, pp. 111–114
- Level B, pp. 115–118
- Level C, p. 119

Advanced students should complete Levels B & C.

Writing a Lab Report, D12–13

Technology Resources

Customize this student lab as needed or look for an alternative. Print rubrics to assess student lab reports.

 Lab Generator CD-ROM

2. Make a data table for Part Two like the one shown on the sample **Science Notebook** below.

3. Test each water sample as in step 2, Part One. Record your observations as you test each unknown sample with each indicator strip. Note all color changes you observe.

4. Consult the chart you completed in Part One as you perform tests to determine which type of contaminant each unknown sample contains. From this information determine which location the sample probably came from.

> **Observe and Analyze** | Write It Up

1. **IDENTIFY CONTROLS** Why was it necessary to test the distilled water in Part One?

2. **IDENTIFY** Use what you have learned in this chapter to determine which location corresponds to the types of pollution you learned to identify in Part One.

3. **ANALYZE** Compare your testing results from the unknown water samples with your testing results from the known water samples. Are your results similar?

> **Conclude** | Write It Up

1. **COMPARE** How did your results in Part One compare with your results in Part Two?

2. **EVALUATE** What part of this investigation was the most difficult? Why?

3. **IDENTIFY LIMITS** What limitations does this type of testing pose for real-life water-quality technicians?

4. **APPLY** A runoff pool is contaminated with bacteria, chemicals, and pesticides. How would your water-testing results appear for a sample from this pool?

> **INVESTIGATE Further**

CHALLENGE Design a procedure to test unknown water samples that have numerous contaminants.

Monitoring Water Quality

Table 1. Positive Test Results of Known Water Samples

	Pure distilled water	Chemical-contaminated water	Bacteria-contaminated water	Pesticide-contaminated water
Indicator A				
Indicator B				
Indicator C				

Table 2. Test Results of Unknown Samples with Probable Locations

	Unknown #1	Unknown #2	Unknown #3	Unknown #4
Indicator A				
Indicator B				
Indicator C				
Type of Contaminant				
Location				

Chapter 2: **Freshwater Resources** 59 **C**

> **Observe and Analyze** | Write It Up

Sample data: Acids turn blue litmus paper red. Bases turn red litmus paper blue. Sugar causes glucose strips to change color (see package instructions). Distilled water will have no effect on any of the strips.

1. *Distilled water was a control so that you knew the indicator strips changed color only when a substance was added to the water.*

2. *distilled water—mountain stream; chemical-contaminated water—river near factory; bacteria-contaminated water—pond on dairy farm; pesticide-contaminated water—runoff from field*

3. *Each unknown sample should match to one of the known samples.*

> **Conclude** | Write It Up

1. *Sample answer: The color changes on the indicator strips showed that each sample in Part One matched only one sample in Part Two.*

2. *Sample answer: Sometimes it was difficult to tell if a strip had changed color or was just darker because it got wet.*

3. *Sample answer: Technicians who check water need to have very accurate testing materials and standards.*

4. *This sample should test positive for each of the three types of indicator strips.*

> **INVESTIGATE Further**

CHALLENGE Answers will vary but should include the use of a control and variables and should show an understanding of the testing procedure used in this investigation. Note that if students mix an acid and a base and actually test the mix with litmus, they may get a neutral reading. Mixing samples could be a valid real-world procedure, however.

Post-Lab Discussion

Discuss the limitations of the tests that the students used in terms of determining the safety level of the water for drinking. *Students used only a few tests. It is possible that other contaminants are contained in the water. Additional tests would need to be done to ensure that the water is safe to drink. Also, these tests don't indicate the number of parts per million of a contaminant.*

◉ Set Learning Goals

Students will

- Explain how overuse causes water shortages.
- Identify ways that water can be conserved.
- Describe how governments and organizations manage water use.

◐ 3-Minute Warm-Up

Display Transparency 13 or copy this exercise on the board:

Draw a diagram to show five major sources of water pollution. Label each source by name, and include one method that could be used to prevent it. *Diagram should show urban and residential areas (including sewage and septic), agriculture, industry, and shipping and boating.*

 3-Minute Warm-Up, p. T13

2.3 MOTIVATE

EXPLORE The Value of Fresh Water

PURPOSE To help students understand how much water costs in relation to a more valued product such as gasoline

TIP *10 min.*

- Students might need help finding the price of water. Direct them to local advertisements, or tell them the price of a half liter and let them calculate the liter price. If necessary, help students convert a price to a liter price.

- Ask students to observe and record the current prices of gasoline as advertised on gas station signs. Have students find the average of several prices and use that as the current price. Take note of prices yourself in case students are not aware of current prices.

WHAT DO YOU THINK? *Bottled water likely will cost about the same as or more than gasoline; water may have a greater value than students realized.*

◀ **BEFORE, you learned**

- Water is treated for drinking
- Wastewater is treated and released
- Pollutants contaminate the water supply

▶ **NOW, you will learn**

- How overuse causes water shortages
- How water can be conserved
- How governments and organizations manage water use

VOCABULARY

drought p. 61
desalination p. 66

EXPLORE The Value of Fresh Water

Does water cost more than gasoline?

PROCEDURE

1. Find out the current price of a liter of bottled water.

2. Find out the current price of a gallon of gasoline.

3. To calculate the price of gasoline in liters, multiply the price per gallon by 0.26.

WHAT DO YOU THINK?
- How do the prices of bottled water and gasoline compare?
- What do your results tell you about the value of drinking water?

MATERIALS
calculator

SUPPORTING MAIN IDEAS
Support the main idea of global water shortages with details and examples.

Water shortages are a global problem.

Most nations in the deserts of northern Africa and in the Middle East have severe water shortages. These are some of the driest regions on Earth, but their populations require more and more water as cities grow. Water that could be used to grow food is piped instead to the growing cities, where it is needed in homes and factories.

So how do people in these regions grow enough food? For the most part, they cannot. There is simply not enough water. Jordan imports, or brings in from other countries, about 91 percent of its grain. Israel imports about 87 percent, and Egypt, once a center of agriculture, imports 40 percent.

RESOURCES FOR DIFFERENTIATED INSTRUCTION

Below Level

UNIT RESOURCE BOOK
- Reading Study Guide A, pp. 95–96
- Decoding Support, p. 108

 AUDIO CDS

R **Additional INVESTIGATION,**
Desalination, A, B, & C, pp. 120–128;
Teacher Instructions, pp. 261–262

Advanced

UNIT RESOURCE BOOK
- Challenge and Extension, p. 101
- Challenge Reading, pp. 104–105

English Learners

UNIT RESOURCE BOOK
Spanish Reading Study Guide, pp. 99–100

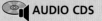 **AUDIO CDS**

- Audio Readings in Spanish
- Audio Readings (English)

All over the world, the water supply is dwindling. Populations are growing everywhere, and people must be fed. Farmers draw water from underground aquifers faster than the water can be replaced.

Even places that normally get regular rainfall can face water shortages. **Drought** (drowt) is a long period of abnormally low rainfall. Drought can destroy crops and dry up water supplies. Usually, trees can survive a dry period because their roots reach into the ground for water. However, severe drought can dry out entire forests. Dry trees are more vulnerable to disease, and wildfires are harder to control.

Overuse can cause water shortages.

As the world's population grows, usable fresh water is becoming scarcer in many places. Agriculture uses two-thirds of the world's available fresh water. Unfortunately, only half of that water reaches the roots of the plants. The other half is lost to evaporation and runoff.

Overuse of underground water can cause an aquifer to be depleted, or consumed faster than its water is replaced. In most places where crops require irrigation, farmers water their fields with groundwater. India is using twice as much water from its aquifers as can be replaced. In the United States, farmers are taking so much water that they are draining the huge Ogallala Aquifer. The problem is that underground stores of water can take thousands of years to refill. Draining an aquifer can also destroy it. When water is removed, the ground may settle and close up the storage space.

River water is also being overused in many places. So much water is being taken out that many major rivers now run dry for a large part of the year. These rivers include the Ganges River in South Asia, the Indus River in Pakistan, and the Colorado River in the southwestern United States. People in seven western states use water from the Colorado. As cities in these states have grown, the demand for the river water has increased.

MARYLAND

A bridge stands over a dried-out part of a reservoir during a drought in Maryland.

CHECK YOUR READING How has overuse of water affected some rivers?

DIFFERENTIATE INSTRUCTION

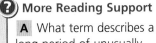 **More Reading Support**

A What term describes a long period of unusually low rainfall? *drought*

B How is the world's population affecting the water supply? *Growth makes fresh water scarcer.*

English Learners Within this section are sentences with a variety of introductory clauses and phrases. To help students identify the subject of the main clause in these sentences, help them separate introductory clauses from main clauses: "As the world's population grows, usable fresh water is becoming scarcer in many places." (The subject of the main clause is *water*.) Encourage students to use subordinate introductory clauses and phrases in their own writing.

Teach from Visuals

To help students interpret the photograph of the dried out reservoir, ask:

- Describe the level of the water in this reservoir if there had been no drought. *The water would be covering most or all of the exposed tan shoreline.*
- What are the narrow curving marks in the dry river bottom in the lower half of the photograph? *They are small eroded stream valleys that have formed in the exposed reservoir bed.*

Develop Critical Thinking

APPLY Challenge students to describe how they could develop an experiment to show the effects of drought on plants. *Sample answer: Grow some plants and then stop watering them. They should have a control plant that they continue to water.*

Real World Example

Several years of drought conditions in the western United States caused many wildfires to burn out of control. During the summer of 2002, 88,458 fires burned across 6,937,584 acres. During the summer of 2000, 122,827 fires burned 8,422,237 acres. The numbers of fires and the numbers of burned acres during both these summers were higher than the 10-year average ending in 2003, which was for 70,241 fires to burn 3,998,705 acres.

EXPLORE (the **BIG** idea)

Revisit "Internet Activity: Aquifers" on p. 39. Have students describe their observations.

Ongoing Assessment

Explain how overuse causes water shortages.

Ask: What results from overuse of underground water? *Water in aquifers is used faster than it is replenished. Draining an aquifer can destroy it.*

CHECK YOUR READING *Answer: Overuse has caused some rivers to run dry for parts of the year.*

Teach from Visuals

To help students interpret the pie chart, ask:

- Which three activities use the most water? *flushing the toilet, using a washing machine, showering*

- What percentage of the water that people use each day comes from the faucet? *12 percent*

- Which two uses make up half of the water used at home each day? *flushing the toilet, and either taking showers or using a washing machine*

- What repair could save 5 percent of the water that people use? *fixing leaking toilets*

Develop Number Sense

Arizona is a state that has a large amount of desert area. The population in 1920 was 334,162. In 1960 it was 1,302,161 and in 1990 it was 3,665,228. In 2000 the population was 5,130,632. Have students make a line graph showing these population statistics. Ask: Based on the slope in the line graph, how do you expect the population has changed since 2000? *It has probably increased.* Should residents of Arizona conserve water? *Yes, they will have more people to supply with a limited supply of water.*

Teacher Demo

Poke several holes in the sides of a container made of thin, clear plastic near the bottom. Close all but one of the holes by covering them with clay from the outside. Have a volunteer hold the container over a bucket. Fill the container with water. Slowly pour more water into the bucket. As you pour, remove the pieces of clay until the water is coming out of the holes at the bottom faster than you are refilling the container. Ask: How does this compare to the depletion of water in an aquifer? *The water is going out faster than it is going in, so the water level is going down.*

SUPPORTING MAIN IDEAS Record in your notes the important details about water conservation.

? **C**

These water-catching devices are used to collect and store rainwater in Hawaii.

Fresh water can be conserved.

Although water shortages are a serious problem, the situation is not entirely hopeless. Conserving can solve a big part of the problem. Conservation is action taken to protect and preserve the natural world. To conserve water means to use less of it.

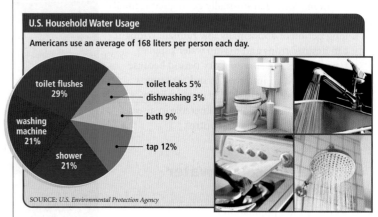

U.S. Household Water Usage

Americans use an average of 168 liters per person each day.

- toilet flushes 29%
- washing machine 21%
- shower 21%
- toilet leaks 5%
- dishwashing 3%
- bath 9%
- tap 12%

SOURCE: *U.S. Environmental Protection Agency*

The chart above shows how Americans use water each day. The amount that each American uses on average—168 liters—is higher than in most parts of the world. Note that 5 percent of the amount—more than 8 liters—is wasted by leaking toilets.

The Need for Conservation

Think about what you already know about the water cycle. When aquifers, lakes, and rivers are depleted—or used up faster than the water in them can be replaced naturally—available fresh water from those water supplies decreases. Because water supplies in many regions are being depleted, conservation is an urgent issue.

Much of the western United States is mostly desert, and yet the population in dry parts of the West is growing each year. What will happen if the aquifers and rivers that supply this region with water dry up? The less water that people use today, the more water there will be to use in the future.

Water shortages are an increasing problem around the world as the population grows in many regions. About half a billion people in 31 countries—mostly in the Middle East and Africa—currently face water shortages. By 2025, the number of people without enough water will increase five times, to about 2.8 billion people.

DIFFERENTIATE INSTRUCTION

? **More Reading Support**

C What can help to solve the water shortage? *conserving water*

Advanced Have students convert the percentages in the circle graph into numbers, using the total of 168 liters per person per day. *By rounding to the nearest ones digit, students will get a total of 167 instead of 168, as follows: toilet flush—49 liters; washing machine—35 liters; shower—35 liters; taps—20 liters; bath—15 liters; dish washing—5 liters; toilet leaks—8 liters*

Have students who are interested in the world's water crisis read the following article:

 Challenge Reading, pp. 104–105

Conservation Practices

People conserve water in three ways. The first way is to use less water. Some cities conserve their supply of water simply by repairing leaks in underground pipes. The second way is to reuse water. Many cities reuse treated wastewater for landscaping. The third method is to recycle water, or use water again for the same purpose.

Farmers can conserve water by using drip irrigation instead of spraying water. They can change the grooves in their fields so the water stays in the soil longer. Most industries can use water at least twice before returning it to a river or lake. For example, water used to cool machines can be recycled back through the same system.

At home, people can change their plumbing and their habits. Low-flow toilets and showerheads can cut water use in half. People conserve water by turning off the faucet while brushing their teeth, taking shorter showers, and running the dishwasher only when it is full. Leaking pipes and dripping faucets in homes cause huge amounts of water to be wasted. Repair and maintenance of plumbing systems would reduce water use greatly.

RESOURCE CENTER
CLASSZONE.COM
Learn more about water conservation.

CHECK YOUR READING What are the three main ways in which people conserve water?

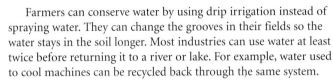
INVESTIGATE Water Conservation

How much water does a dripping faucet use?

① Adjust a faucet so that water drips slowly.

② Set a container under the faucet and collect the dripping water for five minutes.

③ Turn off the faucet. Use the graduated cylinder to measure how much water dripped. Record your results in milliliters.

④ Multiply the amount by 12 to determine how much water would drip in an hour. Then divide that number by 1000 to convert your result to liters.

WHAT DO YOU THINK?
• How much water would one leaky faucet waste in a day?
• In a town with 2000 houses with one leaky faucet in each, how much water would be wasted each day?

CHALLENGE How could you combine your results with those of your classmates to make the results more reliable?

SKILL FOCUS
Measuring

MATERIALS
• water faucet
• container
• funnel
• 100 mL graduated cylinder

TIME
20 minutes

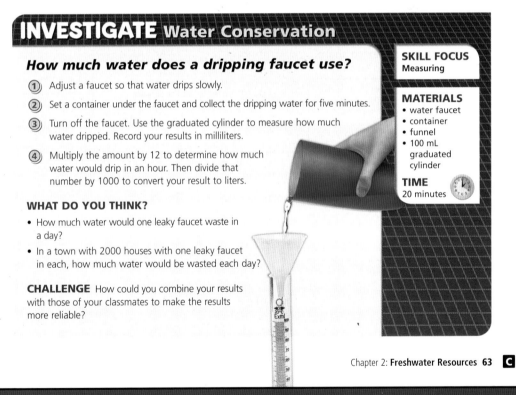

Chapter 2: Freshwater Resources 63 **C**

INVESTIGATE Water Conservation

PURPOSE Collect and measure dripping water for five minutes and calculate the amount of water lost in one hour.

TIPS *20 min.* Pair below-level students with students who have good math skills for doing the calculations. Have students use care when adjusting the faucet.

WHAT DO YOU THINK? *Answers will vary, but students should see that even a seemingly minor drip can waste a lot of water over time when it is multiplied by many households.*

CHALLENGE *You could take an average of the classmates' results.*

 Datasheet, Water Conservation, p. 102

Technology Resources

Customize this student lab as needed or look for an alternative. Print rubrics to assess student lab reports.

Lab Generator CD-ROM

Teaching with Technology

Have students use calculators to make their calculations for "Investigate Water Conservation."

Ongoing Assessment

Identify ways that water can be conserved.

Ask: How does industry conserve water? *uses it more than once*

CHECK YOUR READING *Answer: Use less water, such as by repairing leaks in plumbing, reusing, and recycling.*

DIFFERENTIATE INSTRUCTION

 **More Reading Support**

D How can farmers conserve water? *by using drip irrigation*

Alternative Assessment Have students draw a graduated cylinder to show the amount of water collected in five minutes and another to show the amount of water that would be collected in one hour.

Teach from Visuals

To help students interpret the map, ask:

- Which four areas share the water of the Rio Grande? *Texas, New Mexico, Colorado, and Mexico*

- What are some of the large population centers that use water from the Rio Grande? *Albuquerque, El Paso, Ciudad Juarez, Presidio*

- What sometimes happens to the river between El Paso and Presidio? *It dries up.*

Teach Difficult Concepts

Some students may have a difficult time understanding the problems with sharing the water from the Rio Grande, which are presented in somewhat simplified terms. Point out these problems:

- Regional population growth has outdated the international agreement, or compact.

- The compact tells which percentage of the water each state can use, and a fixed amount, which already is not enough, is given to Mexico.

- Questions exist about whether the water rights of Native American tribes are included in the compact and where the water to sustain the habitat of an endangered fish species living in the Rio Grande will come from.

People can balance water needs and uses.

People around the world have different views about how water should be used. Americans in the hot Southwest might want water for swimming pools and lawns. Developing countries need water to prevent disease and grow food. In some places, farmers use river water before it can reach others downstream. Some industries want water to make products.

As water becomes scarcer, the arguments become more serious. Public officials and experts can help manage water use and enforce fair laws. For example, what happens when a river flows from one state into another or across a national border? In such a situation, people must agree to share the water rights.

The Rio Grande flows through two states and then between Texas and Mexico. The water in this river is an international issue. In 1939 a legal agreement was made between the states of Colorado, New Mexico, and Texas, and between the United States and Mexico. It listed how much water each region could take.

In the past, water from the Rio Grande was used for farming. However, cities along the river are growing rapidly. All the cities need more water from the Rio Grande, and every year they will need more. The international agreement no longer solves this urgent problem. American and Mexican officials are looking for new solutions.

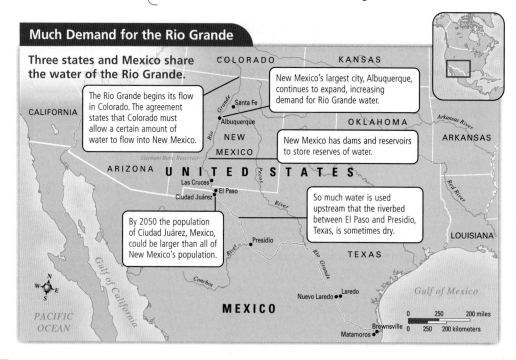

Much Demand for the Rio Grande

Three states and Mexico share the water of the Rio Grande.

The Rio Grande begins its flow in Colorado. The agreement states that Colorado must allow a certain amount of water to flow into New Mexico.

New Mexico's largest city, Albuquerque, continues to expand, increasing demand for Rio Grande water.

New Mexico has dams and reservoirs to store reserves of water.

So much water is used upstream that the riverbed between El Paso and Presidio, Texas, is sometimes dry.

By 2050 the population of Ciudad Juárez, Mexico, could be larger than all of New Mexico's population.

DIFFERENTIATE INSTRUCTION

?) More Reading Support

E What must people do when a river flows from one state to another? *share the water rights*

Advanced Challenge students to make comparisons between the problems of depleted aquifers and the issues over the Rio Grande and to identify the similarities and differences. Alternatively, have students investigate the Rio Grande issue more fully and prepare a debate about it.

R Challenge and Extension, p. 101

Shortages

When there is not enough water, crops will not grow. And when the crops fail to grow, there is not enough food to eat. The Middle East countries that import most of their grain are, in a way, importing water. Billions of tons of water are used to grow the imported grain.

International organizations help out countries where drought and floods have destroyed the crops. For example, in 2002 the World Food Programme alerted the world to a serious lack of food in southeast Africa. The United Nations agencies arranged for food aid. The shrinking of Lake Chad has also caused hardship for many Africans.

In the future, people may solve some of the problems by sharing water around the world. The governor of Alaska has suggested an undersea pipeline. This line would be between 2200 kilometers (1360 mi) and 3400 kilometers (2100 mi) long. Through this pipe, thousands of liters of fresh water would flow from Alaska to California. Some people have also suggested selling Great Lakes water to Japan. Many people in states and Canadian provinces around the lakes have strongly objected, because they think removing water could damage the lakes.

 How can Alaska help solve a water shortage in California?

Pollution

Where water flows across the boundaries of nations, pollution can flow across as well. One example of this problem is the Danube River in Europe. This river begins in the Black Forest in Germany. It empties into the Black Sea on the coast of Romania. As it flows through the cities of Vienna, Budapest, and Belgrade, more and more pollution is added to the water. Seventeen countries border either the Danube River or the Black Sea. To protect the river and the sea, as well as to manage use of the river water, 11 nations made an agreement among themselves and the European Union. They agreed to cooperate to prevent pollution of the water and to conserve and use water from the Danube sensibly. They also agreed to conserve and protect groundwater.

Some national and international water pollution problems are hard to solve. States in the northeastern United States are concerned about acid rain. Particle pollution from factories to the west is collected in clouds. Then the wind blows the clouds across the Eastern states, and acid rain falls in lakes and rivers that are far from the source. The acid rain can kill plants, as well as fish and other animals.

This satellite photograph of Lake Chad in Africa was taken in 1973.

A recent photograph shows how much the lake has shrunk.

Teach from Visuals

To help students interpret the photographs of Lake Chad in Africa, ask:

- These photographs use false colors to distinguish between different kinds of materials. What do you think red stands for? *vegetation*

- How do the two photographs look different? *The more recent one has much more red (vegetation) where water used to be.*

History of Science

Scientists have used models and climate data to understand what has happened to Lake Chad. The lake decreased in size by 30 percent between 1966 and 1975. Five percent of the decrease was due to irrigation, and the rest was due to a drier climate. Between 1983 and 1994, irrigation increased in the area, and accounted for 50 percent of the decrease in the size of the lake during that period. In addition, the lake has been filling up with windblown Sahara sand.

Ongoing Assessment

Describe how governments and organizations manage water use.

Ask: How do some international organizations help with water-related problems? *They help out after floods or droughts by providing food aid.*

 Answer: There has been a proposal to ship water from Alaska to California through a pipeline.

DIFFERENTIATE INSTRUCTION

 More Reading Support

F What is one type of pollution in the northeastern United States that is caused by factories farther west? *acid rain*

Additional Investigation To reinforce Section 2.3 learning goals, use the following full-period investigation:

R Additional **INVESTIGATION,** Desalination, A, B, & C, pp. 120–128, 261–262 (Advanced students should complete Levels B and C.)

Below Level Show students images, available via the Internet, books, and magazines, of forests affected by acid rain. Have them describe the source of the pollution.

Teach from Visuals

To help students interpret the visual on desalination, ask:

- How are the water and salt separated from each other? *When the water is heated, it evaporates into water vapor and the salt is left behind.*

- What happens to the water vapor? *It condenses and falls into collection troughs*

EXPLORE (the BIG idea)

Revisit "What Happens When Salt Water Evaporates?" on p. 39. Have students relate their results to the process of desalination.

Reinforce (the BIG idea)

Have students relate the section to the Big Idea.

 Reinforcing Key Concepts, p. 103

2.3 ASSESS & RETEACH

Assess

 Section 2.3 Quiz, p. 24

Reteach

Set out two one-liter bottles of water on a table. Tell students that they are the members of a committee.

- They must decide how to divide up the water among the students.

- As they decide, have them compare the parts of the model (the water, the students, the committee) with what they learned in this section.

Technology Resources

Have students visit **ClassZone.com** for reteaching of Key Concepts.

 CONTENT REVIEW

 CONTENT REVIEW CD-ROM

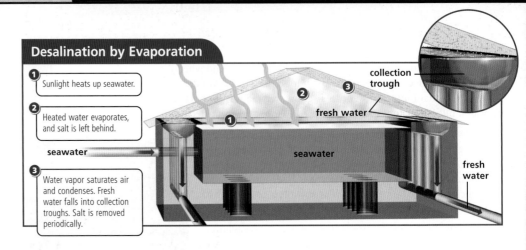

Desalination by Evaporation

1 Sunlight heats up seawater.

2 Heated water evaporates, and salt is left behind.

3 Water vapor saturates air and condenses. Fresh water falls into collection troughs. Salt is removed periodically.

collection trough

fresh water

seawater

seawater

fresh water

 VOCABULARY
Add a description wheel for *desalination* in your notebook.

New Sources

Can people find new sources of fresh water? The answer, at first, seems obvious. Just remove the salt from seawater. In dry regions, such as Israel, Lebanon, and some coastal towns in California and Florida, people are trying to obtain fresh water this way. The process of removing salt from ocean water is called **desalination** (dee-SAL-ih-NAY-shun). Some treatment plants use a method similar to the natural water cycle. Salt water is evaporated, and salt is left behind. Then water vapor is condensed, or returned to liquid form, as fresh water.

If this process were easy and inexpensive, water shortages might never happen. However, desalination can cost five times as much as normal water treatment. Therefore, it is not a solution that will work for most countries. As technology improves, the cost may go down.

Another possible source of fresh water is icebergs. Icebergs contain millions of liters of fresh water. However, the process of towing an iceberg to a city before it melts is too expensive to be practical.

2.3 Review

KEY CONCEPTS

1. What is drought and what problems does it cause?

2. How are aquifers and rivers being depleted?

3. Name two ways to help prevent water shortages.

CRITICAL THINKING

4. **Connect** Draw up a plan that suggests three ways to conserve water at your school. Be sure your ideas are practical, and explain how you might convince people to make the changes.

5. **Infer** Why do you think some people object to building a water pipeline from Alaska to California?

❂ CHALLENGE

6. **Synthesize** Think about what you have learned about national and international water issues. Then think about what you know about aquifers. What usage problems might occur when one aquifer lies under two countries? How might people solve any problems that arise?

ANSWERS

1. a shortage of rainfall over time; can ruin crops and dry up water supplies

2. overuse by growing populations and too much irrigation

3. Sample answer: not watering lawns, better irrigation methods, efficient plumbing, reusing water

4. Sample answer: check toilets and taps for efficiency; groundskeepers use less water; campaign for everyone not to run water when brushing teeth

5. pipeline might disrupt environment; could deplete Alaska's water; might be too expensive

6. One country might use more than its share. Countries could agree to use fair shares and to set the same conservation standards.

Water and Farming

Farmers have used irrigation, the process of supplying water to crops, for at least 7000 years. Today, about 60 percent of the fresh water used in the world goes for irrigation. However, about one-third of this water does not reach the crops. Some of it runs off the field. By building ditches and ponds, farmers can capture runoff water and pump it back into a field.

Irrigation water can also evaporate before crops can use it. Farmers can reduce this loss by understanding how changes in air temperature, relative humidity, and wind speed affect the evaporation rate. Then farmers can adjust when and how much they irrigate.

Spray Irrigation

In some systems, sprinklers as much as 400 meters (1300 ft) long spray water on crops. Since the water is sprayed into the air, evaporation loss can be high. Spray irrigation is used for many crops in the western United States. Spraying at night can reduce evaporation loss.

Drip Irrigation

In drip irrigation, water bubbles out of pipes lying on or just above the ground throughout a field or orchard. The water reaches the ground quickly and in small amounts, so little is lost to runoff or evaporation. Farmers growing fruits and vegetables frequently use this system.

Flood Irrigation

Many farmers send water through small ditches between rows of crops, or sometimes farmers flood entire fields. Compared with other systems, flooding results in higher losses from runoff. Flooding is commonly used by rice farmers in eastern Asia.

EXPLORE

1. **ANALYZING** Compare the amounts of labor, machinery, and water used in each irrigation system. Which system uses water most efficiently? In what climate regions is this most important? Why would farmers choose a system that uses water less efficiently?

2. **CHALLENGE** Create a model of a flood irrigation system. Use dirt in a pan, with toothpicks to represent crops. Make ditches that send water evenly throughout the "field." As you pour water into your system, note any soil loss that may occur. How can you fix this problem?

Set Learning Goal

To explore the ways that fresh water is used by farmers

Present the Science

In the United States about 80 percent of the fresh water is used for farming, and in many western states the figure is 90 percent or even higher.

Discussion Questions

- Ask: How does the amount of water used for irrigation compare with the amount used in other ways? *More water is used for irrigation than for anything else.*

- Ask: What is the problem with using flood irrigation? *A lot of water is lost to runoff.*

- Ask: What is the problem with using sprinkler systems? *A lot of water evaporates into the air.*

- Ask: What is the advantage of using drip irrigation? *Very little is lost.*

DIFFERENTIATION TIP For tactile learners, spray a fine water mist into the air over a paper towel. Ask: What happens to the water that does not land on the towel? *It evaporates.*

Close

Ask students to summarize what they have learned about water and farming. *Sample answer: More than half of the fresh water used in the world goes for irrigation. Flood and spray irrigation result in the loss of a lot of water. Drip irrigation is the most efficient.*

EXPLORE

1. *ANALYZING Drip irrigation is most efficient generally because it uses only what is needed, and little water is lost to evaporation and runoff. This would be especially important in hot, dry climates where water evaporates quickly and may be in short supply or on steep slopes where water runs off quickly. Farmers might use less efficient methods because they are cheaper and because there are no restrictions on how much water they can use.*

2. *CHALLENGE Use less water—modeling conservation practices such as irrigating at night. Add water more slowly, over a longer time period.*

BACK TO

the BIG idea

Have students look back at the photograph on pp. 38–39. Ask them to use the photograph to summarize what they've learned about the uses of fresh water; the need for a clean, safe water supply; and threats of water shortages. *Water is used for farming, industry, transportation, recreation, fisheries, aquaculture, energy, and living organisms. Pollution can harm water, so water must be treated to be safe for drinking. Drought and overuse can cause water shortages.*

◐ KEY CONCEPTS SUMMARY

SECTION 2.1
Ask: Which of the listed uses of fresh water affects your life? *all of them*

SECTION 2.2
Ask: What happens to water from a lake or river before it gets to your faucet? *Water is treated so that dirt and bacteria clump together and settle out. Water is flowed into a clarifying pool where heavy lumps of dirt sink to the bottom and are scraped away. Then the water is filtered to remove tiny particles. Chlorine is added to kill remaining bacteria. The cleaned water is stored and piped to homes and businesses.*

SECTION 2.3
Ask: What caused the change in Lake Chad? *too much water has been taken out, the climate is becoming drier, windblown sand is filling up the lake*

Ask: How can people conserve water? *by being aware of how they use water and taking steps to use or waste less, for example, by fixing leaks*

Review Concepts

- Big Idea Flow Chart, p. T9
- Chapter Outline, pp. T15–T16

---

2 Chapter Review

the BIG idea

Fresh water is a limited resource and is essential for human society.

CONTENT REVIEW
CLASSZONE.COM

◐ KEY CONCEPTS SUMMARY

2.1 Fresh water is an essential resource.
Fresh water is essential for life and is used for many human activities.

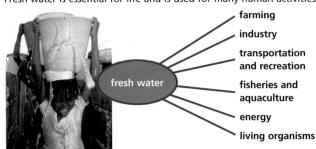

fresh water
- farming
- industry
- transportation and recreation
- fisheries and aquaculture
- energy
- living organisms

VOCABULARY
irrigation p. 43
aquaculture p. 45
dam p. 46
lock p. 46

2.2 Society depends on clean and safe water.
Water is treated for safe drinking. Pollution can harm the water supply.

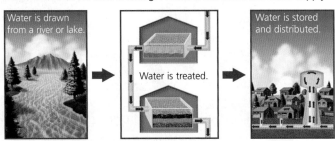

Water is drawn from a river or lake.

Water is treated.

Water is stored and distributed.

VOCABULARY
concentration p. 51
sewage system p. 53
septic system p. 54
point-source pollution p. 54
nonpoint-source pollution p. 54

2.3 Water shortages threaten society.
Drought and overuse can cause water shortages.

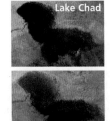
Lake Chad

Americans use an average of 168 liters per person each day.

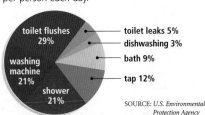
- toilet flushes 29%
- washing machine 21%
- shower 21%
- toilet leaks 5%
- dishwashing 3%
- bath 9%
- tap 12%

SOURCE: U.S. Environmental Protection Agency

VOCABULARY
drought p. 61
desalination p. 66

 68 Unit: Earth's Waters

Technology Resources

Have students visit **ClassZone.com** or use the CD-ROM for a cumulative review of concepts.

 CONTENT REVIEW

 CONTENT REVIEW CD-ROM

Engage students in a whole-class interactive review of Key Concepts. Edit content as you wish.

 POWER PRESENTATIONS

Reviewing Vocabulary

Use words from the box below to answer the next nine questions.

septic system	nonpoint-source pollution	desalination
concentration	sewage system	point-source pollution
aquaculture	drought	irrigation

1. Which word means "fish farming"?

2. What is the term for a method farmers use to bring water to their fields from rivers and aquifers?

3. Which term can be used to describe the amount of a harmful substance in fresh water?

4. Which term would be used for waste flowing from a factory pipe?

5. Select the term for what a city uses to collect and treat wastewater.

6. Which term would describe oil running off from a parking lot during a rainstorm?

7. What word describes a period when there is little or no rainfall?

8. What process is used to obtain fresh water from seawater?

9. Which term describes a method for treating home wastewater in an underground tank?

Reviewing Key Concepts

Multiple Choice Choose the letter of the best answer.

10. Which type of irrigation pours water through canals and waterways?
    a. flood irrigation   c. drip irrigation
    b. spray irrigation   d. reservoir irrigation

11. A channel dug to allow boats to travel from one river to another is an example of a
    a. canal   c. reservoir
    b. lake   d. sewage system

12. A section of a waterway in which ships are raised or lowered is called a
    a. turbine   c. dam
    b. fish ladder d. lock

13. Concentrations of substances are often expressed as
    a. whole parts
    b. parts per million
    c. parts per thousand
    d. parts per hundred

14. In a sewage plant, sludge and oil are consumed by
    a. chlorine   c. bacteria
    b. sand   d. filters

15. In a sewage system, what is added to kill harmful bacteria?
    a. chlorine   c. bacteria
    b. sand   d. soap

16. The term for pollution that can be traced to a specific location is
    a. water pollution
    b. point-source pollution
    c. nonpoint-source pollution
    d. runoff pollution

Short Answer Write a short answer to each question.

17. How are aquifers depleted?

18. How are EPA standards used to protect fresh water?

19. How does the practice of organic farming help prevent water pollution?

20. What problems do people have sharing water from the Rio Grande?

Reviewing Vocabulary

Sample Answers:

1. aquaculture
2. irrigation
3. concentration
4. point-source pollution
5. sewage system
6. nonpoint-source pollution
7. drought
8. desalination
9. septic system

Reviewing Key Concepts

10. a
11. a
12. d
13. b
14. c
15. a
16. b
17. by overuse from cities and towns and irrigation
18. Water providers test water and take action to treat water or prevent the pollution if EPA standards are exceeded.
19. Because it does not use pesticides and chemical weed killers, toxic substances do not run off into the water system.
20. There is more demand for water than the river can supply. People upstream use the water; this leaves too little for those living downstream.

ASSESSMENT RESOURCES

UNIT ASSESSMENT BOOK
- Chapter Test A, pp. 25–28
- Chapter Test B, pp. 29–32
- Chapter Test C, pp. 33–36
- Alternative Assessment, pp. 37–38

SPANISH ASSESSMENT BOOK
Spanish Chapter Test, pp. 157–160

Technology Resources

Edit test items and answer choices.

 Test Generator CD-ROM

Visit **ClassZone.com** to extend test practice.

 Test Practice

Thinking Critically

21. Colorado, Utah, Arizona, Nevada, California (USA), and Mexico
22. irrigation, household use, industry
23. California probably wants Arizona to use less water. Arizona probably says it has first rights to the water.
24. Each city or region will want more water. San Luis will say it's not fair that the water gets used up before it gets to Mexico. The cities need to agree to share the water and use less.
25. Students may think that the level of population should determine how much a state gets, therefore southern California would get the most.
26.

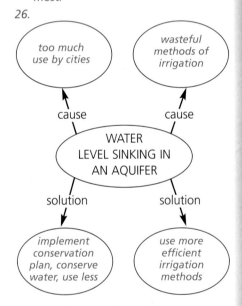

too much use by cities

wasteful methods of irrigation

cause   cause

WATER LEVEL SINKING IN AN AQUIFER

solution   solution

implement conservation plan, conserve water, use less

use more efficient irrigation methods

the **BIG** idea

27. Students probably learned of many ways they "use" water that they had not known (food growing, product manufacturing, leaks).
28. Diagrams should include labels that indicate the treating of water and wastewater, water storage, and its return to the environment.

UNIT PROJECTS

Check to make sure students are working on their projects. Check schedules and work in progress.

 Unit Projects, pp. 5–10

Thinking Critically

Use the map to answer the next five questions.

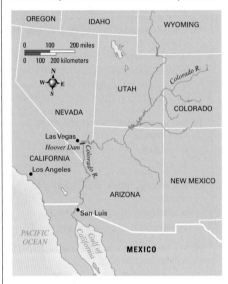

The Colorado River runs from Colorado to the Gulf of California. In California water is needed for 17 million people and also to irrigate 3642 square kilometers (900,000 acres) of farmland. The Colorado provides 60 percent of this water.

21. **OBSERVE** Through which states and countries does the Colorado River flow?

22. **EXAMPLES** What are three ways in which water from the Colorado is probably used?

23. **INFER** What conflicts probably exist between the states of California and Arizona?

24. **PREDICT** As populations grow in Las Vegas, southern California, and San Luis, Mexico, what problems will arise? How can they be solved?

25. **CONNECT** Do you think states should receive equal shares of the water in the Colorado River? Explain your answer.

---

26. **IDENTIFY CAUSE** Copy the concept map below, and complete it by adding two causes of, and two solutions to, the problem of the water level of an aquifer sinking.

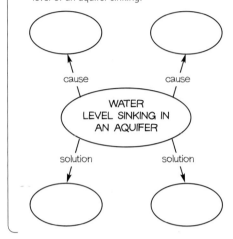

cause   cause

WATER LEVEL SINKING IN AN AQUIFER

solution   solution

the **BIG** idea

27. **PROVIDE EXAMPLES** Look again at the photograph on pages 38–39. Now that you have finished the chapter, how would you change your response to the question on the photograph?

28. **SEQUENCE** Draw a diagram of the path that fresh water travels before and after humans use it. Show where freshwater comes from, how it is treated, how it arrives at our homes, how it leaves our homes as wastewater, how it is treated again, and how it reenters the water cycle.

UNIT PROJECTS

If you need to do an experiment for your unit project, gather the materials. Be sure to allow enough time to observe results before the project is due.

MONITOR AND RETEACH

If students have trouble applying the concepts in Chapter Review items 21–25, suggest that they review the text and map on p. 64, which presents a similar situation. Have them compare the Rio Grande and Colorado River issues. Also, refer them to the visual on p. 62.

Students may benefit from summarizing one or more sections of the chapter.

 Summarizing the Chapter, pp. 129–130

Standardized Test Practice

For practice on your state test, go to . . .
TEST PRACTICE
CLASSZONE.COM

Analyzing a Graph

The line graph below shows the amount of a chemical found in a stream. During the period shown, a factory opened and released water into the stream. Later, a wastewater treatment plant opened and treated water from the factory before it entered the stream. Study the graph and use it to answer the first six questions below.

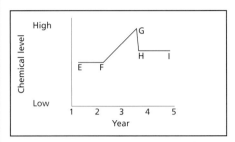

1. Which phrase best describes the concentration of the chemical at Point E?

a. low
b. medium
c. somewhat high
d. very high

2. A new factory opens during year 2. What immediately happens to the concentration of the chemical?

a. It does not change.
b. It decreases sharply.
c. It decreases slightly.
d. It increases sharply.

3. Which point probably marks when a new wastewater treatment plant opened?

a. E
b. F
c. G
d. I

4. Point-source pollution comes from a known source. Which amount is point-source pollution?

a. the difference between E and F
b. the difference between F and G
c. the difference between G and H
d. the difference between H and I

5. How do the concentrations of E and I compare?

a. I is higher.
b. I is lower.
c. I and E are equal.
d. The graph does not include enough data to compare concentrations.

6. Which statement best explains the data on the graph?

a. The factory has less impact than the treatment plant does.
b. The factory and the treatment plant have little influence on the water.
c. The factory and the treatment plant balance each other out.
d. The factory adds more of the chemical than the treatment plant removes.

Extended Response

Answer the two questions below in detail. Include some of the terms shown in the word box. Underline each term you use in your answers.

evaporate	condense	precipitation
groundwater	irrigation	rain

7. Describe the parts of the water cycle that are involved at a desalination plant.

8. For a science fair project, Anthony compared the growth of plants that got their water in different ways. One group grew in soil that he kept moist by providing water through a tube under the surface. For a second group, he poured water on top of the soil each day. In the third group, he sprayed water from a bottle on the plants. How are the three methods Anthony used similar to ways that farmers irrigate crops?

Analyzing a Graph

1. b   3. c   5. a
2. d   4. b   6. d

Extended Response

7. RUBRIC

4 points for a response that describes the water cycle involved in a desalination plant and uses the following terms accurately:

- evaporate
- condense
- precipitation

Sample answer: Salt water <u>evaporates</u>, leaving salt behind. The water vapor <u>condenses</u> and falls as <u>precipitation</u> into collection troughs.

3 points describes the water cycle adequately and uses two terms accurately
2 points describes the water cycle partially and uses one term accurately
1 point describes the water cycle partially but does not use any of the terms

8. RUBRIC

4 points for a response that correctly compares the watering of plants in the project to the watering of crops and uses the following terms accurately:

- groundwater
- irrigation
- rain

Sample answer: Water in the tube under the surface is similar to <u>groundwater</u>, which plants draw up into their roots. Pouring water on the soil is similar to <u>irrigation</u>, particularly flood irrigation, in which water is sent over the field in ditches between rows of crops. The sprayed water is similar to <u>rain</u>, which must soak into the soil before being drawn up through the plant roots.

3 points compares the watering of plants in the project to the watering of crops adequately and uses two terms accurately
2 points compares the watering of project plants and crops partially and uses one term accurately
1 point compares the watering of project plants and crops partially without using any of the terms

METACOGNITIVE ACTIVITY

Have students answer the following questions in their **Science Notebook:**

1. What were you surprised to learn about freshwater resources?

2. What additional information would you like to find out about freshwater resources?

3. What was a challenge or was too easy for you as you continued with your Unit Project?

3 Ocean Systems

Earth Science
UNIFYING PRINCIPLES

PRINCIPLE 1

Heat energy inside Earth and radiation from the Sun provide energy for Earth's processes.

PRINCIPLE 2

Physical forces, such as gravity, affect the movement of all matter on Earth and throughout the universe.

PRINCIPLE 3

Matter and energy move among Earth's rocks and soil, atmosphere, waters, and living things.

PRINCIPLE 4

Earth has changed over time and continues to change.

Unit: Earth's Waters
BIG IDEAS

CHAPTER 1
The Water Planet

Water moves through Earth's atmosphere, oceans, and land in a cycle.

CHAPTER 2
Freshwater Resources

Fresh water is a limited resource and is essential for human society.

CHAPTER 3
Ocean Systems

The oceans are a connected system of water in motion.

CHAPTER 4
Ocean Environments

The ocean supports life and contains natural resources.

CHAPTER 3
KEY CONCEPTS

SECTION 3.1	SECTION 3.2	SECTION 3.3	SECTION 3.4
The oceans are a connected system.	**Ocean water moves in currents.**	**Waves move through oceans.**	**Waters rise and fall in tides.**
1. Ocean water covers much of Earth.	1. The oceans have major currents.	1. Waves form in the open ocean.	1. Coastal waters rise and fall each day.
2. Ocean water contains salts and gases.	2. Currents interact with climate and weather.	2. Waves cause currents near shore.	2. The gravity of the Moon and the Sun causes tides.
3. Ocean temperatures vary.			3. Tides can be used to generate electricity.
4. The ocean floor has many features.			

The Big Idea Flow Chart is available on p. T17 in the **UNIT TRANSPARENCY BOOK.**

Previewing Content

 3.1 The oceans are a connected system.
pp. 75–83

1. Ocean water covers much of Earth.
Scientists theorize that the reason Earth is nearly covered in water has to do with how Earth formed. About 4.6 billion years ago, Earth formed as a ball of molten rock. Heavier materials sank to the core, and lighter materials floated to the surface. Water vapor, which is very light, rose and cooled enough to become a liquid. The liquid water became the global ocean.

2. Ocean water contains salts and gases.
Most of the salt in ocean water is sodium chloride, or table salt. **Salinity** is the measure of dissolved salt contained in the water. The sodium chloride and other dissolved solids make ocean water denser than fresh water. The ocean contains dissolved molecules of the same gases found in the atmosphere. Ocean animals take in oxygen and give off carbon dioxide. Algae and plants use carbon dioxide and release oxygen into the ocean.

3. Ocean temperatures vary.
Ocean water gets colder with increasing depth. The surface water is warmed by sunlight, and because warm water is less dense than cold water, it stays near the surface. The temperature of the surface water varies by location and season. It is warmer near the equator than near the poles, and warmer in summer than in winter.

4. The ocean floor has many features.
Scientists use scuba equipment, submarines, robots, sonar, and satellites to map the ocean floor. The submerged edge of a continent is called a **continental shelf.** Huge canyons slice through the shelf. Farther beyond are deep ocean trenches, flat abyssal plains, seamounts, volcanic islands, and the mid-ocean ridge.

 3.2 Ocean water moves in currents.
pp. 84–88

1. The oceans have major currents.
Ocean currents are masses of moving water. Ocean currents cycle heat and nutrients around the globe. Two types of currents are surface currents and deep currents.
Surface currents
- caused by wind blowing across ocean
- curl clockwise in Northern Hemisphere and counterclockwise in Southern Hemisphere because of Earth's rotation
- help distribute heat around globe by carrying warm water away from equator and cold water away from poles

The satellite image shows the Gulf Stream, a surface current that flows along the eastern coast of the United States.

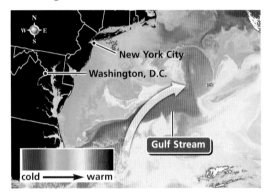

New York City
Washington, D.C.
Gulf Stream
cold ———► warm

Deep currents
- caused by differences in density because of coldness, salinity, or both
- move water across ocean floor from poles to the equator
- help bring nutrients up to the surface in an **upwelling,** which is the vertical movement of deep water to the surface
- help bring oxygen from the surface to the depths in a movement called **downmelting**

2. Currents interact with climate and weather.
Moving air produces movement in water, while the water changes the air above it. Wind-blown currents distribute heat by moving warm water away from the equator and cold water away from the poles. These currents affect the climate of regions around the globe. Changes in a surface current can cause huge changes in weather patterns, as witnessed during **El Niño** years.

Common Misconceptions

THE OCEAN FLOOR Students may think that the ocean floor is flat. In fact, the ocean floor has many features, including canyons and mountains.

 This misconception is addressed on p. 80.

 MISCONCEPTION DATABASE
CLASSZONE.COM Background on student misconceptions

Previewing Content

3.3 Waves move through oceans. pp. 89–95

1. Waves form in the open ocean.

- Most ocean waves form when moving air drags across the water's surface and passes energy to the water. Waves move energy, not water. This diagram shows the parts of a wave.

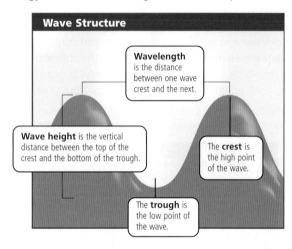

Wave Structure

Wavelength is the distance between one wave crest and the next.

Wave height is the vertical distance between the top of the crest and the bottom of the trough.

The **crest** is the high point of the wave.

The **trough** is the low point of the wave.

- Waves lose speed and topple over, losing their energy, as they break on shore. On the beach, the water runs back down the sand into the ocean. An undertow is the pull of the water as it runs back to sea.

2. Waves cause currents near shore.

- **Longshore currents** move water parallel to the shore. They occur where the waves meet the land at an angle and then wash back straight down the beach into the ocean, creating a zigzag motion.
- **Rip currents** occur where the movement of waves and long-shore currents builds up sandbars in the water near shore, and water collects behind the sandbars. High winds or waves can cause a larger-than-usual amount of water to collect behind a sandbar. Rip currents are narrow streams of water that break through the sandbars and drain rapidly back to sea.

3.4 Waters rise and fall in tides. pp. 96–101

1. Coastal waters rise and fall each day.

The periodic rising and falling of the water level of the ocean is called the **tide.** At high tide, the water level along a coast is at its highest point and submerges parts of the coastline. At low tide, the water level is lowest and exposes parts of the coastline.

2. The gravity of the Moon and the Sun causes tides.

- **Daily Tides** The Moon's gravitational pull causes Earth's water to bulge on the side facing the Moon. The Moon's gravity also pulls on Earth itself, leaving a second bulge of water on the side of Earth facing away from the Moon. At these bulges, it is high tide. In between the two bulges are dips, where it is low tide. As Earth rotates, different parts of the planet pass through the bulges and the dips. As a result, most places near the ocean experience two high tides and two low tides each day. **Tidal range** is affected by the shape of the land along a coastline. It is greater in a narrow bay than on a wide open shore. In addition, coastlines with steeply sloped ocean floors have larger tidal ranges than coastlines with gradually dropping floors.
- **Monthly Tides** The Sun also affects tides. During the Moon's month-long journey around Earth, the Moon, Sun, and Earth line up twice—at times of the new moon and full moon. The gravity of the Sun and of the Moon combine to pull on Earth's waters from the same direction. The result is an extra-high tidal bulge and an extra-low tidal dip called a **spring tide.** During first- and third-quarter moons, the Sun and Moon are not lined up, and the gravity of each pulls on Earth from a different direction. Then the tidal bulge is smaller than normal. **Neap tides** result in less extreme high and low tides.

3. Tides can be used to generate electricity.

A tidal dam traps water during high tides. When the tide is low, the dam gates open and the trapped water rushes out, spinning turbines that generate electricity. Tidal dams cause less pollution than other methods of generating electricity and are a renewable source of energy. However, few places are suitable for tidal dams, the timing of the tides may not be convenient, and marine life can be harmed by the dams.

Common Misconceptions

WAVES Students may think that waves are made of water. In fact, waves carry energy through water. The water itself does not travel in the same direction as the wave. Water particles move in a circular motion, ending up in the same place they started before the wave traveled through.

TE This misconception is addressed on p. 90.

 MISCONCEPTION DATABASE
CLASSZONE.COM Background on student misconceptions

Previewing Labs

Lab Generator CD-ROM
Edit these Pupil Edition labs and generate alternative labs.

EXPLORE the BIG idea

What Makes Things Float or Sink? p. 73
Students observe that the density of water affects whether objects float or sink.

TIME 10 minutes
MATERIALS 2 clear cups, water, spoon, salt, food coloring

How Does Moving Air Affect Water? p. 73
Students are introduced to surface currents.

TIME 10 minutes
MATERIALS pan, water, straw

Internet Activity: The Ocean Floor, p. 73
Students view features of the ocean floor.

TIME 20 minutes
MATERIALS computer with Internet access

SECTION **3.1**

EXPLORE Density, p. 75
Students pour liquids into a straw to observe that liquids of different densities form layers.

TIME 20 minutes
MATERIALS 3 solutions with varying food coloring in clear cups: A is tap water, B is 100 mL salt per 1000 mL water, C is 25 mL salt per 1000 mL water; clear straw; waste cup

INVESTIGATE Density, p. 78
Students predict what will happen when water solutions with different densities combine.

TIME 30 minutes
MATERIALS 2 baby food jars, blue and red food coloring, tap water, salt water solution of 100 mL salt per 1000 mL water, index cards, large pan or bucket

---

SECTION **3.2**

EXPLORE Currents, p. 84
Students create a stream of cold water flowing into warm water to observe that cold water sinks in warm water.

TIME 20 minutes
MATERIALS cold water, ice cubes, food coloring, paper cup, masking tape, clear plastic box, toothpick, water

INVESTIGATE Currents, p. 87
Students create currents with high-salt and low-salt water to observe that high-salt water will flow under low-salt water.

TIME 30 minutes
MATERIALS clear plastic box, foil, masking tape, solution of 100 mL salt per 1000 mL water with blue food coloring, low-salinity tap water, pepper, sharp pencil

---

SECTION **3.3**

EXPLORE Waves, p. 89
Students create waves in water and observe how objects at varying depths are affected.

TIME 20 minutes
MATERIALS aquarium or clear tank, 4 corks, 1 meter of string, 12 metal washers, tap water

CHAPTER INVESTIGATION
Wave Movement, pp. 94–95
Students observe how waves affect a floating object to draw conclusions about the movement of water particles in a passing wave.

TIME 40 minutes
MATERIALS small aquarium or clear container; tap water; small plastic dropping bottle or plastic spice container, with cap; salt

---

SECTION **3.4**

INVESTIGATE Tides, p. 98
Students model how the Moon produces tides.
R Tides Datasheet, p. 172

TIME 15 minutes
MATERIALS Tides Datasheet, scissors, brass paper fastener

R Additional **INVESTIGATION,** Measuring Salinity, A, B, & C, pp. 191–199; Teacher Instructions, pp. 261–262

Previewing Chapter Resources

	INTEGRATED TECHNOLOGY	LABS AND ACTIVITIES

CHAPTER 3
Ocean Systems

 CLASSZONE.COM
- eEdition Plus
- EasyPlanner Plus
- Misconception Database
- Content Review
- Test Practice
- Simulation
- Visualization
- Resource Centers
- Internet Activity: The Ocean Floor
- Math Tutorial

 SCILINKS.ORG
SCI LINKS

 CD-ROMS
- eEdition
- EasyPlanner
- Power Presentations
- Content Review
- Lab Generator
- Test Generator

 AUDIO CDS
- Audio Readings
- Audio Readings in Spanish

 EXPLORE the Big Idea, p. 73
- What Makes Things Float or Sink?
- How Does Moving Air Affect Water?
- Internet Activity: The Ocean Floor

UNIT RESOURCE BOOK
Unit Projects, pp. 5–10

 Lab Generator CD-ROM
Generate customized labs.

SECTION
 3.1 The oceans are a connected system.
pp. 75–83

Time: 2 periods (1 block)
 Lesson Plan, pp. 131–132

 MATH TUTORIAL

UNIT TRANSPARENCY BOOK
- Big Idea Flow Chart, p. T17
- Daily Vocabulary Scaffolding, p. T18
- Note-Taking Model, p. T19
- 3-Minute Warm-Up, p. T20

 • EXPLORE Density, p. 75
- INVESTIGATE Density, p. 78
- Math in Science, p. 83

UNIT RESOURCE BOOK
- Datasheet, Density, p. 140
- Additional INVESTIGATION, Measuring Salinity, A, B, & C, pp. 191–199
- Math Support & Practice, pp. 180–181

SECTION
 3.2 Ocean water moves in currents.
pp. 84–88

Time: 2 periods (1 block)
 Lesson Plan, pp. 142–143

 RESOURCE CENTER, Ocean Currents

 UNIT TRANSPARENCY BOOK
- Daily Vocabulary Scaffolding, p. T18
- 3-Minute Warm-Up, p. T20

 • EXPLORE Currents, p. 84
- INVESTIGATE Currents, p. 87

UNIT RESOURCE BOOK
Datasheet, Currents, p. 151

SECTION
 3.3 Waves move through oceans.
pp. 89–95

Time: 3 periods (1.5 blocks)
 Lesson Plan, pp. 153–154

 RESOURCE CENTER, Ocean Waves

UNIT TRANSPARENCY BOOK
- Daily Vocabulary Scaffolding, p. T18
- 3-Minute Warm-Up, p. T21
- "Ocean Waves" Visual, p. T22

 • EXPLORE Waves, p. 89
- CHAPTER INVESTIGATION, Wave Movement, pp. 94–95

UNIT RESOURCE BOOK
CHAPTER INVESTIGATION, Wave Movement, A, B, & C, pp. 182–190

SECTION
 3.4 Waters rise and fall in tides.
pp. 96–101

Time: 3 periods (1.5 blocks)
 Lesson Plan, pp. 163–164

 • **VISUALIZATION,** Daily Tides
- **RESOURCE CENTER,** Ocean Tides

 UNIT TRANSPARENCY BOOK
- Big Idea Flow Chart, p. T17
- Daily Vocabulary Scaffolding, p. T18
- 3-Minute Warm-Up, p. T21
- Chapter Outline, pp. T23–T24

 • INVESTIGATE Tides, p. 98
- Connecting Sciences, p. 101

UNIT RESOURCE BOOK
- Tides Datasheet, p. 172
- Datasheet, Tides, p. 173

KEY TO ICONS

 CD/CD-ROM

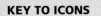 **INTERNET**

 Pupil Edition

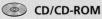 **Teacher Edition**

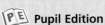 **UNIT RESOURCE BOOK**

UNIT TRANSPARENCY BOOK

UNIT ASSESSMENT BOOK

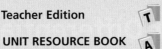 **SPANISH ASSESSMENT BOOK**

SCIENCE TOOLKIT

READING AND REINFORCEMENT

ASSESSMENT

STANDARDS

- Word Triangle, B18–19
- Outline, C43
- Daily Vocabulary Scaffolding, H1–8

 UNIT RESOURCE BOOK
- Vocabulary Practice, pp. 177–178
- Decoding Support, p. 179
- Summarizing the Chapter, pp. 200–201

 Audio Readings CD
Listen to Pupil Edition.

Audio Readings in Spanish CD
Listen to Pupil Edition in Spanish.

- Chapter Review, pp. 103–104
- Standardized Test Practice, p. 105

 UNIT ASSESSMENT BOOK
- Diagnostic Test, pp. 39–40
- Chapter Test, A, B, & C, pp. 45–56
- Alternative Assessment, pp. 57–58

 Spanish Chapter Test, pp. 161–164

Test Generator CD-ROM
Generate customized tests.

Lab Generator CD-ROM
Rubrics for Labs

National Standards
A.2–8, A.9.a–f, D.1.g, D.1.j, D.3.c, E.6.c–d

See p. 72 for the standards.

 UNIT RESOURCE BOOK
- Reading Study Guide, A & B, pp. 133–136
- Spanish Reading Study Guide, pp. 137–138
- Challenge and Extension, p. 139
- Reinforcing Key Concepts, p. 141

 Ongoing Assessment, pp. 77–79, 81–82

 Section 3.1 Review, p. 82

 UNIT ASSESSMENT BOOK
Section 3.1 Quiz, p. 41

National Standards
A.2–8, A.9.a–f, D.1.g

UNIT RESOURCE BOOK
- Reading Study Guide, A & B, pp. 144–147
- Spanish Reading Study Guide, pp. 148–149
- Challenge and Extension, p. 150
- Reinforcing Key Concepts, p. 152
- Challenge Reading, pp. 175–176

 Ongoing Assessment, pp. 85–88

 Section 3.2 Review, p. 88

 UNIT ASSESSMENT BOOK
Section 3.2 Quiz, p. 42

National Standards
A.2–7, A.9.a–b, A.9.e–f, D.1.j

UNIT RESOURCE BOOK
- Reading Study Guide, A & B, pp. 155–158
- Spanish Reading Study Guide, pp. 159–160
- Challenge and Extension, p. 161
- Reinforcing Key Concepts, p. 162

 Ongoing Assessment, pp. 89, 91–92

 Section 3.3 Review, p. 93

 UNIT ASSESSMENT BOOK
Section 3.3 Quiz, p. 43

National Standards
A.2–7, A.9.a–b, A.9.e–f

 UNIT RESOURCE BOOK
- Reading Study Guide, A & B, pp. 165–168
- Spanish Reading Study Guide, pp. 169–170
- Challenge and Extension, p. 171
- Reinforcing Key Concepts, p. 174

 Ongoing Assessment, pp. 96–100

 Section 3.4 Review, p. 100

 UNIT ASSESSMENT BOOK
Section 3.4 Quiz, p. 44

National Standards
A.2–7, A.9.a–b, A.9.d–f, D.3.c, E.6.c–d

Previewing Resources for Differentiated Instruction

CHAPTER INVESTIGATION

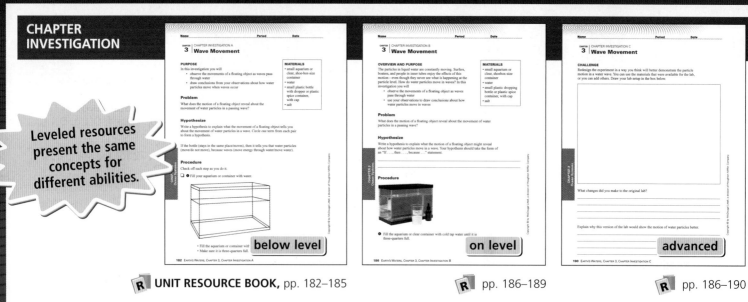

Leveled resources present the same concepts for different abilities.

below level

on level

advanced

R **UNIT RESOURCE BOOK,** pp. 182–185

R pp. 186–189

R pp. 186–190

READING STUDY GUIDE

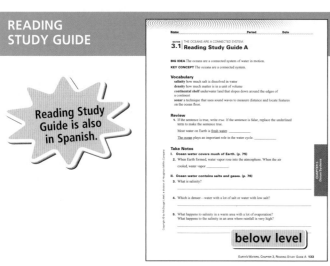

Reading Study Guide is also in Spanish.

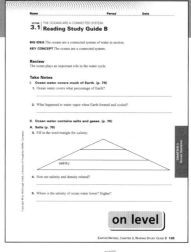

below level

on level

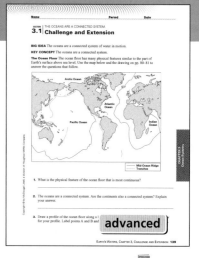

advanced

R **UNIT RESOURCE BOOK,** pp. 133–134

R pp. 135–136

R p. 139

CHAPTER TEST

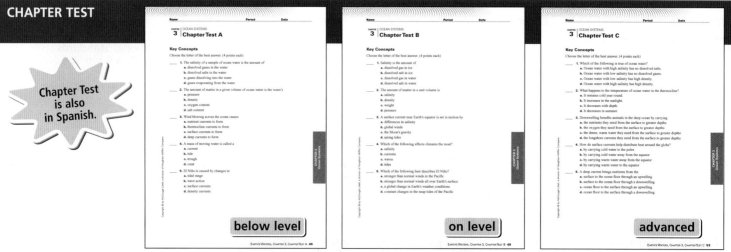

Chapter Test is also in Spanish.

below level

on level

advanced

A **UNIT ASSESSMENT BOOK,** pp. 45–48

A pp. 49–52

A pp. 53–56

C **71G** Unit: Earth's Waters

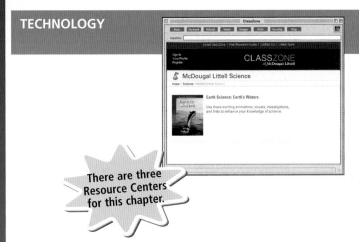

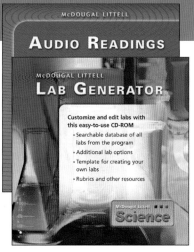

There are three Resource Centers for this chapter.

 CLASSZONE.COM

 CD/CD-ROMS

 CLASSZONE.COM

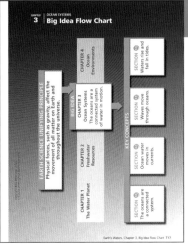

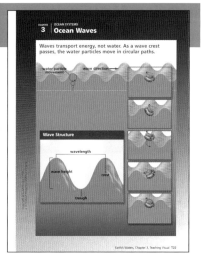

T UNIT TRANSPARENCY BOOK, p. T17

T p. T19

T p. T22

Reinforcing Key Concepts for each section

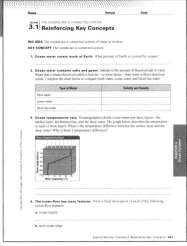

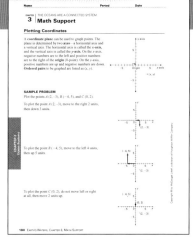

R UNIT RESOURCE BOOK, p. 141

R pp. 177–178

R p. 180

INTRODUCE

the **BIG** idea

Have students look at the photograph of a surfer on a beach and discuss how the question in the box links to the Big Idea:

- How is ocean water like water near you?
- What kind of water movement do you see in the photograph? What do you think causes it?

National Science Education Standards

Content

D.1.g Water is a solvent. As it passes through the water cycle it dissolves minerals and gases and carries them to the oceans.

D.1.j Oceans have a major effect on climate, because water in the oceans holds a large amount of heat.

D.3.c Gravity alone holds us to Earth's surface and explains the phenomena of the tides.

Process

A.2–8 Design and conduct an investigation; use tools to gather and interpret data; use evidence to describe, predict, explain, model; think critically to make relationships between evidence and explanation; recognize different explanations and predictions; communicate scientific procedures and explanations; use mathematics.

A.9.a–f Understand scientific inquiry by using different investigations, methods, mathematics, technology, and explanations based on logic, evidence, and skepticism.

E.6.c–d Science and technology are reciprocal; perfectly designed solutions don't exist, there are tradeoffs.

CHAPTER

Ocean Systems

the **BIG** idea

The oceans are a connected system of water in motion.

What causes these waves?

Key Concepts

 SECTION 3.1 The oceans are a connected system. Learn about ocean water and the ocean floor.

 SECTION 3.2 Ocean water moves in currents. Learn about currents and how they interact with climate and weather.

 SECTION 3.3 Waves move through oceans. Learn how waves form and move through the ocean.

 SECTION 3.4 Waters rise and fall in tides. Learn how tides are related to the Sun and the Moon.

Internet Preview

CLASSZONE.COM

Chapter 3 online resources: Content Review, Simulation, Visualization, three Resource Centers, Math Tutorial, Test Practice

C 72 Unit: Earth's Waters

 INTERNET PREVIEW

CLASSZONE.COM For student use with the following pages:

Review and Practice
- Content Review, pp. 74, 102
- Math Tutorial: Coordinates and Line Graphs, p. 83
- Test Practice, p. 105

Activities and Resources
- Internet Activity: The Ocean Floor, p. 73
- Resource Centers: Ocean Currents, p. 84; Ocean Waves, p. 90; Ocean Tides, p. 99. Visualization: Daily Tides, p. 97

Exploring Earth's Oceans
Code: MDL020

What Makes Things Float or Sink?

Fill two clear cups with water. Add a heaping spoonful of salt to one cup and stir until it dissolves. Gently squeeze two drops of food coloring into each cup.

Observe and Think What happened to the drops of food coloring in each cup?

How Does Moving Air Affect Water?

Fill a pan with water. Use a straw to blow over the surface of the water.

Observe and Think What happened to the water when you blew on it? Draw a diagram to show what happened.

Internet Activity: The Ocean Floor

Go to **ClassZone.com** to expose the ocean floor by draining all of the water out of the ocean.

Observe and Think How are the features of the ocean floor similar to features on land? How are they different?

CLASSZONE

McDougal Littell Science

NSTA scilinks.org SCi*LINKS*

Exploring Earth's Oceans **Code: MDL020**

Chapter 3: **Ocean Systems 73** **C**

TEACHING WITH TECHNOLOGY

CBL and Probeware If probeware is available, you may wish to use a flow-rate sensor for the scenario pictured in "Connecting Sciences" on p. 101.

These inquiry-based activities are appropriate for use at home or as a supplement to classroom instruction.

What Makes Things Float or Sink?

PURPOSE To observe how the density of water affects whether something floats or sinks.

TIP *10 min.* Advise students to keep stirring the salt water until they do not see any grains of salt.

Answer: The drop of food coloring in the plain water sank to the bottom. The drop of food coloring in the salt solution floated to the top.

REVISIT after p. 76.

How Does Moving Air Affect Water?

PURPOSE To observe how moving air produces surface currents.

TIP *10 min.* Have students blow gently and then more strongly to see the effects of varying the force of the air.

Answer: The air that comes through the straw will cause the surface of the water to ripple.

REVISIT after p. 85.

Internet Activity: The Ocean Floor

PURPOSE To observe the features of the ocean floor.

TIP *20 min.* Students should appreciate that the ocean floor has a complex and varied landscape.

Answer: Answers may include the following: Similarities: The ocean floor contains such topographical features as mountains, valleys, and canyons just like the continents. Differences: Ocean floor is underwater and ocean sediment is different from the soil on land.

REVISIT after p. 81.

◗ CONCEPT REVIEW
Activate Prior Knowledge

- Draw a simple diagram of the water cycle on the board without any title or label.
- Call on a volunteer to title and label the diagram. Call on another volunteer to verbally describe the water cycle.
- Remind students that the oceans contain most of the liquid water on Earth.

▶ TAKING NOTES

Outline

Have students discuss the relationship among outline ideas. Suggest that students use their outlines when studying the chapter.

Vocabulary Strategy

Word triangles give students three approaches to word meaning: defining the word, using it in a sentence, and visualizing it.

Vocabulary and Note-Taking Resources

R
- Vocabulary Practice, pp. 177–178
- Decoding Support, p. 179

T
- Daily Vocabulary Scaffolding, p. T18
- Note-Taking Model, p. T19

- Word Triangle, B18–19
- Outline, C43
- Daily Vocabulary Scaffolding, H1–8

◗ CONCEPT REVIEW

- Water covers most of Earth.
- Earth's waters circulate in the water cycle.
- The water in the oceans is salt water.

◗ VOCABULARY REVIEW

salt water p. 11
water cycle p. 12
evaporation p. 13
desalination p. 66

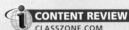

CONTENT REVIEW
CLASSZONE.COM
Review concepts and vocabulary.

▶ TAKING NOTES

OUTLINE

As you read, copy the headings into your notebook in the form of an outline. Then add notes in your own words that summarize what you read.

VOCABULARY STRATEGY

Draw a **word triangle** for each new vocabulary term. At the bottom, write and define the term. Above that, write a sentence in which you use the term correctly. At the top, draw a small picture to represent the term.

See the Note-Taking Handbook on pages R45–R51.

SCIENCE NOTEBOOK

OUTLINE

I. The oceans are a connected system.
  A. Ocean water covers much of Earth.
  B. Ocean water contains salts and gases.
    1.
    2.
  C. Ocean temperatures vary.
    1.
    2.

The salinity of ocean water is about 35 grams of salt per 1000 grams of water

salinity: a measure of the saltiness of water

CHECK READINESS

Administer the Diagnostic Test to determine students' readiness for new science content and their mastery of requisite math skills.

A Diagnostic Test, pp. 39–40

Technology Resources

Students needing content and math skills should visit **ClassZone.com**.

- **CONTENT REVIEW**
- **MATH TUTORIAL**

CONTENT REVIEW CD-ROM

KEY CONCEPT

3.1 The oceans are a connected system.

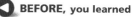

◀ **BEFORE, you learned**

- Most water on Earth is salt water
- The ocean plays an important role in the water cycle

▶ **NOW, you will learn**

- What ocean water contains
- What the ocean floor looks like
- How people explore the ocean

VOCABULARY

salinity p. 76
density p. 76
continental shelf p. 80
sonar p. 82

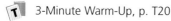

EXPLORE Density

Why do liquids form layers?

PROCEDURE

① Insert the straw into one of the solutions. Cover the top of the straw with your finger and then remove the straw from the solution. The liquid should stay in the straw.

② Using this technique, try to layer the three liquids in your straw so that you can see three distinct layers.

③ Experiment with the order in which you place the liquids into the straw. Between trials, empty the contents of the straw into the waste cup.

MATERIALS

- 3 solutions—A, B, and C—provided by your teacher
- clear straw
- waste cup

WHAT DO YOU THINK?
Did it matter in what order you layered the liquids? If so, can you explain why?

OUTLINE
Remember to start an outline for this section.

I. Main idea
  A. Supporting idea
    1. Detail
    2. Detail
  B. Supporting idea

Ocean water covers much of Earth.

As land animals, we naturally think of our planet as a rocky and solid place. We even named our planet Earth, which means "land" or "soil." But look at a globe and you will see that oceans cover most of Earth. In fact, 71 percent of Earth is covered in seawater.

Looking at a map of the world, you can see the seven continents spread over our planet. These landmasses divide Earth's global ocean into connected sections. Different sections of the ocean have different names, such as Atlantic, Indian, and Pacific. However, all the sections are connected.

Chapter 3: Ocean Systems **75** **C**

RESOURCES FOR DIFFERENTIATED INSTRUCTION

Below Level

UNIT RESOURCE BOOK
- Reading Study Guide A, pp. 133–134
- Decoding Support, p. 179

 AUDIO CDS

R **Additional INVESTIGATION,**
Measuring Salinity, A, B, & C, pp. 191–199; Teacher Instructions, pp. 261–262

Advanced

UNIT RESOURCE BOOK
Challenge and Extension, p. 139

English Learners

UNIT RESOURCE BOOK
Spanish Reading Study Guide, pp. 137–138

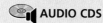 **AUDIO CDS**

- Audio Readings in Spanish
- Audio Readings (English)

3.1 FOCUS

▶ Set Learning Goals
Students will

- Identify what ocean water contains.
- Describe what the ocean floor looks like.
- Explain how the ocean is explored.
- Predict in an experiment that denser water will sink.

◀ 3-Minute Warm-Up

Display Transparency 20 or copy this exercise on the board:

Decide if these statements are true. If not, correct them.

1. Most water on Earth is fresh water. *Most water on Earth is salt water.*

2. Water continually circulates through the atmosphere, the soil, and bodies of water. *true*

3. Rain is a part of the water cycle. *true*

T 3-Minute Warm-Up, p. T20

3.1 MOTIVATE

EXPLORE Density

PURPOSE To observe that liquids of different densities form layers

TIP *20 min.* The three solutions are (A) tap water, (B) 100 mL salt per 1000 mL water, and (C) 25 mL salt per 1000 mL water. All three solutions should be at room temperature. Add several drops of food coloring to each solution, using three different colors.

WHAT DO YOU THINK? *Yes, it did matter in which order the liquids were layered. One of the solutions floated on top of the other solutions. One of the solutions sank to the bottom of the other solutions. It is possible to make three layers only by putting the liquids in the straw in the right order.*

Chapter 3 **75** **C**

Teacher Demo

Show students a large globe and spin it around slowly so that they can see that the world's oceans are connected and actually form one global ocean. Point out how much larger the Pacific Ocean is than the other oceans. Ask: What is one way to show that the global ocean is one connected body of water? *A line could be drawn connecting each body of water to another.*

Integrate the Sciences

Show students the Periodic Table of Elements and point out that the 92 naturally occurring elements have atomic numbers between 1 and 92. Note that water consists of hydrogen (H), number 1 on the table, and oxygen (O), number 8. Another name for salt is sodium chloride. The two elements that make up salt are sodium (Na), number 11, and chlorine (Cl), number 17.

EXPLORE (the BIG idea)

Revisit "What Makes Things Float or Sink?" on p. 73. Have students explain their results.

The global ocean is one connected body of water, divided into sections by the continents.

How did Earth become covered by an ocean? Scientists have several theories. The most commonly accepted explanation has to do with how Earth formed. Earth formed about 4.6 billion years ago as a ball of molten rock. Heavier materials sank to the core, and lighter materials floated toward the surface—the same way oil and vinegar in salad dressing separate into layers. Water vapor, a very light substance, rose to the cooler surface. By about 4 billion years ago, Earth had cooled enough for the water vapor to become liquid. At that time, the vapor condensed—just as water vapor condenses into droplets on a cool glass of lemonade—forming liquid water that became the ocean.

Ocean water contains salts and gases.

Despite its name, the salt water that fills the ocean is much more than just salt and water. Ocean water contains many different dissolved substances. Sodium chloride, which is the same compound as ordinary table salt, is the most plentiful of these substances. The ocean also contains other dissolved solids, as well as dissolved molecules of the same gases found in the atmosphere. In fact, the ocean contains all 92 elements that occur in nature, although most are in very tiny amounts.

Salts

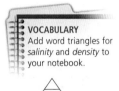

VOCABULARY
Add word triangles for *salinity* and *density* to your notebook.

One taste will convince you that ocean water is salty. Every 1000 grams of seawater contains an average of 35 grams of salt. **Salinity** (suh-LIHN-ih-tee) is a measure of the amount of dissolved salt contained in water. The ocean contains many different kinds of salts. However, sodium chloride accounts for most of the ocean's salinity.

The elements that make up salts are found in rocks and minerals. Over time, rain and rivers wash some of these elements into the sea. The elements that make up salts also enter the ocean when underwater volcanoes erupt. Natural processes also remove salt from the ocean. Because salt is added as well as removed, the ocean's overall salinity does not change much over time. The ocean's salinity has stayed constant for the past 1.5 billion years.

Water that contains dissolved solids, such as salts, is heavier than the same amount of water with no dissolved solids. In other words, salt water has a greater density than fresh water. **Density** is a measure of the amount of matter packed into a given volume.

The higher water's salt content, the greater its density. The denser the water, the more easily things float in it. As you can see in the photograph on page 77, the Dead Sea is so salty (and dense) that people can float easily on the surface.

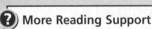

DIFFERENTIATE INSTRUCTION

? More Reading Support

A What is the most plentiful dissolved substance in ocean water? *sodium chloride*

B Is salt water more or less dense than fresh water? *more dense*

English Learners Tell students that phrases and clauses at the beginnings of sentences sometimes show when or why things happen, as in "By about 4 billion years ago," or "Because salt is added as well as removed" on this page. If students are confused by sentences that begin with introductory clauses, have them rearrange the clauses to read the main clause of the sentence first, and then add the subordinate clause.

Salinity and Density

Salt water has a greater density than fresh water.

Fresh Water	Ocean Water	Dead Sea Water
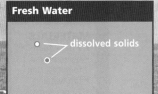 dissolved solids		
Fresh water has fewer dissolved solids than salt water, so it is less dense than salt water.	Ocean water is more dense than fresh water because it has more dissolved solids.	The Dead Sea is about ten times saltier than the ocean, so Dead Sea water is more dense than ocean water.

Located between Israel and Jordan, the Dead Sea is actually a salty lake and not part of the ocean. Its high salinity, and therefore high density, allows people to float more easily in it than in fresh water or in the ocean.

Dead Sea

Some parts of the ocean are saltier than others. When water evaporates from the ocean, the salts are left behind, causing the remaining water to become even saltier. Ocean water is especially salty in places where water evaporates quickly, such as in shallow areas and warm climates. Salinity is also higher in very cold areas, where the ocean water freezes. When ice forms on the ocean, the salt is left in the water below.

Salinity is lower in areas where the ocean is diluted by fresh water. For example, seawater has lower salinity in places where rivers empty into the ocean. Similarly, the ocean's salinity is lower in areas where a lot of rain falls.

CHECK YOUR READING How are salinity and density related?

DIFFERENTIATE INSTRUCTION

? More Reading Support

C How does evaporation affect ocean water? *increases salinity*

D How does fresh water affect salinity? *lowers it*

Additional Investigation To reinforce Section 3.1 learning goals, use the following full-period investigation:

R **Additional INVESTIGATION,** Measuring Salinity, A, B, & C, pp. 191–199, 261–262 (Advanced students should complete Levels B and C.)

Advanced Have interested students find out how the Dead Sea formed and how it became so salty. Encourage them to give an oral report to the class.

R Challenge and Extension, p. 139

Teach from Visuals

To help students interpret the diagrams comparing the salinity of water, ask:

• What do the solid and open circles in the diagrams represent? *two different types of dissolved solids*

• Which kind of water has the fewest dissolved solids? *fresh water*

• Which kind of water is the least dense? *fresh water*

• Is ocean water more or less dense than fresh water? *more dense*

Integrate the Sciences

The equation for finding density is mass divided by volume. In other words, density is the amount of mass in a given unit volume. Density is usually expressed in kilograms per meter cubed. Since density increases as temperature decreases, it is important to note the temperature of the substance being measured. Pure water at 4 degrees Celsius has a density of 1.0 g/cm³. Water behaves differently from other substances and is actually less dense in the form of ice, which has a density of 0.92 g/cm³.

Develop Critical Thinking

APPLY Have students apply their knowledge of how water changes states to infer what processes could be used to desalinate ocean water. *Apply heat so that the water evaporates, leaving the salt behind. Then lower the temperature to cause the water vapor to condense and became liquid water again.*

Ongoing Assessment

CHECK YOUR READING *Answer: The higher the salinity of water, the greater the density. The lower the salinity, the lower the density.*

INVESTIGATE Density

PURPOSE To make predictions about the movement of dense water and then test the predictions

TIP *30 min.* Prepare the salt solution in advance, using 100 mL salt per 1000 mL water. The water should be at room temperature.

WHAT DO YOU THINK? *Answers will vary. The water moved because of differences in density. Salt water is more dense than fresh water and sinks to the bottom.*

CHALLENGE *Saltier water will be at the bottom because it is more dense.*

 Datasheet, Density, p. 140

Technology Resources

Customize this student lab as needed or look for an alternative. Print rubrics to assess student lab reports.

 Lab Generator CD-ROM

Integrate the Sciences

Oxygen is necessary for chemical reactions that release energy in most living things. Fish obtain oxygen from water through structures called gills. Whales, dolphins, and other water mammals obtain oxygen through structures called lungs. Ocean mammals must come to the surface to get oxygen. Humans and other land mammals inhale a mixture of gases, which includes oxygen.

Ongoing Assessment

Identify what ocean water contains.

Ask: What are the main components of ocean water? *water; sodium chloride and other salts; dissolved gases such as oxygen, nitrogen, and carbon dioxide*

CHECK YOUR READING *Answer: Oxygen gets mixed in from the air at the surface and is added by plants that produce oxygen in the process of making food.*

INVESTIGATE Density

How does dense water move?

PROCEDURE

1. Read the instructions below and predict what will happen in steps 3 and 4 before you begin. Record your predictions.

2. Fill one jar with tap water and color it blue. Fill another jar with salt water and color it red. Place an index card over the top of the jar of red salt water.

3. With your hand over the index card, turn the jar over and place it on top of the jar with the blue tap water. Pull out the index card and observe the water movement, if any.

4. Repeat steps 2 and 3, but with the blue tap water on the top.

WHAT DO YOU THINK?

- Describe any ways in which your observations differed from your predictions. On what did you base your predictions?
- Explain why the water moved, if it did, in each of the two setups.

CHALLENGE How do you think water in the ocean might be layered?

SKILL FOCUS
Predicting

MATERIALS
- 2 baby food jars
- blue and red food coloring
- tap water
- 10 percent salt solution
- index cards
- large pan or bucket

TIME
30 minutes

Oxygen and Other Gases

Fish, like other animals, need oxygen to live. Oxygen and other gases dissolve in water, just as sugar dissolves in tea. The ocean contains the same gases as the air, including oxygen, nitrogen, and carbon dioxide. Dissolved gases are essential to ocean life.

You know that when you breathe, you use oxygen and exhale carbon dioxide. Ocean animals also take in oxygen and give off carbon dioxide. Oxygen and carbon dioxide get mixed into the ocean from the air above the ocean surface. Oxygen is also added to the ocean by plants and algae that live near the surface. Plants and algae use sunlight to convert carbon dioxide and water into food, and release oxygen into the water. Besides being used by plants to make food, carbon dioxide is a building block of ocean animals' shells.

Algae use dissolved carbon dioxide to make food, and give off oxygen.

Sea horses take in dissolved oxygen and give off carbon dioxide through their gills.

CHECK YOUR READING Where does the oxygen in the ocean come from? Name two sources.

DIFFERENTIATE INSTRUCTION

? More Reading Support

E What gases does the ocean contain? *oxygen, nitrogen, carbon dioxide*

F What do you exhale, or breathe out, when you breathe? *carbon dioxide*

English Learners Helps students separate out the directions for "Investigate Density" into more steps. Direction 3, for example, could begin with "Hold the index card tightly over the top of the jar."

Inclusion Have students do "Investigate Density" in mixed ability groups. Students with physical disabilities might read the instructions and direct the investigation in their groups.

Ocean temperatures vary.

Oceanographers—people who study the ocean—divide ocean water into three layers on the basis of temperature.

❶ The surface layer, heated by the Sun and mixed by winds and waves, is the warmest layer. Warm water is less dense than cold water, so the heated water stays at the surface.

❷ The thermocline (THUR-muh-KLYN) lies below the surface layer. The temperature of the water in the thermocline drops fast with depth.

❸ The deep water is cold all year. Almost anywhere on the globe—even in the tropics—the temperature of the water at the ocean's bottom is around 0°C–3°C (32°F–37°F), at or barely above freezing.

The temperature of the water at the surface of the ocean varies by location and season. As you can see in the map of satellite data below, the surface layer is warmer near the equator than near the poles. Over much of Earth, the surface layer is warmer in the summer and cooler in the winter.

CHECK YOUR READING Why doesn't the warm water at the ocean's surface sink to the bottom?

Ocean Temperature by Depth

sunlight

① surface layer
② thermocline
③ deep water

Water depth (meters): 0, 200, 400, 600, 800, 1000, 1200
Water temperature (°C): 0, 5, 10, 15, 20, 25

Surface Temperature

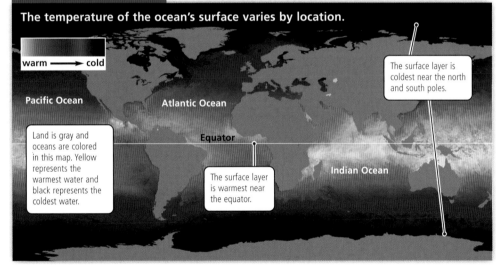

The temperature of the ocean's surface varies by location.

warm ⟶ cold

Pacific Ocean

Atlantic Ocean

Land is gray and oceans are colored in this map. Yellow represents the warmest water and black represents the coldest water.

Equator

The surface layer is warmest near the equator.

Indian Ocean

The surface layer is coldest near the north and south poles.

Chapter 3: **Ocean Systems** 79 **C**

DIFFERENTIATE INSTRUCTION

❓ More Reading Support

G What two things cause the surface temperature of ocean water to vary? *location and season*

Inclusion Encourage students to cover up the bottom visual on this page to study the upper graph and words; then cover the top to study the lower graphic. This will eliminate too much visual distraction.

Teach from Visuals

To help students interpret the graph of ocean temperature:

- Ask: What is the temperature of ocean water at the surface, or at 0 meters? *25°C (about 77°F)*
- Ask: What is the approximate temperature of the water at 600 meters below the surface? *10°C (about 50°F)*
- Have students follow the red line and describe how the water temperature changes with depth. *From 0 to about 360 meters, the water temperature stays at 25°C. From about 360 meters to about 760 meters, the water rapidly drops to 4°C. It stays at that temperature to about 1200 meters.*

Real World Example

Ask students if any of them have ever swum in a large lake or swimming pool. If so, have them recall how the water got cooler as they swam deeper. Tell students that the water in any large body of water, even a large swimming pool, has layers that differ in temperature, going from warmest at the surface to coolest at the bottom.

Teach from Visuals

To help students interpret the satellite image of ocean surface temperatures, ask:

- What does the color yellow represent? *warmest water*
- What does the color black represent? *coldest water*
- What pattern in water temperature does the image show? *Ocean water is warmest near the equator and gets colder toward the poles.*

Ongoing Assessment

CHECK YOUR READING *Answer: because it is less dense than the colder water underneath and so it floats at the top*

Chapter 3 **79** **C**

Teach from Visuals

To help students interpret the diagram of the ocean floor, ask:

- What is the ocean bottom like along coastlines? *It gradually slopes and is cut through by canyons.*

- What land feature drops steeply at the edge of the continental shelf? *the continental slope*

- What features lie beyond the continental slope? *ocean trenches, abyssal plains, the mid-ocean ridge, seamounts, and volcanic islands*

Address Misconceptions

IDENTIFY Ask students to describe or draw the ocean floor. If their drawings show a flat ocean floor, they are unaware of the ocean floor's features.

CORRECT Direct students to the visual "The Ocean Floor" and ask them to find mountains, volcanoes, plains, and canyons.

REASSESS Ask: What features does the ocean floor have in common with dry land? *trenches, mountains, volcanoes, plains, ridges*

The ocean floor has many features.

People have sailed the ocean for thousands of years. However, the landscape of most of the ocean floor remained a mystery until the 1950s. Since then, exploration and improvements in mapping techniques have revealed many spectacular features on the ocean floor, including the tallest mountains and deepest canyons on Earth.

A **continental shelf** is the flat or gently sloping land that lies submerged around the edges of a continent and that extends from the shoreline out to a continental slope. Huge submarine canyons, some similar in size to the Grand Canyon, slice through continental shelves and slopes. Farther out, ocean trenches cut deep into the ocean floor. With a bottom over 11,000 meters (36,000 ft) below sea level, the Mariana Trench is the deepest place in the world. Flat abyssal (uh-BIHS-uhl) plains cover huge portions of the deep-ocean floor. Seamounts are undersea mountains. Tall volcanoes that poke above the surface are volcanic islands. Mid-ocean ridges, the world's longest mountain range, run throughout Earth's ocean like the seams on a baseball.

READING TiP
Abyss means "a very deep place." Abyssal plains are on the deep-ocean floor.

? H

? I

The Ocean Floor

The ocean floor has canyons, mountains, and many other features.

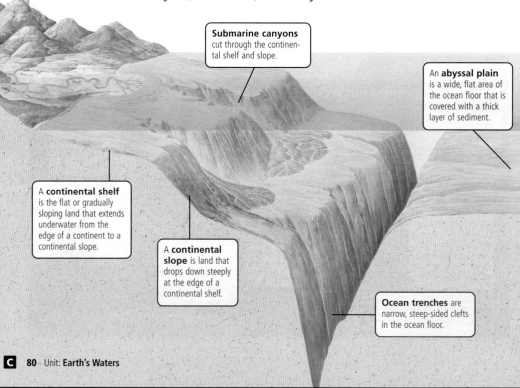

Submarine canyons cut through the continental shelf and slope.

An **abyssal plain** is a wide, flat area of the ocean floor that is covered with a thick layer of sediment.

A **continental shelf** is the flat or gradually sloping land that extends underwater from the edge of a continent to a continental slope.

A **continental slope** is land that drops down steeply at the edge of a continental shelf.

Ocean trenches are narrow, steep-sided clefts in the ocean floor.

C 80 Unit: Earth's Waters

DIFFERENTIATE INSTRUCTION

? More Reading Support

H What is the continental shelf? *submerged land at the edges of continents*

I What are the flat parts of the ocean floor called? *abyssal plains*

Below Level Have students work in small groups to make a model of the ocean floor using clay or other materials. Tell students to label the continental shelf, continental slope, submarine canyons, abyssal plain, ocean trench, seamounts, volcanic islands, and the mid-ocean ridge.

Ocean Exploration

Because the majority of Earth's surface is underwater, until recently it remained largely unexplored. If your ears have ever hurt when you dived to the bottom of a pool, you have felt the effects of water pressure. That pressure is multiplied hundreds of times deep in the ocean. The deeper down you go, the more crushing the weight of the water.

Despite the pressure, darkness, lack of air, chilling cold, and other obstacles to ocean exploration, scientists have developed tools that help them discover what lies beneath the surface. Scuba equipment allows a diver to spend about an hour underwater, breathing air carried in a tank on his or her back. Scuba divers can safely reach depths as great as 40 meters (130 ft). To go even deeper, people use small submarines, such as the one pictured here. Robots equipped with cameras offer views of areas too deep or difficult for humans to reach.

Small submarines carry researchers to depths as great as 6500 meters (21,300 ft).

CHECK YOUR READING What is one obstacle to ocean exploration?

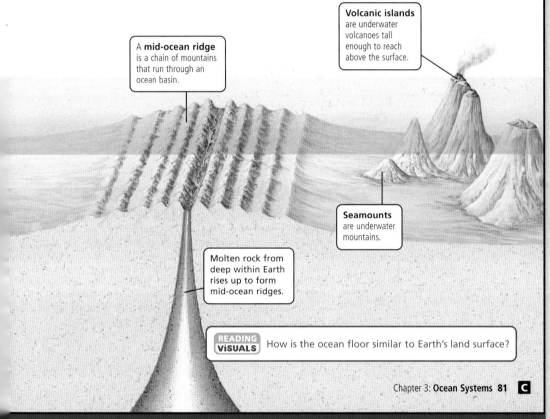

Volcanic islands are underwater volcanoes tall enough to reach above the surface.

A **mid-ocean ridge** is a chain of mountains that run through an ocean basin.

Seamounts are underwater mountains.

Molten rock from deep within Earth rises up to form mid-ocean ridges.

READING VISUALS How is the ocean floor similar to Earth's land surface?

History of Science

The first submersible that could carry researchers into the ocean depths was named *Alvin* and was first used in 1964. It is still operated by the Woods Hole Oceanographic Institution in Massachusetts. Using *Alvin*, researchers have not only discovered features of the ocean floor but also about 300 new species of animals. In 1985, *Alvin* was used to locate the wreckage of the *Titanic*. *Alvin* is used between 150 and 200 times a year, with each dive lasting about 6 hours.

Integrate the Sciences

On land, the pressure in a person's lungs equals the air pressure. Under water, the pressure in the lungs must be kept equal to the water pressure, which increases with depth. Scuba divers breathe compressed air, and their equipment includes a regulator that controls the flow of air to maintain the correct pressure in the lungs.

EXPLORE (the **BIG** idea)

Revisit "Internet Activity: The Ocean Floor" on p. 73. Have students discuss the features of the ocean floor that they viewed in this Internet activity.

Ongoing Assessment

Explain how the ocean is explored.

Ask: What can carry scientists deeper to explore the ocean floor? *small submarines*

CHECK YOUR READING *Sample answer: pressure, darkness, lack of air, or chilling cold*

READING VISUALS *Sample answer: Like land on the continents, the ocean floor has mountains, trenches, hills, plains, and canyons.*

DIFFERENTIATE INSTRUCTION

? More Reading Support

J Does water pressure increase or decrease with depth? *increase*

Advanced Ask students how the pressure problems associated with flying differ from those associated with diving. *At high altitudes, the air pressure is lower than it is at sea level. Deep in the ocean, on the other hand, the pressure is higher.*

Reinforce (the **BIG** idea)

Have students relate the section to the Big Idea.

 Reinforcing Key Concepts, p. 141

3.1 ASSESS & RETEACH

Assess

 Section 3.1 Quiz, p. 41

Reteach

To help students review this section, write these sentences on the board, leaving underlined areas blank. Let students fill in missing words.

- Ocean water covers _71_ percent of Earth.
- Ocean water contains _salts_ and such gases as _oxygen, nitrogen, and carbon dioxide._
- The higher the salinity, the greater the _density_ of ocean water.
- Ocean water is _saltier_ in shallow areas, in warm climates, and in areas where the water freezes.
- Marine animals and plants use the dissolved _gases_ in ocean water.
- The temperature of the ocean water _decreases_ with depth.
- Scientists explore the ocean using _scuba gear, submarines, robots, sonar, and satellites._
- The ocean floor has many of the same landforms as _the continents._

Technology Resources

Have students visit **ClassZone.com** for reteaching of Key Concepts.

 CONTENT REVIEW

 CONTENT REVIEW CD-ROM

 82 Unit: **Earth's Waters**

VOCABULARY Add a word triangle for *sonar* to your notebook.

Mapping the Ocean Floor

Today's detailed maps of the ocean floor would amaze early scientists and sailors, who tested sea-floor depths by dropping weighted lines overboard. Now sailors find depths with **sonar**, a system that uses sound waves to measure distances and locate objects. Ships aim sound waves at the ocean's bottom and measure the time it takes to receive the echo. A fast echo means the bottom is shallow; a slow echo means the bottom is deep.

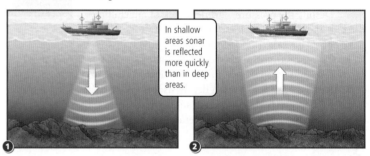

In shallow areas sonar is reflected more quickly than in deep areas.

① To measure sea-floor depth, ships aim sound waves at the ocean floor.

② The time it takes for the echo to return depends on the depth of the ocean floor.

Sonar can provide detailed images of small areas of the ocean floor. For mapping large areas, satellite imaging is much more efficient. Satellites can detect tiny bumps and dips in the ocean's height. These small surface differences reveal the shape of the ocean floor. For example, water levels are slightly higher over seamounts and lower over trenches. Because of its vast size and the challenges of exploring it, the ocean still holds many secrets. Exploration continues to bring new discoveries of geological formations and events.

 CHECK YOUR READING What are two methods used in mapping the ocean floor?

3.1 Review

KEY CONCEPTS

1. What substances are contained in ocean water?
2. Describe or draw five features of the ocean-floor landscape.
3. Describe three kinds of technology or equipment used to explore the ocean.

CRITICAL THINKING

4. **Predict** A shallow pan and a deep bowl hold equal amounts of salt water. If you left both containers in the sun for a day and then measured the salinity of the water in each, which would be saltier? Why?
5. **Analyze** Where in the ocean do you think water pressure is greatest? Explain why.

◯ CHALLENGE

6. **Synthesize** If you wanted to design a submarine to obtain the most information possible during a research voyage, what features would you include and why? First think about what types of information you would like to collect.

ANSWERS

1. dissolved salts and dissolved gases

2. Students could draw continental shelf, continental slope, submarine canyons, seamounts, volcanic islands, mid-ocean ridge, ocean trenches, abyssal plain.

3. scuba equipment: allows divers to spend time underwater; submarines: take scientists as low as 6500 meters; sonar: directs sound waves at ocean floor

4. the shallow pan, because the water would evaporate faster

5. at the bottom, because the pressure increases with depth

6. Answers will vary but may include sonar, satellite connection, robot, headlights, video camera, way to collect water samples, and so on.

MATH in SCIENCE

SKILL: PLOTTING COORDINATES

MATH TUTORIAL
CLASSZONE.COM

Click on Math Tutorial for more help with coordinates and line graphs.

Mapping the Ocean Floor

Before sonar and satellites, scientists used weighted lines to map the ocean floor. They tied a weight to a cable and dropped the weight overboard. When the weight landed on the ocean floor, the length of the cable indicated the depth of the ocean at that point. By combining many measurements, scientists could make approximate maps of sections of the ocean floor.

The table on the right gives depths at eight positions in the ocean off a coast. The positions are at regular intervals along a straight line. Depths are given as negative numbers.

Ocean-Floor Depths

Position	Depth
1	–293
2	–302
3	–381
4	–485
5	–593
6	–624
7	–517
8	–204

Example

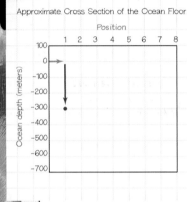

You can draw an approximate cross section of part of the ocean floor by making a line graph of the data. To graph the data, think of each column in the table as an ordered pair: **(Position, Depth)**.

(1) Copy the axes and labels.

(2) Graph each point. The first point has been graphed as an example.

(3) Connect the points with line segments.

Follow the steps above to graph points 2 through 8. Use the data and your graph to answer the following questions.

1. How deep is the ocean at position 2?

2. Which position is the deepest, and what is the depth there?

3. Shade the part of the graph that is underwater.

CHALLENGE Does your graph accurately represent the ocean floor between positions 5 and 6? Explain your reasoning.

The continents are shown in black and the ocean floor is colored in this satellite image. High points are orange and yellow, and the lowest points are deep blue-purple.

Chapter 3: **Ocean Systems** 83 **C**

ANSWERS

1. 302 m

2. Position 6; 624 m

3. All of the graph below the line should be shaded.

CHALLENGE No. The line connecting the points is only an approximation of the ocean floor. For example, if the bottom of the valley is between positions 5 and 6, then the ocean floor is lower than shown between those points.

MATH IN SCIENCE
Math Skills Practice for Science

Set Learning Goal
To graph depth measurements to draw a cross section of the ocean floor

Present the Science
The use of weighted lines to map the ocean floor produced only an approximate picture of large features. At first, such surveys were mainly done to locate shipping hazards close to shore. In the late 1800s, this method was used to explore the deep ocean.

Develop Graphing Skills
Review with students how to plot ordered pairs. Explain that students should first locate the position number, then follow that line up to the number representing the ocean depth and place a dot there. When they have finished plotting the points, they should draw a line connecting the dots.

DIFFERENTIATION TIP For students who have difficulty with math, demonstrate on the board or on an overhead transparency how to plot ordered pairs on a graph.

Close
Ask students to imagine what it would be like to try to map the entire ocean floor using this method, considering the vastness of the ocean. *Students should realize that it could take more than a lifetime of work.*

• Math Support, p. 180
• Math Practice, p. 181

Technology Resources
Students can visit **ClassZone.com** for practice in making line graphs.

 MATH TUTORIAL

○ Set Learning Goals

Students will

- Identify what causes ocean currents.
- Explain how currents distribute heat around the globe.
- Describe how currents interact with climate and weather.
- Observe in an experiment that a current of high-salt water will flow under a current of low-salt water.

○ 3-Minute Warm-Up

Display Transparency 20 or copy this exercise on the board:

Match each definition with the correct term.

Definitions

1. gradually sloping land that lies submerged around the edges of a continent *d*

2. technology system that uses sound waves to measure distance *a*

3. measure of the amount of dissolved salt in water *b*

Terms

a. sonar   c. continental shelf

b. salinity   d. continental slope

 3-Minute Warm-Up, p. T20

EXPLORE Currents

PURPOSE To observe that cold water will sink in warm water

TIP *20 min.* If the tape does not stick, substitute paper clips or clothespins to attach the cup to the side of the container.

WHAT DO YOU THINK? *You know the water is moving because the water is dyed green and you can see the green moving. The cold green water sinks because it is denser.*

KEY CONCEPT

3.2 Ocean water moves in currents.

◀ **BEFORE, you learned**

- The ocean is explored with sonar and satellite imaging
- The ocean floor is a varied landscape
- The ocean contains dissolved salts and gases

▶ **NOW, you will learn**

- What causes ocean currents
- How currents distribute heat around the globe
- How currents interact with climate and weather

VOCABULARY

ocean current p. 84
downwelling p. 86
upwelling p. 86
El Niño p. 88

EXPLORE Currents

How does cold water move?

PROCEDURE

① Stir together cold water, ice, and 3 drops of food coloring in the paper cup. Tape the cup to one inside corner of the plastic box.

② Fill the plastic box with enough room-temperature water to submerge the bottom of the cup.

③ Use a toothpick to carefully poke a hole in the bottom of the cup. Observe the movement of water.

WHAT DO YOU THINK?
How do you know the water is moving? What do you think is the reason for this movement?

MATERIALS
- cold water
- ice cubes
- food coloring
- paper cup
- masking tape
- clear plastic box
- toothpick
- room-temperature water

The oceans have major currents.

Would you ever want to go rafting on the ocean? Thor Heyerdahl of Norway did it in 1947 to demonstrate how early people might have migrated around the world. He floated on a wood raft from South America to Polynesia, without motor or paddles, powered only by an ocean current. An **ocean current** is a mass of moving water. There are many different currents that move water through the ocean. As they move water, ocean currents distribute heat and nutrients around the globe.

ⓘ RESOURCE CENTER
CLASSZONE.COM

Learn more about the different types of ocean currents.

RESOURCES FOR DIFFERENTIATED INSTRUCTION

Below Level

UNIT RESOURCE BOOK
- Reading Study Guide A, pp. 144–145
- Decoding Support, p. 179

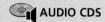 **AUDIO CDS**

Advanced

UNIT RESOURCE BOOK
- Challenge and Extension, p. 150
- Challenge Reading, pp. 175–176

English Learners

UNIT RESOURCE BOOK
Spanish Reading Study Guide, pp. 148–149

 AUDIO CDS

- Audio Readings in Spanish
- Audio Readings (English)

Surface Currents

Strong winds blowing over the ocean are set in motion by the uneven heating of Earth's surface. These winds cause surface currents to flow. The currents extend only about 100 to 200 meters (300–500 ft) down into the ocean, but they cover large areas. The map below shows the major surface currents.

Earth's rotation curls surface currents into giant clockwise whirlpools in the Northern Hemisphere. In the Southern Hemisphere, currents curl counterclockwise because of Earth's rotation. The shapes of continents also affect the paths of surface currents.

Use your finger to trace a few of the surface currents on the map. Surface currents carry warm water away from the equator and cool water away from the poles. In this way, surface currents moderate global temperatures.

New York City

Washington, D.C.

cold ⟶ warm

Gulf Stream

This satellite image shows the Gulf Stream, a surface current that flows along the eastern coast of the United States. The colors indicate the temperature of the water.

CHECK YOUR READING What causes surface currents?

Global Surface Currents

Surface currents are caused by winds. They move warm water away from the equator and cool water away from the poles.

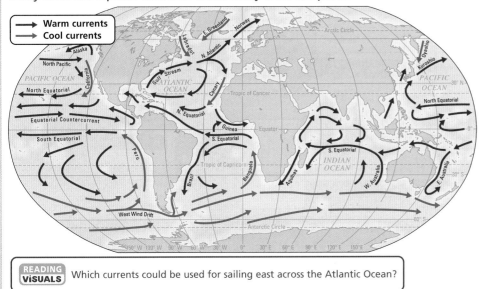

→ Warm currents
→ Cool currents

READING VISUALS Which currents could be used for sailing east across the Atlantic Ocean?

Chapter 3: Ocean Systems **85** **C**

Teach from Visuals

To help students interpret the map of global surface currents, ask:

• What color are the arrows for surface currents? *red and blue*

• What color represents warm water currents? *red*

• What temperature is the Gulf Stream current? *warm*

EXPLORE (the BIG idea)

Revisit "How Does Moving Air Affect Water?" on p. 73. Have students relate their results to surface currents.

Ongoing Assessment

CHECK YOUR READING *Answer: wind*

READING VISUALS *Answer: the Gulf Stream current and the N. Atlantic current*

DIFFERENTIATE INSTRUCTION

More Reading Support

A What do surface currents carry away from the equator? *warm water*

English Learners Alert students to watch for words that signal cause and effect: *because* (p. 87), *a change can . . . result in* (p. 88). Help them sort out the cause and the effect.

Areas of upwelling occur along the coasts of Peru, western North America, Somalia, northwest and southwest Africa, the Arabian Peninsula, and Antarctica. Because upwelled water is high in nutrients and supports large numbers of fish, these areas are home to many major fisheries.

Teach from Visuals

To help students interpret the upwelling diagram, ask:

- What do the arrows in the diagram represent? *the direction the ocean water is moving*

- How would you describe the movement of the water? *As the surface water is blown away from the coast, the deep water rises and takes its place.*

- How does this water movement affect materials? *Nutrients from the ocean bottom are brought to the surface.*

Ongoing Assessment

Identify what causes ocean currents.

Ask: What are some ways that ocean water is made dense? *Ocean water that becomes dense due to cold, salinity, or both sinks and moves slowly across the ocean floor.*

Deep Currents

In addition to surface currents, there are also currents flowing deep in the ocean. Deep currents are driven by differences in water density. Dense water sinks in the ocean the same way that dense chocolate syrup sinks in a glass of milk.

Seawater can become more dense because of cooling, an increase in salinity, or both. The densest water is found in the polar regions. For example, as sea ice forms near Antarctica, the salinity of the cold water beneath the ice increases. The highly dense water sinks down the continental slope of Antarctica and then moves slowly across the ocean floor. It may take 1000 years for water from this current to resurface near the equator. Another deep current flows out from the Arctic Ocean.

The movement of water in deep currents involves two processes important to ocean life. **Downwelling** is the movement of water from the surface to greater depths. As the water sinks, it carries oxygen down from the surface. The oxygen allows animals to live in the deep ocean. **Upwelling** is the movement of water up to the surface. Because this process brings up nutrients from the deep ocean, large numbers of ocean animals live in areas where upwelling occurs.

 B

 VOCABULARY
Add word triangles for *downwelling* and *upwelling* to your notebook.

 C

How Upwelling Affects Ocean Life

Upwelling provides nutrients that support animals and plants in surface waters.

surface water

1. Wind moves water away from the shore.

2. Upwelling occurs as deeper water rises to replace the surface water that has moved away.

The water rising to the surface is rich in nutrients. Many fisheries are located in areas of upwelling because ocean animals thrive there.

DIFFERENTIATE INSTRUCTION

? **More Reading Support**

B In what direction do deep currents move? *from the poles to the equator*

C In what direction does water move in upwelling? *up*

Below Level For students who need to visualize the concepts on this page, have them draw diagrams comparing deep currents, upwelling, and downwelling.

INVESTIGATE Currents

What happens where bodies of water meet?

PROCEDURE

1. Divide the box into two compartments, using masking tape and aluminum foil.

2. Pour one solution into one side of the box while a partner pours the other solution into the opposite side. Be sure you and your partner pour at the same time in order to keep the barrier from breaking.

3. Sprinkle pepper on the high-salinity side.

4. Use the pencil to poke two holes in the aluminum foil—one just below the water surface and another near the bottom of the box. Observe for 10 minutes.

WHAT DO YOU THINK?

- What did you observe in the box? Did you expect this?
- What forces drove any movements of water you observed?

CHALLENGE Compare what you observed with what you have learned about the actual movements of water in the ocean. How could you change the experiment to better model actual ocean currents?

Currents interact with climate and weather.

Imagine mixing red and blue paint in a cup by blowing through a straw. You can move some paint around, but you cannot predict exactly what pattern will result. Similarly, the ocean and the atmosphere interact in unpredictable ways. Moving air produces movement in the water while the water changes the air above it.

Remember that windblown surface currents help distribute heat around the globe by moving warm water away from the equator and cool water away from the north and south poles. The Gulf Stream, for example, is a surface current that moves warm water northeastward toward Great Britain and Europe. Because of the warm Gulf Stream waters, the British climate is mild. No polar bears wander the streets of Great Britain, as they might in places in Canada that are just as far north.

CHECK YOUR READING How does the Gulf Stream affect Great Britain?

DIFFERENTIATE INSTRUCTION

More Reading Support

D What kind of current is the Gulf Stream? *a surface current*

Advanced Briefly explain that every few years a weather pattern known as El Niño causes changes in Pacific Ocean currents. These changes affect worldwide climate patterns, often with devastating effects. Have students research the causes and effects of El Niño, and create a poster or a computer presentation. Refer them to the TAO/Triton Array—a system of buoys in the Pacific that measure conditions such as winds and currents so as to predict an El Niño.

- Challenge Reading, pp. 175–176
- Challenge and Extension, p. 150

INVESTIGATE Currents

PURPOSE To observe that a current of high-salt water will flow under a current of low-salt water

TIPS *30 min.*

- Before class, prepare a high-salinity solution and a low-salinity solution. The high-salinity solution should be 100 mL salt per 1000 mL water, plus a few drops of blue food coloring. The low-salinity solution should be plain tap water dyed red.

- Explain that the pepper is used so that the movement of the water is more visible. Emphasize that the pepper is not a variable in the experiment.

- Duct tape can be used in place of masking tape.

WHAT DO YOU THINK? *The high-salt solution seeped through the bottom hole and the low-salt solution seeped through the top hole. Differences in density caused these movements.*

CHALLENGE *Answers will vary. The experiment could include surface currents too.*

Datasheet, Currents, p. 151

Technology Resources

Customize this student lab as needed or look for an alternative. Print rubrics to assess student lab reports.

Lab Generator CD-ROM

Ongoing Assessment

Explain how currents distribute heat around the globe.

Ask: How do wind-blown surface currents help distribute heat around the globe? *They move warm water away from the equator and cold water away from the North and South poles.*

CHECK YOUR READING *Answer: The Gulf Stream is a surface current that moves warm water away from the equator and toward Great Britain and Western Europe, causing the climate in Great Britain to be mild.*

Ongoing Assessment

Describe how currents interact with climate and weather.

Ask: What are two examples of how currents affect climate and weather? *The Gulf Stream brings warm waters to the shores of Great Britain, moderating the climate. In El Niño years, winds, currents, and upwelling off the western coast of South America are disrupted and weather patterns around the planet change.*

 READING VISUALS *Answer: The warm Gulf Stream causes the climate of the town in the second photograph to be much milder, or warmer, than the other town at the same latitude.*

Reinforce (the **BIG** idea)

Have students relate the section to the Big Idea.

 R Reinforcing Key Concepts, p. 152

3.2 ASSESS & RETEACH

Assess

A Section 3.2 Quiz, p. 42

Reteach

Help students review this section's concepts by calling on volunteers to draw diagrams of the following currents on the board: surface current, deep current, upwelling, and downwelling. Have volunteers explain the cause and effect of each type of current.

Technology Resources

Have students visit **ClassZone.com** for reteaching of Key Concepts.

 i **CONTENT REVIEW**

CONTENT REVIEW CD-ROM

La Scie, Newfoundland

Fowey, England

ATLANTIC OCEAN
La Scie Fowey

READING VISUALS **COMPARE AND CONTRAST** These two towns are at about the same latitude, or distance from the equator. Ice can be found off the coast of La Scie, Newfoundland. Ice is never found off the coast of Fowey, England, which has mild weather year-round. What might explain this difference? **Hint:** the answer has to do with the Gulf Stream.

A change in even one of Earth's surface currents can result in huge changes in weather patterns. Most years, winds blow westward across the tropical Pacific Ocean. Every three to seven years, however, these winds do not blow as strongly as usual. Without the winds, the movement of currents in the Pacific is disrupted. These changes in air and water movements cause a global weather event called **El Niño,** which may last for 12 to 18 months.

During El Niño years, weather patterns change around the planet. Some places get more or less rain or snow than usual. Temperatures may be warmer or cooler than in other years. By using satellite readings of ocean temperatures and floating measurement devices to study conditions in the Pacific, scientists can often predict when El Niño will occur and how severe, or strong, it will be.

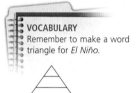
VOCABULARY
Remember to make a word triangle for *El Niño*.

3.2 Review

KEY CONCEPTS

1. What are two causes of currents in the ocean?
2. How do currents distribute heat around the globe?
3. How are climate and weather related to currents? Give two examples.

CRITICAL THINKING

4. **Infer** Describe at least two ways in which upwelled water might differ from the water around it.
5. **Infer** What factor do you think might cause a surface current to change direction?

CHALLENGE

6. **Predict** What would happen if all ocean currents suddenly came to a halt? Describe some effects this change would have.

ANSWERS

1. *wind and differences in density*

2. *by moving warm water away from the equator and cool water away from the poles*

3. *Currents interact with climate and weather. Gulf Stream and El Niño*

4. *It may be colder and it may contain more nutrients.*

5. *a change in the direction of the wind*

6. *change in the distribution of heat on Earth, change in climate in many places on Earth, change in sea life dependent on nutrients from upwellings*

KEY CONCEPT

Waves move through oceans.

◀ **BEFORE, you learned**

- Currents are masses of moving water
- Surface currents are driven mainly by winds
- Deep currents are driven mainly by differences in density

▶ **NOW, you will learn**

- How waves form
- How waves move energy through water
- How wave action changes near the shore
- How waves can cause currents near the shore

VOCABULARY

longshore current p. 92
rip current p. 92

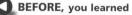

EXPLORE Waves

How does wave motion change with depth?

PROCEDURE

1. Fill an aquarium or another clear rectangular container about three-fourths full of water.

2. Tie several metal washers to each of four corks to make them float at different heights, as shown in the photograph.

3. Using your hand or a piece of cardboard, make steady waves in the water. Experiment with a variety of waves—some small and some large. Observe the cork movements.

MATERIALS

- aquarium or clear container
- corks
- string
- metal washers
- water

WHAT DO YOU THINK?
How does the movement of the corks change with depth?

OUTLINE

Remember to start an outline for this section.

I. Main idea
  A. Supporting idea
    1. Detail
    2. Detail
  B. Supporting idea

Waves form in the open ocean.

If you have ever blown across the surface of hot chocolate, you may have noticed ripples. Each of these ripples is a small wave. A wave is an up-and-down motion along the surface of a body of water. The vast ocean surface is covered with waves of various sizes, which are usually caused by winds. Moving air drags across the water's surface and passes energy to the water, causing waves. Other disturbances—such as earthquakes, landslides, and underwater volcanic eruptions—can also cause waves.

 CHECK YOUR READING What can cause waves to form in the ocean?

RESOURCES FOR DIFFERENTIATED INSTRUCTION

Below Level

UNIT RESOURCE BOOK
- Reading Study Guide A, pp. 155–156
- Decoding Support, p. 179

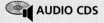 **AUDIO CDS**

Advanced

UNIT RESOURCE BOOK
Challenge and Extension, p. 161

English Learners

UNIT RESOURCE BOOK
Spanish Reading Study Guide, pp. 159–160

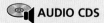 **AUDIO CDS**

- Audio Readings in Spanish
- Audio Readings (English)

3.3 FOCUS

▶ Set Learning Goals

Students will

- Identify how waves form.
- Describe how waves move energy through water.
- Explain how wave action changes near the shore.
- Explain how waves cause currents near the shore.

▶ 3-Minute Warm-Up

Display Transparency 21 or copy this exercise on the board:

Write the term that correctly completes each sentence.

1. A mass of moving water is called a _____. *current*

2. Surface currents are caused by _____ blowing across the ocean. *wind*

3. Deep currents are caused by differences in the _____ of water. *density*

T 3-Minute Warm-Up, p. T21

3.3 MOTIVATE

EXPLORE Waves

PURPOSE To observe how objects at varying depths are affected by waves

TIP *20 min.* This may also be done as a demonstration. Use a grease marker to make a grid across one side of the tank, or tape a clear acetate copy of graph paper to the outside of the tank. Mark the movement of the corks on the grid to allow a more quantitative comparison. Plastic fishing bobbers may be used instead of corks.

WHAT DO YOU THINK? *The waves affect deeper corks less than higher corks.*

Ongoing Assessment

CHECK YOUR READING *Moving air drags across the water's surface and passes energy to the water.*

Teacher Demo

To demonstrate that waves carry energy, bring a rope to class. Ask a student to hold one end of the rope as you hold the other end. Have the student move the rope up and down quickly. Note how the wave passes through the rope, but the rope itself does not move forward.

Address Misconceptions

IDENTIFY Ask: What is a wave? If students respond that it is water, they are mistaking the material through which the wave moves with the energy that is the wave.

CORRECT Explain that the water particles in a water wave actually move in a circle; the particles do not travel in the same direction as the wave. The wave is the energy that moves through the water. Point out that students can make waves in a rope tied to a doorknob; the rope does not move away.

REASSESS Have students describe in their own words the waves shown on the diagram on p. 91.

Technology Resources

Visit **ClassZone.com** for background on common student misconceptions.

 MISCONCEPTION DATABASE

Ongoing Assessment

Identify how waves form.

Ask: What is the primary way that waves form in oceans? *Wind disturbs the surface.* What are some other causes? *earthquakes, landslides, underwater volcanic eruptions*

Explain how wave action changes near shore.

Ask: What happens to waves as they break on shore? *They lose speed and energy and topple over.*

READING TiP

As you read about wave action at the water's surface, look at the illustrations on page 91.

 **RESOURCE CENTER**
CLASSZONE.COM

Explore ocean waves.

Wave Action at the Water's Surface

A wave in the ocean has the same basic shape as many other waves.

- The **crest** is the high point of the wave.
- The **trough** (trawf) is the low point of the wave.
- **Wave height** is the vertical distance between the top of the crest and the bottom of the trough.
- **Wavelength** is the distance between one wave crest and the next. **A**

You have read that currents move water from one place to another. In contrast, waves do not transport water. Waves move energy. They move through water, but the water stays more or less in the same place. Follow the drawings on page 91 to see how water particles move in a circle as a wave passes through. If waves do not transport water, how do surfers zip toward shore on waves? Surfers are powered by the energy traveling in the waves. Waves transport energy, not water.

Most waves affect only the water near the surface of the ocean. Water particles farther down move in smaller circles than particles near the surface. Below a certain depth, the waves no longer affect the water.

Wave Action near Shore

Waves may pass through the ocean for hundreds or thousands of kilometers before moving into shallow water. Then the waves lose speed and eventually topple over, losing their energy as they break on shore.

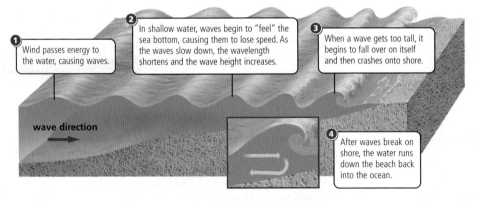

① Wind passes energy to the water, causing waves.

② In shallow water, waves begin to "feel" the sea bottom, causing them to lose speed. As the waves slow down, the wavelength shortens and the wave height increases.

③ When a wave gets too tall, it begins to fall over on itself and then crashes onto shore.

④ After waves break on shore, the water runs down the beach back into the ocean.

wave direction

When waves break on a beach, the water runs back down the sand into the ocean. If the shore is steeply sloped toward the water, the water may rush back to sea forcefully. An undertow is the pull of the water as it runs back to sea. Undertows may be dangerous. Some are strong enough to knock a person off his or her feet and into the waves. **B**

DIFFERENTIATE INSTRUCTION

? **More Reading Support**

A What is the distance between one wave crest and the next called? *wavelength*

B What is the pull of the water as it runs back to sea called? *undertow*

English Learners The steps above describe in detail how waves act near shore. Students from homogenous groups may need to practice describing processes or giving directions so an "outsider" can understand. Ask students to pick a place in their school and write out directions from their classroom to that place. Students should write as if the person reading has never been inside their school before; thus, they would not know landmarks such as the "Principal's office" or "Kim's locker."

Ocean Waves

Waves transport energy, not water. As a wave crest passes, the water particles move in circular paths.

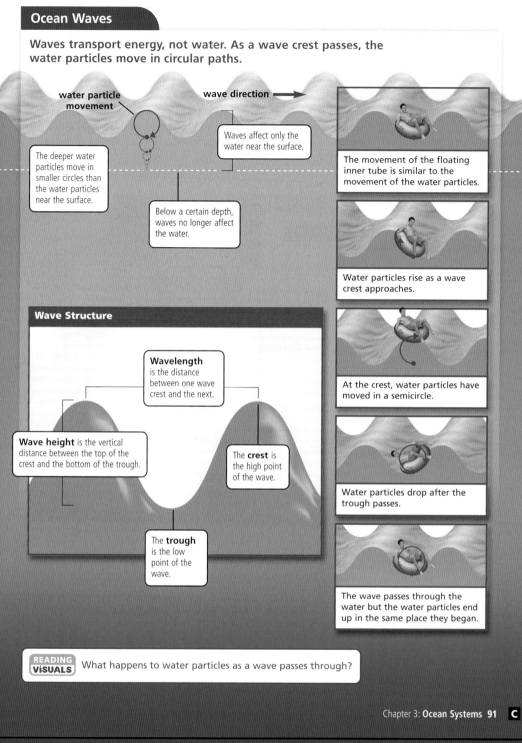

water particle movement

wave direction →

Waves affect only the water near the surface.

The deeper water particles move in smaller circles than the water particles near the surface.

Below a certain depth, waves no longer affect the water.

Wave Structure

Wavelength is the distance between one wave crest and the next.

Wave height is the vertical distance between the top of the crest and the bottom of the trough.

The **crest** is the high point of the wave.

The **trough** is the low point of the wave.

The movement of the floating inner tube is similar to the movement of the water particles.

Water particles rise as a wave crest approaches.

At the crest, water particles have moved in a semicircle.

Water particles drop after the trough passes.

The wave passes through the water but the water particles end up in the same place they began.

READING VISUALS What happens to water particles as a wave passes through?

DIFFERENTIATE INSTRUCTION

Below Level Have students give an oral summary of the science concepts presented in the three sets of diagrams.

Advanced Draw students' attention to the fact that a wave does not affect water below a certain depth, equal to one half the wavelength of the wave. Ask: How does this property of waves affect the ocean floor near the beach? in deeper water? *Ocean floor near beaches is affected by waves more than floor under deeper water.*

R Challenge and Extension, p. 161

Teach from Visuals

To help students interpret the diagrams of ocean waves, ask:

• How do water particles move as a wave passes? *in a circle*

• Where do the water particles end up? *in the same place they began*

• Through what part of ocean water do waves move? *just through the water near the surface*

• What does wave height refer to? *the vertical distance between the top of the crest and the bottom of the trough*

• What does wavelength refer to? *the distance between one wave crest and the next*

• Where is the man on the inner tube when he is at the crest? *at the top of the wave*

 This visual is also available as T22 in the Unit Transparency Book.

Integrate the Sciences

All waves are motions that transport energy. For example, heat, light, and sound also travel in waves. The terms *crest, trough, wavelength,* and *wave height* apply to all types of waves.

Ongoing Assessment

Describe how waves move energy through water.

Ask students to describe where the energy for a wave originally comes from. *Wind passes energy to the water, causing waves to form. Energy is transferred as water particles collide, and waves transfer energy, not water.*

READING VISUALS *Answer: The water particles move in a circle and end up where they began.*

Real World Example

Longshore currents carry large amounts of sand along shorelines, causing beaches to erode in one area and build up in another. One place this process occurs is along the eastern coast of the United States. Longshore currents contribute to the formation and shaping of sandbars, spits, and barrier islands. A spit is an extension of land off the end of a beach. A barrier island is an elongated island that forms parallel to a shore.

Teach from Visuals

To help students interpret the diagram of a longshore current, ask:

- What do the red arrows represent? *the direction of the waves*
- In what direction do the waves strike the beach? *at an angle*
- How do incoming waves affect the sand? *They push the sand up the beach at an angle and then wash it back straight down.*

Develop Critical Thinking

CAUSE AND EFFECT Ask students to identify the cause and effect relationship between longshore currents and rip currents. Tell them that writing these events along a timeline might help illustrate the sequence of events.

Ongoing Assessment

Explain how waves cause currents near the shore.

Ask: How do longshore currents develop? *Longshore currents develop where waves hit a shore at an angle and then wash straight back into the ocean. This zigzag motion moves water and sand parallel to the shore.*

 **CHECK YOUR READING** *Answer: Water builds up behind sandbars and then breaks through in rip currents.*

Waves cause currents near shore.

 C

Sometimes swimmers notice that without trying, they have drifted far down a beach. Their drifting is due to a **longshore current,** which moves water parallel to the shore. Longshore currents occur in places where waves meet the land at an angle rather than head-on. Since waves rarely meet the land exactly head-on, or perpendicular to the shore, there is a longshore current along almost every shore. The waves hit the shore at an angle and then wash back straight down the beach into the ocean. This zigzag motion moves sand along the beach, piling it up at one end.

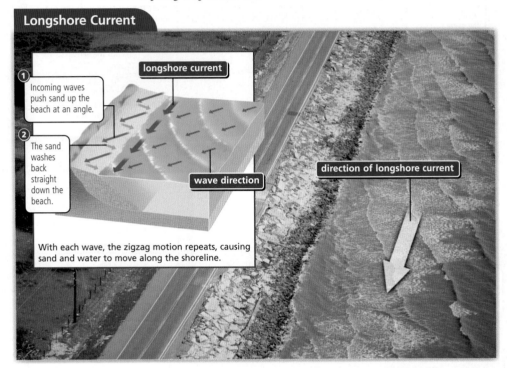

Longshore Current

longshore current

1 Incoming waves push sand up the beach at an angle.

2 The sand washes back straight down the beach.

wave direction

direction of longshore current

With each wave, the zigzag motion repeats, causing sand and water to move along the shoreline.

The movement of waves and longshore currents can build up sandbars in the waters near a shore. Sandbars are long ridges or piles of sand that can form parallel to the coastline. As waves wash over the sandbars and onto shore, water may collect behind the sandbars. Eventually, the pooled water will break through. **Rip currents** are narrow streams of water that break through sandbars and drain rapidly back to sea. Rip currents occur when high winds or waves cause a larger-than-usual amount of water to wash back from the shore.

 D

CHECK YOUR READING What role does a sandbar play in the formation of a rip current?

 **C** 92 Unit: **Earth's Waters**

DIFFERENTIATE INSTRUCTION

? More Reading Support

C In what direction do longshore currents move water? *parallel to a shore*

D In what direction do rip currents move water? *straight out to sea*

Inclusion Supply students who learn best with tactile aids with pans, water, and sand so they can make models of a longshore current and a rip current.

Rip Current

Signs such as this one on a beach in Hawaii warn swimmers of dangerous currents.

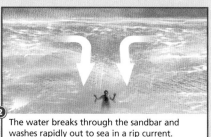

sandbar

① High winds or waves cause a larger-than-usual amount of water to collect behind a sandbar.

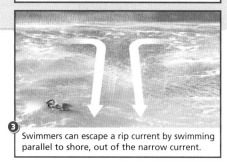

② The water breaks through the sandbar and washes rapidly out to sea in a rip current.

③ Swimmers can escape a rip current by swimming parallel to shore, out of the narrow current.

Like undertows, rip currents can be dangerous for swimmers. In the United States, around 100 people drown in rip currents each year. Most rescues made by lifeguards on U.S. beaches involve swimmers caught in rip currents.

Rip currents are too strong to swim against, but as you can see in the diagram, they are narrow. Swimming parallel to the shore is the best way to escape a rip current. Of course, it is better to avoid rip currents altogether! Many beaches offer daily rip-current forecasts based on information about wind and wave conditions.

3.3 Review

KEY CONCEPTS

1. How does moving air form waves in water?
2. Describe the movement of a water particle as a wave passes through.
3. What happens to waves near shore?
4. Name and describe two kinds of currents that wave action can cause near shore.

CRITICAL THINKING

5. **Compare and Contrast** Describe the similarities and differences between surface currents and waves.
6. **Apply** Imagine you find a piece of wood on the beach. The next day, the wood is 100 meters farther north. How might it have moved? Your answer should refer to currents.

⚠ CHALLENGE

7. **Infer** Some coastlines are more steeply sloped than others. How might wave action on a steeply sloped coastline differ from that on a gently sloped coastline?

Chapter 3: Ocean Systems **93** **C**

ANSWERS

1. It drags along the water and transfers energy to the water to form waves.

2. circular motion; the water particle moves up and forward at the crest, then down and back at the trough.

3. The wave trough drags and the wave slows; the wavelength shortens and the wave height increases until the wave breaks.

4. longshore current: moves water parallel to shore; rip current: water rushes out to sea

5. similarity: caused by wind; differences: currents move water, but waves move energy, not water

6. Longshore currents move water and sand along a beach and could carry the wood.

7. The wave trough begins to drag on the bottom sooner on a gently sloped coastline, so waves break earlier.

Teach from Visuals

To help students interpret the rip current diagrams, ask:

• What do the arrows in the diagrams represent? *the direction of water movement*

• In what direction does a rip current carry a swimmer? *out to sea*

Reinforce (the BIG idea)

Have students relate the section to the Big Idea.

Ⓡ Reinforcing Key Concepts, p. 162

3.3 ASSESS & RETEACH

Assess

Ⓐ Section 3.3 Quiz, p. 43

Reteach

Help students review this section's concepts by writing the following questions on the board and calling on volunteers to answer them:

What causes waves? *moving air dragging across the water's surface and passing energy to water* What do waves move? *energy* How do water particles in a wave move? *in a circular motion* What causes undertows? *water from waves breaking on shore runs back to the ocean and creates a pull* What causes longshore currents? *the zigzag motion of waves hitting the shore at an angle and then washing straight back to the ocean* What causes rip currents? *water breaking through a sandbar and rushing out to sea*

Technology Resources

Have students visit **ClassZone.com** for reteaching of Key Concepts.

ⓘ CONTENT REVIEW

◎ CONTENT REVIEW CD-ROM

Chapter 3 **93** **C**

CHAPTER INVESTIGATION

Focus

PURPOSE To observe how waves affect a floating object in order to draw conclusions about the movement of water particles in a passing wave

OVERVIEW Students will use their hands to create waves in an aquarium filled with water. They will place a bottle in the water and observe the effects of the waves on it. Students will find the following:

- The bottle rocks back and forth but does not move forward.
- The rocking movement of the bottle reflects the circular motion of the water particles in a passing wave.

Lab Preparation

- You might add two items to the lab setup: an aluminum pan for creating waves and a transparent grid on the side of the aquarium for measuring movement.
- Prior to the investigation, have students read through the investigation and prepare their data tables. Or you may wish to copy and distribute datasheets and rubrics.

 UNIT RESOURCE BOOK, pp. 182–190

 SCIENCE TOOLKIT, F14

Lab Management

- Tell students to be careful not to splash the water out of the aquarium.
- Before students leave class, make sure they have all the information they need to answer the first question in "Observe and Analyze," or have them complete the first question in class.

SAFETY If you are using glass aquariums, remind students that they are breakable and should be treated with care. Tell students to notify you immediately if an aquarium breaks; they should not try to clean up the glass themselves.

CHAPTER INVESTIGATION

Wave Movement

OVERVIEW AND PURPOSE The particles in liquid water are constantly moving. Surfers, boaters, and people in inner tubes enjoy the effects of this motion—even though they never see what is happening at the particle level. How do water particles move in waves? In this investigation you will

- observe the movements of a floating object as waves pass through water
- use your observations to draw conclusions about how water particles move in waves

▶ Problem

What does the motion of a floating object reveal about the movement of water particles in a passing wave?

▶ Hypothesize

Write a hypothesis to explain what the motion of a floating object might reveal about how water particles move in a wave. Your hypothesis should take the form of an "If . . . , then . . . , because . . ." statement.

MATERIALS
- small aquarium or clear, shoebox-size container
- water
- small plastic dropping bottle or plastic spice container, with cap
- salt

▶ Procedure

1. Fill the aquarium or clear container with cold tap water until it is three-quarters full.

2. Make the small bottle float with its top just below the surface of the water. You can accomplish this in several ways. First, try adding warm water to the bottle, then securely capping it without air bubbles. See if it will float. You can add salt to the bottle to move the bottle lower in the water. If the bottle is too low, you can trap a small air bubble under the cap to move the bottle higher in the water. Adjust these factors until you successfully float the bottle. The investigation will also work if the top of the bottle just touches the water's surface.

step 2

3. Remove the bottle from the water. Make sure the cap is tightly sealed.

INVESTIGATION RESOURCES

 CHAPTER INVESTIGATION, Wave Movement
- Level A, pp. 182–185
- Level B, pp. 186–189
- Level C, p. 190

Advanced students should complete Levels B & C.

 Writing a Lab Report, D12–13

Technology Resources

Customize this student lab as needed or look for an alternative. Print rubrics to assess student lab reports.

 Lab Generator CD-ROM

4. Push your hand back and forth in the water at one end of the aquarium for about 30 seconds, to produce waves.

5. Gently place the small bottle back into the center of the aquarium. With your eyes level with the water surface, observe the motion of the waves and the bottle. Repeat as many times as needed until you notice the bottle behaving the same way with each passing wave.

▶ Observe and Analyze

1. **RECORD** Make a diagram showing the aquarium setup, including the water, the waves, and the small bottle. Use arrows to show how the bottle moved as waves passed. Or you may draw several diagrams of the aquarium, showing the bottle at different locations as waves passed. Label the various parts of the waves.

2. **ANALYZE** Did the bottle travel with the wave? Why or why not?

▶ Conclude

1. **INTERPRET** Compare your results with your hypothesis. Do your data support your hypothesis?

2. **INTERPRET** Answer the problem question.

3. **INFER** What do your observations tell you about particle movement in waves? Did the results surprise you? Explain.

4. **EVALUATE** Why was it necessary to float the bottle just under the surface of the water rather than letting it float right on top?

5. **IDENTIFY PROBLEMS** What problems, if any, did you encounter in carrying out the procedure?

6. **IDENTIFY LIMITS** In what ways was this experiment limited in showing particle movement? Identify possible sources of error.

7. **PREDICT** How do you think particle motion in a wave with a tall wave height might differ from that in a wave with a short wave height?

8. **SYNTHESIZE** In this lab you made waves with your hand. In the ocean, most waves are caused by wind. Earthquakes, landslides, and other events also cause waves in the ocean. What do earthquakes, landslides, wind, and your hand have in common that allows all of them to make waves?

▶ INVESTIGATE Further

CHALLENGE Redesign this experiment in a way you think will better demonstrate the particle motion in a water wave. You need not limit yourself to the materials you used in this lab. Why will your version of the experiment work better?

Wave Movement

Problem What does the motion of a floating object reveal about the movement of water particles in a passing wave?

Hypothesize

Observe and Analyze

Table 1. Diagram of Setup

no wave	before crest	at crest	after crest	in trough

Conclude

▶ Observe and Analyze

1. Diagrams should show the bottle before, at, and after the crest and in the trough.

2. The bottle did not travel with the wave. Waves move energy through water but do not move the water.

▶ Conclude

1. Sample hypothesis: The bottle will move forward because the wave will push it. (Not supported, because the bottle just moved back and forth.)

2. The motion of the floating object reveals how the water particles move in a passing wave.

3. The floating bottle rocks back and forth as a wave passes. Similarly, the water particles move in a circle as a wave passes. The bottle and the water particles then return to their places.

4. Sample answer: At the surface, currents could move the water bottle. A submerged bottle will move more like the water particles around it.

5. Sample answer: adjusting the bottle

6. Sample answers: The bottle is bigger than water particles so it can only show approximately how water particles move; difficult to make good waves; currents may have affected the movement of the bottle; the movement of the bottle was estimated; bottle was affected by rebound from the other side of the aquarium.

7. The particles might move in larger circles in a wave with a tall wave height.

8. All transfer energy to the water.

▶ INVESTIGATE Further

CHALLENGE Sample answer: use a video camera to record the motion, a large tank to avoid rebound, and an electric wave maker so the waves are even.

Post-Lab Discussion

- Why do you think a dropping bottle was chosen for this experiment? *Air and water can be added or removed to make the bottle float at the right level.*

- How did this experiment show you that the movement you think you see with waves is not really what is happening? *It looks like waves move materials forward, including water, but actually the particles move in a circular motion. Objects floating in or on waves just move up and down.*

◐ Set Learning Goals

Students will

• Explain what causes tides.

• Recognize how tides affect coastlines.

• Describe how tides can be used to generate electricity.

• Make a model in an experiment to show how the Moon makes tides.

◑ 3-Minute Warm-Up

Display Transparency 21 or copy this exercise on the board:

Decide if these statements are true. If not, correct them.

1. Ocean waves are caused by wind moving the water. *Ocean waves are caused by the wind passing energy to the water.*

2. As a wave passes, water particles move in a circular motion. *true*

3. Longshore currents move water perpendicular to the shore. *Longshore currents move water parallel to the shore.*

🅣 3-Minute Warm-Up, p. T21

THINK ABOUT

PURPOSE To think about what causes ocean water levels to change

DISCUSS Have students look at the two photographs of the boat harbor in Lympstone, England. Ask:

• What change do you see in the photographs? *The water level is different.*

• What is the rise and fall in the water level along a coastline called? *tide*

Answer: These are introductory questions to get students thinking. Students may not know the answers, but they will learn the answers in the section.

Ongoing Assessment

CHECK YOUR READING *Answer: It is higher at high tide.*

KEY CONCEPT

3.4 Waters rise and fall in tides.

◀ **BEFORE, you learned**

• Wind provides the energy to form waves in the ocean
• Ocean waves change near shore
• The ocean is a global body of water

▶ **NOW, you will learn**

• What causes tides
• How tides affect coastlines
• How tides can be used to generate electricity

VOCABULARY

tide p. 96
tidal range p. 98
spring tide p. 99
neap tide p. 99

THINK ABOUT

What causes water levels to change in the ocean?

These two photographs were taken on the same day at the boat harbor in Lympstone, England. The change in water level in the harbor occurs every day on a regular and predictable basis. What forces cause shifts in such huge volumes of water? How can we explain the clocklike regularity of the flow?

VOCABULARY
Add a word triangle for *tide* to your notebook.

Coastal waters rise and fall each day.

Have you ever spent a day at a beach along the ocean? Perhaps you placed your blanket and beach chairs in the sand close to the water's edge. An hour later, you may have needed to move your blanket and chairs to keep the advancing waves from washing them away. The water level on coastlines varies with the time of day. This periodic rising and falling of the water level of the ocean is called the **tide.** The water level along a coast is highest at high tide, submerging parts of the coastline. The water level is lowest at low tide, exposing more of the coastline.

What in the world could cause such dramatic changes in the ocean's level? The answer is, nothing in this world. Read on to find out how out-of-this-world objects cause tides.

CHECK YOUR READING How does the water level along a coast differ at high tide and at low tide?

RESOURCES FOR DIFFERENTIATED INSTRUCTION

Below Level
UNIT RESOURCE BOOK
• Reading Study Guide A, pp. 165–166
• Decoding Support, p. 179

💿 AUDIO CDS

Advanced
UNIT RESOURCE BOOK
Challenge and Extension, p. 171

English Learners
UNIT RESOURCE BOOK
Spanish Reading Study Guide, pp. 169–170

💿 AUDIO CDS

• Audio Readings in Spanish
• Audio Readings (English)

The gravity of the Moon and the Sun causes tides.

Over 2000 years ago, people knew that the Moon and the tide were related. But 1700 years passed before the connection was explained in the terms of modern science. In 1687, Sir Isaac Newton developed his theories of gravity and linked the tide to the Moon's gravitational pull. Gravity is a force of attraction between objects. Earth's gravity pulls things toward its center—including you.

The gravity of the Sun and the gravity of the Moon also pull on objects on Earth. In response to the Moon's gravitational pull, Earth's water bulges on the side facing the Moon. The Moon's gravity also pulls on Earth itself. Earth gets pulled toward the Moon, leaving a second bulge of water on the side of Earth facing away from the Moon. The Sun's gravity pulls too, but with less effect because the Sun is so far away.

Daily Tides

The diagram below shows the two bulges of ocean water: one on the side of Earth closest to the Moon, and the other on the opposite side of Earth. At these bulges, it is high tide. Between the two bulges are dips. At these dips, it is low tide. As Earth rotates, different parts of it pass through the bulges and the dips. As a result, most places experience two high tides and two low tides each day.

VISUALIZATION
CLASSZONE.COM
Watch daily tides in action.

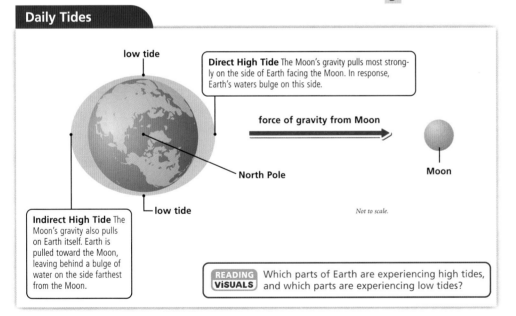

low tide

Direct High Tide The Moon's gravity pulls most strongly on the side of Earth facing the Moon. In response, Earth's waters bulge on this side.

force of gravity from Moon

North Pole

Moon

low tide

Not to scale.

Indirect High Tide The Moon's gravity also pulls on Earth itself. Earth is pulled toward the Moon, leaving behind a bulge of water on the side farthest from the Moon.

READING VISUALS Which parts of Earth are experiencing high tides, and which parts are experiencing low tides?

Teach Difficult Concepts

Students may have difficulty understanding how the Moon's gravity causes daily tides. Remind students that the amount of water in the global ocean is not changing. As students examine the diagram, tell them that they are looking down on Earth from above. You might use a globe to demonstrate the process shown in the diagram. Emphasize that the bulge of water on the side facing *away* from the moon is water that is left behind as the solid Earth is pulled toward the Moon.

Teach from Visuals

To help students interpret the daily tides diagram, ask:

- What does the wide gray area around Earth represent? *high tide*

- What does the thin gray area around Earth represent? *low tide*

- What causes direct high tide? *the Moon's gravity pulling on the Earth's waters on the side of Earth facing the Moon*

- What causes indirect high tide? *the Moon's gravity pulling on Earth itself*

Ongoing Assessment

Explain what causes tides.

Ask: How does the Moon's gravitational pull on Earth cause tides? *In response, Earth's water bulges on the side facing the Moon. The Moon's gravity also pulls on Earth itself, leaving a second bulge of water on the side of Earth facing away from the Moon. These two bulges form high tides. In between the bulges are dips that form low tides.*

READING VISUALS *Answer: In the illustration, the sides of Earth facing the Moon and facing away from the Moon are experiencing high tide (represented by the wide gray area). The parts of Earth that are not in line with the Moon are experiencing low tide (represented by the small gray area).*

DIFFERENTIATE INSTRUCTION

More Reading Support

A What is gravity? *the force of attraction between two objects*

B How many high and low tides do most coastlines experience in a day? *two of each*

English Learners *Pull* is used as both a noun and a verb and may confuse English learners. In "The gravity of the Sun and the Moon also pulls on objects . . . ," *pull* is a verb. It is a noun in "In response to the Moon's gravitational pull . . . ." Help students recognize when a word is used as a noun or a verb.

INVESTIGATE Tides

PURPOSE To make a model that demonstrates how the Moon creates tides

TIPS *15 min.*

- Remind students that they are looking down on Earth from above.
- Tell students that one full turn of the model Earth represents the rotation of Earth on its axis, which equals one day. It does NOT represent the Moon traveling around the Earth, which takes about 27 days.

WHAT DO YOU THINK? *It shows that Earth's waters are pulled toward the Moon. The tidal bulge is fixed in position with the Moon. Each place on Earth experiences two high tides and two low tides each day.*

CHALLENGE *12 hours*

- Tides Datasheet, p. 172
- Datasheet, Tides, p. 173

Ongoing Assessment

 CHECK YOUR READING *Answer: A narrow bay has more extreme tide changes than a wide open shore. Coastlines with steeply sloped ocean floors have more extreme tides than coastlines with gradually sloping ocean floors. Sentences 5–8*

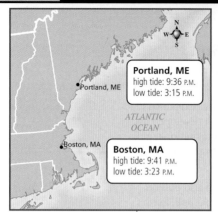

| Portland, ME |
| high tide: 9:36 P.M. |
| low tide: 3:15 P.M. |

ATLANTIC OCEAN

| Boston, MA |
| high tide: 9:41 P.M. |
| low tide: 3:23 P.M. |

A place farther east along a coastline experiences high and low tides earlier in the day, because it passes through the tidal bulge first. Times for high and low tides change daily.

The timing of high and low tides at one location on a coast may differ from the timing at other locations along that coast. As you can see on the map of the coastline of New England, the tides occur later as you move west along the coastline. As Earth rotates, the easternmost points on a coastline will pass through the tidal bulge before places farther west on the same coastline.

The timing of high and low tides is not the only way that tides can differ along a coastline. Some places experience higher high tides and lower low tides than other places. The shape of the land above and below the water affects tidal ranges. A **tidal range** is the difference in height between a high tide and the next low tide. The tidal range is greater in a narrow bay than on a wide-open shore. For example, the narrow harbor of Lympstone, England, shown in the photographs on page 96, has a very large tidal range. A coastline with a steeply sloped ocean floor has a larger tidal range than a coastline with a gradually dropping floor. For example, the coasts of Texas and western Florida have very small tidal ranges because of the gradual slope of the ocean floor there.

 CHECK YOUR READING In what two ways does the shape of the land affect the tidal range? What sentences tell you this?

INVESTIGATE Tides

How does the Moon make tides?

PROCEDURE

1. Cut the Tides datasheet in two, along the dotted line. Cut out the map of Earth on the bottom half of the sheet.
2. Use a paper fastener to connect the two pieces as shown in the photograph.
3. Now you are ready to model the tides. Rotate Earth one full turn in the direction of the arrow. One full turn is equal to one day.

WHAT DO YOU THINK?

- How does the model demonstrate the Moon's role in tides?
- How many times does each place in the ocean experience high tide and low tide each day?

CHALLENGE One full rotation of Earth takes place in a day, or 24 hours. About how much time passes between one high tide and the next high tide at any location on Earth?

SKILL FOCUS Making models

MATERIALS

- Tides datasheet
- scissors
- brass paper fastener

TIME 15 minutes

DIFFERENTIATE INSTRUCTION

 More Reading Support

C What is the difference in height between high tide and the next low tide called? *tidal range*

Advanced Have students use the model they created for the investigation to identify places that would be experiencing high and low tides as they turn the Earth.

Challenge and Extension, p. 171

Monthly Tides

The Moon is the main cause of tides, but the Sun affects tides as well. The Moon takes about a month to move around Earth. Twice during this month-long journey—at the new moon and the full moon—the Moon, the Sun, and Earth line up. The gravity of the Sun and the gravity of the Moon combine to pull Earth's waters in the same directions. The result is an extra-high tidal bulge and an extra-low tidal dip, called a **spring tide.**

During first- and third-quarter moons, the Sun and the Moon are not lined up with Earth. The gravity of each pulls from a different direction. The result is a smaller tidal bulge and tidal dip, called a **neap tide.** During a neap tide, high and low tides are less extreme.

Changes in the timing and the height of tides occur in a regular cycle. The timing of tides may be important to people who live near a coast or use coasts for fishing or boating. In many coastal communities, tide tables printed in newspapers give the exact times and heights of the tides.

RESOURCE CENTER
CLASSZONE.COM

Find out more about ocean tides.

READING TiP

Spring tides occur twice a month all year long, not just in spring. This use of the word *spring* is related to its meaning "to jump."

Monthly Tides

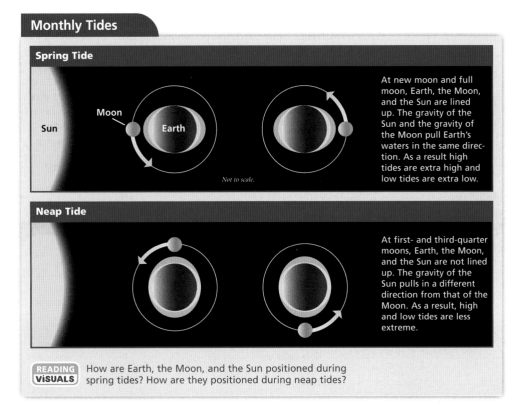

Spring Tide

Sun — Moon — Earth

Not to scale.

At new moon and full moon, Earth, the Moon, and the Sun are lined up. The gravity of the Sun and the gravity of the Moon pull Earth's waters in the same direction. As a result high tides are extra high and low tides are extra low.

Neap Tide

At first- and third-quarter moons, Earth, the Moon, and the Sun are not lined up. The gravity of the Sun pulls in a different direction from that of the Moon. As a result, high and low tides are less extreme.

READING VISUALS How are Earth, the Moon, and the Sun positioned during spring tides? How are they positioned during neap tides?

Chapter 3: **Ocean Systems 99** **C**

Teach from Visuals

To help students interpret the monthly tides diagrams, ask:

• What do the multiple views of Earth and the Moon represent? *the different positions of the Moon in relation to the Earth as it circles the Earth*

• During which phases of the Moon are the tides the greatest? *new moon and full moon*

• During which phases of the Moon are the tides less extreme? *first- and third-quarter moons*

NOTE: As students explore ocean tides on the Internet, have them download helpful graphics to add to their science logs.

Ongoing Assessment

Recognize how tides affect coastlines.

Ask: How do tides affect the activities of people along a coastline? *They occur in a regular cycle and may influence when people fish or boat or go to the beach.*

READING VISUALS *Answer: Earth, the Moon, and the Sun are aligned during spring tides. They are not lined up during neap tides.*

DIFFERENTIATE INSTRUCTION

More Reading Support

D What are spring tides like? *extra-high bulge and extra-low dip*

E What are neap tides like? *less extreme high and low tides*

Below Level Review the phases of the Moon with students, using a globe and a ball to demonstrate.

Ongoing Assessment

Describe how tides can be used to generate electricity.

Ask: How does a tidal dam work? *Water trapped at high tide rushes out at low tide, spinning turbines that generate electricity.*

 CHECK YOUR READING *Answer: Benefits: cause little pollution, renewable energy source. Drawbacks: only possible in some places, timing of tides may not be the same time electricity is needed, may harm wildlife.*

Reinforce (the BIG idea)

Have students relate the section to the Big Idea.

 Reinforcing Key Concepts, p. 174

3.4 ASSESS & RETEACH

Assess

 Section 3.4 Quiz, p. 44

Reteach

Ask students to review by identifying the main ideas associated with daily tides and monthly tides. *Daily Tides: Moon's gravity pulls on Earth, causing tidal bulge on side of Earth facing the Moon and on opposite side. The two bulges form high tides; dips between cause low tides. As Earth rotates, different parts pass through bulges and dips. Monthly Tides: When Earth, Moon, and Sun are aligned, extra high and low tides called spring tides occur. When Earth, Moon, and Sun are not aligned, neap tides occur.*

Technology Resources

Have students visit **ClassZone.com** for reteaching of Key Concepts.

 CONTENT REVIEW

CONTENT REVIEW CD-ROM

Tides can be used to generate electricity.

The energy of tides can be used to generate electricity. A tidal dam is built near a coast in the path of tidal waters. The water flows in during high tide and is trapped behind the gates of the dam. Then, when the tide is low, the gates open and the trapped water rushes out. As the water flows out, it spins turbines that power electric generators.

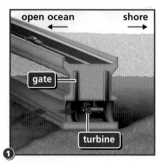

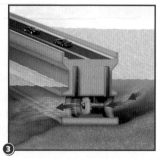
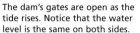

① The dam's gates are open as the tide rises. Notice that the water level is the same on both sides.

② When the tide begins to lower, the gates close, trapping water behind the dam.

③ At low tide, the gates open and the water rushes out, spinning turbines that generate electricity.

Tidal dams cause much less pollution than many other methods of generating electricity. Also, tides are a renewable source of energy; the tides are not used up in the process. However, tidal dams have some drawbacks. Few places in the world are actually suitable for such dams. Another problem is that the times of day when tidal dams generate electricity might not be the times of day when people most need electricity. Tidal dams also sometimes block the paths of migrating fish and might hurt marine life by altering the regular flow of water.

 CHECK YOUR READING What are the benefits and drawbacks of tidal power plants?

3.4 Review

KEY CONCEPTS

1. Describe the appearance of tidal changes at a coastline.
2. Explain the difference between the Sun's role and the Moon's role in creating tides.
3. How are tides used to generate electricity?

CRITICAL THINKING

4. **Synthesize** Contrast the daily and monthly patterns of tides. What role does the Moon's orbit around Earth play in both?
5. **Compare** Tidal range is the daily difference in high and low water levels. Compare the tidal ranges of neap and spring tides.

⬤ CHALLENGE

6. **Draw Conclusions** How would the tides be different if the Moon revolved around Earth twice a month instead of once a month?

ANSWERS

1. high tide: water is high up on shore, rocks submerged and beach narrow; low tide: water is low on shore, rocks exposed, beach wide
2. The gravitational pull of the Moon is the main cause of tides. The gravitational pull of the Sun makes the tides either more or less extreme.

3. Tide rises, gate traps water behind dam. At low tide, water is released and rushes out, spinning turbines to generate electricity.
4. As Earth rotates, different parts of it pass through tidal bulge, causing daily tides. Daily tides are caused by gravitational pull of Moon on

Earth. The monthly pattern of tides depends on whether or not the Moon and Sun are aligned with Earth.
5. neap tides—small tidal range; spring tides—large tidal range
6. four spring tides and four neap tides a month instead of two

The first and largest tidal energy plant in the world is in northern France, where the Rance River enters the English Channel. The plant opened in 1966.

Tidal Energy

Tidal power plants can work only in a few locations in the world. The best locations for tidal energy plants are ones with large differences between high and low tides. Why can't tides make electricity just anywhere?

Under Pressure

Each of these jugs contains the same amount of water. Water sprays out of the hole at the bottom of each—but why does it spray farther out of the narrow jug? The water pressure is greater in the tall, narrow jug because the water is deeper. The width of the jug does not matter—just the depth. The deeper the water, the greater the water pressure. The higher the water pressure, the faster the water comes out of the hole—and the farther the water sprays.

From Pressure to Power

Tidal dams use moving water to turn turbines that power generators. Turning turbines requires work. Work is the use of force to move an object. In this case, the force of the water is doing work on the turbines. The faster the water moves, the more work it can do.

Location, Location, Location

Think again about the two jugs. The water moves faster out of the hole in the tall, narrow jug—the one with the higher water pressure. Tidal power plants work best in places where high water pressure moves the water fast enough to turn the turbines. Remember that deeper water makes for higher water pressure. So tidal power plants work best in places with a large tidal range—the difference between high and low tide.

EXPLORE

1. **APPLY** When the water trapped behind a dam is released, it is channeled through openings in the dam and spins the turbines. From what you've learned about water pressure, where do you think the openings are, toward the top of the dam or toward the bottom? Explain your reasoning.

2. **CHALLENGE** Make a model of a tidal-energy plant. Use the side of a milk jug as a base, modeling clay to make the basin, and pieces of plastic for the dam and gates. Try different shapes for your basin and different sizes of gates to see how fast you can get the water to flow.

Chapter 3: **Ocean Systems 101** **C**

Set Learning Goal

To identify factors that increase water pressure

Present the Science

In physics, pressure is defined as force per unit area and is often measured in kilograms per square centimeter. Water pressure is produced by the weight of the water pressing down on layers of water below. In the example, the water in the taller jug produces more pressure because there is more water—and so a heavier weight—pressing down on the water below.

Discussion Questions

• Ask: Why is the water pressure in the tall, narrow jug greater than the water pressure in the short, wide jug? *because there is more water per square centimeter pressing down on the water below and its weight is greater*

• Ask: How would the water pressure in the short, wide jug be affected if you made the jug the same height as the tall, narrow jug? *It would increase and be the same as that in the tall, narrow jug.*

DIFFERENTIATION TIP For students who learn best through a combination of visual and verbal instruction, demonstrate the concept presented on this page by replicating the situation shown in the illustration.

Teaching with Technology

If probeware is available, you may wish to set this up as an experiment using the flow rate sensor.

Close

Ask: How does water pressure vary with depth? *the greater the depth, the higher the water pressure*

EXPLORE

1. *APPLY* The openings are probably near the bottom because the deeper the water, the greater the water pressure. Therefore, water would flow faster through openings nearer the bottom.

2. *CHALLENGE* Models will vary.

BACK TO

the **BIG** idea

Remind students of this chapter's big idea on p. 72: The oceans are a connected system of water in motion. Ask them to name the kinds of motions they have learned about in the chapter. *surface currents, deep currents, upwelling, downwelling, waves, undertow, longshore currents, rip currents, tides, spring tides, neap tides*

○ KEY CONCEPTS SUMMARY

SECTION 3.1

Ask students to list some substances dissolved in ocean water. *salts, oxygen, and other gases*

Have students name the ocean floor features on the diagram from left to right. Students can refer to pp. 80–81. *continental shelf, continental slope, submarine canyons, ocean trench, abyssal plain, mid-ocean ridge, seamounts, and volcanic islands*

SECTION 3.2

Ask students to name two types of ocean currents. *surface and deep*

Have students look at the diagram and find the Gulf Stream. How does the Gulf Stream affect climate? *moves warm water toward Europe making the climate milder*

SECTION 3.3

Have students explain what the movement of the inner tube represents. *the movement of water particles*

Ask students how water particles move when a wave passes through. *in a circle*

SECTION 3.4

Ask students to look at the diagram and explain what the red arrow represents. *the force of gravity from the Moon*

Ask students where low tides would be located on the diagram. *at the thin part (top and bottom of the picture)*

Review Concepts

• Big Idea Flow Chart, p. T17
• Chapter Outline, pp. T23–24

 102 Unit: **Earth's Waters**

 Chapter Review

the **BIG** idea

The oceans are a connected system of water in motion.

 **CONTENT REVIEW**
CLASSZONE.COM

◄ KEY CONCEPTS SUMMARY

3.1 The oceans are a connected system.

• Much of Earth is covered by ocean water, which contains dissolved salts and gases.

• Ocean temperatures decrease with depth.

• The ocean floor has canyons, mountains, and many other features.

VOCABULARY
salinity p. 76
density p. 76
continental shelf p. 80
sonar p. 82

3.2 Ocean water moves in currents.

• Surface currents are set in motion by winds and carry heat around the globe.

• Deep currents are caused by differences in water density. Dense water sinks at the poles and very slowly flows toward the equator.

VOCABULARY
ocean current p. 84
upwelling p. 86
downwelling p. 86
El Niño p. 88

3.3 Waves move through oceans.

• Ocean waves transport energy, not water. When a wave passes, water particles end up in the same places they began.

• Longshore currents occur when waves hit shores at angles.

• Rip currents are narrow streams of water that break through sandbars.

VOCABULARY
longshore current p. 92
rip current p. 92

3.4 Waters rise and fall in tides.

The Moon's gravity pulls Earth's waters into bulges and dips. As Earth rotates, its movement through these bulges and dips causes tides.

direct high tide

indirect high tide — Earth ——————→ Moon

VOCABULARY
tide p. 96
tidal range p. 98
spring tide p. 99
neap tide p. 99

C 102 Unit: Earth's Waters

Technology Resources

Have students visit **ClassZone.com** or use the CD-ROM for a cumulative review of concepts.

 CONTENT REVIEW

CONTENT REVIEW CD-ROM

Engage students in a whole-class interactive review of Key Concepts. Edit content as you wish.

POWER PRESENTATIONS

Reviewing Vocabulary

Make a description wheel like the one below for each of the following terms. Write the term in the circle. On the spokes, write words or phrases that describe the term.

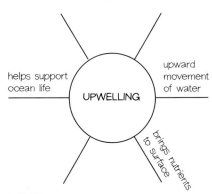

1. El Niño
2. longshore current
3. rip current

Reviewing Key Concepts

Multiple Choice *Choose the letter of the best answer.*

4. Warm water stays at the ocean surface because
   a. it is less dense than cold water
   b. it is more dense than cold water
   c. it is saltier than cold water
   d. it has more carbon dioxide than cold water

5. Sonar measures ocean depth by means of
   a. weighted lines   c. sound waves
   b. light waves   d. magnets

6. Surface currents are caused by
   a. waves   c. density
   b. winds   d. heat

7. El Niño is caused by changes in
   a. wave speed   c. salinity
   b. currents   d. tides

8. Deep currents are caused by differences in
   a. location   c. depth
   b. wind speed   d. density

9. Tides are caused by the gravitational pull of
   a. Earth and the Sun
   b. the Sun and the Moon
   c. Earth alone
   d. Earth and the Moon

10. What does wave action involve?
    a. the transfer of water molecules across the ocean surface
    b. the transfer of energy across the ocean surface
    c. oscillations generated by tides
    d. rip currents

Short Answer *Write a short answer to each question.*

11. What is the connection between salinity and density?

12. Explain why Earth's oceans are actually parts of one connected body of water.

13. Describe the relationship between ocean temperature and depth.

14. What are the characteristics of a wave? Copy the drawing below onto your paper, and label each part.

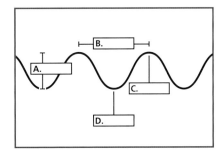

Reviewing Vocabulary

Sample answers:

1. *changes in currents in Pacific; winds not as strong; every 3–7 years; global weather event*

2. *moves water parallel to shore; waves hit shore at angle; zigzag motion piles sand on end of beach*

3. *narrow streams of water; break through sandbars; go back to sea*

Reviewing Key Concepts

4. *a*

5. *c*

6. *b*

7. *b*

8. *d*

9. *b*

10. *b*

11. *the higher the salinity, the higher the density*

12. *The continents divide Earth's oceans into sections, but the sections are all connected.*

13. *The ocean is warmest at the surface. Then the temperature drops quickly with depth at the thermocline. Below the thermocline, in the deep ocean, the water is barely above freezing.*

14. *A: wave height; B: wavelength; C: crest; D: trough*

ASSESSMENT RESOURCES

 UNIT ASSESSMENT BOOK
- Chapter Test A, pp. 45–48
- Chapter Test B, pp. 49–52
- Chapter Test C, pp. 53–56
- Alternative Assessment, pp. 57–58

 SPANISH ASSESSMENT BOOK
Spanish Chapter Test, pp. 161–164

Technology Resources

Edit test items and answer choices.

 Test Generator CD-ROM

Visit **ClassZone.com** to extend test practice.

 Test Practice

Thinking Critically

15. *Evaporate the water from both and see if any salt remains. Or, put a drop of food coloring in each cup and see if it floats or sinks.*

16. *Echoes would return faster as the ship began to cross the ridge, then slower as the ship went over the descending slope on the other side.*

17. *Sample answer: Pressure and breathing are obstacles in both. Pressure is high in the ocean but low in space. Water prevents breathing in the ocean. Lack of oxygen prevents breathing in space.*

18. *Sample answer: It could make the weather cooler if a warm current changed direction.*

19. *Surface currents, waves, upwelling, rip currents*

20. *Waves only affect the water at the surface. Below a certain depth, waves don't affect the water at all.*

21. *Waves: caused by wind. Both: ocean motion. Tides: caused by gravity of Moon and Sun. Summary: Ocean waves and tides are both ocean motions. Waves are caused by wind while tides are caused by gravity of Moon and Sun.*

22. *That the tide is extra low at spring tides, when Earth, Moon, and Sun are aligned. Spring tides happen twice a month.*

the BIG idea

23. *Wind is causing the waves in the photograph. Near the shore, the wavelength gets shorter and the wave height gets taller until the wave breaks. Tides could cause the water level to rise.*

24. *The gravitational pull of Moon and Sun causes tides.*

UNIT PROJECTS

Collect schedules, materials lists, and questions. Be sure dates and materials are obtainable, and questions are focused.

 Unit Projects, pp. 5–10

Thinking Critically

15. **SYNTHESIZE** One of these cups contains salt water, and the other contains fresh water. Without tasting the water, how could you figure out which sample is which? Describe two methods. You may specify tools or materials you would need to carry out the two methods. **Hint:** Think about the water cycle and density when considering the two methods.

16. **INFER** After the development of sonar, oceanographic researchers discovered much about the features of the ocean floor. How would the sonar readings of a research ship be affected as it passes above a mid-ocean ridge?

17. **COMPARE AND CONTRAST** How are space exploration and ocean exploration similar? How are they different?

18. **PROVIDE EXAMPLES** How could a change in the direction of a surface current in the ocean affect weather? Give examples of the weather in an area before and after the change.

19. **INFER** If global winds were to change, which ocean motions would be affected?

20. **APPLY** During a violent storm that causes huge waves to form on the ocean's surface, a submarine glides deep underwater, unaffected by the waves above. Explain why.

21. **COMPARE AND CONTRAST** Copy and fill in the Venn diagram below. In the overlapping section, list at least one characteristic that is shared by waves and tides. In the outer sections, list characteristics that are not shared. Then write a short summary of the information in the Venn diagram.

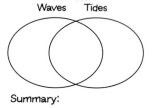

Summary:

22. **APPLY** Maria and her friends like to play soccer on a beach. Sometimes the water is very low at low tide, and there is plenty of room to play. At other times, the water does not get as low at low tide, and there is not enough room to play. What does Maria need to know about monthly tidal cycles so that she can plan to have the soccer games when there is plenty of room on the beach?

the BIG idea

23. **IDENTIFY CAUSE AND EFFECT** Look again at the photograph on pages 72–73. Now that you have finished the chapter, explain what is causing the waves in the photograph. Also explain what might cause the water level to rise and cover the area where the surfer is standing.

24. **SYNTHESIZE** One system can interact with another system. The oceans are a connected system of water in motion. The solar system is the Sun and its family of orbiting planets, moons, and other objects. Describe a connection between the solar system and the ocean system.

UNIT PROJECTS

Check your schedule for your unit project. How are you doing? Be sure that you have placed data or notes from your research in your project folder.

MONITOR AND RETEACH

If students have trouble applying the concepts in items 15–16, divide the class into study groups and have them review the last paragraph on p. 76 and the diagram on p. 82.

Students may benefit from summarizing one or more sections of the chapter.

R Summarizing the Chapter, pp. 200–201

Analyzing a Table

The table below shows the times of high and low tides at a location on the Atlantic Ocean coast. Use the table to answer the questions below.

	Low Tide	High Tide	Low Tide	High Tide
Monday	12:01 A.M.	5:33 A.M.	11:58 A.M.	5:59 P.M.
Tuesday	12:57 A.M.	6:33 A.M.	12:51 P.M.	6:54 P.M.
Wednesday	1:51 A.M.	7:30 A.M.	1:45 P.M.	7:48 P.M.
Thursday	2:43 A.M.	8:25 A.M.	2:38 P.M.	8:40 P.M.

1. On which day was there a high tide at 7:48 P.M.?

  a. Monday   **c.** Wednesday

  b. Tuesday   **d.** Thursday

2. Low tide is a good time to find shells along the beach. What time would be best for finding shells on Wednesday?

  a. 8:00 A.M.   **c.** noon

  b. 10:00 A.M.   **d.** 2:00 P.M.

3. What was happening to the water level along the beach between 12:00 A.M. and 5:33 A.M. on Monday?

  a. The water level was getting higher.

  b. The water level was getting lower.

  c. The water level was at its lowest.

  d. The water level was at its highest.

4. Which of the following graphs best represents the tides during one day?

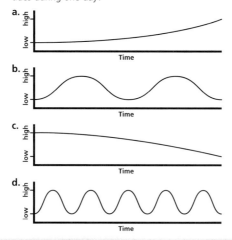

Extended Response

Answer the two questions below in detail.

5. How could you use a cork and a tank of water to demonstrate that waves transport energy, not water? You may include a diagram as part of your response if you wish.

6. The beaker contains both salt water and fresh water. Why do the two liquids form layers? Use the words *salinity* and *density* in your response.

fresh water

salt water

Analyzing a Table

1. c   *2. d*   *3. a*   *4. b*

Extended Response

5. RUBRIC

4 points for a response that explains the concept and describes or has labeled diagrams

Sample: You could make waves in the water with your hand and place the cork in the water. You would observe that the cork rocks back and forth but does not move forward with the waves. The cork reveals the circular motion of the water particles as a wave passes through.

3 points for a response that shows or describes the concept

2 points for a response that shows some understanding of the concept

6. RUBRIC

4 points for a response that correctly answers the question and uses the terms *salinity* and *density* accurately

Sample: The two samples of water form layers because they differ in salinity and density. The salt water is denser than the fresh water. A denser fluid sinks in a less dense fluid.

3 points correctly answers the question and shows understanding and uses one term accurately

2 points correctly answers the question but does not use the terms

Have students answer the following questions in their **Science Notebook:**

1. Which of the motions of ocean water described in this chapter have you personally experienced?

2. Which topic in this chapter do you still have questions about?

3. Are the concepts involved in your Unit Project challenging for you or too easy?

TIMELINES in Science

FOCUS

▶ Set Learning Goals

Students will

- Discuss the history of ocean exploration.
- Distinguish among technologies used to study the ocean.
- Analyze how ocean technology is applied.
- Use data to model the ocean floor.

National Science Education Standards

A.9.a–g Understandings about Scientific Inquiry

E.6.a–c Understandings about Science and Technology

F.5.a–e, F.5.g Science and Technology in Society

G.1.a–b Science as a Human Endeavor

G.2.a Nature of Science

G.3.a–c History of Science

INSTRUCT

The top half of the timeline shows major developments in the study of the ocean. The bottom half discusses advances in technology and gives examples of how this technology is applied. Point out that people have been studying oceans for at least 5000 years. The timeline, however, begins roughly 2300 years ago, when people first developed ways to explore beneath the ocean's surface.

Application

MEASURING OCEAN DEPTH Tell students that sometimes technology is developed to solve a particular problem—scuba equipment, for example, helps people breathe underwater. Sometimes technology is developed simply to further scientific knowledge. Posidonius's method of determining ocean depth had no other application until thousands of years later.

EXPLORING THE OCEAN

People have been studying ocean waves and currents at least since Egyptians sailed in the Mediterranean Sea more than 5000 years ago. Almost 3000 years ago, Phoenicians in the Mediterranean and Polynesians in the South Pacific understood enough to sail the open sea with confidence. More than 2000 years ago, people developed special gear to provide divers with oxygen so that they could explore the undersea world.

The timeline shows some historical events in the study of the ocean. The boxes below the timeline show how technology has made this study possible and useful.

345 B.C.

Alexander Goes Undersea?

According to legend, Macedonia's powerful ruler Alexander the Great has himself lowered into the ocean in a glass ball so that he can explore what lies underwater.

EVENTS

360 B.C.   320 B.C.

APPLICATIONS AND TECHNOLOGY

APPLICATION

Measuring Ocean Depth

Around 85 B.C., the Greek philosopher Posidonius used a simple method to answer a simple question. He wanted to know the depth of the Mediterranean Sea. So he and a crew sailed out into the sea near Italy. There, they dropped a weight tied to a very long rope into the water. When the weight struck bottom, they measured how much rope they had let out. It was almost 2 kilometers (about 1 mi). This was the standard method for measuring depth for almost 2000 years. Today, instruments on ships emit sound waves that bounce off the sea floor. The instruments then calculate depth according to how long the sound waves take to return to the surface.

A sailor in 1916 prepares to lower a weight on a rope to measure the ocean's depth.

C **106** Unit: Earth's Waters

DIFFERENTIATE INSTRUCTION

Below Level To help students understand the timeline, have them describe any patterns that they see, such as gaps in the timeline and number of years between events.

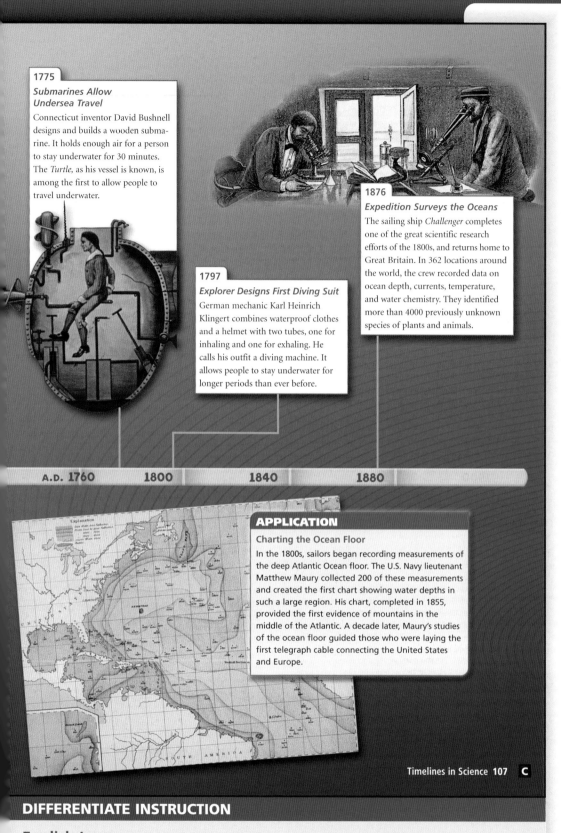

1775
Submarines Allow Undersea Travel
Connecticut inventor David Bushnell designs and builds a wooden submarine. It holds enough air for a person to stay underwater for 30 minutes. The *Turtle*, as his vessel is known, is among the first to allow people to travel underwater.

1797
Explorer Designs First Diving Suit
German mechanic Karl Heinrich Klingert combines waterproof clothes and a helmet with two tubes, one for inhaling and one for exhaling. He calls his outfit a diving machine. It allows people to stay underwater for longer periods than ever before.

1876
Expedition Surveys the Oceans
The sailing ship *Challenger* completes one of the great scientific research efforts of the 1800s, and returns home to Great Britain. In 362 locations around the world, the crew recorded data on ocean depth, currents, temperature, and water chemistry. They identified more than 4000 previously unknown species of plants and animals.

A.D. 1760   1800   1840   1880

APPLICATION

Charting the Ocean Floor

In the 1800s, sailors began recording measurements of the deep Atlantic Ocean floor. The U.S. Navy lieutenant Matthew Maury collected 200 of these measurements and created the first chart showing water depths in such a large region. His chart, completed in 1855, provided the first evidence of mountains in the middle of the Atlantic. A decade later, Maury's studies of the ocean floor guided those who were laying the first telegraph cable connecting the United States and Europe.

Scientific Process

1797 Ask students to imagine that they invented the diving suit. Discuss the problems of making a safe enclosure in a time before plastics for a person to breathe in and observe from. Ask: What purpose did the diving suit serve? *to satisfy curiosity about the ocean by allowing people more time to explore*

Application

CHARTING THE OCEAN FLOOR The mountain range in the middle of the Atlantic Ocean is called the Mid-Atlantic Ridge. Ridge systems form in areas where tectonic plates move apart, or diverge. As the plates separate, a crack forms on the ocean floor. Magma fills the crack, forming new ocean floor. Show students a modern physiographic map of the ocean floor. Have them identify the ridge located in the middle of the Atlantic Ocean.

DIFFERENTIATE INSTRUCTION

English Learners Have students identify several words on pp. 106–107 that include commonly used prefixes and suffixes, such as *submarine* and *powerful*. Tell students to use a dictionary to look up the meanings of the prefixes and suffixes—if necessary, have them look up the meanings of the root words as well.

Technology

SONAR Sonar readings are compiled into echo charts, which show profiles of the ocean floor. Schools of fish can reflect sound waves and distort the profiles. Experienced chart readers can detect the difference between a true reading of the ocean floor and a false reading caused by schools of fish. Ask: What can people who fish learn from sonar? *where the fish are, how deep to lower the nets, what size nets to use, how fast the fish are moving*

Integrate the Sciences

Dolphins and some whales use echoes to locate food, estimate distances, and identify nearby objects. In this process, called echolocation, the aquatic mammals make loud squeaking or clicking sounds. The sounds reflect off objects and return to the animals, who identify the object by its shape and size. Echolocation is also used by bats to hunt and navigate.

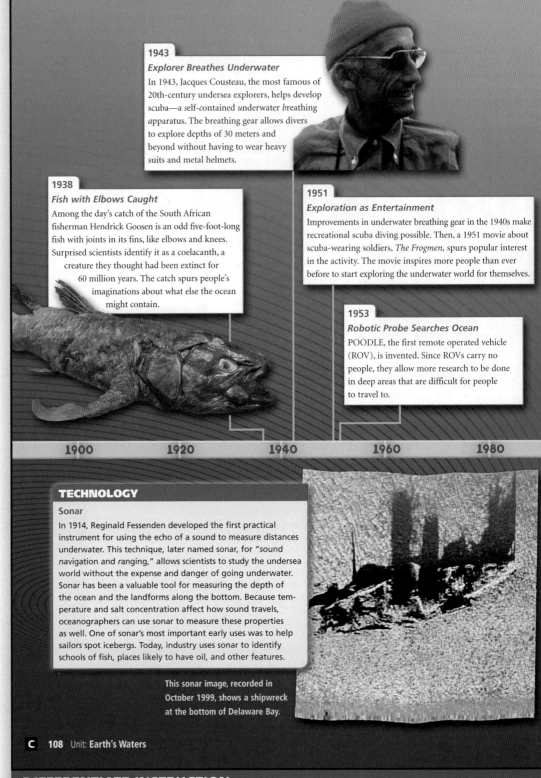

1943

Explorer Breathes Underwater

In 1943, Jacques Cousteau, the most famous of 20th-century undersea explorers, helps develop scuba—a *self*-contained *u*nderwater *b*reathing *a*pparatus. The breathing gear allows divers to explore depths of 30 meters and beyond without having to wear heavy suits and metal helmets.

1938

Fish with Elbows Caught

Among the day's catch of the South African fisherman Hendrick Goosen is an odd five-foot-long fish with joints in its fins, like elbows and knees. Surprised scientists identify it as a coelacanth, a creature they thought had been extinct for 60 million years. The catch spurs people's imaginations about what else the ocean might contain.

1951

Exploration as Entertainment

Improvements in underwater breathing gear in the 1940s make recreational scuba diving possible. Then, a 1951 movie about scuba-wearing soldiers, *The Frogmen*, spurs popular interest in the activity. The movie inspires more people than ever before to start exploring the underwater world for themselves.

1953

Robotic Probe Searches Ocean

POODLE, the first remote operated vehicle (ROV), is invented. Since ROVs carry no people, they allow more research to be done in deep areas that are difficult for people to travel to.

1900   1920   1940   1960   1980

TECHNOLOGY

Sonar

In 1914, Reginald Fessenden developed the first practical instrument for using the echo of a sound to measure distances underwater. This technique, later named sonar, for "*s*ound *n*avigation *a*nd *r*anging," allows scientists to study the undersea world without the expense and danger of going underwater. Sonar has been a valuable tool for measuring the depth of the ocean and the landforms along the bottom. Because temperature and salt concentration affect how sound travels, oceanographers can use sonar to measure these properties as well. One of sonar's most important early uses was to help sailors spot icebergs. Today, industry uses sonar to identify schools of fish, places likely to have oil, and other features.

This sonar image, recorded in October 1999, shows a shipwreck at the bottom of Delaware Bay.

DIFFERENTIATE INSTRUCTION

Below Level Help students understand that, before the development of sonar, it was very difficult to measure the depth of the deep sea. Have them review the method developed by Posidonius to measure ocean depth. Ask: How does sonar improve upon Posidonius's method? *It allows scientists to measure the deepest parts of the ocean using the echo of sound rather than ropes, and it is much faster.*

1998
Aquarius *Keeps Researching*

After renovation, the 12-year-old *Aquarius* lab settles on the ocean floor in the Florida Keys. Its crew is investigating a nearby coral reef. They have studied the impact of sewage, the effects of ultraviolet radiation, and chemicals produced by organisms in the reef.

1994
Life Thrives Under Ocean

The discovery of microorganisms thriving in rock pulled up from 500 meters (1600 ft) below the ocean floor raises new questions for scientists. How did the bacteria get there? How do they survive? How many are there? Scientists call the region the deep biosphere.

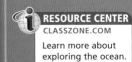

RESOURCE CENTER
CLASSZONE.COM

Learn more about exploring the ocean.

2000

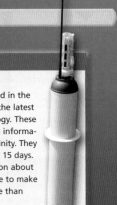

TECHNOLOGY
Ocean Buoys

Starting in 2000, scientists scattered in the ocean 3000 buoys equipped with the latest developments in floating technology. These Argo floats then started collecting information on water temperature and salinity. They transmitted data by satellite every 15 days. With this more detailed information about ocean water, scientists may be able to make weather predictions more accurate than ever before.

INTO THE FUTURE

Over the past 5000 years, people have learned more and more about the ocean. This knowledge has helped scientists understand how ocean systems work, how Earth has changed, and what factors influence the weather. Continuing research is expanding knowledge in these areas. New findings could be just as surprising as the previous discovery of a fish considered extinct or of microorganisms deep under the ocean floor.

People will probably continue to catch fish and to drill for oil in the ocean for many decades. In addition, people might find it profitable to use other ocean resources. For example, they might mine gold or manganese. Or they might use the tremendous energy in ocean tides or waves—or in the winds that blow over the ocean—to generate electricity. The ocean is so large that many possibilities for using its resources remain.

ACTIVITIES

Mapping the Sea Floor

Suppose you are in a boat that is traveling in a straight line. You take a sonar reading every one-half minute. Your readings, which show how long sound waves take to reach bottom and return to the surface, are as follows:

1. 2 seconds   **3.** 3 seconds
2. 0.5 second   **4.** 3 seconds

Sound travels at about 1500 meters per second (4900 ft/s) in seawater.

From this information, draw what the sea floor looks like under the path of your boat.

Writing About Science

Technology has been used for centuries to study the ocean. Trace the history of one piece of technology, such as a submarine, diving gear, sonar, or a depth gauge. Write a short history of that device.

Teach from Visuals

Have students compare and contrast the visuals of the *Aquarius* on p. 109 and the *Turtle* on p. 107. Have them describe advances in the technology of submersibles. *The* Turtle *allowed people to stay underwater for only about 30 minutes. The* Aquarius *holds an entire crew and lab; it allows people to live under water.*

INTO THE FUTURE

Remind students that scientists are still making fascinating discoveries about the ocean. For example, hydrothermal vent communities get their primary energy from dissolved chemicals in heated water rather than from sunlight. Until these communities were discovered, scientists doubted life could survive under such harsh conditions. Ask: What future discoveries might be made in the ocean? *Answers might include new life forms and the locations of natural resources.*

ACTIVITIES

Mapping the Sea Floor

Have students draw a straight line across the bottom of a sheet of paper. This line represents a flat ocean floor. Students can use this baseline as a guide when plotting the sonar readings. Drawings should show a slightly elevated area, a tall ridge, and a deep area.

Writing About Science

Encourage students to make drawings or use visuals of other types to include in their histories. They might make a visual timeline about one device.

Technology Resources

Students can visit **ClassZone.com** for information about the ocean.

DIFFERENTIATE INSTRUCTION

Advanced Have students use the sonar readings in the "Mapping the Sea Floor" activity to calculate the depth of the ocean at all four locations. *1500 m/s × 2 s = 3000 m; 1500 m/s × 0.5 s = 750 m; 1500 m/s × 3 s = 4500 m; 1500 m/s × 3 s = 4500 m*

Ocean Environments

Earth Science
UNIFYING PRINCIPLES

PRINCIPLE 1

Heat energy inside Earth and radiation from the Sun provide energy for Earth's processes.

PRINCIPLE 2

Physical forces, such as gravity, affect the movement of all matter on Earth and throughout the universe.

PRINCIPLE 3

Matter and energy move among Earth's rocks and soil, atmosphere, waters, and living things.

PRINCIPLE 4

Earth has changed over time and continues to change.

Unit: Earth's Waters
BIG IDEAS

CHAPTER 1
The Water Planet

Water moves through Earth's atmosphere, oceans, and land in a cycle.

CHAPTER 2
Freshwater Resources

Fresh water is a limited resource and is essential for human society.

CHAPTER 3
Ocean Systems

The oceans are a connected system of water in motion.

CHAPTER 4
Ocean Environments

The ocean supports life and contains natural resources.

CHAPTER 4
KEY CONCEPTS

SECTION 4.1

Ocean coasts support plant and animal life.

1. Ocean waters contain many environments.
2. The shoreline supports many plants and animals.
3. Fresh water and salt water meet on coasts.
4. Human activity affects shorelines.

SECTION 4.2

Conditions differ away from shore.

1. Ocean environments change with depth and distance from shore.
2. The waters near shore support diverse life forms.
3. Environments in the open ocean change with depth.
4. New discoveries about ocean life continue.

SECTION 4.3

The ocean contains natural resources.

1. The ocean supports living resources.
2. The ocean contains nonliving resources.
3. Pollution affects the ocean.

 The Big Idea Flow Chart is available on p. T25 in the **UNIT TRANSPARENCY BOOK**.

Previewing Content

SECTION

4.1 Ocean coasts support plant and animal life. pp. 113–120

1. Ocean waters contain many environments.

The ocean contains diverse environments, from near-shore habitats to open-ocean zones. Approximately 95 percent of the ocean remains unexplored. Millions of marine species may yet be discovered. Known marine organisms may be classified into three groups according to how they live: benthos (bottom dwellers), nekton (swimmers), and plankton (floaters).

2. The shoreline supports many plants and animals.

A **habitat** is an environment that contains all the requirements for an organism to live. The habitat at the edge of the ocean, between the high tide mark and the low tide mark, is the **intertidal zone.** The intertidal zone is characterized by constantly changing conditions.

- During low tide, the zone is dry and exposed to direct sunlight.
- During high tide, the zone is covered with water.

Organisms in the intertidal zone have adaptations to withstand crashing waves, as well as changes in temperature, salinity, and moisture.

3. Fresh water and salt water meet on coasts.

Fresh water from rivers mixes with salt water from oceans in shoreline areas called **estuaries.** Coastal **wetlands,** such as salt marshes and mangrove forests, are wet, swampy areas along the edges of estuaries. Coastal wetlands and estuaries are habitats for many organisms.

4. Human activity affects shorelines.

About half the world's population lives within 80 kilometers of a coastline. Human activities such as recreation, development, shipping, and dumping can harm coastal environments. Even activities that take place far from shore can impact the ocean when rivers carry runoff into oceans. Improved sewage treatment plants, government regulations, and shoreline sanctuaries help protect coastal habitats.

SECTION

4.2 Conditions differ away from shore. pp. 121–129

1. Ocean environments change with depth and distance from shore.

In the near-shore environment, sunlight reaches nearly to the bottom of the ocean. Nutrients wash in from land. Temperature and salinity are nearly constant from the surface to the bottom. In contrast, temperature and sunlight vary in different parts of the open ocean.

2. The waters near shore support diverse life forms.

Coral reefs are built-up limestone deposits formed by large colonies of tiny organisms called corals. Reefs are found in tropical waters. More than 25 percent of all marine species are found in coral reefs. These diverse habitats are among the most endangered on Earth.

In cold waters, large communities of kelp seaweed form **kelp forests.** Kelp needs sunlight to grow; thus, these habitats are found near shore, where sunlight penetrates to the ocean floor. Kelp forests provide food and shelter to many marine organisms.

3. Environments in the open ocean change with depth.

Open-ocean environments can be classified into surface zones and deep zones.

The surface zone is the sunlit top of the open ocean. It has a depth of roughly 200 meters. Microscopic floating organisms called **phytoplankton** live at or near the surface. Through photosynthesis, phytoplankton produce about as much atmospheric oxygen as all land plants combined. Many surface-zone organisms have adaptations such as air-filled bladders to help them stay buoyant.

The dark, cold deep zone lies under the surface zone. Sunlight does not reach the deep zone so no plants can live there. Deep-zone organisms have adaptations such as glowing extensions on their heads to help them bait prey.

4. New discoveries about ocean life continue.

In 1977, scientists discovered **hydrothermal vents,** which are openings in the ocean floor where heated water gushes out. A type of bacteria that uses dissolved chemicals to produce food in a process called chemosynthesis forms the base of a food chain in hydrothermal vent communities.

Common Misconceptions

PRODUCERS IN THE OCEANS Students may think that producers cannot exist in aquatic environments because carbon dioxide and sunlight cannot get through water to aquatic organisms. Actually, carbon dioxide is dissolved in ocean water, and sunlight penetrates

 MISCONCEPTION DATABASE
CLASSZONE.COM Background on student misconceptions

to a depth of many meters. Phytoplankton use these resources to produce about as much oxygen as all land plants combined.

 This misconception is addressed on p. 126.

Previewing Content

1. The ocean supports living resources.

Algae and seafood are two living resources found in the ocean. The ocean's living resources are used in medicines, cosmetics, and as food. The United States is the third largest consumer of seafood in the world. **Overfishing,** or a decrease in fish populations, has become a growing problem worldwide. A related problem is **by-catch,** which describes the portion of animals that are caught in a net and then thrown away. Global fisheries throw away about 30 percent of their total fish catch as by-catch.

To increase fish harvests, many countries are turning to aquaculture, the farming of both freshwater and marine organisms. Aquaculture can harm the environment when fish waste and chemicals added to fish farms are dumped into oceans. In addition, many wetlands have been cleared to make way for aquaculture.

2. The ocean contains nonliving resources.

Nonliving resources from the ocean include
- energy resources such as oil and gas
- minerals such as phosphorite, iron, copper, lead, gold, and tin
- building materials such as sand and gravel

Many minerals wash into the ocean from land. These deposits are often found near shore. Nodules, however, are lumps of minerals that are scattered across the deep-ocean floor. Nodules build up over millions of years and may reach 1 meter in diameter. They contain minerals such as manganese, iron, and cobalt. Currently, it is too expensive to mine nodules.

3. Pollution affects the ocean.

Because the ocean is one large, interconnected body of water, ocean pollution can circulate around the world. Types of ocean pollution include solid wastes, such as plastics, and chemical contaminants.

Use the following graph when discussing sources of ocean oil pollution.

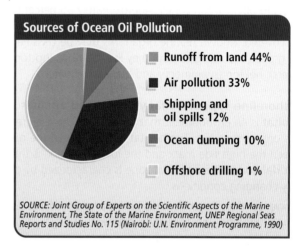

Sources of Ocean Oil Pollution

- Runoff from land 44%
- Air pollution 33%
- Shipping and oil spills 12%
- Ocean dumping 10%
- Offshore drilling 1%

SOURCE: Joint Group of Experts on the Scientific Aspects of the Marine Environment, The State of the Marine Environment, UNEP Regional Seas Reports and Studies No. 115 (Nairobi: U.N. Environment Programme, 1990)

Ocean pollution can be prevented or reduced. Governments can implement laws that restrict the use of toxic chemicals or ban the dumping of wastes into the ocean. People can properly dispose of chemicals that may eventually enter the ocean through runoff.

Common Misconceptions

 MISCONCEPTION DATABASE
CLASSZONE.COM Background on student misconceptions

LIMITED OCEAN RESOURCES Students may think that the oceans of the world provide a limitless source of materials such as seafood and minerals. In fact, a decrease in seafood has already been seen in areas that are overfished. Mining minerals from the ocean floor is too expensive at this time.

 TE This misconception is addressed on p. 135.

Previewing Labs

Lab Generator CD-ROM
Edit these Pupil Edition labs and generate alternative labs.

EXPLORE the BIG idea

It's Alive! p. 111
Students examine fish in an aquarium to learn about characteristics of ocean environments.

TIME 15 minutes
MATERIALS aquarium, fish

Beneath the Surface, p. 111
Students think of questions to identify their knowledge about the ocean environment near shore.

TIME 15 minutes
MATERIALS pencil, paper

Internet Activity: Ocean Environments, p. 111
Students use the Internet to learn about the factors that affect where in the ocean an organism lives.

TIME 20 minutes
MATERIALS computer with Internet access

SECTION 4.1

INVESTIGATE Coastal Environments, p. 116
Students design an experiment using sponges and containers with lids to model how mussels are adapted to their coastal environment.

TIME 30 minutes
MATERIALS 2 small plastic containers with lids, 2 sponges, water

---

SECTION 4.2

EXPLORE Air Bladders, p. 121
Students observe how bubbles of air can lift raisins to model the function of air bladders.

TIME 15 minutes
MATERIALS clear container, soda water, 5 raisins

INVESTIGATE Floating, p. 125
Students manipulate pieces of clay to determine how shape affects the way plankton float.

TIME 30 minutes
MATERIALS clear container, water, modeling clay, watch with a second hand

---

SECTION 4.3

EXPLORE Ocean Pollution, p. 130
Students use oil and a feather to investigate how oil spills affect birds.

TIME 20 minutes
MATERIALS bowl, water, feather, spoon, cooking oil

CHAPTER INVESTIGATION
Population Sampling, pp. 138–139
Students use a quadrat technique to estimate population size.

TIME 40 minutes
MATERIALS calculator, removable tape (masking tape works well)

 Additional INVESTIGATION, Oxygen in Ocean Water, A, B, & C, pp. 250–258; Teacher Instructions, pp. 261–262

Previewing Chapter Resources

	INTEGRATED TECHNOLOGY	LABS AND ACTIVITIES

CHAPTER 4
Ocean Environments

INTEGRATED TECHNOLOGY

 CLASSZONE.COM
- eEdition Plus
- EasyPlanner Plus
- Misconception Database
- Content Review
- Test Practice
- Simulation
- Visualization
- Resource Centers
- Internet Activity: Ocean Environments
- Math Tutorial

 SCILINKS.ORG
SCI LINKS

 CD-ROMS
- eEdition
- EasyPlanner
- Power Presentations
- Content Review
- Lab Generator
- Test Generator

 AUDIO CDS
- Audio Readings
- Audio Readings in Spanish

LABS AND ACTIVITIES

P E EXPLORE the Big Idea, p. 111
- It's Alive!
- Beneath the Surface
- Internet Activity: Ocean Environments

R **UNIT RESOURCE BOOK**
Unit Projects, pp. 5–10

 Lab Generator CD-ROM
Generate customized labs.

SECTION

 4.1

Ocean coasts support plant and animal life.
pp. 113–120

Time: 2 periods (1 block)
 Lesson Plan, pp. 202–203

 MATH TUTORIAL

 UNIT TRANSPARENCY BOOK
- Big Idea Flow Chart, p. T25
- Daily Vocabulary Scaffolding, p. T26
- Note-Taking Model, p. T27
- 3-Minute Warm-Up, p. T28
- "Intertidal Zone" Visual, p. T30

P E
- INVESTIGATE Coastal Environments, p. 116
- Math in Science, p. 120

R **UNIT RESOURCE BOOK**
- Datasheet, Coastal Environments, p. 211
- Math Support, p. 239
- Math Practice, p. 240

SECTION

 4.2

Conditions differ away from shore.
pp. 121–129

Time: 2 periods (1 block)
 Lesson Plan, pp. 213–214

- **RESOURCE CENTERS,** Coral Reefs, Hydrothermal Vents
- **VISUALIZATION,** Life at Hydrothermal Vents

 UNIT TRANSPARENCY BOOK
- Daily Vocabulary Scaffolding, p. T26
- 3-Minute Warm-Up, p. T28

P E
- EXPLORE Air Bladders, p. 121
- INVESTIGATE Floating, p. 125
- Extreme Science, p. 129

R **UNIT RESOURCE BOOK**
Datasheet, Floating, p. 222

SECTION

 4.3

The ocean contains natural resources.
pp. 130–139

Time: 4 periods (2 blocks)
 Lesson Plan, pp. 224–225

 RESOURCE CENTER, Ocean Pollution and Pollution Prevention

 UNIT TRANSPARENCY BOOK
- Big Idea Flow Chart, p. T25
- Daily Vocabulary Scaffolding, p. T26
- 3-Minute Warm-Up, p. T29
- Chapter Outline, pp. T31–T32

P E
- EXPLORE Ocean Pollution, p. 130
- CHAPTER INVESTIGATION, Population Sampling, pp. 138–139

R **UNIT RESOURCE BOOK**
- Additional INVESTIGATION, Oxygen in Ocean Water, A, B, & C, pp. 250–258
- CHAPTER INVESTIGATION, Population Sampling, A, B, & C, pp. 241–249

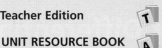
 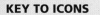
READING AND REINFORCEMENT

- Choose Your Own Strategy, B18–27
- Main Idea Web, C38–39
- Daily Vocabulary Scaffolding, H1–8

 UNIT RESOURCE BOOK
- Vocabulary Practice, pp. 236–237
- Decoding Support, p. 238
- Summarizing the Chapter, pp. 259–260

 Audio Readings CD
Listen to Pupil Edition.

Audio Readings in Spanish CD
Listen to Pupil Edition in Spanish.

 UNIT RESOURCE BOOK
- Reading Study Guide, A & B, pp. 204–207
- Spanish Reading Study Guide, pp. 208–209
- Challenge and Extension, p. 210
- Reinforcing Key Concepts, p. 212

UNIT RESOURCE BOOK
- Reading Study Guide, A & B, pp. 215–218
- Spanish Reading Study Guide, pp. 219–220
- Challenge and Extension, p. 221
- Reinforcing Key Concepts, p. 223

UNIT RESOURCE BOOK
- Reading Study Guide, A & B, pp. 226–229
- Spanish Reading Study Guide, pp. 230–231
- Challenge and Extension, p. 232
- Reinforcing Key Concepts, p. 233
- Challenge Reading, pp. 234–235

ASSESSMENT

- Chapter Review, pp. 141–142
- Standardized Test Practice, p. 143

 UNIT ASSESSMENT BOOK
- Diagnostic Test, pp. 59–60
- Chapter Test, A, B, & C, pp. 64–75
- Alternative Assessment, pp. 76–77
- Unit Test, pp. 78–89

- Spanish Chapter Test, pp. 165–168
- Spanish Unit Test, pp. 169–172

 Test Generator CD-ROM
Generate customized tests.

 Lab Generator CD-ROM
Rubrics for Labs

 Ongoing Assessment, pp. 114–119

 Section 4.1 Review, p. 119

UNIT ASSESSMENT BOOK
Section 4.1 Quiz, p. 61

 Ongoing Assessment, pp. 121, 123–125, 127–128

 Section 4.2 Review, p. 128

 UNIT ASSESSMENT BOOK
Section 4.2 Quiz, p. 62

 Ongoing Assessment, pp. 131–132, 134, 136–137

 Section 4.3 Review, p. 137

 UNIT ASSESSMENT BOOK
Section 4.3 Quiz, p. 63

STANDARDS

National Standards
A.2–8, A.9.a–c, A.9.e–f, C.4.c–d, E.2–5, F.3.b, F.5.b–c, F.5.e

See p. 110 for the standards.

National Standards
A.2–8, A.9.a–c, A.9.e–f, C.4.c, E.2–5, F.3.b

National Standards
A.2–7, A.9.a–b, A.9.e–f, C.4.c, E.2–5, F.5.e

National Standards
A.2–8, A.9.a–c, A.9.e–f, C.4.d, F.3.b, F.5.b–c

Previewing Resources for Differentiated Instruction

CHAPTER INVESTIGATION

Leveled resources present the same concepts for different abilities.

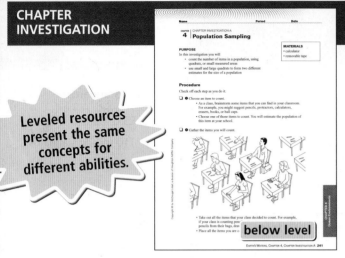

CHAPTER INVESTIGATION A
4 | Population Sampling

PURPOSE
In this investigation you will
- count the number of items in a population, using quadrats, or small measured areas
- use small and large quadrats to form two different estimates for the size of a population

MATERIALS
- calculator
- removable tape

Procedure
Check off each step as you do it.

below level

EARTH'S WATERS, CHAPTER 4, CHAPTER INVESTIGATION A **241**

CHAPTER INVESTIGATION B
4 | Population Sampling

OVERVIEW AND PURPOSE

MATERIALS
- calculator
- removable tape

Procedure

on level

EARTH'S WATERS, CHAPTER 4, CHAPTER INVESTIGATION B **245**

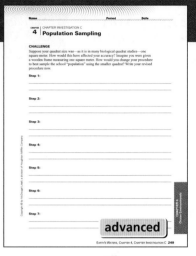

CHAPTER INVESTIGATION C
4 | Population Sampling

CHALLENGE

Step 1:

Step 2:

Step 3:

Step 4:

Step 5:

Step 6:

Step 7:

advanced

EARTH'S WATERS, CHAPTER 4, CHAPTER INVESTIGATION C **249**

R **UNIT RESOURCE BOOK,** pp. 241–244   **R** pp. 245–248   **R** pp. 245–249

READING STUDY GUIDE

Reading Study Guide is also in Spanish.

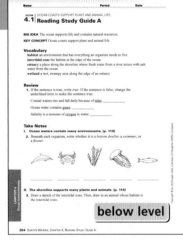

SECTION OCEAN COASTS SUPPORT PLANT AND ANIMAL LIFE.
4.1 | Reading Study Guide A

BIG IDEA The ocean supports life and contains natural resources.
KEY CONCEPT Ocean coasts support plant and animal life.

Vocabulary
habitat an environment that has everything an organism needs to live.
intertidal zone the habitat at the edge of the ocean
estuary a place along the shoreline where fresh water from a river mixes with salt water from the ocean
wetland a wet, swampy area along the edge of an estuary

Review
1. If the sentence is true, write *true*. If the sentence is false, change the underlined term to make the sentence true.

Coastal waters rise and fall daily because of tides.

Ocean water contains gases.

Salinity is a measure of oxygen in water.

Take Notes
I. **Ocean waters contain many environments.** (p. 113)
2. Beneath each organism, write whether it is a *bottom dweller*, a *swimmer*, or a *floater*.

II. **The shoreline supports many plants and animals.** (p. 114)
3. Draw a sketch of the intertidal zone. Then, draw in an animal whose habitat is the intertidal zone.

below level

204 EARTH'S WATERS, CHAPTER 4, READING STUDY GUIDE A

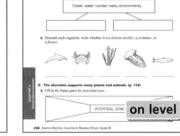

SECTION OCEAN COASTS SUPPORT PLANT AND ANIMAL LIFE.
4.1 | Reading Study Guide B

BIG IDEA The ocean supports life and contains natural resources.
KEY CONCEPT Ocean coasts support plant and animal life.

Review
Ocean water contains gases such as oxygen.

Take Notes
I. **Ocean waters contain many environments.** (p. 113)
1. Fill in the main-idea web for the main idea shown.

Ocean water contain many environments.

2. Beneath each organism, write whether it is a *bottom dweller*, a *swimmer*, or a *floater*.

II. **The shoreline supports many plants and animals.** (p. 114)
3. Fill in the frame game for *intertidal zone*.

INTERTIDAL ZONE

on level

206 EARTH'S WATERS, CHAPTER 4, READING STUDY GUIDE B

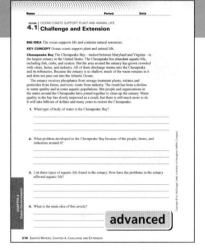

SECTION OCEAN COASTS SUPPORT PLANT AND ANIMAL LIFE.
4.1 | Challenge and Extension

BIG IDEA The ocean supports life and contains natural resources.
KEY CONCEPT Ocean coasts support plant and animal life.

Chesapeake Bay The Chesapeake Bay—tucked between Maryland and Virginia—is the largest estuary in the United States.

1. What type of body of water is the Chesapeake Bay?

2. What problem developed in the Chesapeake Bay because of the people, farms, and industries around it?

3. List three types of aquatic life found in the estuary. How have the problems in the estuary affected aquatic life?

4. What is the main idea of this article?

advanced

210 EARTH'S WATERS, CHAPTER 4, CHALLENGE AND EXTENSION

R **UNIT RESOURCE BOOK,** pp. 204–205   **R** pp. 206–207   **R** p. 210

CHAPTER TEST

Chapter Test is also in Spanish.

CHAPTER OCEAN ENVIRONMENTS
4 | Chapter Test A

Key Concepts
Choose the letter of the best answer. (5 points each)

____ 1. The narrow margin between the low tide and high tide marks is called
  a. a habitat
  b. an estuary
  c. the intertidal zone
  d. the deep zone

____ 2. Fresh water from rivers mixes with the ocean's salt water in
  a. wetlands
  b. mangrove swamps
  c. estuaries
  d. salt marshes

____ 3. What is a wetland?
  a. barren land near a coast
  b. developed land near a coast
  c. farmland near a coast
  d. soggy land near a coast

____ 4. One way that governments protect organisms in coastal areas is by passing laws that
  a. prohibit habitats along shore lines
  b. prohibit dumping along shorelines
  c. increase pollution released along the coast
  d. increase development of wetland areas

____ 5. Which of these describes the waters in many near-shore environments?
  a. dark and full of life
  b. dark with very little life
  c. sunlit and full of life
  d. sunlit with very little life

below level

64 EARTH'S WATERS, CHAPTER 4, CHAPTER TEST A

CHAPTER OCEAN ENVIRONMENTS
4 | Chapter Test B

Key Concepts
Choose the letter of the best answer. (5 points each)

____ 1. All organisms in the intertidal zone must be adapted to
  a. survive in wet and dry conditions
  b. feed only at high tide
  c. see in the dark
  d. get food from hydrothermal vents

____ 2. Floating plants and animals that live in estuaries are well adapted to tolerate daily changes in
  a. sunlight
  b. air temperature
  c. salinity
  d. water temperature

____ 3. In a salt marsh, nutrients in dead grasses are returned to the marsh by
  a. salt
  b. birds
  c. crabs
  d. tiny organisms

____ 4. Unlike solid waste, most ocean pollution is
  a. harmless to bottom dwellers
  b. difficult to see
  c. easy to see
  d. harmless to swimmers

____ 5. In most near-shore environments, sunlight reaches
  a. only the first few meters of the ocean floor
  b. about one-fourth of the way to the ocean floor
  c. about half of the way to the ocean floor
  d. nearly all the way to the ocean floor

on level

68 EARTH'S WATERS, CHAPTER 4, CHAPTER TEST B

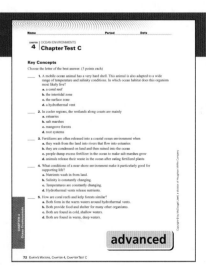

CHAPTER OCEAN ENVIRONMENTS
4 | Chapter Test C

Key Concepts
Choose the letter of the best answer. (5 points each)

____ 1. A mobile ocean animal has a very hard shell. This animal is also adapted to a wide range of temperature and salinity conditions. In which ocean habitat does this organism most likely live?
  a. a coral reef
  b. the intertidal zone
  c. the surface zone
  d. a hydrothermal vent

____ 2. In cooler regions, the wetlands along coasts are mainly
  a. estuaries
  b. salt marshes
  c. mangrove forests
  d. root systems

____ 3. Fertilizers are often released into a coastal ocean environment when
  a. they wash from the land into rivers that flow into estuaries
  b. they are condensed on land and then rained into the ocean
  c. people dump excess fertilizer in the ocean to make salt marshes grow
  d. animals release their waste in the ocean after eating fertilized plants

____ 4. What conditions of a near-shore environment make it particularly good for supporting life?
  a. Nutrients wash in from land.
  b. Salinity is constantly changing.
  c. Temperatures are constantly changing.
  d. Hydrothermal vents release nutrients.

____ 5. How are coral reefs and kelp forests similar?
  a. Both form in the warm waters around hydrothermal vents.
  b. Both provide food and shelter for many other organisms.
  c. Both are found in cold, shallow waters.
  d. Both are found in warm, deep waters.

advanced

72 EARTH'S WATERS, CHAPTER 4, CHAPTER TEST C

A **UNIT ASSESSMENT BOOK,** pp. 64–67   **A** pp. 68–71   **A** pp. 72–75

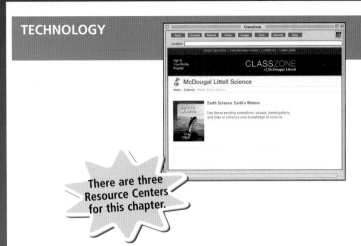

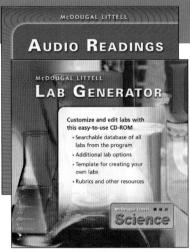

There are three Resource Centers for this chapter.

 CLASSZONE.COM

 CD/CD-ROMS

 CLASSZONE.COM

VISUAL CONTENT

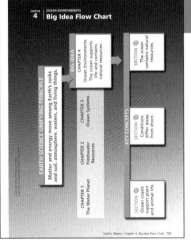

UNIT TRANSPARENCY BOOK, p. T25

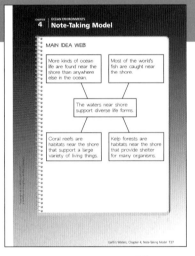

p. T27

p. T30

MORE SUPPORT

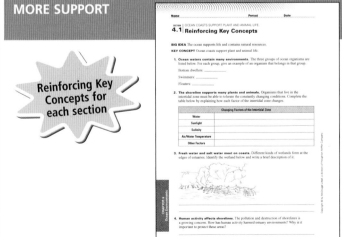

Reinforcing Key Concepts for each section

UNIT RESOURCE BOOK, p. 212

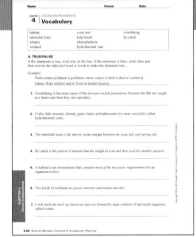

pp. 236–237

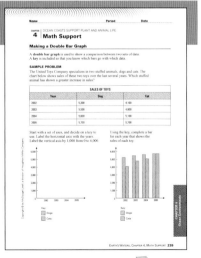

p. 239

INTRODUCE

the BIG idea

Have students look at the photograph of the ocean shore and discuss how the question in the box links to the Big Idea:

- What animals do you see in the photograph? Do you think these same animals might be found in the deep ocean? Why or why not?

- What physical features do you see in the photograph? Would you see these same features in the deep ocean? Why or why not?

National Science Education Standards

Content

C.4.c For ecosystems, the major source of energy is sunlight.

C.4.d The number of organisms an ecosystem can support depends on the resources available and abiotic factors.

Process

A.2–8 Design and conduct an investigation; use tools; use evidence; think critically between evidence and explanation; recognize different explanations and predictions; communicate scientific procedures and explanations; use mathematics.

A.9.a–c, A.9.e–f Understand scientific inquiry by using different investigations, methods, mathematics, and explanations based on logic, evidence, and skepticism.

E.2–5 Design, implement, and evaluate a solution or product; communicate technological design.

F.3.b Human activities, such as resource acquisition, land-use decisions, and waste disposal, can also induce hazards.

F.5.b–c, F.5.e Societal challenges inspire scientific research; technology influences society; scientists work in different settings.

CHAPTER

4 Ocean Environments

the BIG idea

The ocean supports life and contains natural resources.

How is the deep ocean different from the shore?

Key Concepts

SECTION 4.1 Ocean coasts support plant and animal life. Learn about conditions in coastal environments and about the plants and animals that live there.

SECTION 4.2 Conditions differ away from shore. Learn how conditions change as you move away from the shore and deeper into the ocean.

SECTION 4.3 The ocean contains natural resources. Learn about the ocean's living and nonliving resources and how pollution affects the ocean.

Internet Preview

CLASSZONE.COM

Chapter 4 online resources: Content Review, Simulation, Visualization, three Resource Centers, Math Tutorial, Test Practice

INTERNET PREVIEW

NSTA *SCiLINKS*

scilinks.org

Ocean Resources
Code: MDL021

It's Alive!

Carefully observe a fish in a fish tank. Pay attention to all of the fish's movements. Record what the fish does and what the fish's environment is like.

Observe and Think All animals, including fish, need oxygen to live. Where does the fish get its oxygen?

Beneath the Surface

What forms of life would you expect to see underwater in the ocean near shore? Draw a picture to show your ideas.

Observe and Think What do you need to know in order to make your picture more accurate? Write five questions you have about the ocean environment near shore.

Internet Activity: Ocean Environments

Go to **ClassZone.com** to learn more about organisms in the ocean. See which plants and animals live in different ocean environments.

Observe and Think What factors or conditions might affect the kinds of organisms that can live in each part of the ocean?

NSTA
scilinks.org SCI*LINKS*

Ocean Resources **Code: MDL021**

Chapter 4: Ocean Environments **111** **C**

TEACHING WITH TECHNOLOGY

PC Microscope If you have access to a PC microscope, allow students to view different-shaped plankton after they perform "Investigate Floating" on p. 125.

These inquiry-based activities are appropriate for use at home or as a supplement to classroom instruction.

It's Alive!

PURPOSE To introduce students to characteristics of ocean environments.

TIP *15 min.* If you do not have access to a fish tank, arrange a field trip to a pet store where students can view saltwater fish in aquariums. You can also obtain a video showing marine organisms in their natural environments.

Answer: The fish gets its oxygen from the water.

REVISIT after p. 127.

Beneath the Surface

PURPOSE To help students formulate questions about the ocean environment near shore.

TIP *15 min.* Students might try working in groups to brainstorm questions.

Sample questions: What animals live near shore? How deep is the water near shore? How do tides and waves affect ocean organisms? What do the animals eat? How do they get their food?

REVISIT after p. 118.

Internet Activity: Ocean Environments

PURPOSE To introduce students to the factors that affect where organisms live in the ocean.

TIP *20 min.* Students could make a simple diagram in their Science Notebook that shows how the ocean varies with depth. As they learn about an organism and its environment, they could then draw it in the proper place on the diagram.

Answer: temperature, pressure, amount of sunlight that penetrates the water

REVISIT after p. 128.

CONCEPT REVIEW

Activate Prior Knowledge

Help students remember what they have already learned about oceans. Ask:

- What kind of elements are found in ocean water? *all 92, including salts, oxygen, and other gases*

- How do the density and temperature of ocean water change with depth? *deepest water is densest and coldest*

- Do you think density and temperature affect ocean organisms? Why or why not? *yes; some organisms thrive in dense, cold water rather than in less dense, warm water*

▶ TAKING NOTES

Main Idea Web

Tell students that the blue heads in their text can be used to identify main ideas. Other textual clues, such as bold-faced terms and topic sentences, can indicate supporting terms and details.

Choose Your Own Strategy

Have students review these and other strategies found in the Note-Taking Handbook on pp. R45–R51. Each student can then choose the strategy that works best for him or her.

Vocabulary and Note-Taking Resources

- Vocabulary Practice, pp. 236–237
- Decoding Support, p. 238

- Daily Vocabulary Scaffolding, p. T26
- Note-Taking Model, p. T27

- Choose Your Own Strategy, B18–27
- Main Idea Web, C38–39
- Daily Vocabulary Scaffolding, H1–8

Getting Ready to Learn

◀ CONCEPT REVIEW

- The ocean contains oxygen and other gases.
- Deep currents carry oxygen from the surface to the ocean floor.
- Upwelling carries nutrients from the bottom of the ocean to the surface.

◀ VOCABULARY REVIEW

point-source pollution p. 54
nonpoint-source pollution p. 54
continental shelf p. 80
ocean current p. 84

CONTENT REVIEW
CLASSZONE.COM
Review concepts and vocabulary.

▶ TAKING NOTES

MAIN IDEA WEB

Write each new blue heading—a main idea—in a box. Then put notes with important terms and details into boxes around the main idea.

CHOOSE YOUR OWN STRATEGY

Take notes about new vocabulary terms, using one or more of the strategies from earlier chapters—**four square, description wheel,** or **word triangle.** Feel free to mix and match the strategies, or use an entirely different vocabulary strategy.

See the Note-Taking Handbook on pages R45–R51.

SCIENCE NOTEBOOK

Different parts of the ocean have different characteristics.

Almost 95 percent of the ocean is still unexplored.

Ocean waters contain many environments.

Swimmers, floaters, and bottom dwellers are three groups of ocean life.

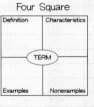

Four Square

Definition	Characteristics
	TERM
Examples	Nonexamples

Description Wheel

feature feature feature TERM feature feature feature

Word Triangle

sketch
sentence using the word
TERM: definition

CHECK READINESS

Administer the Diagnostic Test to determine students' readiness for new science content and their mastery of requisite math skills.

 Diagnostic Test, pp. 59–60

Technology Resources

Students needing content and math skills should visit **ClassZone.com.**

- **CONTENT REVIEW**
- **MATH TUTORIAL**

- **CONTENT REVIEW CD-ROM**

KEY CONCEPT

Ocean coasts support plant and animal life.

◀ BEFORE, you learned

- Ocean water contains gases such as oxygen
- Salinity is a measure of the amount of salt in water
- Coastal waters rise and fall each day because of tides

▶ NOW, you will learn

- What the intertidal zone is
- What coastal environments exist where fresh water and salt water meet
- How human activity affects shoreline environments

VOCABULARY

habitat p. 114
intertidal zone p. 114
estuary p. 116
wetland p. 116

THINK ABOUT

What are the characteristics of shoreline environments?

This map shows the migration route of the osprey, a type of bird. Each fall ospreys fly south to warmer weather. In the spring they fly north. Each dot on the map represents a place where ospreys stop along the way. What do you notice about where the birds stop? What resources might shoreline environments provide for birds?

MAIN IDEA WEB
Remember to start a main idea web in your notebook for this blue heading.

Ocean waters contain many environments.

Where on Earth can you find a living animal that is larger than the largest dinosaur that ever lived? Where can you find birds that use their wings to fly underwater, or animals that can eject their internal organs—and grow another set? Where can you find warm tropical zones thick with plants, or cold, empty plains where no plant can grow? The ocean contains all these and more.

Like the land, the ocean contains many different environments, each with its own special characteristics. Although scientists have learned a lot about the ocean and its environments, almost 95 percent of the ocean remains unexplored. It is possible that many millions more species of ocean life are yet to be discovered.

Chapter 4: **Ocean Environments** 113 **C**

RESOURCES FOR DIFFERENTIATED INSTRUCTION

Below Level

UNIT RESOURCE BOOK
- Reading Study Guide A, pp. 204–205
- Decoding Support, p. 238

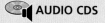 **AUDIO CDS**

Advanced

UNIT RESOURCE BOOK
Challenge and Extension, p. 210

English Learners

UNIT RESOURCE BOOK
Spanish Reading Study Guide, pp. 208–209

AUDIO CDS

- Audio Readings in Spanish
- Audio Readings (English)

4.1 FOCUS

▶ Set Learning Goals

Students will

- Define the intertidal zone.
- Identify what coastal environments exist where fresh water and salt water meet.
- Explain how human activity affects shoreline environments.
- Design an experiment to show how mussels survive in their environment.

◀ 3-Minute Warm-Up

Display Transparency 28 or copy this exercise on the board:

Picture an ocean shore in your mind. Make a list of its characteristics. Then write a short paragraph describing the adaptations an animal might need to survive in this environment. *Shoreline characteristics might include a sandy or rocky beach, crashing waves, and extreme tidal changes. Adaptations might include ways to survive during low tide, such as a crab burrowing into the sand so as not to be exposed to predatory birds, or a bird with a long beak for digging out burrowed animals.*

T 3-Minute Warm-Up, p. T28

4.1 MOTIVATE

THINK ABOUT

PURPOSE To think about the characteristics and resources of shoreline environments

DISCUSS During the discussion about resources provided by shoreline environments, mention to students that ospreys are fish-eating raptors.

Answers: The birds stop along the coastline. Shoreline resources might include food, water, and shelter.

Chapter 4 **113 C**

4.1 INSTRUCT

Integrate the Sciences

Most organisms that live on land need some sort of structural support to withstand the force of gravity. Humans, for example, have muscles and skeletons. Insects have an exoskeleton. In contrast, marine organisms do not necessarily need skeletal systems because they are supported by water. Many ocean organisms, such as jellyfish and sponges, are invertebrates.

Ongoing Assessment

The many known ocean organisms are organized in three groups according to the way the organisms live. Bottom dwellers include plantlike organisms called algae (AL-jee) and other organisms that live on the ocean bottom—for example, seaweeds, crabs, corals, starfish, and shellfish. Swimmers are animals such as fish, dolphins, whales, and octopuses that swim in the ocean. Floaters are organisms that do not swim but float at or near the ocean surface. Some floaters, such as jellyfish, are large, but most are so small you need a microscope to see them. These tiny living things include plants, animals, bacteria, and single-celled organisms called protists (PROH-tihsts).

 CHECK YOUR READING What are the three groups of ocean life?

The shoreline supports many plants and animals.

An environment that has all the necessary requirements for an organism to live is called a **habitat**. In this chapter you will explore some of the many different ocean habitats. Your journey begins on the coastline, where the ocean meets the land. The habitat at the edge of the ocean is the **intertidal zone** (IHN-tuhr-TYD-uhl)—the narrow ocean margin between the high tide mark and the low tide mark. The conditions constantly change in the intertidal zone. Organisms that live here must be able to survive both wet and dry periods. Plants and animals must also withstand the force of waves that constantly crash onto shore.

READING TIP
Word parts can help you remember the meaning of *intertidal zone*. The prefix *inter-* means "between." The root *tidal* means "relating to the tides." The *intertidal zone* is the area between high and low tides.

 A

 B

① At **low tide,** the intertidal zone is dry and exposed to direct sunlight. Organisms must be able to live out of water. They must also be able to tolerate the air temperature, which may differ from the temperature of the water.

② At **high tide,** the intertidal zone is covered with water, so it is not exposed to direct sunlight. Organisms must be able to live completely underwater and tolerate the temperature of the water.

Tidal pools are areas along the shore where water remains at low tide. Plants and animals that live in tidal pools must survive drastic changes in salinity, or salt content. When sunlight causes water to evaporate, the salinity increases. When rain falls, the salinity decreases.

Organisms have different ways of surviving the conditions of the intertidal zone. For example, crabs can move around and seek cover in the sand or in between rocks. Mussels attach themselves to rocks and close their shells to keep from drying out during low tide. Some seaweeds dry out at low tide but are able to regain moisture at high tide.

DIFFERENTIATE INSTRUCTION

 More Reading Support

A What habitat is found at the ocean's edge? *intertidal zone*

B When is the intertidal zone dry and exposed to sunlight? *during low tide*

English Learners English learners may be confused by the different ways they are asked to make conclusions. For example, on p. 113, the sentence "What do you notice about where the birds stop?" might not be clear to English learners. Other instances include "What do you think?" "What can you tell?" and "What can you conclude?" Help students by modeling appropriate answers.

Intertidal Zone

The intertidal zone is the area along the coastline between the high tide mark and the low tide mark.

intertidal zone

① Low Tide

At low tide, the intertidal zone is exposed to the air.

Tidal pools are areas where water remains at low tide.

Some seaweeds can dry out during low tide and absorb water at high tide.

At low tide, mussels close their shells tightly to keep from drying out.

② High Tide

At high tide, the intertidal zone is covered with water.

Plants and animals must survive the constant crashing of waves against the shore.

At high tide, mussels open their shells to eat and take in oxygen.

READING VISUALS What organisms can you see in the photograph of low tide?

115 **C**

DIFFERENTIATE INSTRUCTION

Below Level Have students compare a sponge that was just soaked in water with a sponge that was left on a sunny windowsill all day. Ask: Which sponge is most like a marine organism at low tide? Explain your answer. *The sponge most like a marine organism at low tide is the one left on the windowsill all day. During low tide, organisms are exposed to air and direct sunlight and they may dry up.*

Teach from Visuals

To help students interpret the visual of the intertidal zone:

• Ask: What does the small diagram in the upper right show? *the location of the intertidal zone in relation to a larger environment*

• Have students compare and contrast conditions in the intertidal zone during low tide and high tide. *During low tide, the intertidal zone is exposed to air and direct sunlight. During high tide, the intertidal zone is covered with water.*

• Ask: How do mussels react to these changing conditions? *At low tide, the mussels close their shells to retain moisture. At high tide, the shells reopen so the mussels can eat and take in oxygen.*

• Direct students' attention to the different water levels at high tide and low tide. Ask: What might a lower water level at low tide mean to animals like the seagull? *an opportunity to get food sources that are inaccessible at high tide*

 This visual is also available as T30 in the Unit Transparency Book.

Develop Critical Thinking

INFER Make sure students realize that organisms in intertidal zones are specially adapted to their environment. Tell students that mussels secrete threads. Ask students to infer how those threads help them adapt to the intertidal zone environment. *Waves constantly crash against shore and the mussels use the threads to securely attach themselves to rocks.*

Ongoing Assessment

Define the intertidal zone.

Ask: What is the intertidal zone? *a habitat along the coastline between the high tide mark and the low tide mark*

READING VISUALS *Answer: seagull, mussels, plants, crabs, starfish, and more*

INVESTIGATE Coastal Environments

PURPOSE To design an experiment to determine how mussels are adapted to coastal environments

TIP *30 min.* A few days before conducting this activity, have students bring plastic containers with lids from home.

WHAT DO YOU THINK? *The sponge in the open container dried up. The sponge in the closed container remained moist. Closing the shells during low tide prevents the mussel from drying out. The variable was exposure to air.*

CHALLENGE *Sample answer: Other variables could include exposure to salinity, exposure to waves, or changes in temperature.*

 Datasheet, Coastal Environments, p. 211

Metacognitive Strategy

Ask: What questions came to mind as you conducted the experiment? How did you go about answering these questions? How did you solve any problems encountered as you were designing your procedure?

Ongoing Assessment

CHECK YOUR READING *Answer: Coastal wetlands form along the edges of estuaries.*

INVESTIGATE Coastal Environments

How do mussels survive?

Most intertidal zone organisms require water to survive, and they must endure long dry periods during low tides. Mussels close their shells tightly during low tide and open them during high tide.

PROCEDURE

1. Using the materials listed, design an experiment to demonstrate why mussels close their shells during low tide.

2. Write up your procedure.

3. Test your experiment.

WHAT DO YOU THINK?

- How does your experiment demonstrate why mussels close their shells?
- What were the variables in your experiment?

CHALLENGE How could you redesign your experiment to better model what happens during low tide? What other variables would you include?

SKILL FOCUS
Designing experiments

MATERIALS
- small plastic containers with lids
- sponges
- water

TIME
30 minutes

Fresh water and salt water meet on coasts.

This aerial photograph shows the Pawcatuck River estuary in the northeastern United States. Fresh water from the river mixes with salt water from the ocean.

You have read that rivers flow to the sea. What happens when they get there? The fresh water from rivers mixes with salt water from the ocean in shoreline areas called **estuaries** (EHS-choo-EHR-eez), which include bays, inlets, and harbors. The water in estuaries is not as salty as ocean water, nor as fresh as river water. The salinity changes as the tide flows in and out. Sometimes the water at the surface is fresh, while denser salt water remains below.

Estuaries are bursting with life. Plants and animals thrive on nutrients washed in by rivers. Worms and shellfish live along the bottom. Plants and animals too small to see without a microscope float in the water. Many different kinds of birds and sea animals breed in estuaries. Roots and grasses offer protection for young fish and other animals. These small fish and other animals are an important food source for larger fish and for birds.

Coastal wetlands form along the edges of estuaries. As the name suggests, **wetlands** are wet, swampy areas that are often flooded with water. There are two kinds of coastal wetlands. Away from the equator, in cooler regions, coastal wetlands are salt marshes. Closer to the equator, in tropical regions, coastal wetlands are mangrove forests.

CHECK YOUR READING How are coastal wetlands related to estuaries?

C 116 Unit: Earth's Waters

DIFFERENTIATE INSTRUCTION

 More Reading Support

C Is the water in an estuary fresh, salty, or a mixture of both? *mixture*

D What kind of coastal wetlands are in cool regions? *salt marshes*

Advanced Have students obtain a map of the Gulf of Mexico from an atlas, encyclopedia, CD, or online source. Ask them to identify estuaries by looking for rivers that empty into the Gulf. Challenge them to research any animals that live only in the estuaries.

 Challenge and Extension, p. 210

Salt Marshes

Away from the equator, in cooler regions, grassy salt marshes are found along the edges of estuaries. In the United States, salt marshes are found along the coasts of the Atlantic and Pacific oceans and the Gulf of Mexico. Salt marshes help keep the shoreline from washing away. They also provide an important habitat for fish, birds, and other wildlife.

The rivers that flow into estuaries carry nutrient-rich soil. When the rivers reach the sea, they drop the soil. This rich soil supports thick grasses. The grasses form a protective barrier against waves, tides, and storms. Thick root systems hold the muddy bottom together. Tiny organisms decompose, or break down, dead grasses and return the nutrients the grasses contained to the marsh.

Crabs, snails, and minnows thrive among the grasses. Ospreys and other fish-eating birds find food in salt marshes. Birds that migrate use salt marshes as rest stops when they fly back and forth each season.

In the past, people did not understand the importance of wetlands. Over the last 200 years, about half of all wetlands in the United States were destroyed. Many were drained or filled in with soil to provide solid ground to build on or to farm. In the 1970s, people started working to protect and restore coastal wetlands.

CHECK YOUR READING Why are grasses an important part of the salt marsh environment?

Marsh grasses have thick root systems that help hold the muddy soil together.

Many small fish and other animals live in the sheltered areas among the marsh grasses.

Fish-eating birds find plenty to eat in salt marshes.

Chapter 4: Ocean Environments 117 **C**

DIFFERENTIATE INSTRUCTION

(?) More Reading Support

E What plants are found in salt marshes? *thick grasses*

F Migrating birds use salt marshes as what? *rest stops*

Teach Difficult Concepts

Students may have a difficult time understanding how plant roots can reduce shoreline erosion. Explain that the roots form thick, tangled networks. They not only hold soil together, they also keep the plants anchored in place. This latter function is crucial—without plant cover, the bare soil would rapidly erode. You might try the following demonstration to help clarify the concept.

Teacher Demo

Do this demonstration outside. Place a stalk of celery in a pot of soil. The celery should be standing upright. Place a potted plant with a strong root system next to the celery. Ask students to predict what will happen when a hose is turned on the pots. Then turn on a water hose and, using medium pressure, spray it on both pots. Students should observe that the celery falls over while the plant with roots withstands the water's force. They should also observe that more dirt splatters out of the pot with celery. Ask: How does this model relate to salt marsh grasses? *The potted plant represents salt marsh grasses because it has roots. The roots keep the plant anchored and help reduce soil erosion.*

Ongoing Assessment

CHECK YOUR READING *Answer: Grasses form a protective barrier against waves, tides, and storms. The root systems of grasses hold together the muddy salt marsh bottom. When grasses decompose, nutrients are returned to the salt marsh.*

FLORIDA

Florida Keys

This is an underwater view of mangrove roots.

Teach from Visuals

To help students interpret the visual of a mangrove forest, ask:

- What types of plants make up a mangrove forest? *trees and shrubs*

- In the United States, where would you expect to find mangrove forests? *along the coast of Florida*

PHOTO CAPTION The roots anchor the trees and shrubs in the soil and keep the plants from falling over when buffeted by strong storms or high waves.

History of Science

Aquaculture, or fish farming, was developed by the Chinese more than 4000 years ago. In 1000 B.C., the Chinese were raising carp in artificial ponds. In the 20th century, commercial catches declined due to overfishing and pollution-related problems. Many countries turned to aquaculture to meet their seafood needs. The most current trend in aquaculture is genetically engineered fish and shellfish. For example, flounder can be genetically altered so that all offspring in a fishery are female—female flounders are twice as large as male flounders and thus generate higher profits.

Develop Critical Thinking

PREDICT Tell students that wetlands serve important environmental functions. For example, they absorb excess runoff from heavy rains and they naturally filter pollutants from water. Ask students to predict what could happen to rates of flooding and water quality if a coastal wetland were paved over. *Flooding would increase; water quality would decrease.*

EXPLORE (the BIG idea)

Revisit "Beneath the Surface" on p. 111. Have students answer some of the questions they formulated in the activity.

Ongoing Assessment

Identify what coastal environments exist where fresh water and salt water meet.

Ask: What coastal wetland is found in tropical areas? *mangrove forest*

C 118 Unit: Earth's Waters

INFER This photograph shows mangrove plants along the coast of Florida. How do the roots brace the mangroves against waves and storms?

G

MAIN IDEA WEB
Remember to start a main idea web in your notebook for this blue heading.

?
H

Mangrove Forests

In tropical regions, the main coastal wetland is the mangrove forest. In the United States, mangrove forests are found along the coast of southern Florida. A mangrove forest is a thick group of mangrove shrubs and trees. The mangrove plants' roots brace them against storms and waves. Without the protection of these plants, shorelines in tropical areas would be drastically changed by heavy storms.

The sheltered mangrove forest is home to many living things. Fiddler crabs may live in the shallow waters among the mangrove roots. You may find seaweeds, oysters, shrimp, and snails. You may even see tree-climbing fish! These fish, called mudskippers, climb mangrove roots to catch insects and crabs.

Human activity affects shorelines.

Coastal environments are home not only to many plants and animals, but to many humans as well. About half of the world's population lives within 80 kilometers (50 mi) of a coastline. Big cities and important commercial ports are often located where rivers meet the sea. Many people use coastlines and estuaries for recreation, such as boating, swimming, and fishing.

Human activity can harm the estuary environment. For example, some coastal wetlands are cleared for shrimp farms and for raising crops. Other areas are filled in to make new land for houses and other development. Industry and shipping can disturb wildlife and alter the estuary habitat. In some places, human waste and other sewage drains directly into the water.

C 118 Unit: Earth's Waters

DIFFERENTIATE INSTRUCTION

? **More Reading Support**

G What plants are found in mangrove forests? *mangrove shrubs, trees*

H About half the world's population lives within 80 km of what? *a coastline*

Alternative Assessment Write on the board: Population Density of U.S. Coastal Counties. Write under the title: 1960: 248 people per square mile; 1988: 342 people per square mile; projected 2010: 400 people per square mile. Ask: What trend do you see? *The population in coastal areas is increasing.* Ask: How might this trend affect coastal environments? *Sample answer: It might harm coastal environments because the growing population will need more space for housing and development.*

About half of the world's population lives near a coastline, such as this one in Mexico.

Even pollution that occurs far away from the shore can affect the coast. The rivers that empty into estuaries pass through farms and cities. Along the way, the rivers may pick up pollutants such as pesticides, fertilizers, oil, and other chemicals. Pollution that washes into the river—even kilometers away from the shore—will eventually end up in the estuary.

Governments, local organizations, and individuals work to protect and preserve shoreline environments in many states. Improved sewage treatment plants reduce the amount of human waste that ends up in shoreline environments. Laws that restrict dumping help reduce pollution along shorelines. Many states have shoreline sanctuaries where plants and animals are protected.

 CHECK YOUR READING What are three ways shorelines are protected?

4.1 Review

KEY CONCEPTS

1. Describe the characteristics of the intertidal zone.
2. Name and describe two coastal environments that border estuaries.
3. What human activities are harmful to shoreline environments?

CRITICAL THINKING

4. **Compare and Contrast** What similarities exist between salt marshes and mangrove forests? How are they different?
5. **Infer** Sometimes estuaries are called nursery areas. Why do you think estuaries may have been given that name?

● CHALLENGE

6. **Identify Cause** A salinity meter placed in a tidal pool shows a dramatic decrease in salinity between 2 A.M. and 3 A.M. This decrease is followed by a gradual rise in salinity from 11 A.M. until 4 P.M. the next day. What might explain these changes?

Chapter 4: Ocean Environments **119** **C**

ANSWERS

1. high tide: covered in water, filtered sunlight; low tide: exposed to air and direct sunlight

2. salt marshes: in cooler areas, have grasses with thick root systems; mangrove forests: in tropical areas, have trees and shrubs with

roots that brace the plants against storms and waves

3. clearing wetlands for crops or development; industry; shipping; dumping

4. Both are coastal wetlands, have thick root systems, and are home to many animals. Salt marshes are located in

cooler areas; mangrove forests are located in tropical areas.

5. Many animals breed their young in estuaries.

6. Rain may have diluted the water, causing a decrease in salinity. Sunlight may have caused water to evaporate, increasing salinity.

Ask: How can pollution that occurs far away from shore affect the coast? *Rivers may carry pollutants to the shore.*

 *Answer: improvements in sewage treatment, restrictions on dumping, construction of marine sanctuaries*

Reinforce (the **BIG** idea)

Have students relate the section to the Big Idea.

R Reinforcing Key Concepts, p. 212

4.1 ASSESS & RETEACH

Assess

A Section 4.1 Quiz, p. 61

Reteach

Begin outlining the section by writing the section title on the board. Write the first blue heading on p. 113 as the first Roman numeral entry. Invite students to help you develop the outline using standard outlining format. Suggest that the blue and red headings and the headings for the drawings on p. 115 be used as guides for the outline.

Technology Resources

Have students visit **ClassZone.com** for reteaching of Key Concepts.

 CONTENT REVIEW

 CONTENT REVIEW CD-ROM

Set Learning Goal

To make double bar graphs showing patterns of pollution over time

Present the Science

Lead and arsenic are neurotoxins, or poisons that attack the nervous system. Lead can destroy nerve cells and cause irreversible brain damage. Extreme lead poisoning can induce seizures and comas. Exposure to arsenic at low levels can cause memory impairment, inability to concentrate, and irritability. At high levels, arsenic exposure can cause death. Sources of lead pollution include dust and fumes from factories that make car batteries, rubber, and electronic products. House paint used to contain lead. Arsenic is used in much electrical equipment, rat poisons, and insecticides.

Develop Graphing Skills

Have students use different-colored pencils when drawing the bar graphs to indicate arsenic and lead levels. Colors in the key should explain colors in the graph.

DIFFERENTIATION TIP Students with physical impairments may have trouble drawing the graphs. Enlarge graph paper and encourage them to use rulers to align numbers and graph points. Or allow then to construct graphs on a computer.

Close

Ask: What might account for the large increase in levels of lead between 1880 and 1960? *Sample answer: increased use of cars and leaded gasoline*

   • Math Support, p. 239
   • Math Practice, p. 240

Technology Resources

Students can visit **ClassZone.com** for practice with bar graphs.

 MATH TUTORIAL

MATH in SCIENCE

MATH TUTORIAL
CLASSZONE.COM
Click on Math Tutorial for more help with bar graphs.

Machines mounted on boats drill down into the ocean floor to collect sediment cores.

This tube contains a sediment core.

C **120** Unit: Earth's Waters

Tracking Contaminants

The layered sediments at the bottom of the ocean have formed over time. The particles in the deeper layers settled to the floor long ago, while those in the top layers settled out of the water more recently. By studying the amounts of pollutants in different layers of sediment, scientists can see how the water quality has changed over time. In 1991, scientists collected sediment cores north of Dash Point in Puget Sound. The table below shows levels of two pollutants, lead and arsenic, in the sediment layers for 1880, 1960, and 1990. The levels are measured in milligrams per kilogram dry weight (mg/kg d.w.).

Levels of Lead and Arsenic in Sediments		
Year	Lead (mg/kg d.w.)	Arsenic (mg/kg d.w.)
1880	10	6
1960	62	22
1990	45	17

You can use a double bar graph to analyze the data. A double bar graph shows two sets of data on the same graph. The first two bars of the graph are drawn for you below.

Example

(1) Copy the axes and labels.

(2) Draw bars for the lead data. Use the scale to determine the height of each bar, as shown.

(3) Draw the arsenic bars next to the lead bars.

(4) Shade the bars in different colors. Include a key.

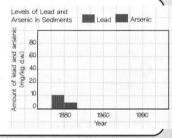

Make a double bar graph of the data by following the steps above. Use your graph to answer the following questions.

1. What happened to the levels of lead and arsenic between 1880 and 1960?

2. What happened to the levels of lead and arsenic between 1960 and 1990?

CHALLENGE Because lead can be harmful to humans, the use of leaded gasoline in new cars was banned in 1975 and the sale of lead-based paint was banned in 1978. How might these bans have affected the amount of lead in Puget Sound? Use evidence from your graph to support your answer.

ANSWERS

1. The levels of both contaminants increased.

2. The levels of both contaminants decreased.

CHALLENGE *Before lead was banned, lead levels in Puget Sound were rising, as shown in the graph. By 1990, more than a decade after the ban, lead levels in Puget Sound decreased significantly. Thus, the ban may have prevented more lead from entering Puget Sound.*

KEY CONCEPT

4.2 Conditions differ away from shore.

◀ **BEFORE, you learned**

- Coasts support plants and animals
- Estuaries and intertidal zones are coastal environments

▶ **NOW, you will learn**

- About ocean environments away from the coast
- How ocean environments change with depth
- How hydrothermal vents support life in the ocean

VOCABULARY

coral reef p. 122
kelp forest p. 124
phytoplankton p. 126
hydrothermal vent p. 128

EXPLORE Air Bladders

How can air make things float?

PROCEDURE

① Fill the container halfway with soda water.

② Add raisins to the container, one by one.

③ Observe for 5 minutes. Record your observations.

WHAT DO YOU THINK?

- How did the air bubbles control the movement of the raisins?
- Many ocean fish have an air-filled organ called an air bladder. The fish can control the amount of air in the bladder. How might the amount of air in the bladder change as a fish dives from the ocean surface to the bottom and then returns to the surface?

MATERIALS

- clear container
- soda water
- 5 raisins

Ocean environments change with depth and distance from shore.

MAIN IDEA WEB
Remember to start a main idea web in your notebook for the blue heading.

Your journey through ocean environments continues as you leave the intertidal zone and move farther out into the ocean. First, you will visit the habitats found in the waters near shore. Next you will move out into the open ocean.

Near shore—in the waters over the continental shelf—sunlight reaches most of the way to the ocean bottom. Nutrients wash in from land. Temperature and salinity are nearly constant from the surface to the bottom. These conditions support many kinds of living things.

CHECK YOUR READING What are some characteristics of the environment near shore?

RESOURCES FOR DIFFERENTIATED INSTRUCTION

Below Level

UNIT RESOURCE BOOK
- Reading Study Guide A, pp. 215–216
- Decoding Support, p. 238

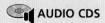 **AUDIO CDS**

Advanced

UNIT RESOURCE BOOK
Challenge and Extension, p. 221

English Learners

UNIT RESOURCE BOOK
Spanish Reading Study Guide, pp. 219–220

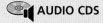 **AUDIO CDS**

- Audio Readings in Spanish
- Audio Readings (English)

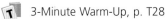

4.2 FOCUS

⊙ Set Learning Goals

Students will

- Describe ocean environments away from the coast.
- Recognize how ocean environments change with depth.
- Explain how hydrothermal vents support life in the ocean.
- Model how plankton float.

◑ 3-Minute Warm-Up

Display Transparency 28 or copy this exercise on the board:

Decide if these statements are true. If not, correct them.

1. Ocean organisms are organized into three groups according to the way the organisms look. *organized according to the way they live.*

2. Bottom dwellers include animals that live on the ocean floor. *true*

3. Swimmers include organisms that float at or near the ocean surface. *Floaters include organisms that float at or near the ocean surface.*

▧ 3-Minute Warm-Up, p. T28

4.2 MOTIVATE

EXPLORE Air Bladders

PURPOSE To introduce students to the function of air bladders

TIP *15 min.* This activity works best with smaller raisins that are gently dropped into the water, one by one.

WHAT DO YOU THINK? *Bubbles accumulated on the raisins and lifted them. When the bubbles burst, the raisins sank. Air leaving the bladder allows the fish to sink. The bladder fills with air when the fish returns to the surface.*

Ongoing Assessment

CHECK YOUR READING *Answer: sunlight, high nutrients, constant temperature and salinity from surface to bottom*

Health Connection

Medical researchers are finding that coral skeletons are excellent materials for grafting human bones. Grafts for injured or diseased bones are often taken from a healthy bone in a person's body. However, this procedure is costly and painful, so other materials, including animal bones and synthetic products, are increasingly used as substitutes. Corals work well because they are porous and easily dissolved. These factors allow human cells and blood vessels to "invade" the graft material and replace it with human bone. As an added bonus, the coral releases calcium as it dissolves and so promotes bone growth. To reduce environmental harm to coral reefs, corals used for bone grafts are usually cultured in laboratories.

Teach Difficult Concepts

Some students may not understand that although coral reefs can be large, corals themselves are actually tiny organisms that live in large colonies. Ask them to summarize how corals live and the role they play in forming reefs. *Corals are small organisms that live in large colonies and produce hard limestone coverings. A coral reef is made up of limestone deposits formed by successive generations of corals.*

Integrate the Sciences

Limestone consists mostly of the mineral calcite. Much of this mineral is dissolved in water from rocks on land. Rivers carry the calcite to the sea in the form of calcium ions. Corals use the ions to produce their hard limestone covering; shellfish use the ions to produce calcium carbonate shells. Over millions of years, the materials of ancient coral reefs and shells become compacted and cemented into thick layers of limestone.

The waters near shore support diverse life forms.

More kinds of ocean life live in the waters near shore than in any other ocean environment. Microscopic organisms including bacteria, protists, plants, and animals live there. They share the waters near shore with plants as tall as ten-story buildings and animals larger than elephants. Each organism is part of a delicate and complex food web. You become part of this food web when you eat a fish from the waters near shore. In fact, most of the world's fish are caught in this ocean environment.

? A Two important habitats near shore are the kelp forest and the coral reef. Kelp forests are found in cooler waters, and coral reefs are found in tropical warm waters.

Coral Reefs

? B In warm, tropical regions of the globe, the waters near shore support coral reefs. **Coral reefs** are built-up limestone deposits formed by large colonies of ant-sized organisms called corals. Corals produce a hard limestone covering that remains after the corals die. New generations of corals grow on top of older limestone coverings. Although individual corals are small, coral reefs can be huge. Australia's Great Barrier Reef is about 2000 kilometers (1250 mi) long—as long as the distance from Chicago, Illinois, to San Antonio, Texas.

Corals rely on a special relationship with a kind of algae for almost all of their food needs. Tiny algae live inside individual corals. Like plants, the algae use sunlight to produce food through photosynthesis. The food algae produces provides the coral with most of its nutrition. In return, the coral provides some nutrients to the algae. Because the algae need sunlight to survive, coral reefs exist only in the ocean environment near shore, where sunlight reaches all the way to the ocean floor.

VOCABULARY
A four square diagram would be a good choice for taking notes about the term *coral reef.*

Coral reefs, which contain over 25 percent of all of the species of ocean life, help protect shorelines from wave and storm damage.

DIFFERENTIATE INSTRUCTION

? More Reading Support

A List two ocean habitats near shore. *kelp forest, coral reef*

B What types of deposits make up coral reefs? *limestone*

English Learners The use of dashes in writing might be confusing to English learners. Explain that dashes can be used to interject an idea into a sentence. Give students the example below. Show students that the sentence would still be complete if the clause inside (or after) the dashes were not there.
"Australia's Great Barrier Reef is about 2000 kilometers (1250 mi) long—as long as the distance from Chicago, Illinois, to San Antonio, Texas." (p. 122)

Coral Reefs

The nutrient-rich, sunlit waters near shore support a greater variety of life than any other part of the ocean.

near shore environment

The **anemone** can paralyze most fish with its stinging tentacles.

The **anemone fish** (also called the clown fish) is covered by mucus that protects it from the anemone. The anemone shelters the fish from predators. The anemone benefits by eating bits of food that the fish drops.

The **parrotfish** uses its hard teeth to chew on coral. It eats the algae that live in and on the coral. The hard coral skeletons get ground into sand as they pass through the parrotfish's digestive system.

The **moray eel** spends days hidden in cracks or holes in the reef. At night the eel comes out to hunt.

The **nudibranch** is related to snails but has no shell. It contains bad-tasting or poisonous chemicals that discourage fish from eating it.

The **giant clam** can grow to be over 1 meter (3 ft) long. It feeds by filtering tiny organisms from the water. Like corals, the giant clam gets some of its nutrients from algae that live within its own tissues.

READING ViSUALS Which organisms in the diagram appear to be using nooks in the reef for shelter?

123 C

Teach from Visuals

To help students interpret the coral reef visual, ask:

- Where are coral reefs generally located? How do you know? *Coral reefs are located near the shore, as shown in the small diagram in the upper right.*
- What are some ways that organisms in a coral reef protect themselves against predators? *The nudibranch contains bad-tasting or poisonous chemicals that discourage fish from eating it. The anemone fish is covered by mucous that allows it to take shelter in the anemone.*
- What are some ways that organisms in the coral reef catch prey? *The anemone paralyzes fish with its stinging tentacles. The moray eel hunts at night.*

Integrate the Sciences

Organisms that live in the same ecosystem often compete for food and shelter. However, some relationships between organisms are cooperative. The anemone and the clown fish, for example, have a symbiotic relationship, meaning that the two different species share a close association. The clown fish receives protection from predators by hiding in the anemone's stinging tentacles. The anemone receives bits of food that the fish drops. This type of symbiosis is called mutualism because both organisms benefit from the relationship.

Ongoing Assessment

READING ViSUALS *Answer: moray eel, nudibranch*

DIFFERENTIATE INSTRUCTION

Inclusion Allow students with visual impairments to handle samples of coral. Ask them to describe its texture. Enlarge the visual "Coral Reefs" and help students identify the different organisms.

Alternative Assessment A food chain shows how energy flows through ecosystems from producers to consumers to decomposers. Have students use some of the organisms in the visual to make a simple food chain. Students can use arrows showing the direction of energy flow.

Teach from Visuals

To help students interpret the photograph of the kelp forest, ask:

• Where was the camera located when it took this picture? *underwater*

• What is the light source? Where is it coming from? *sunlight; above the surface of the water*

Teacher Demo

Show students how air-filled bulbs help keep kelp upright in water. Place a small piece of string in a bucket of water. Tie a second small piece of string to the end of a blown-up balloon and then place it in the water as well. Give students a few moments to observe the strings. Then ask: Which string remained upright? *the one tied to the balloon* What did the balloon represent? *the air-filled bulbs that help kelp stalks remain upright underwater*

Ongoing Assessment

 *Answer: Pollution and destructive fishing practices endanger coral reefs.*

 **RESOURCE CENTER**
CLASSZONE.COM
Explore coral reefs.

The huge amount and variety of life found at coral reefs compares with that found in rain forests. In fact, coral reefs contain over 25 percent of all the species of ocean life. Some reef inhabitants use nooks and crannies in the reef for shelter. Other inhabitants eat corals or feed on seaweed that grows on the corals. Clown fish, sea anemones, (uh-NEHM-uh-neez), sea urchins, starfish, giant clams, and parrotfish are some of the many colorful reef inhabitants.

Coral reefs are now endangered habitats. Pollution that drains off land or that is dumped directly into the water harms coral reefs. Some fishing practices also harm corals and other life at reefs.

 CHECK YOUR READING Why are coral reefs endangered?

Kelp Forests

 In cold waters, a seaweed called kelp attaches itself to the ocean floor and grows as tall as 40 meters (130 ft)—about the length of an airline jet. Air-filled bulbs on the seaweed's stalks help it to float up toward the surface and remain upright underwater. Large communities of this seaweed form **kelp forests.** Like plants, kelps use sunlight to produce food. Because kelps need sunlight and grow in the ocean, kelp forests

Kelp forests, such as this one in California, provide food and shelter for many living things.

Kelp is an ingredient in many common products including ice cream. Kelp can grow up to 33 cm (13 in) each day.

 124 Unit: Earth's Waters

DIFFERENTIATE INSTRUCTION

? More Reading Support

C What percentage of ocean life is found in coral reefs? *over 25 percent*

D What is kelp? *seaweed with air-filled bulbs*

Advanced Tell students that different animals live in different layers of a kelp forest. Have students investigate the animals that live in kelp forests and make a chart that classifies them according to whether they inhabit the kelp canopy, its stalk, or its holdfast (root area). *Sample answer: Fish swim among the fronds of the canopy. Sea urchins feed on red seaweed that covers the stalk. Lobsters scramble around the holdfasts and nearby rocks on the ocean floor.*

R Challenge and Extension, p. 221

A sea otter off the coast of California wraps itself in kelp.

are found only in the waters near shore, where sunlight reaches to the ocean floor. Thick kelp forests provide habitats for many organisms. Worms, starfish, lobsters, crabs, abalones, and octopuses are some of the animals that live among the crowded stands of kelp. Fish find shelter and food there. Sea otters dining on sea urchins anchor themselves to the thick mats that the kelps form on the surface.

CHECK YOUR READING Why are kelp forests found only in waters near shore?

INVESTIGATE Floating

How do plankton float?

DESIGN —YOUR OWN—

Plankton are microscopic organisms that drift in the ocean, where they are moved about by wind, waves, and currents. They must stay near the sunlit surface in order to live. Because plankton have no muscles, they cannot swim to stay afloat. In this lab, you will construct different-shaped clay models to determine how shape helps plankton stay near the ocean surface.

PROCEDURE

(1) Fill the clear container with tap water.

(2) Use the clay to make several different shapes that you think will stay afloat.

(3) One by one, place your clay models on the surface of the water. Time how long each piece takes to reach the bottom. Record your observations.

WHAT DO YOU THINK?

- What were the characteristics of the clay shape that sank the slowest?
- What factors affected how fast your clay shape sunk?

CHALLENGE Some kinds of floating organisms release oil droplets or air bubbles to help them stay afloat. How could oil or air help them float?

SKILL FOCUS Modeling

MATERIALS
- clear container
- water
- modeling clay
- watch with a second hand

TIME 30 minutes

Chapter 4: Ocean Environments **125** **C**

INVESTIGATE Floating

PURPOSE To model the effect of shape on floating plankton

TIPS *30 min.*

- Some clays dissolve easily in water. Obtain a small sample of clay and test it beforehand to make sure it does not dissolve.

- Before students make their models, show them photographs of different-shaped plankton.

WHAT DO YOU THINK? *A very thin flat disk sank the slowest. Thin extensions helped the model stay afloat. The shape and size of the clay model affected how fast it sank.*

CHALLENGE *Because oil is less dense than water, it floats on water—thus, an organism that releases oil droplets would float. Air bubbles also float on water, so an organism could use an air bubble to float.*

R Datasheet, Floating, p. 222

Technology Resources

Customize this student lab as needed or look for an alternative. Print rubrics to assess student lab reports.

Lab Generator CD-ROM

Teaching with Technology

If you have access to a PC microscope, allow students to view different-shaped plankton.

Ongoing Assessment

CHECK YOUR READING *Answer: Kelp needs sunlight to grow so it is only found where sunlight reaches all the way to the ocean floor.*

DIFFERENTIATE INSTRUCTION

More Reading Support

E List three animals found in kelp forests. *any three: worms, starfish, lobsters, crabs, abalones, octopuses*

Alternative Assessment Have students use clay, straws, and other materials to create a model of an ocean environment. Students should explain the physical conditions and the organisms that inhabit the environment.

Real World Example

Invasive species are non-native species that are transported purposely or accidentally into new environments. Some invasive species attached themselves to the wooden hulls of ships and traveled thousands of kilometers from their native habitats. The periwinkle snail is an example of a European species that arrived on the U.S eastern coast hundreds of years ago.

Modern ships are equipped with ballast tanks that are filled with water to stabilize the ship. The ballast is filled at the port of origin and often contains numerous species, including microscopic zooplankton. When the ship completes its journey, the water is released and the hitchhiking species invade new territory.

Invasive species may have no natural predators in their new habitats. For this reason, they can disrupt native ecosystems. For example, an American ship carried marine organisms similar to jellyfish in its ballast water to the Black Sea in 1982. The small organism had no predators and fed on plankton, shrimp, and fish larvae. By the 1990s, fish catches in the Black Sea had plummeted.

Address Misconceptions

IDENTIFY Ask: In what places can organisms get carbon dioxide and sunlight? If students mention only places in the open air, they may hold the misconception that carbon dioxide and sunlight cannot get through water for use by aquatic organisms.

CORRECT Shine a flashlight lengthwise through a tall container of water. Point out the light shining on the bottom of the container. Then open a clear bottle of soda and point out the bubbles of carbon dioxide rising through the soda.

REASSESS Ask: How can organisms underwater get carbon dioxide and sunlight to produce oxygen? *Carbon dioxide is dissolved in the water, and sunlight penetrates water to certain depths.*

Environments in the open ocean change with depth.

Out in the open ocean, conditions are different from these found in the waters near shore. Sunlight reaches through only the very top part of the open ocean. Nutrients sink down to the dark depths. There are no rocks, reefs, or big plants to provide shelter from predators. The open ocean covers a huge area but contains fewer living things than the waters near shore. Life is more spread out in the open ocean.

Surface Zone

The surface zone of the open ocean is the sunlit top 200 meters (650 ft). Microscopic floating organisms called **phytoplankton** (FY-toh-PLANGK-tuhn) live at or near the sunlit surface. Like plants, phytoplankton convert sunlight and carbon dioxide into food and oxygen. In fact, phytoplankton convert about as much carbon dioxide into oxygen as all land plants combined. Phytoplankton are an important source of the oxygen that you are breathing right now. Tiny floating animals called zooplankton eat phytoplankton. Zooplankton and phytoplankton then become food for fish, squids, and ocean mammals, such as whales.

Inhabitants of the surface zone must keep from sinking. To stay afloat, phytoplankton bodies have big surface areas and may use air bubbles or oil droplets to stay near the ocean surface. Many fish have an air-filled organ called an air bladder that helps the fish change depth. Changing the amount of air in the bladder allows these fish to move up and down in the water. When the bladder fills with air, the fish floats up toward the surface. Releasing air from the bladder allows the fish to dive down into deeper water.

> **READING TIP**
> Word parts can help you remember the meaning of *phytoplankton* and *zooplankton*. The prefix *phyto-* means "plant" and the prefix *zoo-* means "animal."

Deep Zone

The dark and cold deep zone of the open ocean lies under the surface zone. Because sunlight does not reach the deep zone, no plants can live there. Without plants for food, many deep-sea animals must either eat each other or rely on food drifting down from above.

The anglerfish in the photograph on page 127 has many of the common features of deep-sea animals. Its huge mouth and sharp teeth are typical of predators—animals that hunt and eat other animals. Many deep-sea animals glow in the dark, as fireflies do. A glowing extension sticks out from the head of the anglerfish and acts as bait to attract prey. Animals of the deepest waters often have small eyes—and some have no eyes at all. Among the animals found in the deep zone are lantern fish, squids, octopuses, and shrimp.

DIFFERENTIATE INSTRUCTION

? More Reading Support

F What are phytoplankton? *microscopic floating organisms*

G The deep zone is under what? *the surface zone*

Below Level For students who have a hard time reading large blocks of text, have them relate the text on p. 126 to the visual of life in the open ocean on p. 127. Tell them to frequently pause while reading and refer to the visual.

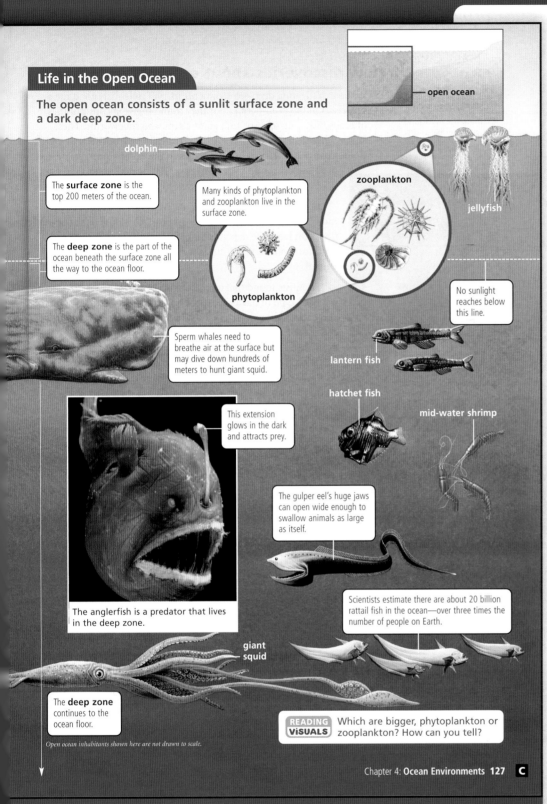

Life in the Open Ocean

The open ocean consists of a sunlit surface zone and a dark deep zone.

— open ocean

dolphin

The **surface zone** is the top 200 meters of the ocean.

Many kinds of phytoplankton and zooplankton live in the surface zone.

zooplankton

jellyfish

The **deep zone** is the part of the ocean beneath the surface zone all the way to the ocean floor.

phytoplankton

No sunlight reaches below this line.

Sperm whales need to breathe air at the surface but may dive down hundreds of meters to hunt giant squid.

lantern fish

hatchet fish

mid-water shrimp

This extension glows in the dark and attracts prey.

The gulper eel's huge jaws can open wide enough to swallow animals as large as itself.

The anglerfish is a predator that lives in the deep zone.

Scientists estimate there are about 20 billion rattail fish in the ocean—over three times the number of people on Earth.

giant squid

The **deep zone** continues to the ocean floor.

Open ocean inhabitants shown here are not drawn to scale.

READING VISUALS Which are bigger, phytoplankton or zooplankton? How can you tell?

Chapter 4: Ocean Environments **127** **C**

Ongoing Assessment

Explain how hydrothermal vents support life in the ocean.

Ask: How do bacteria near hydrothermal vents produce food? *They use dissolved chemicals from the vent.*

 CHECK YOUR READING *Answer: Scientists did not think life was possible without sunlight.*

EXPLORE (the BIG idea)

Revisit "Internet Activity: Ocean Environments" on p. 111. Have students review their answers.

Reinforce (the BIG idea)

Have students relate the section to the Big Idea.

 Reinforcing Key Concepts, p. 223

4.2 ASSESS & RETEACH

Assess

 Section 4.2 Quiz, p. 62

Reteach

Refer students to the visuals on coral reefs (p. 123), and life in the open ocean (p. 127). Have students use the visuals as guides to draw diagrams of marine habitats. Diagrams should include organisms found in kelp forests, coral reefs, and the open ocean, as well as small insets that show the location of these environments.

Technology Resources

Have students visit **ClassZone.com** for reteaching of Key Concepts.

 CONTENT REVIEW

 CONTENT REVIEW CD-ROM

New discoveries about ocean life continue.

VISUALIZATION
CLASSZONE.COM

Examine the life found at hydrothermal vents.

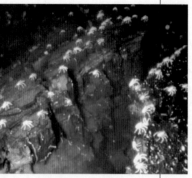

Hydrothermal vents support many kinds of life, including clams, crabs, fish, tubeworms, and bacteria.

While investigating deep-sea sediments in 1977, scientists got quite a surprise. On the deep-ocean floor they found thriving communities of crabs, fish, mussels, shrimp, giant clams, and tubeworms. These animals live near openings in Earth's crust called **hydrothermal vents**. Cold ocean water that seeps into cracks in the ocean floor gets heated deep underground by hot magma. The heated water then rises up and gushes out into the ocean, forming hydrothermal vents.

Before the discovery of animal communities near vents, most scientists thought life was impossible on the dark ocean floor. On land, life depends on plants, which use sunlight to produce food. Without sunlight, how could these deep sea animals live?

Scientists found that animals at hydrothermal vents depend on a special type of bacteria. Instead of making food from sunlight and carbon dioxide, like plants, these bacteria make food from chemicals released by the vents. The bacteria thus form the base of the food chain at the vents. Some of the animals living there eat the bacteria. Other animals, such as tubeworms, have the bacteria living within their bodies. Tubeworms do not eat and have no digestive system—they absorb all their food directly from the bacteria.

Because of its crushing pressure, darkness, and huge size, the deep ocean remains mostly unexplored. The discovery of animal communities at hydrothermal vents is a reminder that life may be possible even in seemingly impossible places. In fact, more recent explorations have even found life deep within the sediments of the ocean floor.

CHECK YOUR READING Why were scientists surprised to find life at hydrothermal vents?

4.2 Review

KEY CONCEPTS

1. What are two environments in the waters near shore? Describe the characteristics of each.
2. How does the surface zone of the open ocean differ from the deep zone?
3. How do hydrothermal vents support life on the deep-ocean floor?

CRITICAL THINKING

4. **Predict** How might a change in the amount of phytoplankton in the ocean affect the world's atmosphere?
5. **Evaluate** Suppose you are seeking a site for a submarine station where scientists could live for months at a time. Which ocean environment would you choose, and why?

CHALLENGE

6. **Apply** Diatoms are tiny ocean organisms that convert carbon dioxide to oxygen. Describe the depth at which diatoms live and where they fit into the ocean food chain.

(magnified 200x)

C 128 Unit: Earth's Waters

ANSWERS

1. coral reefs: sunny, formed by the limestone deposits of corals, home to many species; kelp forests: sunny, formed by large communities of kelp, home to many organisms

2. The surface zone is sunlit and contains plankton. The deep zone is dark and cold.

3. Bacteria use dissolved chemicals from the vents to make food.

4. More phytoplankton might mean more oxygen and less carbon dioxide. Less photoplankton might mean less carbon dioxide and more oxygen.

5. Sample answer: a coral reef because it is near shore and has easy access and dense marine life to study

6. Diatoms live near the ocean surface because they use sunlight to produce food. They are at the bottom of the food chain.

AN EXTREME ENVIRONMENT

RESOURCE CENTER
CLASSZONE.COM
Learn more about hydrothermal vents.

Undersea Hot Spots

Deep within Earth, volcanic activity heats up water. When this water shoots out through a crack in the ocean floor, it forms a hydrothermal vent. These vents are among the world's strangest environments.

- The pressure of the ocean water is so high that the water emerging from the vents does not boil—even though it is as hot as 400°C (750°F).
- The water from the vents is so filled with minerals, particularly hydrogen sulfide, that it would poison most animals.
- Sunlight is so dim that the vents exist in near total darkness. However, they often glow slightly, perhaps due to heat radiation.

When the hot water from the vent hits the nearly freezing ocean water, it cools rapidly. The minerals dissolved in the water settle out, sometimes creating a chimney around the vent. Some chimneys are as tall as 15-story buildings.

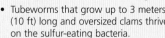

Tubeworms may grow up to 3 meters (10 ft) in length.

Home Sweet Home

Organisms that live anywhere else on Earth would not be able to survive the combination of pressure, heat, poisonous water, and darkness that exists near vents. Yet scientists have identified 300 species living near vents.

- Bacteria convert the sulfur in the water into energy. This is one of the few places on Earth where the living things at the base of a food chain get energy from chemicals rather than from sunlight.
- Tubeworms that grow up to 3 meters (10 ft) long and oversized clams thrive on the sulfur-eating bacteria.
- Crabs with gigantic legs that make them look like enormous spiders from a horror movie survive by eating the worms and other creatures.

Life Far Away

Organisms that live around the vents are like no others on Earth. However, could a different planet with a sulfur-rich environment support similar life forms? As scientists explore the possibility of life on other planets, they will look to hydrothermal vents for lessons on unusual life.

EXPLORE

1. **SEQUENCE** Create a diagram showing the relationship on the hydrothermal vent food chain between bacteria, crabs, and tubeworms.

2. **CHALLENGE** In 1997 scientists discovered features on Jupiter's moon Europa that look like icebergs floating on an ocean. Why did this discovery suggest that life might exist on Europa?

Chapter 4: Ocean Environments **129** **C**

EXPLORE

1. *SEQUENCE Diagrams should show bacteria at the base of the food chain, tubeworms in the middle, and crabs on top.*

2. *CHALLENGE Sample answer: Life on Earth began in the oceans.*

EXTREME SCIENCE
Fun and Motivating Science

Set Learning Goal

To investigate extreme environments such as undersea hot spots

Present the Science

Scientists study hydrothermal vents using technology such as remotely operated vehicles (ROVs). ROVs are tethered to ships or crewed submersibles; operators onboard control the vehicle's movements. Depending on its mission, an ROV may be equipped with cameras, lights, sensors, temperature monitors, and mechanical hands that allow researchers to retrieve objects.

Discussion Questions

Ask: Why doesn't the hot water boil as it comes out of the vent? *The high pressure of ocean water prevents the vent water from boiling.*

Ask: What minerals does water from the vent contain? *at least hydrogen sulfide*

Ask: What process creates chimneys around vents? *Dissolved minerals in the water settle out.*

DIFFERENTIATION TIP Remind English learners that word parts can help them remember new vocabulary terms. Have them look up the meaning of the prefix *hydro-* and the root word *thermal.* *Hydro means "water" and thermal means "relating to heat."*

Close

Ask: What characteristics make hydrothermal vents so unique? *near total darkness, very hot temperatures despite cold surroundings, pressure due to depth*

Technology Resources

Students can visit **ClassZone.com** to find out more about hydrothermal vents.

 RESOURCE CENTER

◉ Set Learning Goals

Students will

- Recognize the living resources the ocean contains.
- Identify the mineral, energy, and other resources the ocean contains.
- Describe how pollution affects the ocean.

◎ 3-Minute Warm-Up

Display Transparency 29 or copy this exercise on the board:

Write a brief paragraph describing the different ocean environments you might encounter if you were to travel from a coastal area to the open ocean in a submersible.

Sample answer: If you start from the intertidal zone, you may be around an estuary, salt marsh, or mangrove forest. As you move away from the intertidal zone and into near shore waters, you might see coral reefs and kelp forests. Once in the open ocean, you may pass from the surface zone to the deep zone. Since sunlight does not penetrate deeper than 200 m (the boundary between the two zones) you will need artificial lights to see sea creatures, and if you go deep enough, the ocean floor and hydrothermal vents.

 3-Minute Warm-Up, p. T29

EXPLORE Ocean Pollution

PURPOSE To investigate how oil spills affect birds

TIP *20 min.* This activity works best when the feather is lightly touched to the surface of the water.

WHAT DO YOU THINK? *The oil changed the feather—the feather did not float when you blew on it after it was put in oily water. Birds would not be able to float or swim in water that has been polluted by an oil spill.*

KEY CONCEPT

4.3 The ocean contains natural resources.

◀ **BEFORE, you learned**

- The waters near shore support diverse life forms
- The ocean environment changes with depth

▶ **NOW, you will learn**

- What living resources the ocean contains
- What mineral, energy, and other resources the ocean contains
- How pollution affects the ocean

VOCABULARY

overfishing p. 131
by-catch p. 132

EXPLORE Ocean Pollution

How do oil spills affect birds?

PROCEDURE

1. Fill the bowl with water.
2. Carefully place the feather on top of the water in the bowl.
3. Holding the end of the feather, blow on it to try to make the feather rise up out of the bowl. Record your observations.
4. Remove the feather and place three spoonfuls of oil into the bowl.
5. Repeat steps 2 and 3.

WHAT DO YOU THINK?

- How did the oil in the water affect the feather?
- Based on your findings, how do you think oil spills might affect birds?

MATERIALS
- bowl
- water
- feather
- spoon
- cooking oil

 MAIN IDEA WEB
Remember to start a main idea web in your notebook for the blue heading.

The ocean supports living resources.

The ocean's many algae and animals are important food sources for people in many areas of the world, including the United States. In fact, the United States is the third largest consumer of seafood in the world. The ocean also supports living resources you do not eat for dinner. You have already read about phytoplankton, tiny ocean organisms. Phytoplankton are a very important resource because they produce much of the oxygen in Earth's air. Chemicals from other ocean organisms are used in medicines—including some that treat cancer. As research continues, scientists may find even more useful chemicals in ocean organisms.

RESOURCES FOR DIFFERENTIATED INSTRUCTION

Below Level
UNIT RESOURCE BOOK
- Reading Study Guide A, pp. 226–227
- Decoding Support, p. 238

 AUDIO CDS

 Additional INVESTIGATION,
Oxygen in Ocean Water, A, B, & C, pp. 250–258; Teacher Instructions, pp. 261–262

Advanced
UNIT RESOURCE BOOK
- Challenge and Extension, p. 232
- Challenge Reading, pp. 234–235

English Learners
UNIT RESOURCE BOOK
Spanish Reading Study Guide, pp. 230–231

 **AUDIO CDS**

- Audio Readings in Spanish
- Audio Readings (English)

Seafood and Algae

Across the United States, supermarkets sell ocean fish and shellfish. Most people, whether they realize it or not, eat seaweeds, too. These ocean algae are commonly used to thicken cheese, ice cream, and pudding. Seaweeds are also ingredients in nonfood products such as shaving cream and pesticides.

When you think of fishing, you might think of a person with a fishing pole catching one fish at a time. This method of fishing, however, is far too slow and inefficient for the commercial fishing industry to use. Instead, the fishing industry uses huge nets bigger than football fields or lines of fishing hooks kilometers long to catch large amounts of fish at a time. As you read this sentence, tens of thousands of nets and fishing lines trail in the ocean. The fishing industry uses sonar, satellites, airplanes, and other technology to find areas in the ocean that contain large numbers of fish.

?
A

Overfishing and By-Catch

?
B

Over the years, people have noticed that there are fewer and fewer fish than there once were. The main cause of the decrease in fish populations is **overfishing,** or catching fish at a faster rate than they can reproduce. Cod is one popular food fish that was nearly killed off by overfishing. Cod were once common in the North Atlantic, but now the cod population is very small. All of the world's fisheries, or main fishing areas of the ocean, are either overfished or very close to being overfished. Overfishing is a major threat to ocean environments.

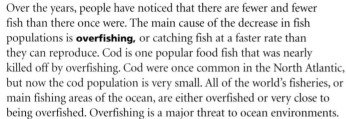
VOCABULARY
You can use a description wheel to take notes about the term *overfishing.*

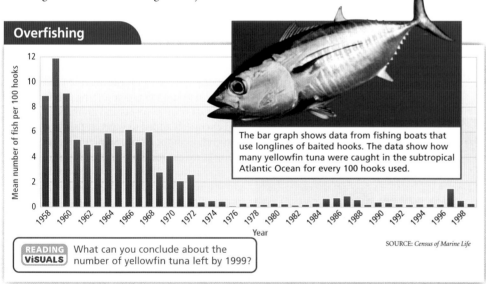
Overfishing

Mean number of fish per 100 hooks

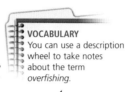

The bar graph shows data from fishing boats that use longlines of baited hooks. The data show how many yellowfin tuna were caught in the subtropical Atlantic Ocean for every 100 hooks used.

Year

SOURCE: *Census of Marine Life*

READING VISUALS What can you conclude about the number of yellowfin tuna left by 1999?

Chapter 4: Ocean Environments **131** **C**

Health Connection

Nutritionally, seaweeds contain many vitamins and minerals. In Asia in particular, they are used in soups, salads, and even candies and cakes. Along the northwest coast of North America, a type of kelp is pickled. In Europe, kelp has also been used to mulch and fertilize crops.

Develop Critical Thinking

INFER Total global catches of fish have—depending on which source you refer to—doubled, tripled, or even quadrupled in the last fifty years. During this time, however, many major fisheries have experienced a decrease in catches. Ask students to infer why global catches have increased overall while catches from major fisheries have declined. *Sample answer: Overfishing has contributed to both the decline in major fisheries and the increase in global catches. New fisheries may have been discovered, adding to the increase in total global catches.*

Teach from Visuals

To help students interpret the visual on overfishing, ask:

• What do the bars on the graph represent? *the mean number of fish caught per 100 hooks*

• Does the graph show a general increase or decrease in fish caught from 1958 to 1999? *decrease*

• What was the mean number of fish caught per 100 hooks in 1959? *12* in 1999? *less than one*

Ongoing Assessment

Recognize the living resources the ocean contains.

Ask: What are the ocean's algae and animals used for? *food and non-food products*

READING VISUALS *Answer: The yellowfin tuna population had decreased significantly in the past 40 years.*

DIFFERENTIATE INSTRUCTION

? **More Reading Support**

A What technology is used to catch fish? *sonar, satellites, and airplanes*

B What is the main cause of the decrease in fish populations? *overfishing*

English Learners English learners may be confused by the different ways prepositions are used in phrases such as *wash into* and *end up*. Point out that in the phrase *wash into* the preposition is literal; "minerals wash into the ocean" (p. 134). Conversely, *end up* is an idiom; "chemicals . . . can end up in the ocean" (p. 136). Students should not read *up* literally as a direction. Rather, in this context it is part of a phrase that means "be transported" or "move to."

Students may have a hard time understanding how nets can be designed to prevent turtles and dolphins from being caught. Explain that the nets are mainly used in the U.S. shrimp industry. They are designed so that small organisms, such as shrimp, stay in the net while larger organisms, such as turtles, slip out through an opening known as a Turtle Excluder Device (TED). The opening is barred and swings open only when hit by a large animal. To help students understand, you might try the following demonstration.

Teacher Demo

Cut a screen into a circle about 5 cm in diameter. Hold the circle by its edge over an open paper bag. Sprinkle some sand over the screen—students should observe that the sand easily passes through the screen and is "caught" in the bag. Then push against the screen with your finger, so that the screen gives way and your finger is deflected away from the opening of the bag. Ask: What does the circle of screen represent? *a TED* What does the bag represent? *a fishing net* What does the sand represent? *small organisms such as shrimp* What does the finger pushing against the circle represent? *large animals such as turtles* Did the large animal get caught in the net? *No, it escaped.*

Ongoing Assessment

 Answer: Overfishing reduces fish populations.

Everything except the shrimp will be thrown away as by-catch from this boat in the Gulf of Mexico.

Fishing nets catch nearly everything in their path. A net that is being used to catch shrimp, for example, may also catch fish, turtles, sharks, dolphins, and other sea animals. The extra catch—everything besides the shrimp—gets tossed back into the ocean either dead or dying. **By-catch,** or by-kill, is the portion of animals that are caught in a net and then thrown away. Sometimes the by-catch is greater than the portion of fish or other animals the net is meant to catch.

To help reduce by-catch, fisheries started using nets designed to prevent animals such as turtles and dolphins from getting caught. Although these efforts have lessened the number of turtles and dolphins caught in fishing nets, fisheries worldwide still throw away about 30 percent of the fish they catch.

CHECK YOUR READING What harm does overfishing cause?

A shrimp farm extends out into the water off the island of Bora Bora in French Polynesia.

Pacific Ocean

SOCIETY ISLANDS, FRENCH POLYNESIA

Saltwater Aquaculture

As you read in Chapter 2, aquaculture is the farming of both freshwater and ocean organisms. Saltwater farmers may raise fish, oysters, mussels, shrimp, seaweeds, or other organisms.

Most aquaculture harms the environment. Huge amounts of fish waste are often released into the ocean waters surrounding fish farms, causing damage to plants and animals. Nutrients and chemicals added to water at fish farms may also end up in the ocean. Sometimes plants and animals are cleared from an area to make space for aquaculture. About half of the world's mangrove forests have been cleared for shrimp farms and similar uses.

Some methods of aquaculture cause more damage than others. For 4000 years, farmers in China have raised fish without causing much harm. Chinese fish farms are often small, so they release less waste than larger farms.

More Reading Support

C The portion of animals caught in a net and then thrown away is called what? *by-catch*

Alternative Assessment As you discuss by-catch, have students develop analogies that correspond to the lack of selectivity of that fishing nets that catch nearly everything in their path. For example, an analogy might be cutting down an entire forest to harvest one species of tree or reaching blindly into the refrigerator for a certain food and throwing away everything else.

The ocean contains nonliving resources.

Ocean water itself is a valuable resource for people living in regions with little fresh water. As you read in Chapter 2, desalination is the process by which salt is removed from seawater. Desalinated seawater is a major portion of the fresh water used by many Middle Eastern countries, such as Saudi Arabia.

Many of the natural resources found on land are also found in the ocean. It is often less expensive to remove resources from the land than from the ocean, so many of the ocean's resources are not currently mined. However, as resources on land are used up and new technology makes ocean exploration and mining easier, ocean mining may increase.

Energy Resources

Oil and gas form from the remains of living organisms. In the ocean, organisms are concentrated in the waters over the continental shelf. Oil deposits, therefore, are found near shore. Oil and gas are pumped from the continental shelf of every continent but Antarctica. About 30 percent of the world's oil is pumped from deposits under the ocean floor.

Huge anchored platforms serve as artificial islands that house workers and the necessary equipment for drilling offshore oil wells. The platforms are built to withstand ocean currents, tides, and weather conditions such as storms. Underwater pipelines carry the oil to shore.

Oil is pumped from the ocean floor at huge anchored platforms such as this one in the North Sea.

Offshore Drilling

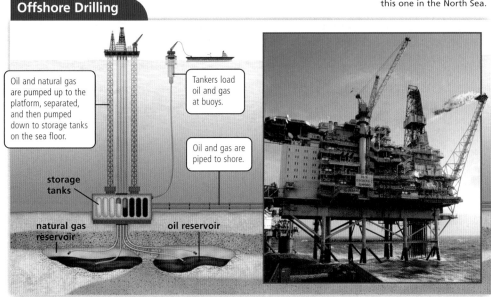

Oil and natural gas are pumped up to the platform, separated, and then pumped down to storage tanks on the sea floor.

Tankers load oil and gas at buoys.

Oil and gas are piped to shore.

storage tanks

natural gas reservoir

oil reservoir

Teacher Demo

Show students how to desalinate water. Use the following materials: salt water, hot plate, cake pan filled with ice, two glass beakers, aluminum foil, and rubber tubing. Pour salt water into one beaker, then cover both beakers with aluminum foil. Carefully insert the ends of the rubber tubing in the foil lids. Place the empty beaker in the pan of ice. Place the beaker containing salt water on the hot plate; bring the salt water to a boil. Pure water will accumulate in the beaker placed in ice.

Integrate the Sciences

Oil and gas are hydrocarbons, or compounds made up of both hydrogen and carbon atoms. When these energy sources are burned for residential or industrial uses, they combine with oxygen and emit heat. Byproducts of this reaction include water and carbon dioxide. Many scientists theorize that carbon dioxide given off by the burning of fossil fuels has caused an increase in levels of atmospheric carbon dioxide. The rising level of atmospheric CO_2 has contributed to the overall increase in Earth's temperatures, a phenomenon known as global warming.

DIFFERENTIATE INSTRUCTION

 More Reading Support

D What is the process by which salt is removed from seawater? *desalination*

E Oil and gas form from what? *the remains of living organisms*

Advanced Ask students to use the information presented in the statement "Oil and gas form from the remains of living organisms" to infer why oil and gas are called fossil fuels. *Just as fossils are the remains or traces of once-living organisms, oil and gas (both fuels) form from the remains of once-living organisms.*

R Challenge and Extension, p. 232

Teach from Visuals

To help students interpret the map of the ocean's energy and mineral resources:

- Ask: What do the upside down triangles represent? *diamonds*

- Ask: Where are most nodules found? *away from shore, in the open ocean*

- Ask: Which ocean resource seems most plentiful? Which seems scarcest? *nodules; diamonds*

- Have students describe any general pattern in the location of minerals and resources. *Oil, gas, gold, tin, diamonds, and phosphorite are found near shorelines. Nodules are often located in the open ocean.*

Teach Difficult Concepts

Help students understand that economics play a large role in decisions to mine ocean resources. Explain that many ocean resources are valuable, and that we have the technology to mine them. However, the cost of mining a resource should not outweigh the profit gained from selling it. Ask: If it cost $2 million to mine an ocean resource, and the resource sold for $1.5 million, would you mine the resource? Why or why not? *You would not mine the resource because you would lose money.*

Ongoing Assessment

Identify the minerals, energy, and other resources the ocean contains.

Name some of the nonliving resources that people harvest from the ocean. *oil, gas, minerals such as salt* What are some of the challenges to obtaining these resources? *It is often too expensive to mine them, especially in areas away from shore.*

Minerals and Rocks

When rivers empty into the sea, sediments carried by the rivers drop to the bottom. These sediments may contain phosphorite, iron, copper, lead, gold, tin, diamonds, and other minerals. Because these minerals wash into the ocean from land, most of them are found in areas near shore. It is currently too expensive to mine many of these minerals.

? F

? G

Some minerals are found away from shore. Nodules (NAHJ-oolz) are lumps of minerals that are scattered across the deep-ocean floor. The nodules are small at first, but they can build up over millions of years to a size of as much as a meter across. Nodules contain valuable manganese, iron, and cobalt, which are used to make metals such as steel. Nodules are not mined because it would be very expensive to remove them from the ocean floor. In the future, however, nodules may be removed—perhaps with giant vacuums.

Nodules are found away from the coast on the deep-ocean floor.

The Ocean's Energy and Mineral Resources

The ocean floor contains valuable energy and mineral resources.

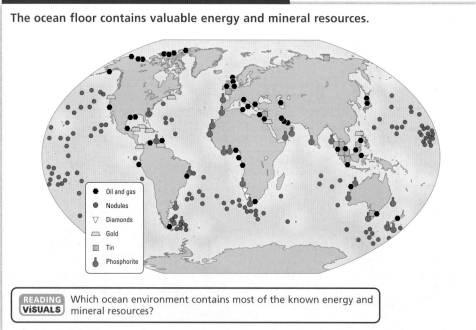

Legend:
- ● Oil and gas
- ● Nodules
- ▽ Diamonds
- ⬭ Gold
- ▣ Tin
- ⬱ Phosphorite

READING VISUALS Which ocean environment contains most of the known energy and mineral resources?

DIFFERENTIATE INSTRUCTION

Inclusion Make enlarged copies of the map on this page for students with visual impairments. Have them use this to participate in class discussions and answer the following questions: Where are diamonds most common? *southern Africa* gold? *the Western Hemisphere, particularly the Caribbean*

When ocean water evaporates, salt is left behind.

Each of these mounds is a pile of salt harvested from ocean water in Thailand.

A mineral you eat is also removed from the ocean. About one-third of the world's table salt comes from the ocean. Ocean water is left to evaporate in flat, shallow areas. As the water evaporates, salts are left behind.

Sand and gravel might not be the first things you think of when you think of important resources. However, they are building materials used in concrete and cement. Sand and gravel are currently scraped off the sea floor in many locations near shore.

Pollution affects the ocean.

Every part of the ocean is polluted. Solid waste—such as plastic garbage, tar balls, and hypodermic needles—is a visible form of pollution along ocean shorelines. Trash washes up on beaches worldwide, even on the beaches of remote islands. Sea animals may mistake trash for food and eat plastic that can block their digestive systems. Animals also get tangled in and even strangled by plastic waste.

Although you may not see this much garbage on every beach, trash washes up on beaches all over the world—even on remote islands.

Most ocean pollution is harder to see than solid waste. Chemical pollutants, nuclear wastes, and heavy metals like mercury and lead are found in all parts of the ocean. These pollutants are known to harm and kill ocean life. They are also harmful to humans. Pregnant women are sometimes advised not to eat tuna and other fish because the fish may contain low levels of toxic mercury. Although the small amounts of mercury may not harm an adult, they could damage the developing child.

Human waste, sewage, and fertilizers have caused dead zones in the ocean—areas where no plants or animals can live. These pollutants contain nutrients and cause a huge increase in the amount of algae that live in an area. When the algae die, bacteria consume them. The large numbers of bacteria use up all the oxygen in an area of ocean. Without oxygen, the animals in the area cannot survive.

135 C

History of Science

In 1956, doctors in the Japanese village of Minamata began seeing cases of patients who suffered from brain damage, cause unknown. Two years later, doctors noticed an increase in babies born with physical disabilities. By 1959, a team of researchers identified the culprit—mercury poisoning. The villagers had been eating seafood contaminated with mercury discharged from an industrial plant. This type of mercury poisoning is now called Minamata Disease. Since the discovery of the disease, the Japanese government has restricted the manufacture of the disease-inducing toxins.

Real World Example

A dead zone exists near the area where the Mississippi River empties into the Gulf of Mexico. The zone appears each year from late spring through late summer. Autumn storms stir up the waters and bring more oxygen into the area. The dead zone is thought to be caused by runoff from farms from among the 31 states that are included in the river's drainage basin.

Address Misconceptions

IDENTIFY Ask: What ocean resources could never be used up? If students indicate that seafood and ocean minerals are so plentiful that they can never be used up, they may hold the misconception that ocean resources are limitless.

CORRECT Invite students to take cups of popcorn from a full bag as you add a few kernels at a time back to the bag. Soon the bag will be empty. Compare this activity to overfishing in areas of the ocean.

REASSESS Ask: How can an ocean's resources run out? *if they are removed faster than they can be replaced*

Teach from Visuals

To help students interpret the ocean oil pollution graph:

- Ask: What does the circle graph represent? *sources of ocean oil pollution*

- Ask: What is the biggest source of ocean oil pollution? *runoff from land*

- Have students rank the sources of ocean oil pollution from highest contributor to lowest contributor. *runoff from land (44 percent), air pollution (33 percent), shipping and oil spills (12 percent), ocean dumping (10 percent), offshore drilling (1 percent)*

Real World Example

The toxic chemical used in ship paint is called tributyltin (TBT). TBT was known to be toxic—in fact, it was selected for its toxicity to keep barnacles and other organisms from attaching to ships' hulls. However, the poisons affected many marine organisms in general, such as oysters, and its use has since been restricted.

Ongoing Assessment

Infer how pollution affects the ocean.

Ask: What can happen when contaminants such as human waste, sewage, and fertilizers are dumped into the ocean? *Nutrients in the contaminants can cause a huge increase in algae populations. When the algae die, bacteria consume them. The bacteria use up all the oxygen in an area of the ocean, causing other organisms to die.*

CHECK YOUR READING *Answer: runoff from land*

Sources of Ocean Oil Pollution

- Runoff from land 44%
- Air pollution 33%
- Shipping and oil spills 12%
- Ocean dumping 10%
- Offshore drilling 1%

SOURCE: *Joint Group of Experts on the Scientific Aspects of the Marine Environment, The State of the Marine Environment,* UNEP Regional Seas Reports and Studies No. 115 (Nairobi: U.N. Environment Programme, 1990)

Oil spills are dramatic and disastrous events. However, most oil pollution in the ocean is washed in from land.

Some pollutants are dumped directly into the ocean. Many other pollutants wash from the land into the ocean or into rivers that flow into the ocean. Although oil spills are dramatic events that kill many animals, they account for only a small percentage of the oil pollution in the ocean. More oil enters the ocean by washing off the land than by being spilled. In addition to oil, pesticides, fertilizers, and many other pollutants wash into the ocean from land.

 K

CHECK YOUR READING What is the source of most of the ocean's oil pollution?

RESOURCE CENTER
CLASSZONE.COM

Find out more about ocean pollution and pollution prevention.

Preventing Ocean Pollution

Ocean pollution can be prevented or reduced. In 1988, for example, the United States government restricted the use of a harmful chemical that had been used in ship paint. As a result, levels of the chemical dropped in certain areas of the ocean, and the health of some types of sea life, such as oysters, improved. Government organizations have also banned the dumping of some chemicals into the ocean. These bans have successfully reduced some kinds of pollution.

Individuals can help prevent or reduce ocean pollution. Many people may not realize that oil or other chemicals dumped in a drain or sewer or on the ground can end up in the ocean. The proper disposal of household chemicals and other toxic substances could reduce ocean pollution. The Environmental Protection Agency (EPA) has information about the proper disposal of many common chemicals.

? **L**

DIFFERENTIATE INSTRUCTION

? More Reading Support

K How does most oil enter the ocean? *by washing off land*

L What agency offers information about chemical disposal? *EPA*

Alternative Assessment Have students create pamphlets that describe what people can do to prevent ocean pollution. Pamphlets may include tips such as "Do not litter beaches" and "Use organic fertilizers in your garden." Encourage students to access the EPA Web site for ideas.

Advanced Provide students with world maps that show major ocean currents. Tell them that trash has been dumped into the ocean in a certain area. Have them use the world map to predict where the currents will carry the trash.

Some oyster populations recovered after the use of a toxic chemical in ship paint was restricted. This photo shows an oyster farm in Washington State.

oyster

Global Pollution Problems

Remember that the ocean is a connected global body of water. Ocean currents circulate water around the globe and carry pollutants to all parts of the ocean. Pollution that occurs in any part of the world can affect the whole ocean.

The United Nations, through its 1994 Law of the Sea, attempts to manage ocean resources and to conserve ocean environments. The law calls on all countries to enforce pollution controls. It also sets pollution rules for ships operating in international waters, regulates fishing, and attempts to divide rights to undersea resources. This international law is an important step toward protecting the ocean and its resources for future generations.

 CHECK YOUR READING Why is ocean pollution a global problem?

KEY CONCEPTS

1. Describe one living resource contained in the ocean and how its use affects the ocean environment.

2. Describe one nonliving resource contained in the ocean and how its use affects the ocean environment.

3. How does pollution affect the ocean?

CRITICAL THINKING

4. **Connect** How could ocean pollution affect your life?

5. **Sequence** Describe how oil from a car many miles away from the shore could reach the ocean.

CHALLENGE

6. **Evaluate** Most of the ocean does not belong to any country or government. Who do you think should be responsible for limiting pollution in areas outside country borders? Who should be able to claim ownership of resources in these areas?

Chapter 4: Ocean Environments **137** **C**

ANSWERS

1. Sample: When fish farms are used to raise more fish, huge amounts of fish waste pollute the waters nearby.

2. Oil is used as an energy resource. Oil spills can harm many animals.

3. Pollution affects all parts of the ocean. Solid wastes can harm animals. Chemical

pollutants can cause dead zones, which are areas where no organisms can live.

4. A person could become sick from eating fish that contained toxins.

5. Oil could drip from a car, then get washed away by rain into a river. The river

eventually carries the oil to the ocean.

6. Sample answer: A global organization, such as the United Nations, should be responsible for limiting pollution outside country borders. Ownership of resources should belong to all nations.

Ongoing Assessment

CHECK YOUR READING *Answer: The ocean is a connected body of water. Ocean currents circulate water around the world and carry pollutants to all parts of the ocean.*

Reinforce (the **BIG** idea)

Have students relate the section to the Big Idea.

 Reinforcing Key Concepts, p. 233

4.3 ASSESS & RETEACH

Assess

 Section 4.3 Quiz, p. 63

Reteach

Ask students to name the different resources in the ocean. Make a list of their responses on the board. Solicit specific information, such as specific minerals. Then draw a simple diagram on the board that includes an ocean, a shoreline, and a factory near the shore. The factory should have a smokestack that is emitting pollutants into the air. Draw clouds over the ocean. Add arrows to the diagram showing the processes of the water cycle: evaporation from the ocean to the clouds, condensation within the clouds, and precipitation falling from the clouds to the ocean. Then ask: How can pollutants in the air eventually end up in the ocean? *The pollutants can combine with water droplets in the clouds and fall as precipitation.*

Technology Resources

Have students visit **ClassZone.com** for reteaching of Key Concepts.

 CONTENT REVIEW

 CONTENT REVIEW CD-ROM

CHAPTER INVESTIGATION

Focus

PURPOSE To estimate populations using quadrat methods

OVERVIEW Students will use a quadrat technique to estimate population size. Students will find that

- the quadrat technique involves counting the number of individuals within a measured area
- estimates calculated from small and large quadrats differ

Lab Preparation

- Find out how many classrooms are in your school before beginning this activity.
- Measure the classroom ahead of time. Students can use your measurement to divide the class into four equal areas.
- Prior to the investigation have students read through the investigation and prepare their data tables. Or you may wish to copy and distribute datasheets and rubrics.

  UNIT RESOURCE BOOK, pp. 241–249

SCIENCE TOOLKIT, F15

Lab Management

- Divide students into four groups. Each group will be responsible for counting the population within one quadrat.
- Allow students to select which object to count.

SAFETY Discourage students from choosing objects that might present safety hazards, such as scissors or glass beakers.

CHAPTER INVESTIGATION

Population Sampling

OVERVIEW AND PURPOSE Scientists have found that overfishing is decreasing the population of many organisms. They have also found that the population of some other organisms are increasing. How do scientists know this? They count the number of individuals in a small measured area, called a quadrat, then estimate from their counts how many organisms live in a larger area. Repeated samplings over time allow them to determine whether populations are growing or decreasing. In this investigation you will

- count the number of items in a "population" using a quadrat technique
- use small and large quadrats to form two different estimates for the size of a "population"

MATERIALS
- calculator
- removable tape

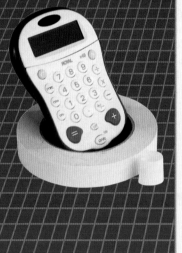

▶ Procedure

1. As a class, brainstorm some objects that you might find in your classroom—for example: pencil, protractor, calculator, or ball cap. Choose one of those objects to count. You will estimate the population at your school of this object.

2. Remove all of the objects that your class decided to count from bags and drawers. For example, if your class is counting pencils, everyone should remove all of their pencils from their bags and place them on their desks.

3. Divide your classroom into four equal-sized pieces. Use removable tape to mark the boundaries of each quadrat. Label the quadrats A, B, C, and D.

4. Count the items in one of the quadrats—either A, B, C, or D. Record the number of objects in your **Science Notebook.**

5. Find the total classroom population of your object by combining your data with the data from groups who counted other quadrats. Record the total classroom population.

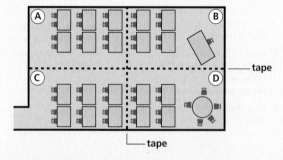

INVESTIGATION RESOURCES

 CHAPTER INVESTIGATION, Population Sampling
- Level A, pp. 241–244
- Level B, pp. 245–248
- Level C, p. 249

Advanced students should complete Levels B & C.

 Writing a Lab Report, D12–13

Technology Resources

Customize this student lab as needed or look for an alternative. Print rubrics to assess student lab reports.

 Lab Generator CD-ROM

Observe and Analyze

1. **RECORD** Make a data table like the one in the notebook.

2. **CALCULATE** Multiply the number of each item you counted in your quadrat by four. This will give you an estimate of the number of each item in your classroom. Record your answer.

3. **CALCULATE** For this investigation, assume that each classroom in your school is the same size as your classroom. Your teacher will provide you with the number of classrooms in your entire school. Multiply your answer from question 2 by the number of classrooms in your school. This will give you an estimate of the number of each item in your school. Record your answer.

4. **CALCULATE** Now estimate the population of the object in the whole school using the total count from the classroom. Multiply the total classroom population by the number of classrooms in your school. This will give you a second estimate for the population of each item in your school. Record your answer.

Conclude

1. **COMPARE** How does your school population estimate based on your small quadrat count compare with your school population estimate based on your total classroom estimate?

2. **INFER** If there was a difference between your two total population estimates, what do you think could explain the difference?

3. **INFER** Do you think your total population estimate for your object in the school is accurate? Explain.

4. **COMPARE** How would your population estimate compare to one done the same way ten years ago? ten years from now? Explain your reasoning.

5. **IDENTIFY LIMITS** What possible limitations or sources of error could have affected your results?

6. **CONNECT** How would you need to change your procedure if you were sampling an ocean fish population? Give at least two examples.

▶ INVESTIGATE Further

CHALLENGE Suppose your quadrat size was one square meter. How would this have affected your accuracy? Imagine that you were given a wooden frame measuring one square meter in size. How would you change your procedure to best sample the school "population" using this smaller quadrat?

Population Sampling
Observe and Analyze
Table 1. Population Data

Quadrat	Number of Items	Classroom Population Estimate	School Population Estimate (No. in classroom × No. of classrooms in school)
A	7	7 × 4 = 28	
B			
C			
D			
Total: classroom count			

Chapter 4: **Ocean Environments** 139

Observe and Analyze

1. *SAMPLE DATA Quadrat A: Number of Items: 7; Classroom Population Estimate: 7 × 4 = 28; School Population Estimate: 28 × 30 = 840; Quadrat B: Number of Items: 5; Classroom Population Estimate: 5 × 4 = 20; School Population Estimate: 20 × 30 = 600; Quadrat C: Number of Items: 10; Classroom Population Estimate: 10 × 4 = 40; School Population Estimate: 40 × 30 = 1200; Quadrat D: Number of Items: 3; Classroom Population Estimate: 3 × 4 = 12; School Population Estimate: 12 × 30 = 360; Total classroom count: 25; School Population Estimate: 25 × 30 = 750*

2–4. *Answers will vary. See students' data tables.*

Conclude

1. *Answers will vary; it may be larger or smaller.*

2. *The populations within the four small quadrats varied widely.*

3. *Sample answer: The estimate may be off because the item might not be used in all classrooms.*

4. *The number of students may change and affect the number of the object. Common tools and technology change, so the item may not have existed before or might not be used in the future.*

5. *Sample answer: Errors could have been made in counting the populations or measuring the quadrats.*

6. *Sample answer: You would need to find a way to count moving organisms that are underwater; you would need a way to partition an area into quadrants.*

▶ INVESTIGATE Further

CHALLENGE Estimating from a single smaller quadrat could make the results less accurate. If the object is small, or very abundant, a smaller quadrat might give a more accurate count. You could change the procedure to use the wooden frame to measure different quadrats in the room.

Post-Lab Discussion

Ask: Suppose you repeated this lab in four other classrooms. How might that affect the accuracy of your school population estimate? *The school population estimate would likely be more accurate because the greater the sample, the more accurate the count.*

the BIG idea

Refer students back to the photograph on pp. 110–111. Ask them to think about all the parts of the ocean they learned about. Have them draw a cross-section of the ocean, showing the following ocean environments: intertidal zone, coral reef, surface zone, deep zone, and hydrothermal vent. Students should show each environment in its proper location—that is, the intertidal zone should be near shore and the deep zone should be in the open ocean. Students should also include labels, listing which organisms and natural resources are found in each environment.

◐ KEY CONCEPTS SUMMARY

SECTION 4.1

Have students point to the intertidal zone in the illustration on the left. *Students should point to the space between the high tide mark and the low tide mark.*

SECTION 4.2

Ask: What is different about the amount of sea life shown in the left illustration compared with that in the right illustration? Why is there a difference? *The amount of sea life shown at left is less and more spread out than that shown at right. The left illustration represents the open ocean and the right illustration represents the near-shore environment.*

SECTION 4.3

Have students name two living ocean resources. *sea animals and algae*

Have students name three nonliving ocean resources. *oil, natural gas, minerals*

Review Concepts

- Big Idea Flow Chart, p. T25
- Chapter Outline, pp. T31–T32

 Chapter Review

the BIG idea

The ocean supports life and contains natural resources.

 **CONTENT REVIEW**
CLASSZONE.COM

◀ KEY CONCEPTS SUMMARY

4.1 Ocean coasts support plant and animal life.

Organisms in the intertidal zone are covered by water during high tide and exposed to the air during low tide.

high tide mark

low tide mark

intertidal zone

- Fresh water and salt water mix in estuaries.
- Salt marshes and mangrove forests form along coasts.

VOCABULARY
habitat p. 114
intertidal zone p. 114
estuary p. 116
wetland p. 116

4.2 Conditions differ away from shore.

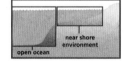
near shore environment
open ocean

Life in the open ocean is more spread out. The surface zone is lit by the Sun. The deep zone is dark.

The waters near shore support more life than any other part of the ocean.

VOCABULARY
coral reef p. 122
kelp forest p. 124
phytoplankton p. 126
hydrothermal vent p. 128

4.3 The ocean contains natural resources.

Living ocean resources include seafood and algae. Overfishing and pollution threaten ocean environments.

Nonliving ocean resources include oil, natural gas, and minerals.

VOCABULARY
overfishing p. 131
by-catch p. 132

Technology Resources

Have students visit **ClassZone.com** or use the CD-ROM for a cumulative review of concepts.

 CONTENT REVIEW

 CONTENT REVIEW CD-ROM

Engage students in a whole-class interactive review of Key Concepts. Edit content as you wish.

◎ **POWER PRESENTATIONS**

Reviewing Vocabulary

Copy and complete the chart below. In the middle column, list characteristics of each environment. In the last column, list examples of organisms that live in each environment.

Vocabulary Term	Characteristics	Organisms
1. intertidal zone		
2. estuary		
3. coral reef		
4. kelp forest		
5. hydrothermal vent		

Reviewing Key Concepts

Multiple Choice *Choose the letter of the best answer.*

6. An environment that contains all the necessary requirements for an organism to live is called
   a. the surface zone   c. a habitat
   b. a nodule   d. an estuary

7. Where would you expect to find ocean organisms that are able to survive out of water and withstand drastic changes in salinity?
   a. the intertidal zone c. the open ocean
   b. a coral reef   d. a hydrothermal vent

8. Two kinds of wetlands that border estuaries are
   a. coral reefs and mangrove forests
   b. salt marshes and mangrove forests
   c. tidal pools and salt marshes
   d. mangrove forests and tidal pools

9. Tiny plantlike organisms that float at the surface of the ocean are called
   a. phytoplankton   c. corals
   b. kelps   d. bottom dwellers

10. Where are hydrothermal vents located?
    a. in the intertidal zone
    b. on the deep-ocean floor
    c. on coral reefs
    d. in kelp forests

11. The bacteria that form the base of the food chain at hydrothermal vents convert
    a. dim sunlight that filters down into food
    b. heat from the vents into food
    c. phytoplankton that drift down into food
    d. chemicals released by the vents into food

12. Overfishing is best described as catching
    a. more fish than people can eat
    b. fish at a faster rate than they can reproduce
    c. other kinds of fish than the ones intended
    d. fish with huge nets and long lines of hooks

13. Why are 30 percent of the fish that are caught by commercial fishing boats thrown away?
    a. Fishing nets catch everything in their path.
    b. Smaller fish are thrown back into the ocean.
    c. Oil pollution has damaged many of the fish.
    d. Large phytoplankton interfere with nets and lines.

Short Answer *Write a short answer to each question.*

14. How does human activity affect shoreline environments?

15. Name the three categories of ocean life, and give an example of an organism for each category.

16. What resources does the ocean contain?

17. What kinds of pollution are found in the ocean?

18. Why is ocean pollution a global problem?

Reviewing Vocabulary

1. characteristics: constantly changing conditions; organisms: crabs, mussels, seaweeds

2. characteristics: mixture of fresh and salt water; organisms: worms, shellfish

3. characteristics: made of built-up limestone deposits; organisms: corals, algae, moray eels

4. characteristics: large community of tall kelp seaweed; organisms: lobsters, sea otters

5. characteristics: heated water gushes out from vent on ocean floor; organisms: bacteria, tubeworms, fish

Reviewing Key Concepts

6. *c*

7. *a*

8. *b*

9. *a*

10. *b*

11. *d*

12. *b*

13. *a*

14. *Human activities such as construction, pollution, recreation, and shipping can disturb shoreline environments.*

15. *bottom dwellers: crab; swimmers: fish; floaters: phytoplankton*

16. *living and nonliving resources, such as fish, seaweed, energy sources, and mineral resources*

17. *solid waste, sewage, and fertilizers*

18. *The ocean is interconnected; pollution in one place is carried by currents around the world.*

ASSESSMENT RESOURCES

UNIT ASSESSMENT BOOK
- Chapter Test A, pp. 64–67
- Chapter Test B, pp. 68–71
- Chapter Test C, pp. 72–75
- Alternative Assessment, pp. 76–77
- Unit Test, pp. 78–89

SPANISH ASSESSMENT BOOK
- Spanish Chapter Test, pp. 165–168
- Spanish Unit Test, pp. 169–172

Technology Resources

Edit test items and answer choices.

 Test Generator CD-ROM

Visit **ClassZone.com** to extend test practice.

 Test Practice

Thinking Critically

19. Populations have decreased.

20. Perhaps the fishing boats had to travel farther to find fish to catch.

21. A current map would be similar to the 1999 map, but would have even less red, yellow, purple, and blue areas and more green areas.

22. Both are found near shore. Both support a wide variety of organisms. Kelp forests are found in cooler waters; coral reefs are found in tropical waters.

23. Sample answer: intertidal zone or near shore, in a place where sunlight can reach the bottom; alternatively, students may infer that life first appeared at hydrothermal vents.

24. intertidal zone or near shore; not in the open ocean; if it lives on algae that are attached to the ocean floor, then it must live in an environment where sunlight reaches all the way to the ocean floor.

25. In their letters, students should support their ideas with examples and reasons. For example, students might suggest that a near-shore environment, including a coast with tidal pools, would be a good place, as there is a lot of marine life there.

the BIG idea

26.

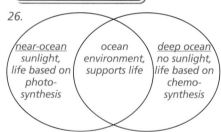

| near-ocean sunlight, life based on photosynthesis | ocean environment, supports life | deep ocean no sunlight, life based on chemosynthesis |

27. Ocean contains habitats such as intertidal zone, near-shore environment, open ocean. Ocean contains resources such as living resources, nonliving resources.

UNIT PROJECTS

Have students present their projects. Use rubrics to evaluate their work.

 Unit Projects, pp. 5–10

Thinking Critically

Use the maps shown below to answer the next three questions.

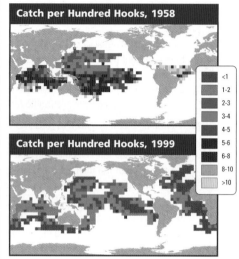

Catch per Hundred Hooks, 1958

Catch per Hundred Hooks, 1999

	<1
	1-2
	2-3
	3-4
	4-5
	5-6
	6-8
	8-10
	>10

SOURCE: *Census of Marine Life*

These maps show data from Japanese fishing boats of the total numbers of fish that were caught in 1958 and 1999. The color code shows the number of fish caught per 100 hooks on longlines.

19. **INTERPRET** What do these data show about how ocean fish populations have changed between 1958 and 1999?

20. **INFER** The data for 1999 were collected over a wider area than were the data for 1958. What might explain the wider area for the 1999 data?

21. **PREDICT** What would you expect a map with data for the current year to look like? Describe it in terms of color and the extent of the data.

22. **COMPARE AND CONTRAST** What similarities exist between kelp forests and coral reefs? How are they different?

23. **INFER** It is believed that life on Earth first appeared in the oceans. In which ocean zone might life have first appeared? Explain your reasoning.

---

24. **APPLY** The sargassum frogfish lives among sargassum algae, a type of algae that grows attached to the ocean floor. In which ocean zones could this species of frogfish possibly live? In which could it not live? Explain.

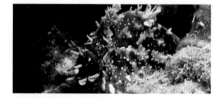

25. **SYNTHESIZE** A marine sanctuary is an area of the ocean that is protected from fishing and most human use. An environmental organization is trying to decide whether to establish a marine sanctuary. Based on what you have learned, write a short letter telling the organization whether you think a marine sanctuary is a good idea and in which ocean zone the sanctuary should be established.

the BIG idea

26. **COMPARE AND CONTRAST** Look again at the photograph on pages 110–111. Now that you have finished the chapter, make a Venn diagram to answer the question on the photograph in more detail. For information about Venn diagrams, see page R49.

27. **PROVIDE EXAMPLES** What types of habitats and resources does the ocean contain? To answer, copy the concept map below into your notebook and add to it. For information about concept maps, see page R49.

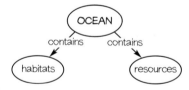

OCEAN
contains   contains
habitats   resources

UNIT PROJECTS

Check your schedule for your unit project. How are you doing? Be sure that you've placed data or notes from your research in your project folder.

MONITOR AND RETEACH

If students are having trouble using the concepts in Chapter Review items 19–21, have them review the overfishing bar graph on p. 131. Point out that both the maps above and the bar graph on p. 131 are making the same point on overfishing, using different formats.

Students may benefit from summarizing one or more sections of the chapter.

 Summarizing the Chapter, pp. 259–260

Standardized Test Practice

For practice on your state test, go to . . . **TEST PRACTICE** CLASSZONE.COM

Analyzing a Diagram

The diagram below shows a side view of part of the ocean. Use the diagram to answer the questions below.

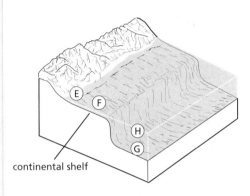

continental shelf

1. Which area is most affected by tides?
  a. E   **c.** G
  b. F   **d.** H

2. Kelps are plantlike algae that grow attached to the ocean bottom. At which points could kelps live?
  a. H and F   **c.** F and G
  b. F only   **d.** G only

3. Where is water the coldest?
  a. E   **c.** G
  b. F   **d.** H

4. Which statement best explains why plantlike algae do not live at G?
  a. The water is too salty at position G.
  b. The water is too cold at position G.
  c. There is not enough oxygen at position G.
  d. There is not enough sunlight at position G.

5. Which trait is most useful for fish in position H as they try to escape predators?
  a. the ability to hide in rocks
  b. the ability to blend in with plants
  c. the ability to swim very fast
  d. the ability to swim without sunlight

6. A limpet is an ocean snail whose flat shape allows it to remain attached to rocks even when waves are pounding against the rocks. Where does the limpet probably live?
  a. E   **c.** G
  b. F   **d.** H

Extended Response

The illustration on the right shows part of an ocean food web. Use the illustration to answer the next two questions in detail.

7. Describe how the killer whale, salmon, and zooplankton in the illustration are linked.

8. What would happen if overfishing caused herring to be removed from the food web? Describe how the other organisms would be affected.

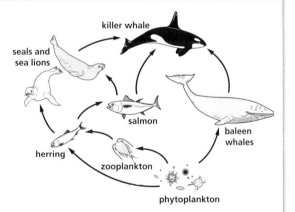

killer whale
seals and sea lions
salmon
baleen whales
herring
zooplankton
phytoplankton

Chapter 4: Ocean Environments 143 **C**

METACOGNITIVE ACTIVITY

Have students answer the following questions in their **Science Notebook:**

1. Which ocean environment did you find most interesting? Why?

2. Why do you think people continue to pollute the ocean?

3. Did the Unit Project help you to better understand this chapter? Why or why not?

Analyzing a Diagram

1. *a*   3. *c*   5. *c*
2. *b*   4. *d*   6. *a*

Extended Response

7. RUBRIC
4 points for a response that correctly answers the question and describes the following organisms' roles accurately:
• killer whale   • salmon   • zooplankton

Sample: The three organisms are related in a food chain. <u>*Zooplankton*</u> *are eaten by herring. The herring are eaten by* <u>*salmon*</u>*. The salmon are eaten by* <u>*killer whales.*</u>

3 points correctly describes two organisms' roles
2 points partially answers the question and describes one organism's roles accurately
1 point partially answers the question, but does not describe any organisms' roles

8. RUBRIC
4 points for a response that correctly answers the question and describes at least six of the following organisms' roles accurately:

• phytoplankton   • seal
• zooplankton   • sea lion
• herring   • killer whale
• salmon   • baleen whale

Sample: If <u>*herring*</u> *was removed from the food web, all the other organisms would be affected.* <u>*Salmon, seals,*</u> *and* <u>*sea lions*</u> *would lose a food source so populations could decline.* <u>*Killer whales*</u> *would then have to find something other than salmon, seals, and sea lions to eat. With less to eat, there would be fewer killer whales. Killer whales would probably eat more* <u>*baleen whales*</u>*. Removing herring from the food web would also affect the organisms herring eat. There might be an overpopulation of* <u>*zooplankton*</u> *and* <u>*phytoplankton*</u> *because herring no longer ate them.*

3 points correctly answers the question and describes four organisms' roles
2 points partially answers the question and describes two organisms' roles accurately
1 point partially answers the question, but does not describe any organisms' roles

Student Resource Handbooks

Scientific Thinking Handbook

Making Observations

An **observation** is an act of noting and recording an event, character-istic, behavior, or anything else detected with an instrument or with the senses.

Observations allow you to make informed hypotheses and to gather data for experiments. Careful observations often lead to ideas for new experiments. There are two categories of observations:

- **Quantitative observations** can be expressed in numbers and include records of time, temperature, mass, distance, and volume.

- **Qualitative observations** include descriptions of sights, sounds, smells, and textures.

EXAMPLE

A student dissolved 30 grams of Epsom salts in water, poured the solution into a dish, and let the dish sit out uncovered overnight. The next day, she made the following observations of the Epsom salt crystals that grew in the dish.

Table 1. Observations of Epsom Salt Crystals

To determine the mass, the student found the mass of the dish before and after growing the crystals and then used subtraction to find the difference.

The student measured several crystals and calculated the mean length. (To learn how to calculate the mean of a data set, see page R36.)

Quantitative Observations	Qualitative Observations
• mass = 30 g • mean crystal length = 0.5 cm • longest crystal length = 2 cm	• Crystals are clear. • Crystals are long, thin, and rectangular. • White crust has formed around edge of dish.

Photographs or sketches are useful for recording qualitative observations.

 Epsom salt crystals

MORE ABOUT OBSERVING

- Make quantitative observations whenever possible. That way, others will know exactly what you observed and be able to compare their results with yours.

- It is always a good idea to make qualitative observations too. You never know when you might observe something unexpected.

Predicting and Hypothesizing

A **prediction** is an expectation of what will be observed or what will happen. A **hypothesis** is a tentative explanation for an observation or scientific problem that can be tested by further investigation.

EXAMPLE

Suppose you have made two paper airplanes and you wonder why one of them tends to glide farther than the other one.

1. Start by asking a question.

2. Make an educated guess. After examination, you notice that the wings of the airplane that flies farther are slightly larger than the wings of the other airplane.

3. Write a prediction based upon your educated guess, in the form of an "If . . . , then . . ." statement. Write the independent variable after the word *if*, and the dependent variable after the word *then*.

4. To make a hypothesis, explain why you think what you predicted will occur. Write the explanation after the word *because*.

1. Why does one of the paper airplanes glide farther than the other?

2. The size of an airplane's wings may affect how far the airplane will glide.

3. Prediction: If I make a paper airplane with larger wings, then the airplane will glide farther.

To read about independent and dependent variables, see page R30.

4. Hypothesis: If I make a paper airplane with larger wings, then the airplane will glide farther, because the additional surface area of the wing will produce more lift.

Notice that the part of the hypothesis after *because* adds an explanation of why the airplane will glide farther.

MORE ABOUT HYPOTHESES

- The results of an experiment cannot prove that a hypothesis is correct. Rather, the results either support or do not support the hypothesis.

- Valuable information is gained even when your hypothesis is not supported by your results. For example, it would be an important discovery to find that wing size is not related to how far an airplane glides.

- In science, a hypothesis is supported only after many scientists have conducted many experiments and produced consistent results.

Inferring

An **inference** is a logical conclusion drawn from the available evidence and prior knowledge. Inferences are often made from observations.

EXAMPLE

A student observing a set of acorns noticed something unexpected about one of them. He noticed a white, soft-bodied insect eating its way out of the acorn.

> The student recorded these observations.

Observations

- There is a hole in the acorn, about 0.5 cm in diameter, where the insect crawled out.
- There is a second hole, which is about the size of a pinhole, on the other side of the acorn.
- The inside of the acorn is hollow.

> Here are some inferences that can be made on the basis of the observations.

Inferences

- The insect formed from the material inside the acorn, grew to its present size, and ate its way out of the acorn.
- The insect crawled through the smaller hole, ate the inside of the acorn, grew to its present size, and ate its way out of the acorn.
- An egg was laid in the acorn through the smaller hole. The egg hatched into a larva that ate the inside of the acorn, grew to its present size, and ate its way out of the acorn.

> When you make inferences, be sure to look at all of the evidence available and combine it with what you already know.

MORE ABOUT INFERENCES

Inferences depend both on observations and on the knowledge of the people making the inferences. Ancient people who did not know that organisms are produced only by similar organisms might have made an inference like the first one. A student today might look at the same observations and make the second inference. A third student might have knowledge about this particular insect and know that it is never small enough to fit through the smaller hole, leading her to the third inference.

Identifying Cause and Effect

In a **cause-and-effect relationship,** one event or characteristic is the result of another. Usually an effect follows its cause in time.

There are many examples of cause-and-effect relationships in everyday life.

Cause	Effect
Turn off a light.	Room gets dark.
Drop a glass.	Glass breaks.
Blow a whistle.	Sound is heard.

Scientists must be careful not to infer a cause-and-effect relationship just because one event happens after another event. When one event occurs after another, you cannot infer a cause-and-effect relationship on the basis of that information alone. You also cannot conclude that one event caused another if there are alternative ways to explain the second event. A scientist must demonstrate through experimentation or continued observation that an event was truly caused by another event.

EXAMPLE

Make an Observation

Suppose you have a few plants growing outside. When the weather starts getting colder, you bring one of the plants indoors. You notice that the plant you brought indoors is growing faster than the others are growing. You cannot conclude from your observation that the change in temperature was the cause of the increased plant growth, because there are alternative explanations for the observation. Some possible explanations are given below.

- The humidity indoors caused the plant to grow faster.

- The level of sunlight indoors caused the plant to grow faster.

- The indoor plant's being noticed more often and watered more often than the outdoor plants caused it to grow faster.

- The plant that was brought indoors was healthier than the other plants to begin with.

To determine which of these factors, if any, caused the indoor plant to grow faster than the outdoor plants, you would need to design and conduct an experiment.

See pages R28–R35 for information about designing experiments.

Recognizing Bias

Television, newspapers, and the Internet are full of experts claiming to have scientific evidence to back up their claims. How do you know whether the claims are really backed up by good science?

Bias is a slanted point of view, or personal prejudice. The goal of scientists is to be as objective as possible and to base their findings on facts instead of opinions. However, bias often affects the conclusions of researchers, and it is important to learn to recognize bias.

When scientific results are reported, you should consider the source of the information as well as the information itself. It is important to critically analyze the information that you see and read.

SOURCES OF BIAS

There are several ways in which a report of scientific information may be biased. Here are some questions that you can ask yourself:

1. **Who is sponsoring the research?**

   Sometimes, the results of an investigation are biased because an organization paying for the research is looking for a specific answer. This type of bias can affect how data are gathered and interpreted.

2. **Is the research sample large enough?**

   Sometimes research does not include enough data. The larger the sample size, the more likely that the results are accurate, assuming a truly random sample.

3. **In a survey, who is answering the questions?**

   The results of a survey or poll can be biased. The people taking part in the survey may have been specifically chosen because of how they would answer. They may have the same ideas or lifestyles. A survey or poll should make use of a random sample of people.

4. **Are the people who take part in a survey biased?**

   People who take part in surveys sometimes try to answer the questions the way they think the researcher wants them to answer. Also, in surveys or polls that ask for personal information, people may be unwilling to answer questions truthfully.

SCIENTIFIC BIAS

It is also important to realize that scientists have their own biases because of the types of research they do and because of their scientific viewpoints. Two scientists may look at the same set of data and come to completely different conclusions because of these biases. However, such disagreements are not necessarily bad. In fact, a critical analysis of disagreements is often responsible for moving science forward.

Identifying Faulty Reasoning

Faulty reasoning is wrong or incorrect thinking. It leads to mistakes and to wrong conclusions. Scientists are careful not to draw unreasonable conclusions from experimental data. Without such caution, the results of scientific investigations may be misleading.

EXAMPLE

Scientists try to make generalizations based on their data to explain as much about nature as possible. If only a small sample of data is looked at, however, a conclusion may be faulty. Suppose a scientist has studied the effects of the El Niño and La Niña weather patterns on flood damage in California from 1989 to 1995. The scientist organized the data in the bar graph below.

The scientist drew the following conclusions:

1. The La Niña weather pattern has no effect on flooding in California.

2. When neither weather pattern occurs, there is almost no flood damage.

3. A weak or moderate El Niño produces a small or moderate amount of flooding.

4. A strong El Niño produces a lot of flooding.

Flood and Storm Damage in California

Estimated damage (millions of dollars)

- Weak–moderate El Niño
- Strong El Niño

1989   1992   1995

Starting year of season
(July 1–June 30)

SOURCE: *Governor's Office of Emergency Services, California*

For the six-year period of the scientist's investigation, these conclusions may seem to be reasonable. However, a six-year study of weather patterns may be too small of a sample for the conclusions to be supported. Consider the following graph, which shows information that was gathered from 1949 to 1997.

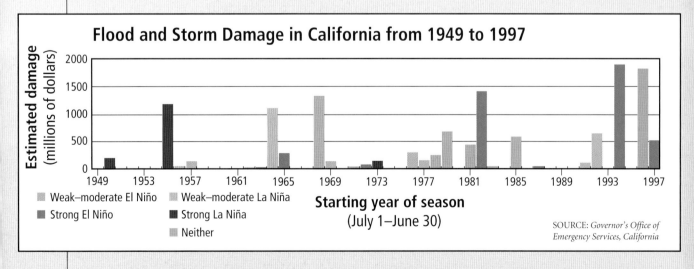

Flood and Storm Damage in California from 1949 to 1997

Estimated damage (millions of dollars)

1949   1953   1957   1961   1965   1969   1973   1977   1981   1985   1989   1993   1997

- Weak–moderate El Niño
- Weak–moderate La Niña
- Strong El Niño
- Strong La Niña
- Neither

Starting year of season
(July 1–June 30)

SOURCE: *Governor's Office of Emergency Services, California*

The only one of the conclusions that all of this information supports is number 3: a weak or moderate El Niño produces a small or moderate amount of flooding. By collecting more data, scientists can be more certain of their conclusions and can avoid faulty reasoning.

Analyzing Statements

To **analyze** a statement is to examine its parts carefully. Scientific findings are often reported through media such as television or the Internet. A report that is made public often focuses on only a small part of research. As a result, it is important to question the sources of information.

Evaluate Media Claims

To **evaluate** a statement is to judge it on the basis of criteria you've established. Sometimes evaluating means deciding whether a statement is true.

Reports of scientific research and findings in the media may be misleading or incomplete. When you are exposed to this information, you should ask yourself some questions so that you can make informed judgments about the information.

1. **Does the information come from a credible source?**

   Suppose you learn about a new product and it is stated that scientific evidence proves that the product works. A report from a respected news source may be more believable than an advertisement paid for by the product's manufacturer.

2. **How much evidence supports the claim?**

   Often, it may seem that there is new evidence every day of something in the world that either causes or cures an illness. However, information that is the result of several years of work by several different scientists is more credible than an advertisement that does not even cite the subjects of the experiment.

3. **How much information is being presented?**

   Science cannot solve all questions, and scientific experiments often have flaws. A report that discusses problems in a scientific study may be more believable than a report that addresses only positive experimental findings.

4. **Is scientific evidence being presented by a specific source?**

   Sometimes scientific findings are reported by people who are called experts or leaders in a scientific field. But if their names are not given or their scientific credentials are not reported, their statements may be less credible than those of recognized experts.

Differentiate Between Fact and Opinion

Sometimes information is presented as a fact when it may be an opinion. When scientific conclusions are reported, it is important to recognize whether they are based on solid evidence. Again, you may find it helpful to ask yourself some questions.

1. **What is the difference between a fact and an opinion?**

   A **fact** is a piece of information that can be strictly defined and proved true. An **opinion** is a statement that expresses a belief, value, or feeling. An opinion cannot be proved true or false. For example, a person's age is a fact, but if someone is asked how old they feel, it is impossible to prove the person's answer to be true or false.

2. **Can opinions be measured?**

   Yes, opinions can be measured. In fact, surveys often ask for people's opinions on a topic. But there is no way to know whether or not an opinion is the truth.

HOW TO DIFFERENTIATE FACT FROM OPINION

Human Activities and the Environment

Opinions
Notice words or phrases that express beliefs or feelings. The words *unfortunately* and *careless* show that opinions are being expressed.

Unfortunately, human use of fossil fuels is one of the most significant developments of the past few centuries. Humans rely on fossil fuels, a non-renewable energy resource, for more than 90 percent of their energy needs.

Opinion
Look for statements that speculate about events. These statements are opinions, because they cannot be proved.

This careless misuse of our planet's resources has resulted in pollution, global warming, and the destruction of fragile ecosystems. For example, oil pipelines carry more than one million barrels of oil each day across tundra regions. Transporting oil across such areas can only result in oil spills that poison the land for decades.

Facts
Statements that contain statistics tend to be facts. Writers often use facts to support their opinions.

Lab Handbook

Safety Rules

Before you work in the laboratory, read these safety rules twice. Ask your teacher to explain any rules that you do not completely understand. Refer to these rules later on if you have questions about safety in the science classroom.

Directions

- Read all directions and make sure that you understand them before starting an investigation or lab activity. If you do not understand how to do a procedure or how to use a piece of equipment, ask your teacher.
- Do not begin any investigation or touch any equipment until your teacher has told you to start.
- Never experiment on your own. If you want to try a procedure that the directions do not call for, ask your teacher for permission first.
- If you are hurt or injured in any way, tell your teacher immediately.

Dress Code

goggles

apron

gloves

- Wear goggles when
  — using glassware, sharp objects, or chemicals
  — heating an object
  — working with anything that can easily fly up into the air and hurt someone's eye
- Tie back long hair or hair that hangs in front of your eyes.
- Remove any article of clothing—such as a loose sweater or a scarf—that hangs down and may touch a flame, chemical, or piece of equipment.
- Observe all safety icons calling for the wearing of eye protection, gloves, and aprons.

Heating and Fire Safety

fire safety

heating safety

- Keep your work area neat, clean, and free of extra materials.
- Never reach over a flame or heat source.
- Point objects being heated away from you and others.
- Never heat a substance or an object in a closed container.
- Never touch an object that has been heated. If you are unsure whether something is hot, treat it as though it is. Use oven mitts, clamps, tongs, or a test-tube holder.
- Know where the fire extinguisher and fire blanket are kept in your classroom.
- Do not throw hot substances into the trash. Wait for them to cool or use the container your teacher puts out for disposal.

Electrical Safety

electrical safety

- Never use lamps or other electrical equipment with frayed cords.
- Make sure no cord is lying on the floor where someone can trip over it.
- Do not let a cord hang over the side of a counter or table so that the equipment can easily be pulled or knocked to the floor.
- Never let cords hang into sinks or other places where water can be found.
- Never try to fix electrical problems. Inform your teacher of any problems immediately.
- Unplug an electrical cord by pulling on the plug, not the cord.

Chemical Safety

chemical safety

poison

fumes

- If you spill a chemical or get one on your skin or in your eyes, tell your teacher right away.
- Never touch, taste, or sniff any chemicals in the lab. If you need to determine odor, waft. Wafting consists of holding the chemical in its container 15 centimeters (6 in.) away from your nose, and using your fingers to bring fumes from the container to your nose.
- Keep lids on all chemicals you are not using.
- Never put unused chemicals back into the original containers. Throw away extra chemicals where your teacher tells you to.
- Pour chemicals over a sink or your work area, not over the floor.
- If you get a chemical in your eye, use the eyewash right away.
- Always wash your hands after handling chemicals, plants, or soil.

Wafting

Glassware and Sharp-Object Safety

sharp objects

- If you break glassware, tell your teacher right away.
- Do not use broken or chipped glassware. Give these to your teacher.
- Use knives and other cutting instruments carefully. Always wear eye protection and cut away from you.

Animal Safety

- Never hurt an animal.
- Touch animals only when necessary. Follow your teacher's instructions for handling animals.
- Always wash your hands after working with animals.

Cleanup

disposal

- Follow your teacher's instructions for throwing away or putting away supplies.
- Clean your work area and pick up anything that has dropped to the floor.
- Wash your hands.

Using Lab Equipment

Different experiments require different types of equipment. But even though experiments differ, the ways in which the equipment is used are the same.

Beakers

- Use beakers for holding and pouring liquids.
- Do not use a beaker to measure the volume of a liquid. Use a graduated cylinder instead. (See page R16.)
- Use a beaker that holds about twice as much liquid as you need. For example, if you need 100 milliliters of water, you should use a 200- or 250-milliliter beaker.

Test Tubes

- Use test tubes to hold small amounts of substances.
- Do not use a test tube to measure the volume of a liquid.
- Use a test tube when heating a substance over a flame. Aim the mouth of the tube away from yourself and other people.
- Liquids easily spill or splash from test tubes, so it is important to use only small amounts of liquids.

Test-Tube Holder

- Use a test-tube holder when heating a substance in a test tube.
- Use a test-tube holder if the substance in a test tube is dangerous to touch.
- Make sure the test-tube holder tightly grips the test tube so that the test tube will not slide out of the holder.
- Make sure that the test-tube holder is above the surface of the substance in the test tube so that you can observe the substance.

Test-Tube Rack

- Use a test-tube rack to organize test tubes before, during, and after an experiment.

- Use a test-tube rack to keep test tubes upright so that they do not fall over and spill their contents.

- Use a test-tube rack that is the correct size for the test tubes that you are using. If the rack is too small, a test tube may become stuck. If the rack is too large, a test tube may lean over, and some of its contents may spill or splash.

Forceps

- Use forceps when you need to pick up or hold a very small object that should not be touched with your hands.

- Do not use forceps to hold anything over a flame, because forceps are not long enough to keep your hand safely away from the flame. Plastic forceps will melt, and metal forceps will conduct heat and burn your hand.

Hot Plate

- Use a hot plate when a substance needs to be kept warmer than room temperature for a long period of time.

- Use a hot plate instead of a Bunsen burner or a candle when you need to carefully control temperature.

- Do not use a hot plate when a substance needs to be burned in an experiment.

- Always use "hot hands" safety mitts or oven mitts when handling anything that has been heated on a hot plate.

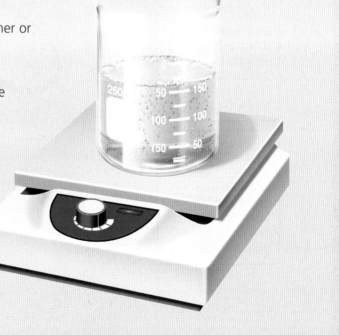

Microscope

Scientists use microscopes to see very small objects that cannot easily be seen with the eye alone. A microscope magnifies the image of an object so that small details may be observed. A microscope that you may use can magnify an object 400 times—the object will appear 400 times larger than its actual size.

Body The body separates the lens in the eyepiece from the objective lenses below.

Nosepiece The nosepiece holds the objective lenses above the stage and rotates so that all lenses may be used.

High-Power Objective Lens This is the largest lens on the nosepiece. It magnifies an image approximately 40 times.

Stage The stage supports the object being viewed.

Diaphragm The diaphragm is used to adjust the amount of light passing through the slide and into an objective lens.

Mirror or Light Source Some microscopes use light that is reflected through the stage by a mirror. Other microscopes have their own light sources.

Eyepiece Objects are viewed through the eyepiece. The eyepiece contains a lens that commonly magnifies an image 10 times.

Coarse Adjustment This knob is used to focus the image of an object when it is viewed through the low-power lens.

Fine Adjustment This knob is used to focus the image of an object when it is viewed through the high-power lens.

Low-Power Objective Lens This is the smallest lens on the nosepiece. It magnifies an image approximately 10 times.

Arm The arm supports the body above the stage. Always carry a microscope by the arm and base.

Stage Clip The stage clip holds a slide in place on the stage.

Base The base supports the microscope.

VIEWING AN OBJECT

1. Use the coarse adjustment knob to raise the body tube.

2. Adjust the diaphragm so that you can see a bright circle of light through the eyepiece.

3. Place the object or slide on the stage. Be sure that it is centered over the hole in the stage.

4. Turn the nosepiece to click the low-power lens into place.

5. Using the coarse adjustment knob, slowly lower the lens and focus on the specimen being viewed. Be sure not to touch the slide or object with the lens.

6. When switching from the low-power lens to the high-power lens, first raise the body tube with the coarse adjustment knob so that the high-power lens will not hit the slide.

7. Turn the nosepiece to click the high-power lens into place.

8. Use the fine adjustment knob to focus on the specimen being viewed. Again, be sure not to touch the slide or object with the lens.

MAKING A SLIDE, OR WET MOUNT

1 Place the specimen in the center of a clean slide.

2 Place a drop of water on the specimen.

3 Place a cover slip on the slide. Put one edge of the cover slip into the drop of water and slowly lower it over the specimen.

4 Remove any air bubbles from under the cover slip by gently tapping the cover slip.

5 Dry any excess water before placing the slide on the microscope stage for viewing.

Spring Scale (Force Meter)

- Use a spring scale to measure a force pulling on the scale.

- Use a spring scale to measure the force of gravity exerted on an object by Earth.

- To measure a force accurately, a spring scale must be zeroed before it is used. The scale is zeroed when no weight is attached and the indicator is positioned at zero.

- Do not attach a weight that is either too heavy or too light to a spring scale. A weight that is too heavy could break the scale or exert too great a force for the scale to measure. A weight that is too light may not exert enough force to be measured accurately.

Graduated Cylinder

- Use a graduated cylinder to measure the volume of a liquid.

- Be sure that the graduated cylinder is on a flat surface so that your measurement will be accurate.

- When reading the scale on a graduated cylinder, be sure to have your eyes at the level of the surface of the liquid.

- The surface of the liquid will be curved in the graduated cylinder. Read the volume of the liquid at the bottom of the curve, or meniscus (muh-NIHS-kuhs).

- You can use a graduated cylinder to find the volume of a solid object by measuring the increase in a liquid's level after you add the object to the cylinder.

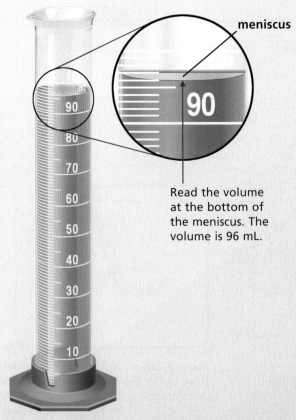

meniscus

Read the volume at the bottom of the meniscus. The volume is 96 mL.

Metric Rulers

- Use metric rulers or meter sticks to measure objects' lengths.

- Do not measure an object from the end of a metric ruler or meter stick, because the end is often imperfect. Instead, measure from the 1-centimeter mark, but remember to subtract a centimeter from the apparent measurement.

- Estimate any lengths that extend between marked units. For example, if a meter stick shows centimeters but not millimeters, you can estimate the length that an object extends between centimeter marks to measure it to the nearest millimeter.

- **Controlling Variables** If you are taking repeated measurements, always measure from the same point each time. For example, if you're measuring how high two different balls bounce when dropped from the same height, measure both bounces at the same point on the balls—either the top or the bottom. Do not measure at the top of one ball and the bottom of the other.

EXAMPLE

How to Measure a Leaf

1. Lay a ruler flat on top of the leaf so that the 1-centimeter mark lines up with one end. Make sure the ruler and the leaf do not move between the time you line them up and the time you take the measurement.

2. Look straight down on the ruler so that you can see exactly how the marks line up with the other end of the leaf.

3. Estimate the length by which the leaf extends beyond a marking. For example, the leaf below extends about halfway between the 4.2-centimeter and 4.3-centimeter marks, so the apparent measurement is about 4.25 centimeters.

4. Remember to subtract 1 centimeter from your apparent measurement, since you started at the 1-centimeter mark on the ruler and not at the end. The leaf is about 3.25 centimeters long (4.25 cm – 1 cm = 3.25 cm).

Triple-Beam Balance

This balance has a pan and three beams with sliding masses, called riders. At one end of the beams is a pointer that indicates whether the mass on the pan is equal to the masses shown on the beams.

1. Make sure the balance is zeroed before measuring the mass of an object. The balance is zeroed if the pointer is at zero when nothing is on the pan and the riders are at their zero points. Use the adjustment knob at the base of the balance to zero it.

2. Place the object to be measured on the pan.

3. Move the riders one notch at a time away from the pan. Begin with the largest rider. If moving the largest rider one notch brings the pointer below zero, begin measuring the mass of the object with the next smaller rider.

4. Change the positions of the riders until they balance the mass on the pan and the pointer is at zero. Then add the readings from the three beams to determine the mass of the object.

300 g	position of largest rider
90 g	position of middle rider
+ 3 g	position of smallest rider
393 g	mass of beaker

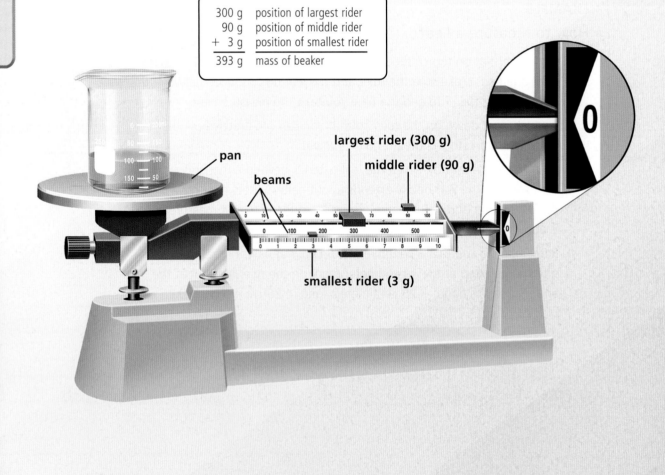

pan

beams

largest rider (300 g)

middle rider (90 g)

smallest rider (3 g)

Double-Pan Balance

This type of balance has two pans. Between the pans is a pointer that indicates whether the masses on the pans are equal.

1. Make sure the balance is zeroed before measuring the mass of an object. The balance is zeroed if the pointer is at zero when there is nothing on either of the pans. Many double-pan balances have sliding knobs that can be used to zero them.

2. Place the object to be measured on one of the pans.

3. Begin adding standard masses to the other pan. Begin with the largest standard mass. If this adds too much mass to the balance, begin measuring the mass of the object with the next smaller standard mass.

4. Add standard masses until the masses on both pans are balanced and the pointer is at zero. Then add the standard masses together to determine the mass of the object being measured.

LAB HANDBOOK

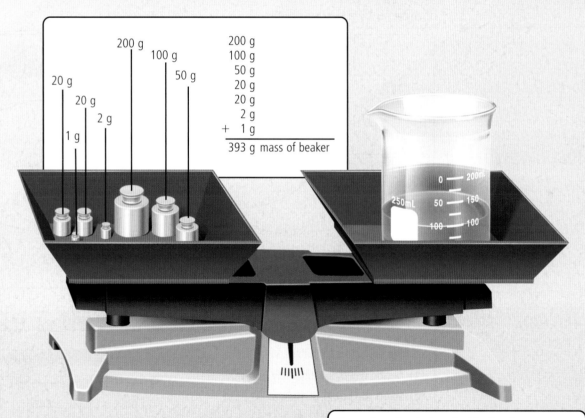

| 20 g |
| 20 g |
| 1 g |
| 2 g |
| 200 g |
| 100 g |
| 50 g |

| 200 g |
| 100 g |
| 50 g |
| 20 g |
| 20 g |
| 2 g |
| + 1 g |
| 393 g mass of beaker |

Never place chemicals or liquids directly on a pan. Instead, use the following procedure:

1. Determine the mass of an empty container, such as a beaker.

2. Pour the substance into the container, and measure the total mass of the substance and the container.

3. Subtract the mass of the empty container from the total mass to find the mass of the substance.

The Metric System and SI Units

Scientists use International System (SI) units for measurements of distance, volume, mass, and temperature. The International System is based on multiples of ten and the metric system of measurement.

Basic SI Units		
Property	Name	Symbol
length	meter	m
volume	liter	L
mass	kilogram	kg
temperature	kelvin	K

SI Prefixes		
Prefix	Symbol	Multiple of 10
kilo-	k	1000
hecto-	h	100
deca-	da	10
deci-	d	$0.1 \left(\frac{1}{10}\right)$
centi-	c	$0.01 \left(\frac{1}{100}\right)$
milli-	m	$0.001 \left(\frac{1}{1000}\right)$

Changing Metric Units

You can change from one unit to another in the metric system by multiplying or dividing by a power of 10.

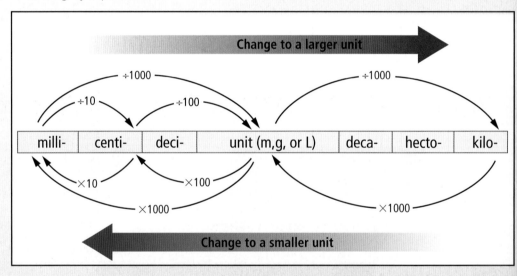

Example

Change 0.64 liters to milliliters.

(1) Decide whether to multiply or divide.

(2) Select the power of 10.

ANSWER 0.64 L = 640 mL

Change to a smaller unit by multiplying.

mL ◄——— × 1000 ——— L

0.64 × 1000 = **640.**

Example

Change 23.6 grams to kilograms.

(1) Decide whether to multiply or divide.

(2) Select the power of 10.

ANSWER 23.6 g = 0.0236 kg

Change to a larger unit by dividing.

g ——— ÷ 1000 ——► kg

23.6 ÷ 1000 = **0.0236**

Temperature Conversions

Even though the kelvin is the SI base unit of temperature, the degree Celsius will be the unit you use most often in your science studies. The formulas below show the relationships between temperatures in degrees Fahrenheit (°F), degrees Celsius (°C), and kelvins (K).

$$°C = \frac{5}{9}(°F - 32)$$

$$°F = \frac{9}{5}°C + 32$$

$$K = °C + 273$$

See page R42 for help with using formulas.

Examples of Temperature Conversions		
Condition	Degrees Celsius	Degrees Fahrenheit
Freezing point of water	0	32
Cool day	10	50
Mild day	20	68
Warm day	30	86
Normal body temperature	37	98.6
Very hot day	40	104
Boiling point of water	100	212

Converting Between SI and U.S. Customary Units

Use the chart below when you need to convert between SI units and U.S. customary units.

SI Unit	From SI to U.S. Customary			From U.S. Customary to SI		
Length	When you know	multiply by	to find	When you know	multiply by	to find
kilometer (km) = 1000 m	kilometers	0.62	miles	miles	1.61	kilometers
meter (m) = 100 cm	meters	3.28	feet	feet	0.3048	meters
centimeter (cm) = 10 mm	centimeters	0.39	inches	inches	2.54	centimeters
millimeter (mm) = 0.1 cm	millimeters	0.04	inches	inches	25.4	millimeters
Area	When you know	multiply by	to find	When you know	multiply by	to find
square kilometer (km^2)	square kilometers	0.39	square miles	square miles	2.59	square kilometers
square meter (m^2)	square meters	1.2	square yards	square yards	0.84	square meters
square centimeter (cm^2)	square centimeters	0.155	square inches	square inches	6.45	square centimeters
Volume	When you know	multiply by	to find	When you know	multiply by	to find
liter (L) = 1000 mL	liters	1.06	quarts	quarts	0.95	liters
	liters	0.26	gallons	gallons	3.79	liters
	liters	4.23	cups	cups	0.24	liters
	liters	2.12	pints	pints	0.47	liters
milliliter (mL) = 0.001 L	milliliters	0.20	teaspoons	teaspoons	4.93	milliliters
	milliliters	0.07	tablespoons	tablespoons	14.79	milliliters
	milliliters	0.03	fluid ounces	fluid ounces	29.57	milliliters
Mass	When you know	multiply by	to find	When you know	multiply by	to find
kilogram (kg) = 1000 g	kilograms	2.2	pounds	pounds	0.45	kilograms
gram (g) = 1000 mg	grams	0.035	ounces	ounces	28.35	grams

Precision and Accuracy

When you do an experiment, it is important that your methods, observations, and data be both precise and accurate.

low precision

precision, but not accuracy

precision and accuracy

Precision

In science, **precision** is the exactness and consistency of measurements. For example, measurements made with a ruler that has both centimeter and millimeter markings would be more precise than measurements made with a ruler that has only centimeter markings. Another indicator of precision is the care taken to make sure that methods and observations are as exact and consistent as possible. Every time a particular experiment is done, the same procedure should be used. Precision is necessary because experiments are repeated several times and if the procedure changes, the results will change.

EXAMPLE

Suppose you are measuring temperatures over a two-week period. Your precision will be greater if you measure each temperature at the same place, at the same time of day, and with the same thermometer than if you change any of these factors from one day to the next.

Accuracy

In science, it is possible to be precise but not accurate. **Accuracy** depends on the difference between a measurement and an actual value. The smaller the difference, the more accurate the measurement.

EXAMPLE

Suppose you look at a stream and estimate that it is about 1 meter wide at a particular place. You decide to check your estimate by measuring the stream with a meter stick, and you determine that the stream is 1.32 meters wide. However, because it is hard to measure the width of a stream with a meter stick, it turns out that you didn't do a very good job. The stream is actually 1.14 meters wide. Therefore, even though your estimate was less precise than your measurement, your estimate was actually more accurate.

Making Data Tables and Graphs

Data tables and graphs are useful tools for both recording and communicating scientific data.

Making Data Tables

You can use a **data table** to organize and record the measurements that you make. Some examples of information that might be recorded in data tables are frequencies, times, and amounts.

EXAMPLE

Suppose you are investigating photosynthesis in two elodea plants. One sits in direct sunlight, and the other sits in a dimly lit room. You measure the rate of photosynthesis by counting the number of bubbles in the jar every ten minutes.

1. Title and number your data table.
2. Decide how you will organize the table into columns and rows.
3. Any units, such as seconds or degrees, should be included in column headings, not in the individual cells.

Table 1. Number of Bubbles from Elodea

Time (min)	Sunlight	Dim Light
0	0	0
10	15	5
20	25	8
30	32	7
40	41	10
50	47	9
60	42	9

Always number and title data tables.

The data in the table above could also be organized in a different way.

Table 1. Number of Bubbles from Elodea

Light Condition	Time (min)						
	0	10	20	30	40	50	60
Sunlight	0	15	25	32	41	47	42
Dim light	0	5	8	7	10	9	9

Put units in column heading.

Making Line Graphs

You can use a **line graph** to show a relationship between variables. Line graphs are particularly useful for showing changes in variables over time.

EXAMPLE

Suppose you are interested in graphing temperature data that you collected over the course of a day.

Table 1. Outside Temperature During the Day on March 7

	Time of Day						
	7:00 A.M.	9:00 A.M.	11:00 A.M.	1:00 P.M.	3:00 P.M.	5:00 P.M.	7:00 P.M.
Temp (°C)	8	9	11	14	12	10	6

1. Use the vertical axis of your line graph for the variable that you are measuring—temperature.

2. Choose scales for both the horizontal axis and the vertical axis of the graph. You should have two points more than you need on the vertical axis, and the horizontal axis should be long enough for all of the data points to fit.

3. Draw and label each axis.

4. Graph each value. First find the appropriate point on the scale of the horizontal axis. Imagine a line that rises vertically from that place on the scale. Then find the corresponding value on the vertical axis, and imagine a line that moves horizontally from that value. The point where these two imaginary lines intersect is where the value should be plotted.

5. Connect the points with straight lines.

Be sure to add a number and a title to your graph.

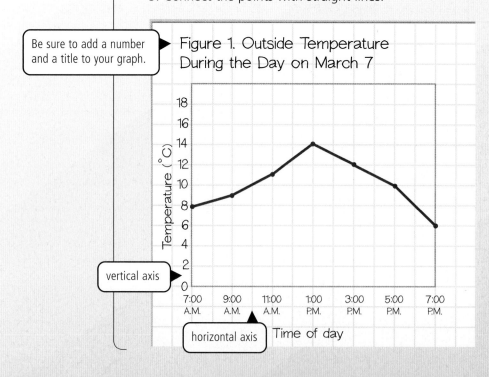

Figure 1. Outside Temperature During the Day on March 7

vertical axis

horizontal axis

Making Circle Graphs

You can use a **circle graph,** sometimes called a pie chart, to represent data as parts of a circle. Circle graphs are used only when the data can be expressed as percentages of a whole. The entire circle shown in a circle graph is equal to 100 percent of the data.

EXAMPLE

Suppose you identified the species of each mature tree growing in a small wooded area. You organized your data in a table, but you also want to show the data in a circle graph.

1. To begin, find the total number of mature trees.

   $56 + 34 + 22 + 10 + 28 = 150$

2. To find the degree measure for each sector of the circle, write a fraction comparing the number of each tree species with the total number of trees. Then multiply the fraction by 360°.

   Oak: $\frac{56}{150} \times 360° = 134.4°$

3. Draw a circle. Use a protractor to draw the angle for each sector of the graph.

4. Color and label each sector of the graph.

5. Give the graph a number and title.

Table 1. Tree Species in Wooded Area

Species	Number of Specimens
Oak	56
Maple	34
Birch	22
Willow	10
Pine	28

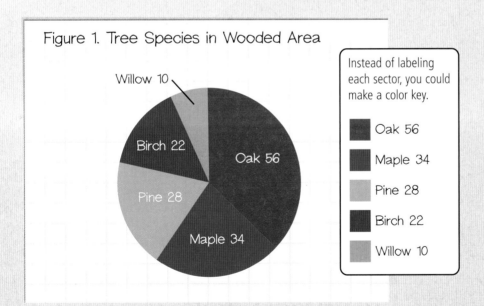

Figure 1. Tree Species in Wooded Area

Willow 10
Birch 22
Oak 56
Pine 28
Maple 34

Instead of labeling each sector, you could make a color key.

■ Oak 56
■ Maple 34
■ Pine 28
■ Birch 22
■ Willow 10

Bar Graph

A **bar graph** is a type of graph in which the lengths of the bars are used to represent and compare data. A numerical scale is used to determine the lengths of the bars.

EXAMPLE

To determine the effect of water on seed sprouting, three cups were filled with sand, and ten seeds were planted in each. Different amounts of water were added to each cup over a three-day period.

Table 1. Effect of Water on Seed Sprouting

Daily Amount of Water (mL)	Number of Seeds That Sprouted After 3 Days in Sand
0	1
10	4
20	8

1. Choose a numerical scale. The greatest value is 8, so the end of the scale should have a value greater than 8, such as 10. Use equal increments along the scale, such as increments of 2.

2. Draw and label the axes. Mark intervals on the vertical axis according to the scale you chose.

3. Draw a bar for each data value. Use the scale to decide how long to make each bar.

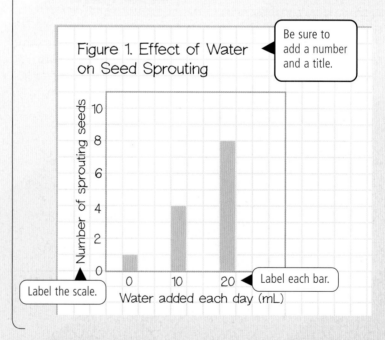

Figure 1. Effect of Water on Seed Sprouting

Be sure to add a number and a title.

Label the scale.

Label each bar.

Double Bar Graph

A **double bar graph** is a bar graph that shows two sets of data. The two bars for each measurement are drawn next to each other.

EXAMPLE

The seed-sprouting experiment was done using both sand and potting soil. The data for sand and potting soil can be plotted on one graph.

1. Draw one set of bars, using the data for sand, as shown below.

2. Draw bars for the potting-soil data next to the bars for the sand data. Shade them a different color. Add a key.

Table 2. Effect of Water and Soil on Seed Sprouting

Daily Amount of Water (mL)	Number of Seeds That Sprouted After 3 Days in Sand	Number of Seeds That Sprouted After 3 Days in Potting Soil
0	1	2
10	4	5
20	8	9

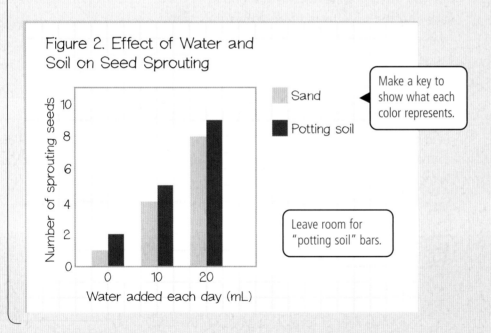

Figure 2. Effect of Water and Soil on Seed Sprouting

Make a key to show what each color represents.

Leave room for "potting soil" bars.

Designing an Experiment

Use this section when designing or conducting an experiment.

Determining a Purpose

You can find a purpose for an experiment by doing research, by examining the results of a previous experiment, or by observing the world around you. An **experiment** is an organized procedure to study something under controlled conditions.

> Don't forget to learn as much as possible about your topic before you begin.

1. Write the purpose of your experiment as a question or problem that you want to investigate.

2. Write down research questions and begin searching for information that will help you design an experiment. Consult the library, the Internet, and other people as you conduct your research.

EXAMPLE

Middle school students observed an odor near the lake by their school. They also noticed that the water on the side of the lake near the school was greener than the water on the other side of the lake. The students did some research to learn more about their observations. They discovered that the odor and green color in the lake  came from algae. They also discovered that a new fertilizer was being used on a field nearby. The students inferred that the use of the fertilizer might be related to the presence of the algae and designed a controlled experiment to find out whether they were right.

Problem
How does fertilizer affect the presence of algae in a lake?

Research Questions
- Have other experiments been done on this problem? If so, what did those experiments show?
- What kind of fertilizer is used on the field? How much?
- How do algae grow?
- How do people measure algae?
- Can fertilizer and algae be used safely in a lab? How?

> **Research**
> As you research, you may find a topic that is more interesting to you than your original topic, or learn that a procedure you wanted to use is not practical or safe. It is OK to change your purpose as you research.

Writing a Hypothesis

A **hypothesis** is a tentative explanation for an observation or scientific problem that can be tested by further investigation. You can write your hypothesis in the form of an "If . . . , then . . . , because . . ." statement.

Hypothesis

If the amount of fertilizer in lake water is increased, then the amount of algae will also increase, because fertilizers provide nutrients that algae need to grow.

◄ **Hypotheses**
For help with hypotheses, refer to page R3.

Determining Materials

Make a list of all the materials you will need to do your experiment. Be specific, especially if someone else is helping you obtain the materials. Try to think of everything you will need.

Materials
- 1 large jar or container
- 4 identical smaller containers
- rubber gloves that also cover the arms
- sample of fertilizer-and-water solution
- eyedropper
- clear plastic wrap
- scissors
- masking tape
- marker
- ruler

Determining Variables and Constants

EXPERIMENTAL GROUP AND CONTROL GROUP

An experiment to determine how two factors are related always has two groups—a control group and an experimental group.

1. Design an experimental group. Include as many trials as possible in the experimental group in order to obtain reliable results.

2. Design a control group that is the same as the experimental group in every way possible, except for the factor you wish to test.

Experimental Group: two containers of lake water with one drop of fertilizer solution added to each

Control Group: two containers of lake water with no fertilizer solution added

Go back to your materials list and make sure you have enough items listed to cover both your experimental group and your control group.

VARIABLES AND CONSTANTS

Identify the variables and constants in your experiment. In a controlled experiment, a **variable** is any factor that can change. **Constants** are all of the factors that are the same in both the experimental group and the control group.

1. Read your hypothesis. The **independent variable** is the factor that you wish to test and that is manipulated or changed so that it can be tested. The independent variable is expressed in your hypothesis after the word *if*. Identify the independent variable in your laboratory report.

2. The **dependent variable** is the factor that you measure to gather results. It is expressed in your hypothesis after the word *then*. Identify the dependent variable in your laboratory report.

Hypothesis
If the amount of fertilizer in lake water is increased, then the amount of algae will also increase, because fertilizers provide nutrients that algae need to grow.

Table 1. Variables and Constants in Algae Experiment

Independent Variable	Dependent Variable	Constants
Amount of fertilizer in lake water	Amount of algae that grow	• Where the lake water is obtained • Type of container used • Light and temperature conditions where water will be stored

Set up your experiment so that you will test only one variable.

MEASURING THE DEPENDENT VARIABLE

Before starting your experiment, you need to define how you will measure the dependent variable. An **operational definition** is a description of the one particular way in which you will measure the dependent variable.

Your operational definition is important for several reasons. First, in any experiment there are several ways in which a dependent variable can be measured. Second, the procedure of the experiment depends on how you decide to measure the dependent variable. Third, your operational definition makes it possible for other people to evaluate and build on your experiment.

EXAMPLE 1

An operational definition of a dependent variable can be qualitative. That is, your measurement of the dependent variable can simply be an observation of whether a change occurs as a result of a change in the independent variable. This type of operational definition can be thought of as a "yes or no" measurement.

Table 2. Qualitative Operational Definition of Algae Growth

Independent Variable	Dependent Variable	Operational Definition
Amount of fertilizer in lake water	Amount of algae that grow	Algae grow in lake water

A qualitative measurement of a dependent variable is often easy to make and record. However, this type of information does not provide a great deal of detail in your experimental results.

EXAMPLE 2

An operational definition of a dependent variable can be quantitative. That is, your measurement of the dependent variable can be a number that shows how much change occurs as a result of a change in the independent variable.

Table 3. Quantitative Operational Definition of Algae Growth

Independent Variable	Dependent Variable	Operational Definition
Amount of fertilizer in lake water	Amount of algae that grow	Diameter of largest algal growth (in mm)

A quantitative measurement of a dependent variable can be more difficult to make and analyze than a qualitative measurement. However, this type of data provides much more information about your experiment and is often more useful.

Writing a Procedure

Write each step of your procedure. Start each step with a verb, or action word, and keep the steps short. Your procedure should be clear enough for someone else to use as instructions for repeating your experiment.

> If necessary, go back to your materials list and add any materials that you left out.

Controlling Variables
The same amount of fertilizer solution must be added to two of the four containers.

Controlling Variables
All four containers must receive the same amount of light.

Procedure

1. Put on your gloves. Use the large container to obtain a sample of lake water.

2. Divide the sample of lake water equally among the four smaller containers.

3. Use the eyedropper to add one drop of fertilizer solution to two of the containers.

4. Use the masking tape and the marker to label the containers with your initials, the date, and the identifiers "Jar 1 with Fertilizer," "Jar 2 with Fertilizer," "Jar 1 without Fertilizer," and "Jar 2 without Fertilizer."

5. Cover the containers with clear plastic wrap. Use the scissors to punch ten holes in each of the covers.

6. Place all four containers on a window ledge. Make sure that they all receive the same amount of light.

7. Observe the containers every day for one week.

8. Use the ruler to measure the diameter of the largest clump of algae in each container, and record your measurements daily.

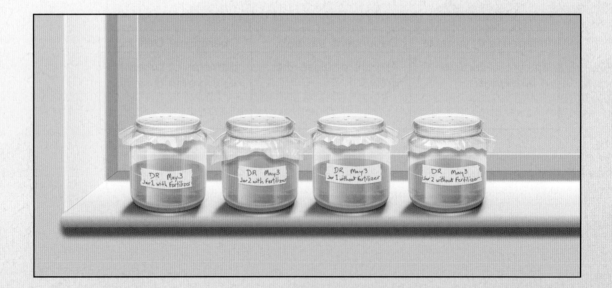

LAB HANDBOOK

Recording Observations

Once you have obtained all of your materials and your procedure has been approved, you can begin making experimental observations. Gather both quantitative and qualitative data. If something goes wrong during your procedure, make sure you record that too.

Observations
For help with making qualitative and quantitative observations, refer to page R2.

For more examples of data tables, see page R23.

Table 4. Fertilizer and Algae Growth

Date and Time	Experimental Group		Control Group		
	Jar 1 with Fertilizer (diameter of algae in mm)	Jar 2 with Fertilizer (diameter of algae in mm)	Jar 1 without Fertilizer (diameter of algae in mm)	Jar 2 without Fertilizer (diameter of algae in mm)	Observations
5/3 4:00 P.M.	0	0	0	0	condensation in all containers
5/4 4:00 P.M.	0	3	0	0	tiny green blobs in jar 2 with fertilizer
5/5 4:15 P.M.	4	5	0	3	green blobs in jars 1 and 2 with fertilizer and jar 2 without fertilizer
5/6 4:00 P.M.	5	6	0	4	water light green in jar 2 with fertilizer
5/7 4:00 P.M.	8	10	0	6	water light green in jars 1 and 2 with fertilizer and in jar 2 without fertilizer
5/8 3:30 P.M.	10	18	0	6	cover off jar 2 with fertilizer
5/9 3:30 P.M.	14	23	0	8	drew sketches of each container

Notice that on the sixth day, the observer found that the cover was off one of the containers. It is important to record observations of unintended factors because they might affect the results of the experiment.

Use technology, such as a microscope, to help you make observations when possible.

Drawings of Samples Viewed Under Microscope on 5/9 at 100x

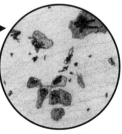

Jar 1
with Fertilizer

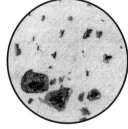

Jar 2
with Fertilizer

Jar 1
without Fertilizer

Jar 2
without Fertilizer

Summarizing Results

To summarize your data, look at all of your observations together. Look for meaningful ways to present your observations. For example, you might average your data or make a graph to look for patterns. When possible, use spreadsheet software to help you analyze and present your data. The two graphs below show the same data.

EXAMPLE 1

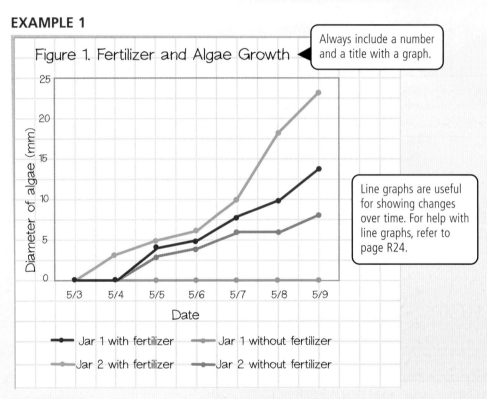

Figure 1. Fertilizer and Algae Growth

> Always include a number and a title with a graph.

> Line graphs are useful for showing changes over time. For help with line graphs, refer to page R24.

EXAMPLE 2

> Bar graphs are useful for comparing different data sets. This bar graph has four bars for each day. Another way to present the data would be to calculate averages for the tests and the controls, and to show one test bar and one control bar for each day.

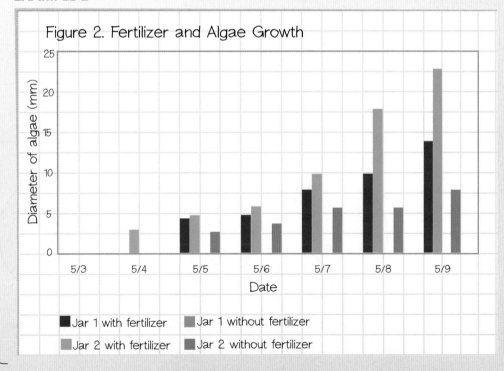

Figure 2. Fertilizer and Algae Growth

Drawing Conclusions

RESULTS AND INFERENCES

To draw conclusions from your experiment, first write your results. Then compare your results with your hypothesis. Do your results support your hypothesis? Be careful not to make inferences about factors that you did not test.

> For help with making inferences, see page R4.

Results and Inferences

The results of my experiment show that more algae grew in lake water to which fertilizer had been added than in lake water to which no fertilizer had been added. My hypothesis was supported. I infer that it is possible that the growth of algae in the lake was caused by the fertilizer used on the field.

> Notice that you cannot conclude from this experiment that the presence of algae in the lake was due only to the fertilizer.

QUESTIONS FOR FURTHER RESEARCH

Write a list of questions for further research and investigation. Your ideas may lead you to new experiments and discoveries.

Questions for Further Research

- What is the connection between the amount of fertilizer and algae growth?
- How do different brands of fertilizer affect algae growth?
- How would algae growth in the lake be affected if no fertilizer were used on the field?
- How do algae affect the lake and the other life in and around it?
- How does fertilizer affect the lake and the life in and around it?
- If fertilizer is getting into the lake, how is it getting there?

Math Handbook

Describing a Set of Data

Means, medians, modes, and ranges are important math tools for describing data sets such as the following widths of fossilized clamshells.

13 mm   25 mm   14 mm   21 mm   16 mm   23 mm   14 mm

Mean

The **mean** of a data set is the sum of the values divided by the number of values.

> **Example**
>
> To find the mean of the clamshell data, add the values and then divide the sum by the number of values.
>
> $$\frac{13 \text{ mm} + 25 \text{ mm} + 14 \text{ mm} + 21 \text{ mm} + 16 \text{ mm} + 23 \text{ mm} + 14 \text{ mm}}{7} = \frac{126 \text{ mm}}{7} = 18 \text{ mm}$$
>
> **ANSWER** The mean is 18 mm.

Median

The **median** of a data set is the middle value when the values are written in numerical order. If a data set has an even number of values, the median is the mean of the two middle values.

> **Example**
>
> To find the median of the clamshell data, arrange the values in order from least to greatest. The median is the middle value.
>
> 13 mm   14 mm   14 mm   16 mm   21 mm   23 mm   25 mm
>
> **ANSWER** The median is 16 mm.

Mode

The **mode** of a data set is the value that occurs most often.

Example

To find the mode of the clamshell data, arrange the values in order from least to greatest and determine the value that occurs most often.

13 mm   14 mm   14 mm   16 mm   21 mm   23 mm   25 mm

ANSWER The mode is 14 mm.

A data set can have more than one mode or no mode. For example, the following data set has modes of 2 mm and 4 mm:

2 mm   2 mm   3 mm   4 mm   4 mm

The data set below has no mode, because no value occurs more often than any other.

2 mm   3 mm   4 mm   5 mm

Range

The **range** of a data set is the difference between the greatest value and the least value.

Example

To find the range of the clamshell data, arrange the values in order from least to greatest.

13 mm   14 mm   14 mm   16 mm   21 mm   23 mm   25 mm

Subtract the least value from the greatest value.

13 mm is the least value.
25 mm is the greatest value.

25 mm − 13 mm = 12 mm

ANSWER The range is 12 mm.

Using Ratios, Rates, and Proportions

You can use ratios and rates to compare values in data sets. You can use proportions to find unknown values.

Ratios

A **ratio** uses division to compare two values. The ratio of a value a to a nonzero value b can be written as $\frac{a}{b}$.

Example

The height of one plant is 8 centimeters. The height of another plant is 6 centimeters. To find the ratio of the height of the first plant to the height of the second plant, write a fraction and simplify it.

$$\frac{8 \text{ cm}}{6 \text{ cm}} = \frac{4 \times \overset{1}{\cancel{2}}}{3 \times \underset{1}{\cancel{2}}} = \frac{4}{3}$$

ANSWER The ratio of the plant heights is $\frac{4}{3}$.

You can also write the ratio $\frac{a}{b}$ as "a to b" or as $a:b$. For example, you can write the ratio of the plant heights as "4 to 3" or as $4:3$.

Rates

A **rate** is a ratio of two values expressed in different units. A unit rate is a rate with a denominator of 1 unit.

Example

A plant grew 6 centimeters in 2 days. The plant's rate of growth was $\frac{6 \text{ cm}}{2 \text{ days}}$. To describe the plant's growth in centimeters per day, write a unit rate.

Divide numerator and denominator by 2: $\quad \dfrac{6 \text{ cm}}{2 \text{ days}} = \dfrac{6 \text{ cm} \div 2}{2 \text{ days} \div 2}$

> You divide 2 days by 2 to get 1 day, so divide 6 cm by 2 also.

Simplify: $\quad = \dfrac{3 \text{ cm}}{1 \text{ day}}$

ANSWER The plant's rate of growth is 3 centimeters per day.

Proportions

A **proportion** is an equation stating that two ratios are equivalent. To solve for an unknown value in a proportion, you can use cross products.

Example

If a plant grew 6 centimeters in 2 days, how many centimeters would it grow in 3 days (if its rate of growth is constant)?

Write a proportion:	$\dfrac{6 \text{ cm}}{2 \text{ days}} = \dfrac{x}{3 \text{ days}}$
Set cross products:	$6 \text{ cm} \cdot 3 = 2x$
Multiply 6 and 3:	$18 \text{ cm} = 2x$
Divide each side by 2:	$\dfrac{18 \text{ cm}}{2} = \dfrac{2x}{2}$
Simplify:	$9 \text{ cm} = x$

ANSWER The plant would grow 9 centimeters in 3 days.

Using Decimals, Fractions, and Percents

Decimals, fractions, and percentages are all ways of recording and representing data.

Decimals

A **decimal** is a number that is written in the base-ten place value system, in which a decimal point separates the ones and tenths digits. The values of each place is ten times that of the place to its right.

Example

A caterpillar traveled from point *A* to point *C* along the path shown.

A   **36.9 cm**   **B**   **52.4 cm**   C

ADDING DECIMALS To find the total distance traveled by the caterpillar, add the distance from *A* to *B* and the distance from *B* to *C*. Begin by lining up the decimal points. Then add the figures as you would whole numbers and bring down the decimal point.

```
  36.9 cm
+ 52.4 cm
  89.3 cm
```

ANSWER The caterpillar traveled a total distance of 89.3 centimeters.

Example *continued*

SUBTRACTING DECIMALS To find how much farther the caterpillar traveled on the second leg of the journey, subtract the distance from *A* to *B* from the distance from *B* to *C*.

$$\begin{array}{r} 52.4 \text{ cm} \\ -\ 36.9 \text{ cm} \\ \hline 15.5 \text{ cm} \end{array}$$

ANSWER The caterpillar traveled 15.5 centimeters farther on the second leg of the journey.

Example

A caterpillar is traveling from point *D* to point *F* along the path shown. The caterpillar travels at a speed of 9.6 centimeters per minute.

D   E   **33.6 cm**   F

MULTIPLYING DECIMALS You can multiply decimals as you would whole numbers. The number of decimal places in the product is equal to the sum of the number of decimal places in the factors.

For instance, suppose it takes the caterpillar 1.5 minutes to go from *D* to *E*. To find the distance from *D* to *E*, multiply the caterpillar's speed by the time it took.

Align as shown.

$$\begin{array}{rl} 9.6 & \quad 1 \quad \text{decimal place} \\ \times\ 1.5 & \quad +\ 1 \quad \text{decimal place} \\ \hline 480 & \\ 96 & \\ \hline 14.40 & \quad 2 \quad \text{decimal places} \end{array}$$

ANSWER The distance from *D* to *E* is 14.4 centimeters.

DIVIDING DECIMALS When you divide by a decimal, move the decimal points the same number of places in the divisor and the dividend to make the divisor a whole number.

For instance, to find the time it will take the caterpillar to travel from *E* to *F*, divide the distance from *E* to *F* by the caterpillar's speed.

$$9.6\,\overline{)33.6}$$

Move each decimal point one place to the right.

$$\begin{array}{r} 3.5 \\ 96\,\overline{)336.} \\ \underline{288} \\ 480 \\ \underline{480} \\ 0 \end{array}$$

Line up decimal points.

ANSWER The caterpillar will travel from *E* to *F* in 3.5 minutes.

Fractions

A **fraction** is a number in the form $\frac{a}{b}$, where b is not equal to 0. A fraction is in **simplest form** if its numerator and denominator have a greatest common factor (GCF) of 1. To simplify a fraction, divide its numerator and denominator by their GCF.

Example

A caterpillar is 40 millimeters long. The head of the caterpillar is 6 millimeters long. To compare the length of the caterpillar's head with the caterpillar's total length, you can write and simplify a fraction that expresses the ratio of the two lengths.

Write the ratio of the two lengths: $\dfrac{\text{Length of head}}{\text{Total length}} = \dfrac{6 \text{ mm}}{40 \text{ mm}}$

Write numerator and denominator as products of numbers and the GCF: $= \dfrac{3 \times 2}{20 \times 2}$

Divide numerator and denominator by the GCF: $= \dfrac{3 \times \overset{1}{\cancel{2}}}{20 \times \underset{1}{\cancel{2}}}$

Simplify: $= \dfrac{3}{20}$

ANSWER In simplest form, the ratio of the lengths is $\dfrac{3}{20}$.

Percents

A **percent** is a ratio that compares a number to 100. The word *percent* means "per hundred" or "out of 100." The symbol for *percent* is %.

For instance, suppose 43 out of 100 caterpillars are female. You can represent this ratio as a percent, a decimal, or a fraction.

Percent	Decimal	Fraction
43%	0.43	$\frac{43}{100}$

Example

In the preceding example, the ratio of the length of the caterpillar's head to the caterpillar's total length is $\frac{3}{20}$. To write this ratio as a percent, write an equivalent fraction that has a denominator of 100.

Multiply numerator and denominator by 5: $\dfrac{3}{20} = \dfrac{3 \times 5}{20 \times 5}$

$= \dfrac{15}{100}$

Write as a percent: $= 15\%$

ANSWER The caterpillar's head represents 15 percent of its total length.

Using Formulas

A **formula** is an equation that shows the general relationship between two or more quantities.

In science, a formula often has a word form and a symbolic form. The formula below expresses Ohm's law.

Word Form

$$\text{Current} = \frac{\text{voltage}}{\text{resistance}}$$

Symbolic Form

$$I = \frac{V}{R}$$

> The term *variable* is also used in science to refer to a factor that can change during an experiment.

In this formula, I, V, and R are variables. A mathematical **variable** is a symbol or letter that is used to represent one or more numbers.

Example

Suppose that you measure a voltage of 1.5 volts and a resistance of 15 ohms. You can use the formula for Ohm's law to find the current in amperes.

Write the formula for Ohm's law: $\quad I = \dfrac{V}{R}$

Substitute 1.5 volts for V and 15 ohms for R: $\quad I = \dfrac{1.5 \text{ volts}}{15 \text{ ohms}}$

Simplify: $\quad I = 0.1 \text{ amp}$

ANSWER The current is 0.1 ampere.

If you know the values of all variables but one in a formula, you can solve for the value of the unknown variable. For instance, Ohm's law can be used to find a voltage if you know the current and the resistance.

Example

Suppose that you know that a current is 0.2 amperes and the resistance is 18 ohms. Use the formula for Ohm's law to find the voltage in volts.

Write the formula for Ohm's law: $\quad I = \dfrac{V}{R}$

Substitute 0.2 amp for I and 18 ohms for R: $\quad 0.2 \text{ amp} = \dfrac{V}{18 \text{ ohms}}$

Multiply both sides by 18 ohms: $\quad 0.2 \text{ amp} \cdot 18 \text{ ohms} = V$

Simplify: $\quad 3.6 \text{ volts} = V$

ANSWER The voltage is 3.6 volts.

MATH HANDBOOK

R42

R42 Student Resources

Finding Areas

The area of a figure is the amount of surface the figure covers.

Area is measured in square units, such as square meters (m²) or square centimeters (cm²). Formulas for the areas of three common geometric figures are shown below.

Area = (side length)²
$A = s^2$

Area = length × width
$A = lw$

Area = $\frac{1}{2}$ × base × height
$A = \frac{1}{2} bh$

Example

Each face of a halite crystal is a square like the one shown. You can find the area of the square by using the steps below.

3 mm

3 mm

Write the formula for the area of a square: $A = s^2$

Substitute 3 mm for s: $= (3 \text{ mm})^2$

Simplify: $= 9 \text{ mm}^2$

ANSWER The area of the square is 9 square millimeters.

Finding Volumes

The volume of a solid is the amount of space contained by the solid.

Volume is measured in cubic units, such as cubic meters (m³) or cubic centimeters (cm³). The volume of a rectangular prism is given by the formula shown below.

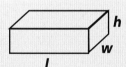

Volume = length × width × height
$V = lwh$

Example

A topaz crystal is a rectangular prism like the one shown. You can find the volume of the prism by using the steps below.

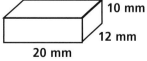

10 mm

12 mm

20 mm

Write the formula for the volume of a rectangular prism: $V = lwh$

Substitute dimensions: $= 20 \text{ mm} \times 12 \text{ mm} \times 10 \text{ mm}$

Simplify: $= 2400 \text{ mm}^3$

ANSWER The volume of the rectangular prism is 2400 cubic millimeters.

Using Significant Figures

The **significant figures** in a decimal are the digits that are warranted by the accuracy of a measuring device.

When you perform a calculation with measurements, the number of significant figures to include in the result depends in part on the number of significant figures in the measurements. When you multiply or divide measurements, your answer should have only as many significant figures as the measurement with the fewest significant figures.

Example

Using a balance and a graduated cylinder filled with water, you determined that a marble has a mass of 8.0 grams and a volume of 3.5 cubic centimeters. To calculate the density of the marble, divide the mass by the volume.

$$\text{Write the formula for density:} \quad \text{Density} = \frac{\text{mass}}{\text{Volume}}$$

$$\text{Substitute measurements:} \quad = \frac{8.0 \text{ g}}{3.5 \text{ cm}^3}$$

$$\text{Use a calculator to divide:} \quad \approx 2.285714286 \text{ g/cm}^3$$

ANSWER Because the mass and the volume have two significant figures each, give the density to two significant figures. The marble has a density of 2.3 grams per cubic centimeter.

Using Scientific Notation

Scientific notation is a shorthand way to write very large or very small numbers. For example, 73,500,000,000,000,000,000,000 kg is the mass of the Moon. In scientific notation, it is 7.35×10^{22} kg.

Example

You can convert from standard form to scientific notation.

Standard Form	Scientific Notation
720,000	7.2×10^5
5 decimal places left	Exponent is 5.
0.000291	2.91×10^{-4}
4 decimal places right	Exponent is −4.

You can convert from scientific notation to standard form.

Scientific Notation	Standard Form
4.63×10^7	46,300,000
Exponent is 7.	7 decimal places right
1.08×10^{-6}	0.00000108
Exponent is −6.	6 decimal places left

Note-Taking Handbook

Note-Taking Strategies

Taking notes as you read helps you understand the information. The notes you take can also be used as a study guide for later review. This handbook presents several ways to organize your notes.

Content Frame

1. Make a chart in which each column represents a category.
2. Give each column a heading.
3. Write details under the headings.

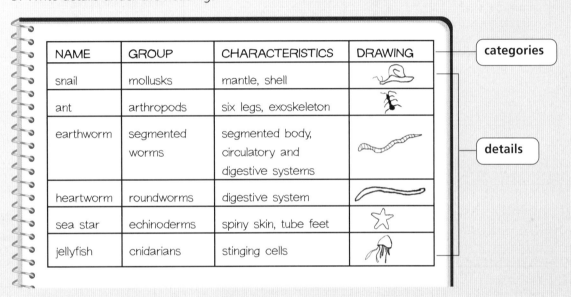

NAME	GROUP	CHARACTERISTICS	DRAWING
snail	mollusks	mantle, shell	
ant	arthropods	six legs, exoskeleton	
earthworm	segmented worms	segmented body, circulatory and digestive systems	
heartworm	roundworms	digestive system	
sea star	echinoderms	spiny skin, tube feet	
jellyfish	cnidarians	stinging cells	

categories

details

Combination Notes

1. For each new idea or concept, write an informal outline of the information.
2. Make a sketch to illustrate the concept, and label it.

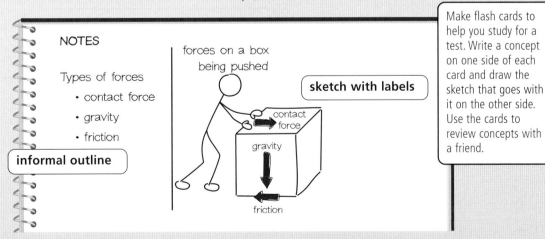

NOTES

Types of forces
- contact force
- gravity
- friction

informal outline

forces on a box being pushed

sketch with labels

contact force

gravity

friction

Make flash cards to help you study for a test. Write a concept on one side of each card and draw the sketch that goes with it on the other side. Use the cards to review concepts with a friend.

Main Idea and Detail Notes

1. In the left-hand column of a two-column chart, list main ideas. The blue headings express main ideas throughout this textbook.

2. In the right-hand column, write details that expand on each main idea.

You can shorten the headings in your chart. Be sure to use the most important words.

When studying for tests, cover up the detail notes column with a sheet of paper. Then use each main idea to form a question—such as "How does latitude affect climate?" Answer the question, and then uncover the detail notes column to check your answer.

MAIN IDEAS	DETAIL NOTES
1. Latitude affects climate. **main idea 1**	1. Places close to the equator are usually warmer than places close to the poles. **details about main idea 1** 1. Latitude has the same effect in both hemispheres.
2. Altitude affects climate. **main idea 2**	2. Temperature decreases with altitude. **details about main idea 2** 2. Altitude can overcome the effect of latitude on temperature.

Main Idea Web

1. Write a main idea in a box.

2. Add boxes around it with related vocabulary terms and important details.

You can find definitions near highlighted terms.

definition of *work*
Work is the use of force to move an object.

formula
Work = force · distance

main idea
Force is necessary to do work.

The joule is the unit used to measure work.
definition of *joule*

Work depends on the size of a force.
important detail

Mind Map

1. Write a main idea in the center.

2. Add details that relate to one another and to the main idea.

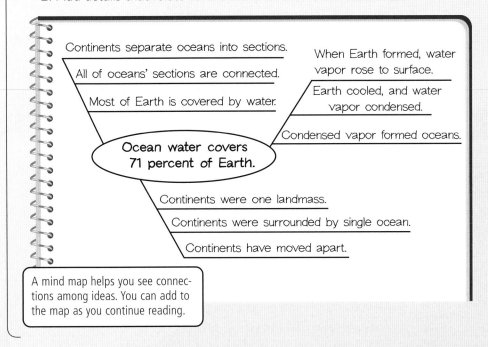

Continents separate oceans into sections.

All of oceans' sections are connected.

Most of Earth is covered by water.

When Earth formed, water vapor rose to surface.

Earth cooled, and water vapor condensed.

Condensed vapor formed oceans.

Ocean water covers 71 percent of Earth.

Continents were one landmass.

Continents were surrounded by single ocean.

Continents have moved apart.

A mind map helps you see connections among ideas. You can add to the map as you continue reading.

Supporting Main Ideas

1. Write a main idea in a box.

2. Add boxes underneath with information—such as reasons, explanations, and examples—that supports the main idea.

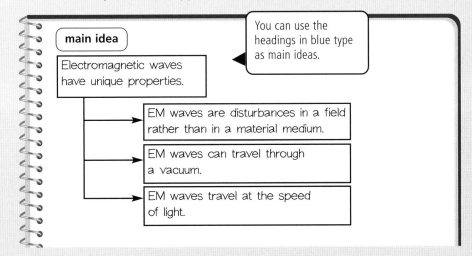

main idea

Electromagnetic waves have unique properties.

You can use the headings in blue type as main ideas.

EM waves are disturbances in a field rather than in a material medium.

EM waves can travel through a vacuum.

EM waves travel at the speed of light.

Outline

1. Copy the chapter title and headings from the book in the form of an outline.

2. Add notes that summarize in your own words what you read.

Cell Processes

1st key idea

I. Cells capture and release energy.

1st subpoint of I

    A. All cells need energy.

2nd subpoint of I

    B. Some cells capture light energy.

1st detail about B

        1. Process of photosynthesis

2nd detail about B

        2. Chloroplasts (site of photosynthesis)

        3. Carbon dioxide and water as raw materials

        4. Glucose and oxygen as products

    C. All cells release energy.

        1. Process of cellular respiration

        2. Fermentation of sugar to carbon dioxide

        3. Bacteria that carry out fermentation

II. Cells transport materials through membranes.

    A. Some materials move by diffusion.

        1. Particle movement from higher to lower concentrations

        2. Movement of water through membrane (osmosis)

    B. Some transport requires energy.

        1. Active transport

        2. Examples of active transport

Correct Outline Form

Include a title.

Arrange key ideas, subpoints, and details as shown.

Indent the divisions of the outline as shown.

Use the same grammatical form for items of the same rank. For example, if A is a sentence, B must also be a sentence.

You must have at least two main ideas or subpoints. That is, every A must be followed by a B, and every 1 must be followed by a 2.

Concept Map

1. Write an important concept in a large oval.

2. Add details related to the concept in smaller ovals.

3. Write linking words on arrows that connect the ovals.

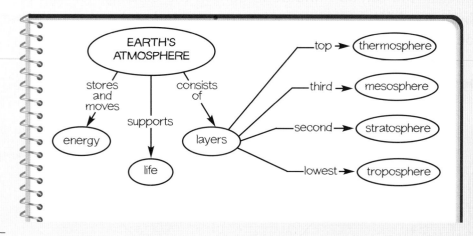

The main ideas or concepts can often be found in the blue headings. An example is "The atmosphere stores and moves energy." Use nouns from these concepts in the ovals, and use the verb or verbs on the lines.

Venn Diagram

1. Draw two overlapping circles, one for each item that you are comparing.

2. In the overlapping section, list the characteristics that are shared by both items.

3. In the outer sections, list the characteristics that are peculiar to each item.

4. Write a summary that describes the information in the Venn diagram.

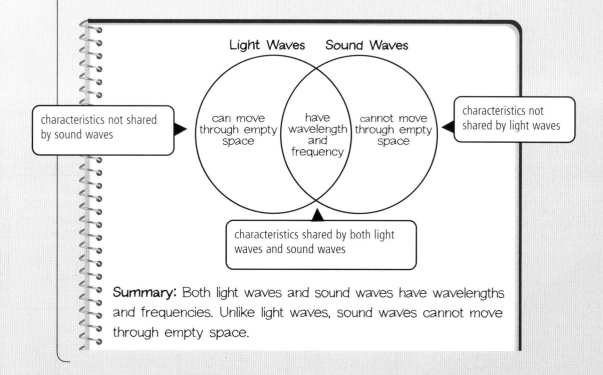

Summary: Both light waves and sound waves have wavelengths and frequencies. Unlike light waves, sound waves cannot move through empty space.

Vocabulary Strategies

Important terms are highlighted in this book. A definition of each term can be found in the sentence or paragraph where the term appears. You can also find definitions in the Glossary. Taking notes about vocabulary terms helps you understand and remember what you read.

Description Wheel

1. Write a term inside a circle.
2. Write words that describe the term on "spokes" attached to the circle.

When studying for a test with a friend, read the phrases on the spokes one at a time until your friend identifies the correct term.

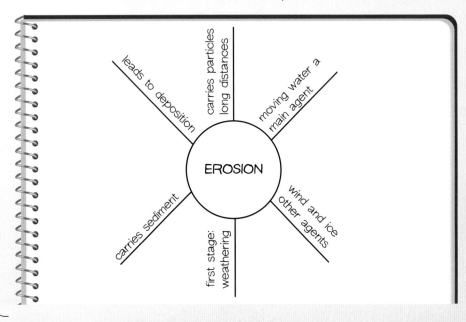

EROSION

leads to deposition
carries particles long distances
moving water a main agent
wind and ice other agents
first stage: weathering
carries sediment

Four Square

1. Write a term in the center.
2. Write details in the four areas around the term.

Definition	Characteristics
any living thing	needs food, water, air; needs energy; grows, develops, reproduces

ORGANISM

Examples	Nonexamples
dogs, cats, birds, insects, flowers, trees	rocks, water, dirt

Include a definition, some characteristics, and examples. You may want to add a formula, a sketch, or examples of things that the term does *not* name.

NOTE-TAKING HANDBOOK

Frame Game

1. Write a term in the center.
2. Frame the term with details.

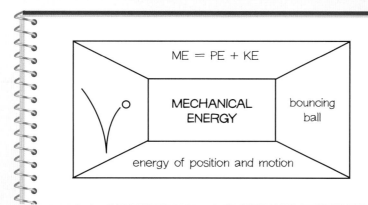

Include examples, descriptions, sketches, or sentences that use the term in context. Change the frame to fit each new term.

Magnet Word

1. Write a term on the magnet.
2. On the lines, add details related to the term.

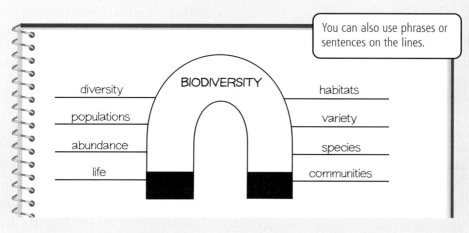

You can also use phrases or sentences on the lines.

Word Triangle

1. Write a term and its definition in the bottom section.
2. In the middle section, write a sentence in which the term is used correctly.
3. In the top section, draw a small picture to illustrate the term.

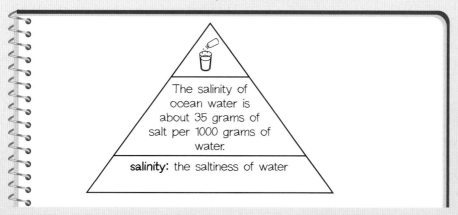

NOTE-TAKING HANDBOOK

Glossary

A, B

aquaculture
The science and business of raising and harvesting fish in a controlled situation. (p. 45)

acuacultura La ciencia y el negocio de criar y cosechar peces en una situación controlada.

aquifer
An underground layer of permeable rock that contains water. (p. 26)

acuífero Una capa subterránea de roca permeable que contiene agua.

artesian well
A well in which pressurized water flows upward to the surface. (p. 28)

pozo artesiano Un pozo en el cual el agua bajo presión fluye hacia arriba hasta la superficie.

atmosphere (AT-muh-SFEER)
The outer layer of gases of a large body in space, such as a planet or star; the mixture of gases that surrounds the solid Earth; one of the four parts of the Earth system. (p. xix)

atmósfera La capa externa de gases de un gran cuerpo que se encuentra en el espacio, como un planeta o una estrella; la mezcla de gases que rodea la Tierra sólida; una de las cuatro partes del sistema terrestre.

atom
The smallest particle of an element that has the chemical properties of that element. (p. xvii)

átomo La partícula más pequeña de un elemento que tiene las propiedades químicas de ese elemento.

biosphere (BY-uh-SFEER)
All living organisms on Earth in the air, on the land, and in the waters; one of the four parts of the Earth system. (p. xix)

biosfera Todos los organismos vivos de la Tierra, en el aire, en la tierra y en las aguas; una de las cuatro partes del sistema de la Tierra.

by-catch
The portion of animals that are caught in a net and then thrown away as unwanted. (p. 132)

captura incidental La porción de los animales que se capturan en una red y luego se desechan como no deseados.

C

climate
The characteristic weather conditions in an area over a long period of time. (p. xxi)

clima Las condiciones meteorológicas características de un lugar durante un largo período de tiempo.

compound
A substance made up of two or more different types of atoms bonded together.

compuesto Una sustancia formada por dos o más diferentes tipos de átomos enlazados.

concentration
The amount of a substance that is contained in another substance—such as dissolved sugar in water—often expressed as parts per million or parts per billion. (p. 51)

concentración La cantidad de una sustancia contenida en otra sustancia, como el azúcar disuelto en agua; a menudo se expresa como partes por millón o partes por mil millones.

condensation
The process by which a gas changes into a liquid. (p. 13)

condensación El proceso por el cual un gas se transforma en líquido.

continental shelf
The flat or gently sloping land that lies submerged around the edges of a continent and that extends from the shoreline out to the continental slope. (p. 80)

plataforma continental La tierra plana o ligeramente inclinada que está sumergida alrededor de las orillas de un continente y que se extiende desde la costa hasta el talud continental.

convection
The transfer of energy from place to place by the motion of heated gas or liquid; in Earth's mantle, convection is thought to transfer energy by the motion of solid rock, which when under great heat and pressure can move like a liquid. (p. xv)

convección La transferencia de energía de un lugar a otro por el movimiento de un líquido o gas calentado; se piensa que en el manto terrestre la convección transfiere energía mediante el movimiento de roca sólida, la cual puede moverse como un líquido cuando está muy caliente y bajo alta presión.

coral reef
A built-up limestone deposit formed by small ant-sized organisms called corals. (p. 122)

   arrecife de coral Un depósito de piedra caliza formado por organismos pequeños del tamaño de una hormiga llamados corales.

cycle
n. A series of events or actions that repeat themselves regularly; a physical and/or chemical process in which one material continually changes locations and/or forms. Examples include the water cycle, the carbon cycle, and the rock cycle.

v. To move through a repeating series of events or actions.

   ciclo s. Una serie de eventos o acciones que se repiten regularmente; un proceso físico y/o químico en el cual un material cambia continuamente de lugar y/o forma. Ejemplos: el ciclo del agua, el ciclo del carbono y el ciclo de las rocas.

D

dam
A structure that holds back and controls the flow of water in a river or other body of water. (p. 46)

   presa Una estructura que retiene y controla el flujo de agua en un río u otro cuerpo de agua.

data
Information gathered by observation or experimentation that can be used in calculating or reasoning. *Data* is a plural word; the singular is *datum.*

   datos Información reunida mediante observación o experimentación y que se puede usar para calcular o para razonar.

density
A property of matter representing the mass per unit volume.

   densidad Una propiedad de la materia que representa la masa por unidad de volumen.

desalination (de-SAL-ih-NAY-shun)
The process of removing salt from ocean water. Desalination is used to obtain fresh water. (p. 66)

   desalinización El proceso de eliminar la sal del agua de mar. La desalinización se usa para obtener agua dulce.

divide
A continuous high line of land—or ridge—from which water drains to one side or the other. (p. 17)

   línea divisoria de aguas Una línea continua de tierra alta, o un cerro, desde donde el agua escurre hacia un lado o hacia el otro.

downwelling
The movement of water from the surface to greater depths. (p. 86)

   sumergencia El movimiento de agua de la superficie hacia mayores profundidades.

drainage basin
An area of land in which water drains into a stream system. The borders of a drainage basin are called divides. (p. 17)

   cuenca tributaria Un área de tierra en la cual el agua escurre a un sistema de corrientes. Los límites de una cuenca tributaria se denominan líneas divisorias de aguas.

drought (drowt)
A long period of abnormally low amounts of rainfall. (p. 61)

   sequía Un período largo con cantidades inusualmente bajas de lluvia.

E

element
A substance that cannot be broken down into a simpler substance by ordinary chemical changes. An element consists of atoms of only one type.

   elemento Una sustancia que no puede descomponerse en otra sustancia más simple por medio de cambios químicos normales. Un elemento consta de átomos de un solo tipo.

El Niño (el NEEN-yoh)
A disturbance of wind patterns and ocean currents in the Pacific Ocean that causes temporary climate changes in many parts of the world. (p. 88)

   El Niño Un disturbio en los patrones de viento y las corrientes oceánicas del océano Pacifico que causa cambios climáticos temporales en muchas partes del mundo.

energy
The ability to do work or to cause a change. For example, the energy of a moving bowling ball knocks over pins; energy from food allows animals to move and to grow; and energy from the Sun heats Earth's surface and atmosphere, which causes air to move. (p. xv)

   energía La capacidad para trabajar o causar un cambio. Por ejemplo, la energía de una bola de boliche en movimiento tumba los pinos; la energía proveniente de su alimento permite a los animales moverse y crecer; la energía del Sol calienta la superficie y la atmósfera de la Tierra, lo que ocasiona que el aire se mueva.

estuary (EHS-choo-EHR-ee)
A shoreline area where fresh water from a river mixes with salt water from the ocean. (p. 116)

> **estuario** Un litoral donde se mezcla agua dulce de un río con agua salada del océano.

eutrophication (yoo-TRAF-ih-KAY-shun)
An increase in nutrients in a lake or pond. Eutrophication can occur naturally or as a result of pollution, and causes increased growth of algae and plants. (p. 20)

> **eutrofización** Un aumento en los nutrientes de un lago o una laguna. La eutrofización puede ocurrir de manera natural o como resultado de la contaminación y ocasiona un aumento en el crecimiento de algas y plantas.

evaporation
The process by which liquid changes into gas. (p. 13)

> **evaporación** El proceso por el cual un líquido se transforma en gas.

experiment
An organized procedure to study something under controlled conditions. (p. xxiv)

> **experimento** Un procedimiento organizado para estudiar algo bajo condiciones controladas.

F

force
A push or a pull; something that changes the motion of an object. (p. xvii)

> **fuerza** Un empuje o un jalón; algo que cambia el movimiento de un objeto.

fossil
A trace or the remains of a once-living thing from long ago. (p. xxi)

> **fósil** Un rastro o los restos de un organismo que vivió hace mucho tiempo.

fresh water
Water that is not salty and has little or no taste, color, or smell. Most lakes and rivers are made up of fresh water. (p. 11)

> **agua dulce** Agua que no es salada y que tiene muy poco o ningún sabor, color u olor. La mayoría de los lagos y los ríos están compuestos de agua dulce.

friction
A force that resists the motion between two surfaces in contact. (p. xxi)

> **fricción** Una fuerza que resiste el movimiento entre dos superficies en contacto.

G

geosphere (JEE-uh-SFEER)
All the features on Earth's surface—continents, islands, and seafloor—and everything below the surface—the inner and outer core and the mantle; one of the four parts of the Earth system. (p. xix)

> **geosfera** Todas las características de la superficie de la Tierra, es decir, continentes, islas y el fondo marino, y de todo bajo la superficie, es decir, el núcleo externo e interno y el manto; una de las cuatro partes del sistema de la Tierra.

glacier
A large mass of ice that exists year-round and moves over land.

> **glaciar** Una gran masa de hielo que existe durante todo el año y se mueve sobre la tierra.

gravity
The force that objects exert on each other because of their mass. (p. xvii)

> **gravedad** La fuerza que los objetos ejercen entre sí debido a su masa.

groundwater
Water that collects and is stored underground. (p. 24)

> **agua subterránea** Agua que se acumula y almacena bajo tierra.

H

habitat
The natural environment in which a living thing gets all that it needs to live; examples include a desert, a coral reef, and a freshwater lake. (p. 114)

> **hábitat** El medio ambiente natural en el cual un organismo vivo consigue todo lo que requiere para vivir; ejemplos incluyen un desierto, un arrecife coralino y un lago de agua dulce.

hydrothermal vent
An opening in the sea floor from which heated water rises and mixes with the ocean water above. (p. 128)

> **abertura hidrotermal** Una salida en el fondo marino desde la cual asciende agua caliente que se mezcla con el agua del océano.

hydrosphere (HY-druh-SFEER)
All water on Earth—in the atmosphere and in the oceans, lakes, glaciers, rivers, streams, and underground reservoirs; one of the four parts of the Earth system. (p. xix)

hidrosfera Toda el agua de la Tierra: en la atmósfera y en los océanos, lagos, glaciares, ríos, arroyos y depósitos subterráneos; una de las cuatro partes del sistema de la Tierra.

hypothesis
A tentative explanation for an observation or phenomenon. A hypothesis is used to make testable predictions. (p. xxiv)

hipótesis Una explicación provisional de una observación o de un fenómeno. Una hipótesis se usa para hacer predicciones que se pueden probar.

I, J

iceberg
A mass of floating ice that broke away from a glacier. (p. 22)

iceberg Una masa de hielo flotante que se separó de un glaciar.

impermeable
Resistant to the passage of water. (p. 25)

impermeable Resistente al paso del agua.

intertidal zone
The narrow ocean margin between the high-tide mark and the low-tide mark. (p. 114)

zona intermareal El estrecho margen oceánico entre el límite de la marea alta y el límite de la marea baja.

irrigation
The process of supplying water to land to grow crops. (p. 43)

irrigación El proceso de suministrar agua a las tierras de cultivo.

K

kelp forest
A large community of kelp, a type of seaweed that can attach to the ocean floor. (p. 124)

bosque de kelp Una comunidad grande de kelp, un tipo de alga marina que puede adherirse al fondo marino.

L

law
In science, a rule or principle describing a physical relationship that always works in the same way under the same conditions. The law of conservation of energy is an example.

ley En las ciencias, una regla o un principio que describe una relación física que siempre funciona de la misma manera bajo las mismas condiciones. La ley de la conservación de la energía es un ejemplo.

lock
A section of a waterway, closed off by gates, in which the water level is rasied or lowered to move ships through. (p. 46)

esclusa Una sección de un canal cerrado con compuertas, en la cual se eleva o se baja el nivel del agua para que pasen barcos.

longshore current
The overall direction and movement of the waves that strike the shore at an angle. (p. 92)

corriente litoral La dirección y el movimiento general de las olas que golpean la costa en ángulo.

M, N

mass
A measure of how much matter an object is made of.

masa Una medida de la cantidad de materia de la que está compuesto un objeto.

matter
Anything that has mass and volume. Matter exists ordinarily as a solid, a liquid, or a gas. (p. xvii)

materia Todo lo que tiene masa y volumen. Generalmente la materia existe como sólido, líquido o gas.

molecule
A group of atoms that are held together by covalent bonds so that they move as a single unit.

molécula Un grupo de átomos que están unidos mediante enlaces covalentes de tal manera que se mueven como una sola unidad.

neap tide
A tide of small range occurring during the first- and third-quarter phases of the Moon. (p. 99)

marea muerta Una marea de poco rango que ocurre durante las fases cuarto menguante y cuarto creciente de la Luna.

nonpoint-source pollution
Pollution with a source that is hard to find or scattered. (p. 54)

> **contaminación por fuentes difusas** Contaminación de fuentes que son dispersas o difíciles de encontrar.

O, P, Q

ocean current
A mass of moving ocean water. (p. 84)

> **corriente oceánica** Una masa de agua oceánica en movimiento.

overfishing
The catching of fish at a faster rate than they can reproduce. (p. 131)

> **sobrepesca** La captura de peces a un ritmo mayor a la que pueden reproducirse.

permeable
Allowing the passage of water. (p. 24)

> **permeable** Que permite el paso del agua.

phytoplankton (fy-toh-PLANGK-tuhn)
Microscopic floating organisms that live in water and, like plants, convert sunlight and carbon dioxide into food. (p. 126)

> **fitoplancton** Organismos microscópicos que flotan y viven en el agua y, al igual que las plantas, convierten la luz del Sol y el dióxido de carbono en alimento.

point-source pollution
Pollution that enters water from a known source. (p. 54)

> **contaminación por fuentes puntuales** Contaminación que entra al agua proveniente de una fuente conocida.

precipitation
Any type of liquid or solid water that falls to Earth's surface, such as rain, snow, or hail. (p. 13)

> **precipitación** Cualquier tipo de agua líquida o sólida que cae a la superficie de la Tierra, como por ejemplo lluvia, nieve o granizo.

R

radiation (ray-dee-AY-shuhn)
Energy that travels across distances as certain types of waves. (p. xv)

> **radiación** Energía que viaja a través de las distancias en forma de ciertos tipos de ondas.

rip current
A narrow stream of water that breaks through sandbars and drains rapidly back into deeper water. (p. 92)

> **corriente de retorno** Una estrecha corriente de agua que atraviesa barras de arena y drena rápidamente hacia aguas más profundas.

S

salinity (suh-LIHN-ih-tee)
The measure of the amount of dissolved salt contained in water. (p. 76)

> **salinidad** La medida de la cantidad de sal disuelta en el agua.

salt water
Water that contains dissolved salts and other minerals. Oceans consist of salt water. (p. 11)

> **agua salada** Agua que contiene sales disueltas y otros minerales. Los océanos están compuestos de agua salada.

septic system
A small sewage system, often for one home or business, that uses an underground tank to treat wastewater. (p. 54)

> **sistema séptico** Un pequeño sistema de aguas residuales, a menudo para un hogar o un negocio, que usa un tanque subterráneo para tratar las aguas de desecho.

sewage system
A system that collects and treats wastewater from a city or a town. (p. 53)

> **sistema de aguas residuales** Un sistema que recolecta y trata las aguas de desecho de una ciudad o población.

sonar (SO-NAHR)
A system that uses underwater sound waves to measure distance and locate objects. (p. 82)

> **sonar** Un sistema que usa ondas sonoras subacuáticas para medir distancias y ubicar objetos.

spring
A flow of water from the ground at a place where the surface of the land dips below the water table. (p. 28)

> **manantial** Un flujo de agua proveniente del suelo en un punto donde la superficie de la tierra desciende por debajo del nivel freático.

spring tide

A tide of large range occurring during the new and full moons, resulting in an extra-high tidal bulge and an extra-low tidal dip. (p. 99)

marea viva Una marea de amplio rango que ocurre durante la luna nueva y la luna llena y que resulta en una protuberancia mareal más alta de lo normal y un descenso de la marea más bajo de lo normal.

system

A group of objects or phenomena that interact. A system can be as simple as a rope, a pulley, and a mass. It also can be as complex as the interaction of energy and matter in the four spheres of the Earth system.

sistema Un grupo de objetos o fenómenos que interactúan. Un sistema puede ser algo tan sencillo como una cuerda, una polea y una masa. También puede ser algo tan complejo como la interacción de la energía y la materia en las cuatro esferas del sistema de la Tierra.

T

technology

The use of scientific knowledge to solve problems or engineer new products, tools, or processes.

tecnología El uso de conocimientos científicos para resolver problemas o para diseñar nuevos productos, herramientas o procesos.

theory

In science, a set of widely accepted explanations of observations and phenomena. A theory is a well-tested explanation that is consistent with all available evidence.

teoría En las ciencias, un conjunto de explicaciones de observaciones y fenómenos que es ampliamente aceptado. Una teoría es una explicación bien probada que es consecuente con la evidencia disponible.

tidal range

The difference in height between high tide and low tide. (p. 98)

rango de marea La diferencia en altura entre la marea alta y la marea baja.

tide

The periodic rising and falling of the water level of the ocean due to the gravitational pulls of the Moon and the Sun. (p. 96)

marea La subida y caída periódica del nivel del agua del océano debido a las atracciones gravitacionales de la Luna y del Sol.

turnover

The yearly rising and sinking of cold and warm water layers in a lake. (p. 19)

renovación La ascensión y el hundimiento anual de las capas de agua fría y agua cálida en un lago.

U, V

upwelling

The vertical movement of deep water up to the surface. (p. 86)

surgencia El movimiento vertical del agua profunda a la superficie.

variable

Any factor that can change in a controlled experiment, observation, or model. (p. R30)

variable Cualquier factor que puede cambiar en un experimento controlado, en una observación o en un modelo.

volume

An amount of three-dimensional space, often used to describe the space that an object takes up.

volumen Una cantidad de espacio tridimensional; a menudo se usa este término para describir el espacio que ocupa un objeto.

W, X, Y, Z

water cycle

The continuous movement of water on Earth, through its atmosphere, and in the living things on Earth. (p. 12)

ciclo del agua El movimiento continuo de agua sobre la Tierra, por su atmósfera y dentro de los organismos vivos de la Tierra.

water table

The highest part in the ground that is saturated, or completely filled with water. (p. 25)

nivel freático La parte más alta del suelo que está saturada, o completamente llena de agua.

wetland

A wet, swampy area that is often flooded with water. (p. 116)

humedal Un área húmeda y pantanosa que a menudo está inundada de agua.

Index

Page numbers for definitions are printed in **boldface** type.
Page numbers for illustrations, maps, and charts are printed in *italics*.

INDEX

P, Q, R

INDEX

Acknowledgments

Photography

Cover © Denis Scott/Corbis; **i** © Denis Scott/Corbis; **iii** *left (top to bottom)* Photograph of James Trefil by Evan Cantwell; Photograph of Rita Ann Calvo by Joseph Calvo; Photograph of Linda Carnine by Amilcar Cifuentes; Photograph of Sam Miller by Samuel Miller; *right (top to bottom)* Photograph of Kenneth Cutler by Kenneth A. Cutler; Photograph of Donald Steely by Marni Stamm; Photograph of Vicky Vachon by Redfern Photographics; **vi** © Photographer's Choice/Getty Images; **vii** © Darrell Jones/Getty Images; **ix** Photographs by Sharon Hoogstraten; **xiv–xv** Doug Scott/age fotostock; **xvi–xvii** © Aflo Foto Agency; **xviii–ix** © Tim Fitzharris/Masterfile; **xx–xxi** AP/Wide World Photos; **xxii** © Vince Streano/Corbis; **xxiii** © Roger Ressmeyer/Corbis; **xxiv** *left* University of Florida Lightning Research Laboratory; *center* © Roger Ressmeyer/Corbis; **xxv** *center* © Mauro Fermariello/Science Researchers; *bottom* © Alfred Pasieka/Photo Researchers; **xxvi–xxvii** © Stocktrek/Corbis; *center* NOAA; **xxvii** *top* © Alan Schein Photography/Corbis; *right* Vaisala Oyj, Finland; **xxxii** © The Chedd-Angier Production Company; **2–3** © Ralph White/Corbis; **3** *center* © Roger Steene/imagequestmarine.com; *bottom* Wolcott Henry/National Geographic Image Collection; **4** *top* NOAA/Pacific Marine Environmental Laboratory; *bottom* © The Chedd-Angier Production Company; **5** © Orbital Imaging Corporation and processing by NASA Goddard Space Flight Center. Image provided by ORBIMAGE; **6–7** © John Lawrence/Getty Images; **7** *top* © Anderson Ross/Getty Images; *bottom* Photograph by Sharon Hoogstraten; **9, 12** Photograph by Sharon Hoogstraten; **14** © Jagdish Agarwal/Alamy Images; **15** *left, inset* AP/WideWorld Photos/NASA Jet Propulsion Laboratories; **16** Photograph by Sharon Hoogstraten; **18** *center inset* © NASA/Getty Images; *bottom* © Claver Carroll/photolibrary/PictureQuest; **20** © Bruce Heinemann/Photodisc/PictureQuest; **21** Photograph by Sharon Hoogstraten; **22** © The Image Bank/Getty Images; **23** © Ron Erwin Photography; **24, 27** Photograph by Sharon Hoogstraten; **28** Peter Essick/Aurora; **30** © Michael S. Lewis/Corbis; **31** *left, right* © Jon Arnold/Jon Arnold Images/Alamy Images; **32** *top* Peter Essick/Aurora ; *bottom* Photograph by Sharon Hoogstraten; **36** Photograph by Sharon Hoogstraten; **38–39** © Photographer's Choice/Getty Images; **39** *top, bottom* Photograph by Sharon Hoogstraten; **41** AP/Wide World Photos; **42** © Charles E. Rotkin/Corbis; **43** *top* Photograph by Sharon Hoogstraten; *bottom* © Michael Andrews/Animals Animals/Earth Scenes; **44** *top* © Geoff Tompkinson/Photo Researchers; *bottom* AP/Wide World Photos; **45** © Macduff Everton/Corbis; **46** © Shubroto Chattopadhyay/Index Stock Imagery/PictureQuest; **47** © 1987 Tom Bean; **48** AP/Wide World Photos; **49** © J.C. Carton/Bruce Coleman, Inc./PictureQuest; **50** Photograph by Sharon Hoogstraten; **51** AP/Wide World Photos; **56** *left* © Brand X Pictures; *right* © Photodisc/Getty Images; **57** AP/Wide World Photos; **58** *top* © William Taufic/Corbis; *bottom left, right* Photograph by Sharon Hoogstraten; **60** © Dieter Melhorn/Alamy Images; **61** AP/Wide World Photos; **62** *top left* © Digital Vision; *top right* © Bob Melnychuk/Getty Images; *center left* © Photodisc/Getty Images; *center right* © Digital Vision; *bottom* AP/Wide World Photos; **63** Photograph by Sharon Hoogstraten; **65** NASA Goddard Space Flight Center Scientific Visualization Studio; **67** *left* © Denny Eilers/Grant Heilman Photography; *left inset* © Bob Rowan/Progressive Image/Corbis; *right* AP/WideWorld Photos; **68** *top* AP/Wide World Photos; *bottom* NASA Goddard Space Flight Center Scientific Visualization Studio; **72–73** © Darrell Jones/Getty Images; **73** *top, center* Photograph by Sharon Hoogstraten; **75** Photograph by Sharon Hoogstraten; **77** © Roger Antrobus/Corbis; **78** *top* Photograph by Sharon Hoogstraten; *bottom* © Jane Burton/Bruce Coleman, Inc.; **79** *bottom* NASA/Photo Researchers; **81** Emory Kristof/National Geographic Image Collection; **83** Walter H. F. Smith/NOAA; **84** Photograph by Sharon Hoogstraten; **85** © AFP/Corbis/NASA; **86** © Dan Gair Photographic/Index Stock Imagery/PictureQuest; **87** Photograph by Sharon Hoogstraten; **88** *left* Ron Erwin Photography; *right* © Bettmann/Corbis; **89** Photograph by Sharon Hoogstraten; **92** © C.C. Lockwood/Bruce Coleman, Inc.; **93** © Buddy Mays/Corbis; **94** *top* AP/Wide World Photos; *bottom left, right* Photograph by Sharon Hoogstraten; **96** *top, bottom* © M. H. Black/Bruce Coleman, Inc.; **98** Photograph by Sharon Hoogstraten; **101** *left* © Attar Maher/Corbis; **104** Photograph by Sharon Hoogstraten; **106** *top* NOAA/OAR/National Undersea Research Program; *bottom* NOAA; **107** *top left* NOAA/OAR/National Undersea Research Program; *top right* The Granger Collection, New York; *bottom* NOAA Central Library; **108** *top* AP Wide World Photos; *center* © Silva Joao/Corbis Sygma; *bottom* Alan Schietzch/ARSTI/NOAA; **109** *top* OAR/National Undersea Research Program/Fairleigh Dickinson University; *bottom* Photograph by Ben Allsup/Webb Research Corporation; **110–111** © Brandon Cole; *top right* © Maximilian Weinzierl/Alamy Images; *center right* Photograph by Sharon Hoogstraten; **113** © Eric and David Hosking/Corbis; **115** *top, bottom* © Brandon Cole; **116** *top* Photograph by Sharon Hoogstraten; *bottom* © Robert Perron; **117** © W.K. Almond/Stock Boston/PictureQuest ; **118** *top* © Lee Foster/Bruce Coleman, Inc.; *right inset* © Masa Ushioda/V&W/Bruce Coleman, Inc.; **119** AP/Wide World Photos; **120** *left, inset* © Lowell Georgia/Corbis; **121** Photograph by Sharon Hoogstraten; **122, 124** © Stone/Getty Images; **125** *top* © Mark A. Johnson/Alamy; *bottom* Photograph by Sharon Hoogstraten; **127** © Norbert Wu; **128** *top* © Dr. Ken Mac Donald/Photo Researchers; *center left* © The Natural History Museum, London; *bottom* © John Burbidge/Photo Researchers; **129** *left* © B. Murton/Southampton Oceanography Centre/Photo Researchers; *inset* © NSF Oasis Project/Norbert Wu Productions; **130** Photograph by Sharon Hoogstraten; **131** © Stephen Frink Collection/Alamy Images; **132** *top* © Norbert Wu; *bottom* © Dani/Jeske/Animals Animals/Earth Scenes; **133** *bottom* Jan Stromme/Strom/Bruce Coleman, Inc.; **134** © Institute of Oceanographic Sciences/NERC/Photo Researchers; **135** *top* © James Marshall/Corbis; *bottom* © Dr. Morley Read/Photo Researchers; **136** © Simon Fraser/Photo Researchers; **137** *top left* © Richard A. Cooke/Corbis; *top right* © Dorling Kindersley; **138** *top* © Gary Bell/Alamy Images; *bottom* Photograph by Sharon Hoogstraten; **140** *bottom left* © Norbert Wu; *bottom right* Jan Stromme/Strom/Bruce Coleman, Inc.; **142** © Lawson Wood/Corbis; **R28** © Photodisc/Getty Images.

Illustrations and Maps

Accurate Art Inc. **143**
Ampersand Design Group **93**
Richard Bronson/Wildlife Art Ltd. **13, 19, 25, 26, 29, 34**
Peter Bull/Wildlife Art Ltd. **52, 53, 55, 68**
Steve Cowden **91**
Stephen Durke **11, 31, 47, 54, 66, 133**
Chris Forsey **17, 20, 34**

Gary Hincks **80–81**
Ian Jackson **115, 123, 127, 140**
Mapquest.com, Inc. **10, 30, 42, 44, 45, 47, 56, 61, 64, 65, 76, 77, 85, 88, 98, 101, 113, 117, 118, 122, 132, 134**
Morgan, Cain & Assoc. **77, 82, 85, 100, 133**
Dan Stuckenschneider **R11–R19, R22, R32, 101**
Raymond Turvey **86, 90–92**

Content Standards: 5–8

A. Science as Inquiry

As a result of activities in grades 5–8, all students should develop

Abilities Necessary to do Scientific Inquiry

A.1   Identify questions that can be answered through scientific investigations. Students should develop the ability to refine and refocus broad and ill-defined questions. An important aspect of this ability consists of students' ability to clarify questions and inquiries and direct them toward objects and phenomena that can be described, explained, or predicted by scientific investigations. Students should develop the ability to identify their questions with scientific ideas, concepts, and quantitative relationships that guide investigation.

A.2   Design and conduct a scientific investigation. Students should develop general abilities, such as systematic observation, making accurate measurements, and identifying and controlling variables. They should also develop the ability to clarify their ideas that are influencing and guiding the inquiry, and to understand how those ideas compare with current scientific knowledge. Students can learn to formulate questions, design investigations, execute investigations, interpret data, use evidence to generate explanations, propose alternative explanations, and critique explanations and procedures.

A.3   Use appropriate tools and techniques to gather, analyze, and interpret data. The use of tools and techniques, including mathematics, will be guided by the question asked and the investigations students design. The use of computers for the collection, summary, and display of evidence is part of this standard. Students should be able to access, gather, store, retrieve, and organize data, using hardware and software designed for these purposes.

A.4   Develop descriptions, explanations, predictions, and models using evidence. Students should base their explanation on what they observed, and as they develop cognitive skills, they should be able to differentiate explanation from description—providing causes for effects and establishing relationships based on evidence and logical argument. This standard requires a subject matter knowledge base so the students can effectively conduct investigations, because developing explanations establishes connections between the content of science and the contexts within which students develop new knowledge.

A.5   Think critically and logically to make the relationships between evidence and explanations. Thinking critically about evidence includes deciding what evidence should be used and accounting for anomalous data. Specifically, students should be able to review data from a simple experiment, summarize the data, and form a logical argument about the cause-and-effect relationships in the experiment. Students should begin to state some explanations in terms of the relationship between two or more variables.

A.6   Recognize and analyze alternative explanations and predictions. Students should develop the ability to listen to and respect the explanations proposed by other students. They should remain open to and acknowledge different ideas and explanations, be able to accept the skepticism of others, and consider alternative explanations.

A.7   Communicate scientific procedures and explanations. With practice, students should become competent at communicating experimental methods, following instructions, describing observations, summarizing the results of other groups, and telling other students about investigations and explanations.

A.8   Use mathematics in all aspects of scientific inquiry. Mathematics is essential to asking and answering questions about the natural world. Mathematics can be used to ask questions; to gather, organize, and present data; and to structure convincing explanations.

Understandings about Scientific Inquiry

A.9.a   Different kinds of questions suggest different kinds of scientific investigations. Some investigations involve observing and describing objects, organisms, or events; some involve collecting specimens; some involve experiments; some involve seeking more information; some involve discovery of new objects and phenomena; and some involve making models.

A.9.b   Current scientific knowledge and understanding guide scientific investigations. Different scientific domains employ different methods, core theories, and standards to advance scientific knowledge and understanding.

A.9.c   Mathematics is important in all aspects of scientific inquiry.

A.9.d   Technology used to gather data enhances accuracy and allows scientists to analyze and quantify results of investigations.

A.9.e   Scientific explanations emphasize evidence, have logically consistent arguments, and use scientific principles, models, and theories. The scientific community accepts and uses such explanations until displaced by better scientific ones. When such displacement occurs, science advances.

A.9.f   Science advances through legitimate skepticism. Asking questions and querying other scientists' explanations is part of scientific inquiry. Scientists evaluate the explanations proposed by other scientists by examining evidence, comparing evidence, identifying faulty reasoning, pointing out statements that go beyond the evidence, and suggesting alternative explanations for the same observations.

A.9.g   Scientific investigations sometimes result in new ideas and phenomena for study, generate new methods or procedures for an investigation, or develop new technologies to improve the collection of data. All of these results can lead to new investigations.

B. Physical Science

As a result of their activities in grades 5–8, all students should develop an understanding of

Properties and Changes of Properties in Matter

B.1.a   A substance has characteristic properties, such as density, a boiling point, and solubility, all of which are independent of the amount of the sample. A mixture of substances often can be separated into the original substances using one or more of the characteristic properties.

B.1.b   Substances react chemically in characteristic ways with other substances to form new substances (compounds) with different characteristic properties. In chemical reactions, the total mass is conserved. Substances often are placed in categories or groups if they react in similar ways; metals is an example of such a group.

B.1.c   Chemical elements do not break down during normal laboratory reactions involving such treatments as heating, exposure to electric current, or reaction with acids. There are more than 100 known elements that combine in a multitude of ways to produce compounds, which account for the living and nonliving substances that we encounter.

Motions and Forces

B.2.a   The motion of an object can be described by its position, direction of motion, and speed. That motion can be measured and represented on a graph.

B.2.b   An object that is not being subjected to a force will continue to move at a constant speed and in a straight line.

B.2.c   If more than one force acts on an object along a straight line, then the forces will reinforce or cancel one another, depending on their direction and magnitude. Unbalanced forces will cause changes in the speed or direction of an object's motion.

Transfer of Energy

B.3.a   Energy is a property of many substances and is associated with heat, light, electricity, mechanical motion, sound, nuclei, and the nature of a chemical. Energy is transferred in many ways.

B.3.b   Heat moves in predictable ways, flowing from warmer objects to cooler ones, until both reach the same temperature.

B.3.c   Light interacts with matter by transmission (including refraction), absorption, or scattering (including reflection). To see an object, light from that object—emitted by or scattered from it—must enter the eye.

B.3.d   Electrical circuits provide a means of transferring electrical energy when heat, light, sound, and chemical changes are produced.

B.3.e   In most chemical and nuclear reactions, energy is transferred into or out of a system. Heat, light, mechanical motion, or electricity might all be involved in such transfers.

B.3.f   The sun is a major source of energy for changes on the earth's surface. The sun loses energy by emitting light. A tiny fraction of that light reaches the earth, transferring energy from the sun to the earth. The sun's energy arrives as light with a range of wavelengths, consisting of visible light, infrared, and ultraviolet radiation.

C. Life Science

As a result of their activities in grades 5–8, all students should develop understanding of

Structure and Function in Living Systems

C.1.a   Living systems at all levels of organization demonstrate the complementary nature of structure and function. Important levels of organization for structure and function include cells, organs, tissues, organ systems, whole organisms, and ecosystems.

C.1.b   All organisms are composed of cells—the fundamental unit of life. Most organisms are single cells; other organisms, including humans, are multicellular.

C.1.c   Cells carry on the many functions needed to sustain life. They grow and divide, thereby producing more cells. This requires that they take in nutrients, which they use to provide energy for the work that cells do and to make the materials that a cell or an organism needs.

C.1.d   Specialized cells perform specialized functions in multicellular organisms. Groups of specialized cells cooperate to form a tissue, such as a muscle. Different tissues are in turn grouped together to form larger functional units, called organs. Each type of cell, tissue, and organ has a distinct structure and set of functions that serve the organism as a whole.

C.1.e   The human organism has systems for digestion, respiration, reproduction, circulation, excretion, movement, control, and coordination, and for protection from disease. These systems interact with one another.

C.1.f   Disease is a breakdown in structures or functions of an organism. Some diseases are the result of intrinsic failures of the system. Others are the result of damage by infection by other organisms.

Reproduction and Heredity

C.2.a   Reproduction is a characteristic of all living systems; because no individual organism lives forever, reproduction is essential to the continuation of every species. Some organisms reproduce asexually. Other organisms reproduce sexually.

C.2.b   In many species, including humans, females produce eggs and males produce sperm. Plants also reproduce sexually—the egg and sperm are produced in the flowers of flowering plants. An egg and sperm unite to begin development of a new individual. That new individual receives genetic information from its mother (via the egg) and its father (via the sperm). Sexually produced offspring never are identical to either of their parents.

C.2.c   Every organism requires a set of instructions for specifying its traits. Heredity is the passage of these instructions from one generation to another.

C.2.d   Hereditary information is contained in genes, located in the chromosomes of each cell. Each gene carries a single unit of information. An inherited trait of an individual can be determined by one or by many genes, and a single gene can influence more than one trait. A human cell contains many thousands of different genes.

C.2.e   The characteristics of an organism can be described in terms of a combination of traits. Some traits are inherited and others result from interactions with the environment.

Regulation and Behavior

C.3.a   All organisms must be able to obtain and use resources, grow, reproduce, and maintain stable internal conditions while living in a constantly changing external environment.

C.3.b   Regulation of an organism's internal environment involves sensing the internal environment and changing physiological activities to keep conditions within the range required to survive.

C.3.c   Behavior is one kind of response an organism can make to an internal or environmental stimulus. A behavioral response requires coordination and communication at many levels, including cells, organ systems, and whole organisms. Behavioral response is a set of actions determined in part by heredity and in part from experience.

C.3.d   An organism's behavior evolves through adaptation to its environment. How a species moves, obtains food, reproduces, and responds to danger are based in the species' evolutionary history.

Populations and Ecosystems

C.4.a   A population consists of all individuals of a species that occur together at a given place and time. All populations living together and the physical factors with which they interact compose an ecosystem.

C.4.b   Populations of organisms can be categorized by the function they serve in an ecosystem. Plants and some microorganisms are producers—they make their own food. All animals, including humans, are consumers, which obtain food by eating other organisms. Decomposers, primarily bacteria and fungi, are consumers that use waste materials and dead organisms for food. Food webs identify the relationships among producers, consumers, and decomposers in an ecosystem.

C.4.c   For ecosystems, the major source of energy is sunlight. Energy entering ecosystems as sunlight is transferred by producers into chemical energy through photosynthesis. That energy then passes from organism to organism in food webs.

C.4.d   The number of organisms an ecosystem can support depends on the resources available and abiotic factors, such as quantity of light and water, range of temperatures, and soil composition. Given adequate biotic and abiotic resources and no disease or predators, populations (including humans) increase at rapid rates. Lack of resources and other factors, such as predation and climate, limit the growth of populations in specific niches in the ecosystem.

Diversity and Adaptations of Organisms

C.5.a   Millions of species of animals, plants, and microorganisms are alive today. Although different species might look dissimilar, the unity among organisms becomes apparent from an analysis of internal structures, the similarity of their chemical processes, and the evidence of common ancestry.

C.5.b   Biological evolution accounts for the diversity of species developed through gradual processes over many generations. Species acquire many of their unique characteristics through biological adaptation, which involves the selection of naturally occurring variations in populations. Biological adaptations include changes in structures, behaviors, or physiology that enhance survival and reproductive success in a particular environment.

C.5.c   Extinction of a species occurs when the environment changes and the adaptive characteristics of a species are insufficient to allow its survival. Fossils indicate that many organisms that lived long ago are extinct. Extinction of species is common; most of the species that have lived on the earth no longer exist.

D. Earth and Space Science

As a result of their activities in grades 5–8, all students should develop an understanding of

Structure of the Earth System

D.1.a The solid earth is layered with a lithosphere; hot, convecting mantle; and dense, metallic core.

D.1.b Lithospheric plates on the scales of continents and oceans constantly move at rates of centimeters per year in response to movements in the mantle. Major geological events, such as earthquakes, volcanic eruptions, and mountain building, result from these plate motions.

D.1.c Land forms are the result of a combination of constructive and destructive forces. Constructive forces include crustal deformation, volcanic eruption, and deposition of sediment, while destructive forces include weathering and erosion.

D.1.d Some changes in the solid earth can be described as the "rock cycle." Old rocks at the earth's surface weather, forming sediments that are buried, then compacted, heated, and often recrystallized into new rock. Eventually, those new rocks may be brought to the surface by the forces that drive plate motions, and the rock cycle continues.

D.1.e Soil consists of weathered rocks and decomposed organic material from dead plants, animals, and bacteria. Soils are often found in layers, with each having a different chemical composition and texture.

D.1.f Water, which covers the majority of the earth's surface, circulates through the crust, oceans, and atmosphere in what is known as the "water cycle." Water evaporates from the earth's surface, rises and cools as it moves to higher elevations, condenses as rain or snow, and falls to the surface where it collects in lakes, oceans, soil, and in rocks underground.

D.1.g Water is a solvent. As it passes through the water cycle it dissolves minerals and gases and carries them to the oceans.

D.1.h The atmosphere is a mixture of nitrogen, oxygen, and trace gases that include water vapor. The atmosphere has different properties at different elevations.

D.1.i Clouds, formed by the condensation of water vapor, affect weather and climate.

D.1.j Global patterns of atmospheric movement influence local weather. Oceans have a major effect on climate, because water in the oceans holds a large amount of heat.

D.1.k Living organisms have played many roles in the earth system, including affecting the composition of the atmosphere, producing some types of rocks, and contributing to the weathering of rocks.

Earth's History

D.2.a The earth processes we see today, including erosion, movement of lithospheric plates, and changes in atmospheric composition, are similar to those that occurred in the past. Earth history is also influenced by occasional catastrophes, such as the impact of an asteroid or comet.

D.2.b Fossils provide important evidence of how life and environmental conditions have changed.

Earth in the Solar System

D.3.a The earth is the third planet from the sun in a system that includes the moon, the sun, eight other planets and their moons, and smaller objects, such as asteroids and comets. The sun, an average star, is the central and largest body in the solar system.

D.3.b Most objects in the solar system are in regular and predictable motion. Those motions explain such phenomena as the day, the year, phases of the moon, and eclipses.

D.3.c Gravity is the force that keeps planets in orbit around the sun and governs the rest of the motion in the solar system. Gravity alone holds us to the earth's surface and explains the phenomena of the tides.

D.3.d The sun is the major source of energy for phenomena on the earth's surface, such as growth of plants, winds, ocean currents, and the water cycle. Seasons result from variations in the amount of the sun's energy hitting the surface, due to the tilt of the earth's rotation on its axis and the length of the day.

E. Science and Technology

As a result of activities in grades 5–8, all students should develop

Abilities of Technological Design

E.1 Identify appropriate problems for technological design. Students should develop their abilities by identifying a specified need, considering its various aspects, and talking to different potential users or beneficiaries. They should appreciate that for some needs, the cultural backgrounds and beliefs of different groups can affect the criteria for a suitable product.

E.2 Design a solution or product. Students should make and compare different proposals in the light of the criteria they have selected. They must consider constraints—such as cost, time, trade-offs, and materials needed—and communicate ideas with drawings and simple models.

E.3 Implement a proposed design. Students should organize materials and other resources, plan their work, make good use of group collaboration where appropriate, choose suitable tools and techniques, and work with appropriate measurement methods to ensure adequate accuracy.

E.4 Evaluate completed technological designs or products. Students should use criteria relevant to the original purpose or need, consider a variety of factors that might affect acceptability and suitability for intended users or beneficiaries, and develop measures of quality with respect to such criteria and factors; they should also suggest improvements and, for their own products, try proposed modifications.

E.5 Communicate the process of technological design. Students should review and describe any completed piece of work and identify the stages of problem identification, solution design, implementation, and evaluation.

Understandings about Science and Technology

E.6.a Scientific inquiry and technological design have similarities and differences. Scientists pro-pose explanations for questions about the natural world, and engineers propose solutions relating to human problems, needs, and aspirations. Technological solutions are temporary; technologies exist within nature and so they cannot contravene physical or biological princi-ples; technological solutions have side effects; and technologies cost, carry risks, and provide benefits.

E.6.b Many different people in different cultures have made and continue to make contributions to science and technology.

E.6.c Science and technology are reciprocal. Science helps drive technology, as it addresses ques-tions that demand more sophisticated instruments and provides principles for better instrumentation and technique. Technology is essential to science, because it provides instruments and techniques that enable observations of objects and phenomena that are otherwise unobservable due to factors such as quantity, distance, location, size, and speed. Technology also provides tools for investigations, inquiry, and analysis.

E.6.d Perfectly designed solutions do not exist. All technological solutions have trade-offs, such as safety, cost, efficiency, and appearance. Engineers often build in back-up systems to provide safety. Risk is part of living in a highly technological world. Reducing risk often results in new technology.

E.6.e Technological designs have constraints. Some constraints are unavoidable, for example, properties of materials, or effects of weather and friction; other constraints limit choices in the design, for example, environmental protection, human safety, and aesthetics.

E.6.f Technological solutions have intended benefits and unintended consequences. Some conse-quences can be predicted, others cannot.

F. Science in Personal and Social Perspectives

As a result of activities in grades 5–8, all students should develop understanding of

Personal Health

F.1.a Regular exercise is important to the maintenance and improvement of health. The benefits of physical fitness include maintaining healthy weight, having energy and strength for rou-tine activities, good muscle tone, bone strength, strong heart/lung systems, and improved mental health. Personal exercise, especially developing cardiovascular endurance, is the foundation of physical fitness.

F.1.b The potential for accidents and the existence of hazards imposes the need for injury prevention. Safe living involves the development and use of safety precautions and the recognition of risk in personal decisions. Injury prevention has personal and social dimensions.

F.1.c The use of tobacco increases the risk of illness. Students should understand the influence of short-term social and psychological factors that lead to tobacco use, and the possible long-term detrimental effects of smoking and chewing tobacco.

F.1.d Alcohol and other drugs are often abused substances. Such drugs change how the body functions and can lead to addiction.

F.1.e Food provides energy and nutrients for growth and development. Nutrition requirements vary with body weight, age, sex, activity, and body functioning.

F.1.f   Sex drive is a natural human function that requires understanding. Sex is also a prominent means of transmitting diseases. The diseases can be prevented through a variety of precautions.

F.1.g   Natural environments may contain substances (for example, radon and lead) that are harmful to human beings. Maintaining environmental health involves establishing or monitoring quality standards related to use of soil, water, and air.

Populations, Resources, and Environments

F.2.a   When an area becomes overpopulated, the environment will become degraded due to the increased use of resources.

F.2.b   Causes of environmental degradation and resource depletion vary from region to region and from country to country.

Natural Hazards

F.3.a   Internal and external processes of the earth system cause natural hazards, events that change or destroy human and wildlife habitats, damage property, and harm or kill humans. Natural hazards include earthquakes, landslides, wildfires, volcanic eruptions, floods, storms, and even possible impacts of asteroids.

F.3.b   Human activities also can induce hazards through resource acquisition, urban growth, land-use decisions, and waste disposal. Such activities can accelerate many natural changes.

F.3.c   Natural hazards can present personal and societal challenges because misidentifying the change or incorrectly estimating the rate and scale of change may result in either too little attention and significant human costs or too much cost for unneeded preventive measures.

Risks and Benefits

F.4.a   Risk analysis considers the type of hazard and estimates the number of people that might be exposed and the number likely to suffer consequences. The results are used to determine the options for reducing or eliminating risks.

F.4.b   Students should understand the risks associated with natural hazards (fires, floods, tornadoes, hurricanes, earthquakes, and volcanic eruptions), with chemical hazards (pollutants in air, water, soil, and food), with biological hazards (pollen, viruses, bacterial, and parasites), social hazards (occupational safety and transportation), and with personal hazards (smoking, dieting, and drinking).

F.4.c   Individuals can use a systematic approach to thinking critically about risks and benefits. Examples include applying probability estimates to risks and comparing them to estimated personal and social benefits.

F.4.d   Important personal and social decisions are made based on perceptions of benefits and risks.

Science and Technology in Society

F.5.a   Science influences society through its knowledge and world view. Scientific knowledge and the procedures used by scientists influence the way many individuals in society think about themselves, others, and the environment. The effect of science on society is neither entirely beneficial nor entirely detrimental.

F.5.b   Societal challenges often inspire questions for scientific research, and social priorities often influence research priorities through the availability of funding for research.

F.5.c   Technology influences society through its products and processes. Technology influences the quality of life and the ways people act and interact. Technological changes are often accompanied by social, political, and economic changes that can be beneficial or detrimental to individuals and to society. Social needs, attitudes, and values influence the direction of technological development.

F.5.d   Science and technology have advanced through contributions of many different people, in different cultures, at different times in history. Science and technology have contributed enormously to economic growth and productivity among societies and groups within societies.

F.5.e   Scientists and engineers work in many different settings, including colleges and universities, businesses and industries, specific research institutes, and government agencies.

F.5.f   Scientists and engineers have ethical codes requiring that human subjects involved with research be fully informed about risks and benefits associated with the research before the individuals choose to participate. This ethic extends to potential risks to communities and property. In short, prior knowledge and consent are required for research involving human subjects or potential damage to property.

F.5.g   Science cannot answer all questions and technology cannot solve all human problems or meet all human needs. Students should understand the difference between scientific and other questions. They should appreciate what science and technology can reasonably contribute to society and what they cannot do. For example, new technologies often will decrease some risks and increase others.

G. History and Nature of Science

As a result of activities in grades 5–8, all students should develop understanding of

Science as a Human Endeavor

G.1.a   Women and men of various social and ethnic backgrounds—and with diverse interests, talents, qualities, and motivations—engage in the activities of science, engineering, and related fields such as the health professions. Some scientists work in teams, and some work alone, but all communicate extensively with others.

G.1.b   Science requires different abilities, depending on such factors as the field of study and type of inquiry. Science is very much a human endeavor, and the work of science relies on basic human qualities, such as reasoning, insight, energy, skill, and creativity—as well as on scientific habits of mind, such as intellectual honesty, tolerance of ambiguity, skepticism, and openness to new ideas.

Nature of Science

G.2.a   Scientists formulate and test their explanations of nature using observation, experiments, and theoretical and mathematical models. Although all scientific ideas are tentative and subject to change and improvement in principle, for most major ideas in science, there is much experimental and observational confirmation. Those ideas are not likely to change greatly in the future. Scientists do and have changed their ideas about nature when they encounter new experimental evidence that does not match their existing explanations.

G.2.b   In areas where active research is being pursued and in which there is not a great deal of experimental or observational evidence and understanding, it is normal for scientists to differ with one another about the interpretation of the evidence or theory being considered. Different scientists might publish conflicting experimental results or might draw different conclusions from the same data. Ideally, scientists acknowledge such conflict and work towards finding evidence that will resolve their disagreement.

G.2.c   It is part of scientific inquiry to evaluate the results of scientific investigations, experiments, observations, theoretical models, and the explanations proposed by other scientists. Evaluation includes reviewing the experimental procedures, examining the evidence, identifying faulty reasoning, pointing out statements that go beyond the evidence, and suggesting alternative explanations for the same observations. Although scientists may disagree about explanations of phenomena, about interpretations of data, or about the value of rival theories, they do agree that questioning, response to criticism, and open communication are integral to the process of science. As scientific knowledge evolves, major disagreements are eventually resolved through such interactions between scientists.

History of Science

G.3.a   Many individuals have contributed to the traditions of science. Studying some of these individuals provides further understanding of scientific inquiry, science as a human endeavor, the nature of science, and the relationships between science and society.

G.3.b   In historical perspective, science has been practiced by different individuals in different cultures. In looking at the history of many peoples, one finds that scientists and engineers of high achievement are considered to be among the most valued contributors to their culture.

G.3.c   Tracing the history of science can show how difficult it was for scientific innovators to break through the accepted ideas of their time to reach the conclusions that we currently take for granted.

1. The Nature of Science

By the end of the 8th grade, students should know that

1.A The Scientific World View

1.A.1 When similar investigations give different results, the scientific challenge is to judge whether the differences are trivial or significant, and it often takes further studies to decide. Even with similar results, scientists may wait until an investigation has been repeated many times before accepting the results as correct.

1.A.2 Scientific knowledge is subject to modification as new information challenges prevailing theories and as a new theory leads to looking at old observations in a new way.

1.A.3 Some scientific knowledge is very old and yet is still applicable today.

1.A.4 Some matters cannot be examined usefully in a scientific way. Among them are matters that by their nature cannot be tested objectively and those that are essentially matters of morality. Science can sometimes be used to inform ethical decisions by identifying the likely consequences of particular actions but cannot be used to establish that some action is either moral or immoral.

1.B Scientific Inquiry

1.B.1 Scientists differ greatly in what phenomena they study and how they go about their work. Although there is no fixed set of steps that all scientists follow, scientific investigations usually involve the collection of relevant evidence, the use of logical reasoning, and the application of imagination in devising hypotheses and explanations to make sense of the collected evidence.

1.B.2 If more than one variable changes at the same time in an experiment, the outcome of the experiment may not be clearly attributable to any one of the variables. It may not always be possible to prevent outside variables from influencing the outcome of an investigation (or even to identify all of the variables), but collaboration among investigators can often lead to research designs that are able to deal with such situations.

1.B.3 What people expect to observe often affects what they actually do observe. Strong beliefs about what should happen in particular circumstances can prevent them from detecting other results. Scientists know about this danger to objectivity and take steps to try and avoid it when designing investigations and examining data. One safeguard is to have different investigators conduct independent studies of the same questions.

1.C The Scientific Enterprise

1.C.1 Important contributions to the advancement of science, mathematics, and technology have been made by different kinds of people, in different cultures, at different times.

1.C.2 Until recently, women and racial minorities, because of restrictions on their education and employment opportunities, were essentially left out of much of the formal work of the science establishment; the remarkable few who overcame those obstacles were even then likely to have their work disregarded by the science establishment.

1.C.3 No matter who does science and mathematics or invents things, or when or where they do it, the knowledge and technology that result can eventually become available to everyone in the world.

1.C.4 Scientists are employed by colleges and universities, business and industry, hospitals, and many government agencies. Their places of work include offices, classrooms, laboratories, farms, factories, and natural field settings ranging from space to the ocean floor.

1.C.5 In research involving human subjects, the ethics of science require that potential subjects be fully informed about the risks and benefits associated with the research and of their right to refuse to participate. Science ethics also demand that scientists must not knowingly subject coworkers, students, the neighborhood, or the community to health or property risks without their prior knowledge and consent. Because animals cannot make informed choices, special care must be taken in using them in scientific research.

1.C.6 Computers have become invaluable in science because they speed up and extend people's ability to collect, store, compile, and analyze data, prepare research reports, and share data and ideas with investigators all over the world.

1.C.7 Accurate record-keeping, openness, and replication are essential for maintaining an investigator's credibility with other scientists and society.

3. The Nature of Technology

By the end of the 8th grade, students should know that

3.A Technology and Science

3.A.1 In earlier times, the accumulated information and techniques of each generation of workers were taught on the job directly to the next generation of workers. Today, the knowledge base for technology can be found as well in libraries of print and electronic resources and is often taught in the classroom.

3.A.2 Technology is essential to science for such purposes as access to outer space and other remote locations, sample collection and treatment, measurement, data collection and storage, computation, and communication of information.

3.A.3 Engineers, architects, and others who engage in design and technology use scientific knowledge to solve practical problems. But they usually have to take human values and limitations into account as well.

3.B Design and Systems

3.B.1   Design usually requires taking constraints into account. Some constraints, such as gravity or the properties of the materials to be used, are unavoidable. Other constraints, including economic, political, social, ethical, and aesthetic ones, limit choices.

3.B.2   All technologies have effects other than those intended by the design, some of which may have been predictable and some not. In either case, these side effects may turn out to be unacceptable to some of the population and therefore lead to conflict between groups.

3.B.3   Almost all control systems have inputs, outputs, and feedback. The essence of control is comparing information about what is happening to what people want to happen and then making appropriate adjustments. This procedure requires sensing information, processing it, and making changes. In almost all modern machines, microprocessors serve as centers of performance control.

3.B.4   Systems fail because they have faulty or poorly matched parts, are used in ways that exceed what was intended by the design, or were poorly designed to begin with. The most common ways to prevent failure are pretesting parts and procedures, overdesign, and redundancy.

3.C Issues in Technology

3.C.1   The human ability to shape the future comes from a capacity for generating knowledge and developing new technologies—and for communicating ideas to others.

3.C.2   Technology cannot always provide successful solutions for problems or fulfill every human need.

3.C.3   Throughout history, people have carried out impressive technological feats, some of which would be hard to duplicate today even with modern tools. The purposes served by these achievements have sometimes been practical, sometimes ceremonial.

3.C.4   Technology has strongly influenced the course of history and continues to do so. It is largely responsible for the great revolutions in agriculture, manufacturing, sanitation and medicine, warfare, transportation, information processing, and communications that have radically changed how people live.

3.C.5   New technologies increase some risks and decrease others. Some of the same technologies that have improved the length and quality of life for many people have also brought new risks.

3.C.6   Rarely are technology issues simple and one-sided. Relevant facts alone, even when known and available, usually do not settle matters entirely in favor of one side or another. That is because the contending groups may have different values and priorities. They may stand to gain or lose in different degrees, or may make very different predictions about what the future consequences of the proposed action will be.

3.C.7   Societies influence what aspects of technology are developed and how these are used. People control technology (as well as science) and are responsible for its effects.

4. The Physical Setting

By the end of the 8th grade, students should know that

4.A The Universe

4.A.1 The sun is a medium-sized star located near the edge of a disk-shaped galaxy of stars, part of which can be seen as a glowing band of light that spans the sky on a very clear night. The universe contains many billions of galaxies, and each galaxy contains many billions of stars. To the naked eye, even the closest of these galaxies is no more than a dim, fuzzy spot.

4.A.2 The sun is many thousands of times closer to the earth than any other star. Light from the sun takes a few minutes to reach the earth, but light from the next nearest star takes a few years to arrive. The trip to that star would take the fastest rocket thousands of years. Some distant galaxies are so far away that their light takes several billion years to reach the earth. People on earth, therefore, see them as they were that long ago in the past.

4.A.3 Nine planets of very different size, composition, and surface features move around the sun in nearly circular orbits. Some planets have a great variety of moons and even flat rings of rock and ice particles orbiting around them. Some of these planets and moons show evidence of geologic activity. The earth is orbited by one moon, many artificial satellites, and debris.

4.A.4 Large numbers of chunks of rock orbit the sun. Some of those that the earth meets in its yearly orbit around the sun glow and disintegrate from friction as they plunge through the atmosphere—and sometimes impact the ground. Other chunks of rocks mixed with ice have long, off-center orbits that carry them close to the sun, where the sun's radiation (of light and particles) boils off frozen material from their surfaces and pushes it into a long, illuminated tail.

4.B The Earth

4.B.1 We live on a relatively small planet, the third from the sun in the only system of planets definitely known to exist (although other, similar systems may be discovered in the universe).

4.B.2 The earth is mostly rock. Three-fourths of its surface is covered by a relatively thin layer of water (some of it frozen), and the entire planet is surrounded by a relatively thin blanket of air. It is the only body in the solar system that appears able to support life. The other planets have compositions and conditions very different from the earth's.

4.B.3 Everything on or anywhere near the earth is pulled toward the earth's center by gravitational force.

4.B.4 Because the earth turns daily on an axis that is tilted relative to the plane of the earth's yearly orbit around the sun, sunlight falls more intensely on different parts of the earth during the year. The difference in heating of the earth's surface produces the planet's seasons and weather patterns.

4.B.5 The moon's orbit around the earth once in about 28 days changes what part of the moon is lighted by the sun and how much of that part can be seen from the earth—the phases of the moon.

4.B.6 Climates have sometimes changed abruptly in the past as a result of changes in the earth's crust, such as volcanic eruptions or impacts of huge rocks from space. Even relatively small changes in atmospheric or ocean content can have widespread effects on climate if the change lasts long enough.

4.B.7 The cycling of water in and out of the atmosphere plays an important role in determining climatic patterns. Water evaporates from the surface of the earth, rises and cools, condenses into rain or snow, and falls again to the surface. The water falling on land collects in rivers and lakes, soil, and porous layers of rock, and much of it flows back into the ocean.

4.B.8 Fresh water, limited in supply, is essential for life and also for most industrial processes. Rivers, lakes, and groundwater can be depleted or polluted, becoming unavailable or unsuitable for life.

4.B.9 Heat energy carried by ocean currents has a strong influence on climate around the world.

4.B.10 Some minerals are very rare and some exist in great quantities, but—for practical purposes—the ability to recover them is just as important as their abundance. As minerals are depleted, obtaining them becomes more difficult. Recycling and the development of substitutes can reduce the rate of depletion but may also be costly.

4.B.11 The benefits of the earth's resources—such as fresh water, air, soil, and trees—can be reduced by using them wastefully or by deliberately or inadvertently destroying them. The atmosphere and the oceans have a limited capacity to absorb wastes and recycle materials naturally. Cleaning up polluted air, water, or soil or restoring depleted soil, forests, or fishing grounds can be very difficult and costly.

4.C Processes that Shape the Earth

4.C.1 The interior of the earth is hot. Heat flow and movement of material within the earth cause earthquakes and volcanic eruptions and create mountains and ocean basins. Gas and dust from large volcanoes can change the atmosphere.

4.C.2 Some changes in the earth's surface are abrupt (such as earthquakes and volcanic eruptions) while other changes happen very slowly (such as uplift and wearing down of mountains). The earth's surface is shaped in part by the motion of water and wind over very long times, which act to level mountain ranges.

4.C.3 Sediments of sand and smaller particles (sometimes containing the remains of organisms) are gradually buried and are cemented together by dissolved minerals to form solid rock again.

4.C.4 Sedimentary rock buried deep enough may be reformed by pressure and heat, perhaps melting and recrystallizing into different kinds of rock. These re-formed rock layers may be forced up again to become land surface and even mountains. Subsequently, this new rock too will erode. Rock bears evidence of the minerals, temperatures, and forces that created it.

4.C.5 Thousands of layers of sedimentary rock confirm the long history of the changing surface of the earth and the changing life forms whose remains are found in successive layers. The youngest layers are not always found on top, because of folding, breaking, and uplift of layers.

4.C.6 Although weathered rock is the basic component of soil, the composition and texture of soil and its fertility and resistance to erosion are greatly influenced by plant roots and debris, bacteria, fungi, worms, insects, rodents, and other organisms.

4.C.7 Human activities, such as reducing the amount of forest cover, increasing the amount and variety of chemicals released into the atmosphere, and intensive farming, have changed the earth's land, oceans, and atmosphere. Some of these changes have decreased the capacity of the environment to support some life forms.

4.D Structure of Matter

4.D.1 All matter is made up of atoms, which are far too small to see directly through a micro-scope. The atoms of any element are alike but are different from atoms of other elements. Atoms may stick together in well-defined molecules or may be packed together in large arrays. Different arrangements of atoms into groups compose all substances.

4.D.2 Equal volumes of different substances usually have different weights.

4.D.3 Atoms and molecules are perpetually in motion. Increased temperature means greater average energy, so most substances expand when heated. In solids, the atoms are closely locked in position and can only vibrate. In liquids, the atoms or molecules have higher energy, are more loosely connected, and can slide past one another; some molecules may get enough energy to escape into a gas. In gases, the atoms or molecules have still more energy and are free of one another except during occasional collisions.

4.D.4 The temperature and acidity of a solution influence reaction rates. Many substances dis-solve in water, which may greatly facilitate reactions between them.

4.D.5 Scientific ideas about elements were borrowed from some Greek philosophers of 2,000 years earlier, who believed that everything was made from four basic substances: air, earth, fire, and water. It was the combinations of these "elements" in different proportions that gave other substances their observable properties. The Greeks were wrong about those four, but now over 100 different elements have been identified, some rare and some plenti-ful, out of which everything is made. Because most elements tend to combine with others, few elements are found in their pure form.

4.D.6 There are groups of elements that have similar properties, including highly reactive metals, less-reactive metals, highly reactive nonmetals (such as chlorine, fluorine, and oxygen), and some almost completely nonreactive gases (such as helium and neon). An especially impor-tant kind of reaction between substances involves combination of oxygen with something else—as in burning or rusting. Some elements don't fit into any of the categories; among them are carbon and hydrogen, essential elements of living matter.

4.D.7 No matter how substances within a closed system interact with one another, or how they combine or break apart, the total weight of the system remains the same. The idea of atoms explains the conservation of matter: If the number of atoms stays the same no matter how they are rearranged, then their total mass stays the same.

4.E Energy Transformations

4.E.1 Energy cannot be created or destroyed, but only changed from one form into another.

4.E.2 Most of what goes on in the universe—from exploding stars and biological growth to the operation of machines and the motion of people—involves some form of energy being transformed into another. Energy in the form of heat is almost always one of the products of an energy transformation.

4.E.3 Heat can be transferred through materials by the collisions of atoms or across space by radiation. If the material is fluid, currents will be set up in it that aid the transfer of heat.

4.E.4 Energy appears in different forms. Heat energy is in the disorderly motion of molecules; chemical energy is in the arrangement of atoms; mechanical energy is in moving bodies or in elastically distorted shapes; gravitational energy is in the separation of mutually attracting masses.

4.F Motion

4.F.1 Light from the sun is made up of a mixture of many different colors of light, even though to the eye the light looks almost white. Other things that give off or reflect light have a different mix of colors.

4.F.2 Something can be "seen" when light waves emitted or reflected by it enter the eye—just as something can be "heard" when sound waves from it enter the ear.

4.F.3 An unbalanced force acting on an object changes its speed or direction of motion, or both. If the force acts toward a single center, the object's path may curve into an orbit around the center.

4.F.4 Vibrations in materials set up wavelike disturbances that spread away from the source. Sound and earthquake waves are examples. These and other waves move at different speeds in different materials.

4.F.5 Human eyes respond to only a narrow range of wavelengths of electromagnetic radiation— visible light. Differences of wavelength within that range are perceived as differences in color.

4.G Forces of Nature

4.G.1 Every object exerts gravitational force on every other object. The force depends on how much mass the objects have and on how far apart they are. The force is hard to detect unless at least one of the objects has a lot of mass.

4.G.2 The sun's gravitational pull holds the earth and other planets in their orbits, just as the planets' gravitational pull keeps their moons in orbit around them.

4.G.3 Electric currents and magnets can exert a force on each other.

5. The Living Environment

By the end of the 8th grade, students should know that

5.A Diversity of Life

5.A.1   One of the most general distinctions among organisms is between plants, which use sunlight to make their own food, and animals, which consume energy-rich foods. Some kinds of organisms, many of them microscopic, cannot be neatly classified as either plants or animals.

5.A.2   Animals and plants have a great variety of body plans and internal structures that contribute to their being able to make or find food and reproduce.

5.A.3   Similarities among organisms are found in internal anatomical features, which can be used to infer the degree of relatedness among organisms. In classifying organisms, biologists consider details of internal and external structures to be more important than behavior or general appearance.

5.A.4   For sexually reproducing organisms, a species comprises all organisms that can mate with one another to produce fertile offspring.

5.A.5   All organisms, including the human species, are part of and depend on two main interconnected global food webs. One includes microscopic ocean plants, the animals that feed on them, and finally the animals that feed on those animals. The other web includes land plants, the animals that feed on them, and so forth. The cycles continue indefinitely because organisms decompose after death to return food material to the environment.

5.B Heredity

5.B.1   In some kinds of organisms, all the genes come from a single parent, whereas in organisms that have sexes, typically half of the genes come from each parent.

5.B.2   In sexual reproduction, a single specialized cell from a female merges with a specialized cell from a male. As the fertilized egg, carrying genetic information from each parent, multiplies to form the complete organism with about a trillion cells, the same genetic information is copied in each cell.

5.B.3   New varieties of cultivated plants and domestic animals have resulted from selective breeding for particular traits.

5.C Cells

5.C.1   All living things are composed of cells, from just one to many millions, whose details usually are visible only through a microscope. Different body tissues and organs are made up of different kinds of cells. The cells in similar tissues and organs in other animals are similar to those in human beings but differ somewhat from cells found in plants.

5.C.2   Cells repeatedly divide to make more cells for growth and repair. Various organs and tissues function to serve the needs of cells for food, air, and waste removal.

5.C.3   Within cells, many of the basic functions of organisms—such as extracting energy from food and getting rid of waste—are carried out. The way in which cells function is similar in all living organisms.

5.C.4   About two-thirds of the weight of cells is accounted for by water, which gives cells many of their properties.

5.D Interdependence of Life

5.D.1 In all environments—freshwater, marine, forest, desert, grassland, mountain, and others—organisms with similar needs may compete with one another for resources, including food, space, water, air, and shelter. In any particular environment, the growth and survival of organisms depend on the physical conditions.

5.D.2 Two types of organisms may interact with one another in several ways: They may be in a producer/consumer, predator/prey, or parasite/host relationship. Or one organism may scavenge or decompose another. Relationships may be competitive or mutually beneficial. Some species have become so adapted to each other that neither could survive without the other.

5.E Flow of Matter and Energy

5.E.1 Food provides molecules that serve as fuel and building material for all organisms. Plants use the energy in light to make sugars out of carbon dioxide and water. This food can be used immediately for fuel or materials or it may be stored for later use. Organisms that eat plants break down the plant structures to produce the materials and energy they need to survive. Then they are consumed by other organisms.

5.E.2 Over a long time, matter is transferred from one organism to another repeatedly and between organisms and their physical environment. As in all material systems, the total amount of matter remains constant, even though its form and location change.

5.E.3 Energy can change from one form to another in living things. Animals get energy from oxidizing their food, releasing some of its energy as heat. Almost all food energy comes originally from sunlight.

5.F Evolution of Life

5.F.1 Small differences between parents and offspring can accumulate (through selective breeding) in successive generations so that descendants are very different from their ancestors.

5.F.2 Individual organisms with certain traits are more likely than others to survive and have offspring. Changes in environmental conditions can affect the survival of individual organisms and entire species.

5.F.3 Many thousands of layers of sedimentary rock provide evidence for the long history of the earth and for the long history of changing life forms whose remains are found in the rocks. More recently deposited rock layers are more likely to contain fossils resembling existing species.

6. The Human Organism

By the end of the 8th grade, students should know that

6.A Human Identity

6.A.1   Like other animals, human beings have body systems for obtaining and providing energy, defense, reproduction, and the coordination of body functions.

6.A.2   Human beings have many similarities and differences. The similarities make it possible for human beings to reproduce and to donate blood and organs to one another throughout the world. Their differences enable them to create diverse social and cultural arrangements and to solve problems in a variety of ways.

6.A.3   Fossil evidence is consistent with the idea that human beings evolved from earlier species.

6.A.4   Specialized roles of individuals within other species are genetically programmed, whereas human beings are able to invent and modify a wider range of social behavior.

6.A.5   Human beings use technology to match or excel many of the abilities of other species. Technology has helped people with disabilities survive and live more conventional lives.

6.A.6   Technologies having to do with food production, sanitation, and disease prevention have dramatically changed how people live and work and have resulted in rapid increases in the human population.

6.B Human Development

6.B.1   Fertilization occurs when sperm cells from a male's testes are deposited near an egg cell from the female ovary, and one of the sperm cells enters the egg cell. Most of the time, by chance or design, a sperm never arrives or an egg isn't available.

6.B.2   Contraception measures may incapacitate sperm, block their way to the egg, prevent the release of eggs, or prevent the fertilized egg from implanting successfully.

6.B.3   Following fertilization, cell division produces a small cluster of cells that then differentiate by appearance and function to form the basic tissues of an embryo. During the first three months of pregnancy, organs begin to form. During the second three months, all organs and body features develop. During the last three months, the organs and features mature enough to function well after birth. Patterns of human development are similar to those of other vertebrates.

6.B.4   The developing embryo—and later the newborn infant—encounters many risks from faults in its genes, its mother's inadequate diet, her cigarette smoking or use of alcohol or other drugs, or from infection. Inadequate child care may lead to lower physical and mental ability.

6.B.5   Various body changes occur as adults age. Muscles and joints become less flexible, bones and muscles lose mass, energy levels diminish, and the senses become less acute. Women stop releasing eggs and hence can no longer reproduce. The length and quality of human life are influenced by many factors, including sanitation, diet, medical care, sex, genes, environmental conditions, and personal health behaviors.

6.C Basic Functions

6.C.1 Organs and organ systems are composed of cells and help to provide all cells with basic needs.

6.C.2 For the body to use food for energy and building materials, the food must first be digested into molecules that are absorbed and transported to cells.

6.C.3 To burn food for the release of energy stored in it, oxygen must be supplied to cells, and carbon dioxide removed. Lungs take in oxygen for the combustion of food and they eliminate the carbon dioxide produced. The urinary system disposes of dissolved waste molecules, the intestinal tract removes solid wastes, and the skin and lungs rid the body of heat energy. The circulatory system moves all these substances to or from cells where they are needed or produced, responding to changing demands.

6.C.4 Specialized cells and the molecules they produce identify and destroy microbes that get inside the body.

6.C.5 Hormones are chemicals from glands that affect other body parts. They are involved in helping the body respond to danger and in regulating human growth, development, and reproduction.

6.C.6 Interactions among the senses, nerves, and brain make possible the learning that enables human beings to cope with changes in their environment.

6.D Learning

6.D.1 Some animal species are limited to a repertoire of genetically determined behaviors; others have more complex brains and can learn a wide variety of behaviors. All behavior is affected by both inheritance and experience.

6.D.2 The level of skill a person can reach in any particular activity depends on innate abilities, the amount of practice, and the use of appropriate learning technologies.

6.D.3 Human beings can detect a tremendous range of visual and olfactory stimuli. The strongest stimulus they can tolerate may be more than a trillion times as intense as the weakest they can detect. Still, there are many kinds of signals in the world that people cannot detect directly.

6.D.4 Attending closely to any one input of information usually reduces the ability to attend to others at the same time.

6.D.5 Learning often results from two perceptions or actions occurring at about the same time. The more often the same combination occurs, the stronger the mental connection between them is likely to be. Occasionally a single vivid experience will connect two things permanently in people's minds.

6.D.6 Language and tools enable human beings to learn complicated and varied things from others.

6.E Physical Health

6.E.1   The amount of food energy (calories) a person requires varies with body weight, age, sex, activity level, and natural body efficiency. Regular exercise is important to maintain a healthy heart/lung system, good muscle tone, and bone strength.

6.E.2   Toxic substances, some dietary habits, and personal behavior may be bad for one's health. Some effects show up right away, others may not show up for many years. Avoiding toxic substances, such as tobacco, and changing dietary habits to reduce the intake of such things as animal fat increases the chances of living longer.

6.E.3   Viruses, bacteria, fungi, and parasites may infect the human body and interfere with normal body functions. A person can catch a cold many times because there are many varieties of cold viruses that cause similar symptoms.

6.E.4   White blood cells engulf invaders or produce antibodies that attack them or mark them for killing by other white cells. The antibodies produced will remain and can fight off subsequent invaders of the same kind.

6.E.5   The environment may contain dangerous levels of substances that are harmful to human beings. Therefore, the good health of individuals requires monitoring the soil, air, and water and taking steps to keep them safe.

6.F Mental Health

6.F.1   Individuals differ greatly in their ability to cope with stressful situations. Both external and internal conditions (chemistry, personal history, values) influence how people behave.

6.F.2   Often people react to mental distress by denying that they have any problem. Sometimes they don't know why they feel the way they do, but with help they can sometimes uncover the reasons.

8. The Designed World

By the end of the 8th grade, students should know that

8.A Agriculture

8.A.1   Early in human history, there was an agricultural revolution in which people changed from hunting and gathering to farming. This allowed changes in the division of labor between men and women and between children and adults, and the development of new patterns of government.

8.A.2   People control the characteristics of plants and animals they raise by selective breeding and by preserving varieties of seeds (old and new) to use if growing conditions change.

8.A.3   In agriculture, as in all technologies, there are always trade-offs to be made. Getting food from many different places makes people less dependent on weather in any one place, yet more dependent on transportation and communication among far-flung markets. Specializing in one crop may risk disaster if changes in weather or increases in pest populations wipe out that crop. Also, the soil may be exhausted of some nutrients, which can be replenished by rotating the right crops.

8.A.4   Many people work to bring food, fiber, and fuel to U.S. markets. With improved technology, only a small fraction of workers in the United States actually plant and harvest the products that people use. Most workers are engaged in processing, packaging, transporting, and selling what is produced.

8.B Materials and Manufacturing

8.B.1 The choice of materials for a job depends on their properties and on how they interact with other materials. Similarly, the usefulness of some manufactured parts of an object depends on how well they fit together with the other parts.

8.B.2 Manufacturing usually involves a series of steps, such as designing a product, obtaining and preparing raw materials, processing the materials mechanically or chemically, and assembling, testing, inspecting, and packaging. The sequence of these steps is also often important.

8.B.3 Modern technology reduces manufacturing costs, produces more uniform products, and creates new synthetic materials that can help reduce the depletion of some natural resources.

8.B.4 Automation, including the use of robots, has changed the nature of work in most fields, including manufacturing. As a result, high-skill, high-knowledge jobs in engineering, computer programming, quality control, supervision, and maintenance are replacing many routine, manual-labor jobs. Workers therefore need better learning skills and flexibility to take on new and rapidly changing jobs.

8.C Energy Sources and Use

8.C.1 Energy can change from one form to another, although in the process some energy is always converted to heat. Some systems transform energy with less loss of heat than others.

8.C.2 Different ways of obtaining, transforming, and distributing energy have different environmental consequences.

8.C.3 In many instances, manufacturing and other technological activities are performed at a site close to an energy source. Some forms of energy are transported easily, others are not.

8.C.4 Electrical energy can be produced from a variety of energy sources and can be transformed into almost any other form of energy. Moreover, electricity is used to distribute energy quickly and conveniently to distant locations.

8.C.5 Energy from the sun (and the wind and water energy derived from it) is available indefinitely. Because the flow of energy is weak and variable, very large collection systems are needed. Other sources don't renew or renew only slowly.

8.C.6 Different parts of the world have different amounts and kinds of energy resources to use and use them for different purposes.

8.D Communication

8.D.1 Errors can occur in coding, transmitting, or decoding information, and some means of checking for accuracy is needed. Repeating the message is a frequently used method.

8.D.2 Information can be carried by many media, including sound, light, and objects. In this century, the ability to code information as electric currents in wires, electromagnetic waves in space, and light in glass fibers has made communication millions of times faster than is possible by mail or sound.

8.E Information Processing

8.E.1 Most computers use digital codes containing only two symbols, 0 and 1, to perform all operations. Continuous signals (analog) must be transformed into digital codes before they can be processed by a computer.

8.E.2 What use can be made of a large collection of information depends upon how it is organized. One of the values of computers is that they are able, on command, to reorganize information in a variety of ways, thereby enabling people to make more and better uses of the collection.

8.E.3 Computer control of mechanical systems can be much quicker than human control. In situations where events happen faster than people can react, there is little choice but to rely on computers. Most complex systems still require human oversight, however, to make certain kinds of judgments about the readiness of the parts of the system (including the computers) and the system as a whole to operate properly, to react to unexpected failures, and to evaluate how well the system is serving its intended purposes.

8.E.4 An increasing number of people work at jobs that involve processing or distributing information. Because computers can do these tasks faster and more reliably, they have become standard tools both in the workplace and at home.

8.F Health Technology

8.F.1 Sanitation measures such as the use of sewers, landfills, quarantines, and safe food handling are important in controlling the spread of organisms that cause disease. Improving sanitation to prevent disease has contributed more to saving human life than any advance in medical treatment.

8.F.2 The ability to measure the level of substances in body fluids has made it possible for physicians to make comparisons with normal levels, make very sophisticated diagnoses, and monitor the effects of the treatments they prescribe.

8.F.3 It is becoming increasingly possible to manufacture chemical substances such as insulin and hormones that are normally found in the body. They can be used by individuals whose own bodies cannot produce the amounts required for good health.

9. The Mathematical World

By the end of the 8th grade, students should know that

9.A Numbers

9.A.1   There have been systems for writing numbers other than the Arabic system of place values based on tens. The very old Roman numerals are now used only for dates, clock faces, or ordering chapters in a book. Numbers based on 60 are still used for describing time and angles.

9.A.2   A number line can be extended on the other side of zero to represent negative numbers. Negative numbers allow subtraction of a bigger number from a smaller number to make sense, and are often used when something can be measured on either side of some reference point (time, ground level, temperature, budget).

9.A.3   Numbers can be written in different forms, depending on how they are being used. How fractions or decimals based on measured quantities should be written depends on how precise the measurements are and how precise an answer is needed.

9.A.4   The operations + and − are inverses of each other—one undoes what the other does; likewise x and ÷ .

9.A.5   The expression a/b can mean different things: a parts of size $1/b$ each, a divided by b, or a compared to b.

9.A.6   Numbers can be represented by using sequences of only two symbols (such as 1 and 0, on and off); computers work this way.

9.A.7   Computations (as on calculators) can give more digits than make sense or are useful.

9.B Symbolic Relationships

9.B.1   An equation containing a variable may be true for just one value of the variable.

9.B.2   Mathematical statements can be used to describe how one quantity changes when another changes. Rates of change can be computed from differences in magnitudes and vice versa.

9.B.3   Graphs can show a variety of possible relationships between two variables. As one variable increases uniformly, the other may do one of the following: increase or decrease steadily, increase or decrease faster and faster, get closer and closer to some limiting value, reach some intermediate maximum or minimum, alternately increase and decrease indefinitely, increase or decrease in steps, or do something different from any of these.

9.C Shapes

9.C.1   Some shapes have special properties: triangular shapes tend to make structures rigid, and round shapes give the least possible boundary for a given amount of interior area. Shapes can match exactly or have the same shape in different sizes.

9.C.2   Lines can be parallel, perpendicular, or oblique.

9.C.3   Shapes on a sphere like the earth cannot be depicted on a flat surface without some distortion.

9.C.4   The graphic display of numbers may help to show patterns such as trends, varying rates of change, gaps, or clusters. Such patterns sometimes can be used to make predictions about the phenomena being graphed.

9.C.5   It takes two numbers to locate a point on a map or any other flat surface. The numbers may be two perpendicular distances from a point, or an angle and a distance from a point.

9.C.6   The scale chosen for a graph or drawing makes a big difference in how useful it is.

9.D Uncertainty

9.D.1   How probability is estimated depends on what is known about the situation. Estimates can be based on data from similar conditions in the past or on the assumption that all the possibilities are known.

9.D.2   Probabilities are ratios and can be expressed as fractions, percentages, or odds.

9.D.3   The mean, median, and mode tell different things about the middle of a data set.

9.D.4   Comparison of data from two groups should involve comparing both their middles and the spreads around them.

9.D.5   The larger a well-chosen sample is, the more accurately it is likely to represent the whole. But there are many ways of choosing a sample that can make it unrepresentative of the whole.

9.D.6   Events can be described in terms of being more or less likely, impossible, or certain.

9.E Reasoning

9.E.1   Some aspects of reasoning have fairly rigid rules for what makes sense; other aspects don't. If people have rules that always hold, and good information about a particular situation, then logic can help them to figure out what is true about it. This kind of reasoning requires care in the use of key words such as if, and, not, or, all, and some. Reasoning by similarities can suggest ideas but can't prove them one way or the other.

9.E.2   Practical reasoning, such as diagnosing or troubleshooting almost anything, may require many-step, branching logic. Because computers can keep track of complicated logic, as well as a lot of information, they are useful in a lot of problem-solving situations.

9.E.3   Sometimes people invent a general rule to explain how something works by summarizing observations. But people tend to overgeneralize, imagining general rules on the basis of only a few observations.

9.E.4   People are using incorrect logic when they make a statement such as "If A is true, then B is true; but A isn't true, therefore B isn't true either."

9.E.5   A single example can never prove that something is always true, but sometimes a single example can prove that something is not always true.

9.E.6   An analogy has some likenesses to but also some differences from the real thing.

10. Historical Perspectives

By the end of the 8th grade, students should know that

10.A Displacing the Earth from the Center of the Universe

10.A.1 The motion of an object is always judged with respect to some other object or point and so the idea of absolute motion or rest is misleading.

10.A.2 Telescopes reveal that there are many more stars in the night sky than are evident to the unaided eye, the surface of the moon has many craters and mountains, the sun has dark spots, and Jupiter and some other planets have their own moons.

10.F Understanding Fire

10.F.1 From the earliest times until now, people have believed that even though millions of different kinds of material seem to exist in the world, most things must be made up of combinations of just a few basic kinds of things. There has not always been agreement, however, on what those basic kinds of things are. One theory long ago was that the basic substances were earth, water, air, and fire. Scientists now know that these are not the basic substances. But the old theory seemed to explain many observations about the world.

10.F.2 Today, scientists are still working out the details of what the basic kinds of matter are and of how they combine, or can be made to combine, to make other substances.

10.F.3 Experimental and theoretical work done by French scientist Antoine Lavoisier in the decade between the American and French revolutions led to the modern science of chemistry.

10.F.4 Lavoisier's work was based on the idea that when materials react with each other many changes can take place but that in every case the total amount of matter afterward is the same as before. He successfully tested the concept of conservation of matter by conducting a series of experiments in which he carefully measured all the substances involved in burning, including the gases used and those given off.

10.F.5 Alchemy was chiefly an effort to change base metals like lead into gold and to produce an elixir that would enable people to live forever. It failed to do that or to create much knowledge of how substances react with each other. The more scientific study of chemistry that began in Lavoisier's time has gone far beyond alchemy in understanding reactions and producing new materials.

10.G Splitting the Atom

10.G.1 The accidental discovery that minerals containing uranium darken photographic film, as light does, led to the idea of radioactivity.

10.G.2 In their laboratory in France, Marie Curie and her husband, Pierre Curie, isolated two new elements that caused most of the radioactivity of the uranium mineral. They named one radium because it gave off powerful, invisible rays, and the other polonium in honor of Madame Curie's country of birth. Marie Curie was the first scientist ever to win the Nobel prize in two different fields—in physics, shared with her husband, and later in chemistry.

10.I Discovering Germs

10.I.1 Throughout history, people have created explanations for disease. Some have held that disease has spiritual causes, but the most persistent biological theory over the centuries was that illness resulted from an imbalance in the body fluids. The introduction of germ theory by Louis Pasteur and others in the 19th century led to the modern belief that many diseases are caused by microorganisms—bacteria, viruses, yeasts, and parasites.

10.I.2 Pasteur wanted to find out what causes milk and wine to spoil. He demonstrated that spoilage and fermentation occur when microorganisms enter from the air, multiply rapidly, and produce waste products. After showing that spoilage could be avoided by keeping germs out or by destroying them with heat, he investigated animal diseases and showed that microorganisms were involved. Other investigators later showed that specific kinds of germs caused specific diseases.

10.I.3 Pasteur found that infection by disease organisms—germs—caused the body to build up an immunity against subsequent infection by the same organisms. He then demonstrated that it was possible to produce vaccines that would induce the body to build immunity to a disease without actually causing the disease itself.

10.I.4 Changes in health practices have resulted from the acceptance of the germ theory of disease. Before germ theory, illness was treated by appeals to supernatural powers or by trying to adjust body fluids through induced vomiting, bleeding, or purging. The modern approach emphasizes sanitation, the safe handling of food and water, the pasteurization of milk, quarantine, and aseptic surgical techniques to keep germs out of the body; vaccinations to strengthen the body's immune system against subsequent infection by the same kind of microorganisms; and antibiotics and other chemicals and processes to destroy microorganisms.

10.I.5 In medicine, as in other fields of science, discoveries are sometimes made unexpectedly, even by accident. But knowledge and creative insight are usually required to recognize the meaning of the unexpected.

10.J Harnessing Power

10.J.1 Until the 1800s, most manufacturing was done in homes, using small, handmade machines that were powered by muscle, wind, or running water. New machinery and steam engines to drive them made it possible to replace craftsmanship with factories, using fuels as a source of energy. In the factory system, workers, materials, and energy could be brought together efficiently.

10.J.2 The invention of the steam engine was at the center of the Industrial Revolution. It converted the chemical energy stored in wood and coal, which were plentiful, into mechanical work. The steam engine was invented to solve the urgent problem of pumping water out of coal mines. As improved by James Watt, it was soon used to move coal, drive manufacturing machinery, and power locomotives, ships, and even the first automobiles.

11. Common Themes

By the end of the 8th grade, students should know that

11.A Systems

11.A.1 A system can include processes as well as things.

11.A.2 Thinking about things as systems means looking for how every part relates to others. The output from one part of a system (which can include material, energy, or information) can become the input to other parts. Such feedback can serve to control what goes on in the system as a whole.

11.A.3 Any system is usually connected to other systems, both internally and externally. Thus a system may be thought of as containing subsystems and as being a subsystem of a larger system.

11.B Models

11.B.1 Models are often used to think about processes that happen too slowly, too quickly, or on too small a scale to observe directly, or that are too vast to be changed deliberately, or that are potentially dangerous.

11.B.2 Mathematical models can be displayed on a computer and then modified to see what happens.

11.B.3 Different models can be used to represent the same thing. What kind of a model to use and how complex it should be depends on its purpose. The usefulness of a model may be limited if it is too simple or if it is needlessly complicated. Choosing a useful model is one of the instances in which intuition and creativity come into play in science, mathematics, and engineering.

11.C Constancy and Change

11.C.1 Physical and biological systems tend to change until they become stable and then remain that way unless their surroundings change.

11.C.2 A system may stay the same because nothing is happening or because things are happening but exactly counterbalance one another.

11.C.3 Many systems contain feedback mechanisms that serve to keep changes within specified limits.

11.C.4 Symbolic equations can be used to summarize how the quantity of something changes over time or in response to other changes.

11.C.5 Symmetry (or the lack of it) may determine properties of many objects, from molecules and crystals to organisms and designed structures.

11.C.6 Cycles, such as the seasons or body temperature, can be described by their cycle length or frequency, what their highest and lowest values are, and when these values occur. Different cycles range from many thousands of years down to less than a billionth of a second.

11.D Scale

11.D.1 Properties of systems that depend on volume, such as capacity and weight, change out of proportion to properties that depend on area, such as strength or surface processes.

11.D.2 As the complexity of any system increases, gaining an understanding of it depends increasingly on summaries, such as averages and ranges, and on descriptions of typical examples of that system.

12. Habits of Mind

By the end of the 8th grade, students should know that

12.A Values and Attitudes

12.A.1 Know why it is important in science to keep honest, clear, and accurate records.

12.A.2 Know that hypotheses are valuable, even if they turn out not to be true, if they lead to fruitful investigations.

12.A.3 Know that often different explanations can be given for the same evidence, and it is not always possible to tell which one is correct.

12.B Computation and Estimation

12.B.1 Find what percentage one number is of another and figure any percentage of any number.

12.B.2 Use, interpret, and compare numbers in several equivalent forms such as integers, fractions, decimals, and percents.

12.B.3 Calculate the circumferences and areas of rectangles, triangles, and circles, and the volumes of rectangular solids.

12.B.4 Find the mean and median of a set of data.

12.B.5 Estimate distances and travel times from maps and the actual size of objects from scale drawings.

12.B.6 Insert instructions into computer spreadsheet cells to program arithmetic calculations.

12.B.7 Determine what unit (such as seconds, square inches, or dollars per tankful) an answer should be expressed in from the units of the inputs to the calculation, and be able to convert compound units (such as yen per dollar into dollar per yen, or miles per hour into feet per second).

12.B.8 Decide what degree of precision is adequate and round off the result of calculator operations to enough significant figures to reasonably reflect those of the inputs.

12.B.9 Express numbers like 100, 1,000, and 1,000,000 as powers of 10.

12.B.10 Estimate probabilities of outcomes in familiar situations, on the basis of history or the number of possible outcomes.

12.C Manipulation and Observation

12.C.1 Use calculators to compare amounts proportionally.

12.C.2 Use computers to store and retrieve information in topical, alphabetical, numerical, and key-word files, and create simple files of their own devising.

12.C.3 Read analog and digital meters on instruments used to make direct measurements of length, volume, weight, elapsed time, rates, and temperature, and choose appropriate units for reporting various magnitudes.

12.C.4 Use cameras and tape recorders for capturing information.

12.C.5 Inspect, disassemble, and reassemble simple mechanical devices and describe what the various parts are for; estimate what the effect that making a change in one part of a system is likely to have on the system as a whole.

12.D Communication Skills

12.D.1 Organize information in simple tables and graphs and identify relationships they reveal.

12.D.2 Read simple tables and graphs produced by others and describe in words what they show.

12.D.3 Locate information in reference books, back issues of newspapers and magazines, compact disks, and computer databases.

12.D.4 Understand writing that incorporates circle charts, bar and line graphs, two-way data tables, diagrams, and symbols.

12.D.5 Find and describe locations on maps with rectangular and polar coordinates.

12.E Critical-Response Skills

12.E.1 Question claims based on vague attributions (such as "Leading doctors say...") or on statements made by celebrities or others outside the area of their particular expertise.

12.E.2 Compare consumer products and consider reasonable personal trade-offs among them on the basis of features, performance, durability, and cost.

12.E.3 Be skeptical of arguments based on very small samples of data, biased samples, or samples for which there was no control sample.

12.E.4 Be aware that there may be more than one good way to interpret a given set of findings.

12.E.5 Notice and criticize the reasoning in arguments in which (1) fact and opinion are intermingled or the conclusions do not follow logically from the evidence given, (2) an analogy is not apt, (3) no mention is made of whether the control groups are very much like the experimental group, or (4) all members of a group (such as teenagers or chemists) are implied to have nearly identical characteristics that differ from those of other groups.